A MUSICAL
PEACEMAKER

To Juliet

A MUSICAL PEACEMAKER

The Life and Work of Sir Edward German

· BRIAN REES ·

THE
KENSAL
PRESS

© Brian Rees 1986

British Library Cataloguing in Publication Data

Rees, Brian
  A musical peacemaker: the life and music of Sir Edward German.
  1. German, Edward   2. Composers——Great Britain——Biography
  I. Title
  780'.92'4   ML410.G2854

  ISBN 0-946041-49-0

Published by The Kensal Press.
Kensal House, Abbotsbrook, Bourne End, Buckinghamshire.

Printed by Hollen Street Press, Slough.

Contents

List of Illustrations

Preface

Edward German's place in English music may be compared with that of Charles Lamb in English literature. Both had a liking for the antique style and imaginary phraseology of the past. Both wrote fancifully in a way which gives immediate pleasure, avoiding strident passions and sombre philosophical intentions. There are personal parallels also. Both were shy men in public, but loved the theatre and relaxed in convivial company. Both were captivated by Shakespeare's many worlds and transmitted something of the magic to others. Each had a deep relationship with a sister, though in the case of German and Rachel it was she who was more forcefully the guide and protector. Both men had the ability to dissolve life's pain and disappointments into humour.

Yet, in his early days, German had much the bolder aspirations. His remarkable skills as a player and his promise as a composer led to hopes and prophecies of high mastery and renown. But the years at the turn of the century, which saw him established as 'Sullivan's Successor' also witnessed the appearance of the first great works of Elgar, and thenceforward his achievements, unique in their sphere, were to be overshadowed. With the grace and tactful shyness that were in his nature he accepted his lesser role. His admiration for Elgar's works was as strong as Elgar's affection for his. He nevertheless insisted that his art demanded the same care and precision as the heavier and more tragic compositions of others and much of his later correspondence was devoted to ensuring this.

His letters to Rachel are quoted frequently in the following pages, for they have hitherto been unpublished and indeed unknown, and they give a livelier picture of his personality than W.H. Scott's Biography published in 1932 in the composer's lifetime. Scott, a friend since childhood, was determined to tell a story of uninterrupted progress from youthful prodigy to revered genius. German's own reticence and the desire to suppress and forget difficulties in the past, such as the crucial episode of 'Fallen Faries', did not help Scott, valuable though his book is, to paint in sharper tones. In addition to German's letters a number of press criticisms and reviews have been included, in an endeavour to portray the extraordinary popularity and acclaim which German enjoyed in the 1890's and after, though critical superlatives (except from Bernard Shaw) gradually gave way to total silence as the present century progressed.

I owe an immense debt of thanks to Mrs Winifred German, herself a most active and enterprising musician, for giving me access to all the papers bequeathed by Rachel and maintained by her late husband, Arthur German, as well as the manuscript of German's unpublished early compositions. Thanks must be gratefully accorded also to Miss Margery Jones, pianist and composer, who has lent family photographs and German's letters to his Whitchurch cousins. Mr Dennis Earnshaw of Whitchurch has been indefatigable in hunting out details of the Jones family history and an expert guide to the locality of German's boyhood. Mr Dominic Guyver, generously gave permission for me to use material from his article in the Elgar Journal, on the friendship between the two composers. I gratefully acknowledge the help the Pierpont Morgan Library, New York, and permission of the Royal General Theatrical Fund to quote from W.S. Gilbert's correspondence, the assistance generously given by staff at the British Library, Manuscript and Music sections, as well as the principal departments at Bloomsbury and Colindale, the London Library, Westminster City Library, Theatre Museum (Victoria and Albert), Leeds University and Southampton University Libraries, the Performing Rights Society, National Sound Archives, Record Office House of Lords, Chertsey Museum, Chester, Shrewsbury, Birmingham and Norwich City Archives, the Guildhall School of Music and the Worshipful Company of Musicians. Mr Robin Golding, Registrar, and Miss M.J. Harrington Librarian of the Royal Academy of Music brought interesting material to my attention.

I should like to thank also the Headmasters and Librarians of Shrewsbury School, Wimbledon College, Wellington College, Sir John Talbot's School, Whitchurch and King's School, Wimbledon, for the work they have done on my behalf. Individual thanks must be accorded to The Countess of Sutherland, Lord Strathnaver, Mrs Jocelyn Mcdowell (great niece), Mr Peter White (Master of Music Leicester Cathedral), Mr Robin Langley (Publisher of Novello), Professor Erlich of Belfast University, Michael Hurd, Tris Penna (of Chappell Music), Dr Bernard Massey of the Hymn Society, Mr Graham Lee, Mr Cyril Taylor, Mr Edward Pease-Watkins, Mrs Susan Barnard, Mr Barry Mann (Archivist of the Savage Club) and Mr and Mrs Menzies for permission to view 'The Laurels' Whitchurch. To friends who have given encouragement to commence and continue the biography, William Llewellyn (Director of Music, Charterhouse), Kenneth Rose, Celia Davis of Heritage Music and Ursula Vaughan Williams, I am especially indebted.

Finally, I must render heartfelt thanks to the Leverhulme trustees whose grant enabled the work to be completed. The new edition of Grove's. Dictionary of Music and Musicians has been valuable at every stage. Hesketh Pearson's *Gilbert, His Life and Strife* provides a most useful prelude to the story of the collaboration with German.

As so little of German's splendid music is on record, and hence available on radio, this is not a detailed study or analysis of his works, though I have endeavoured to give descriptions especially of many of the lesser known compositions. The few musical examples are given solely to emphasise a point in the text. A revival of appreciation would warrant such a study and I hope this story of the composer's life may do something to initiate it.

Brian Rees

CHAPTER ONE

A Shropshire Lad

In the late 1850s the nineteen year-old Miss Elizabeth Cox of Whitchurch, Shropshire, kept a detailed journal of her courtship by John David Jones, a young suitor who brought to his task unbounded romantic ardour coupled with deep non-conformist piety.

> Wed. 16th. Came at 7. We went to walk up Alkington Road and returned at 8.30. We then went and sat in the Bottom Garden. He leaned his hand on my knees, pressed my right hand to his heart and with his right arm encircled my waist. Thus we sat. It was a beautiful evening. The heavens being beautifully studded with stars. 'How truly Betsy,' he observed 'does the Psalmist say, "The heavens declare the glory of God and the firmament showeth his handiwork!" I looked around me a few moments and was lost in adoration and wonder when I viewed those countless orbs of light, and that verse of David's occurred to my mind, 'He telleth the number of the stars and calleth them all by their names.' When I again looked downward he was gazing intently in my face with a look of fondness and love, a look that would read my very inmost soul.

In meticulous detail she recorded the hours and minutes of the frequent visits which he made to her home several times each day and added them up at the end of each month. ('The time he has spent with me during the month is 63 hours 15 minutes.') She noted each country road and pathway which they took on their evening walks, the moments which they spent in psalm reading, prayer and, often, in dialogue form, his protestations of total devotion and her own somewhat prolonged hesitancies. John was a lover set firmly in the post-Byronic period. When Elizabeth announced that she was about to spend some time with her cousins seven miles distant, his response was made in the same terms as if she had decided to cross the Atlantic:

> Is it possible, Betsy, that you will be seven miles from me this time tomorrow night! – well, I suppose it must be, but it is only for a short

time: if we are absent in the body I shall never be absent from you in the spirit, for you are always in my prayers and in my thoughts by night and by day, at home and abroad. Father has promised to give me something, but, if I had nothing, I could be happy with you.

A 'degree of painfulness' crept over him when she refused to let him know how long she intended to be absent.

> Kneeling by my side, he said, 'But Betsy, absence makes the heart grow fonder. It only makes those who love fonder of each other when that love is true; doesn't it Betsy?'
> 'Sometimes,' I replied.
> 'Oh yes, Betsy,' he said with a sigh, 'I am sure it does in our case.'

He left at 20 m to 10.

Great was the young man's joy when he heard that Elizabeth at her cousin's had danced with no one but her sister and a certain Mrs Heywood. He wrote immediately:

> My dear, I can truly assure you, you will never have cause to regret what you then did in days and years to come. One word, dear Betsy, with regard to my fidelity. As I before said, I now repeat that I love you fervently, earnestly and affectionately and faithfully, and can you for a moment doubt me? Do not you think that in those solemn moments after which with calm reflection, serious forethought and mature consideration I gave myself to you, and said I would be yours, dear Betsy, and were I for a moment to think that you cherished a thought towards me, that I should act wrong towards you?

John was an apprentice in his father's wine and spirit business. His father, Edward Jones, was a local Whitchurch brewer, a man of comparative wealth, who generously supported the Dodington Congregational Chapel. The first organ installed was presented by the son, though it was presumably paid for by the father, out of the profits of the brewery and the drink trade carried on in The Vaults, a quaint public house behind the old Town Hall. Major hostilities between drink and nonconformity had not yet assumed their full proportions, though John David's elder brother Edward Junior, had a severe crisis of conscience over the evils of his trade. He renounced his profitable share of revenue from The Vaults, learnt the grocery business and opened a shop in the High Street becoming a dedicated leader of temperance movements. He also helped to found a mechanics' institute where workmen could spend their time more profitably than in the taverns.

Although John David earned his living at The Vaults his principal interests lay in the Chapel and his preaching in non-conformist chapels in the Shropshire villages. To the end of his days he retained his warm and trusting nature. His daughter, Rachel, later recalled that he was a loving and indulgent father and would have spoilt his children utterly, if it had not been for the wiser judgement and firmness of his wife. On one occasion having whipped both his sons, German and Clifford in accordance with Victorian custom, for some naughtiness, and then locked them in the bedroom, he could stand the atmosphere of sorrow no longer, and crept stealthily to press sixpence into the hand of each small sinner without his wife's knowledge.

While German was a student at the Academy, Rachel wrote a poem on her father's birthday to atone for her tardiness in finishing the slippers she was embroidering as a present, and in it she paid tribute to the benign influence which he shed over the household.

The flair of language which had sustained his wooing infused his sermons and the listeners observed tears in his eyes when he reached the climax of his addresses. At the wedding of his youngest daughter, Mabel, he broke down in tears at the opening lines of a hymn he himself had chosen: 'O Love, divine and golden'.

Elizabeth was more circumspect and practical. Though she was not immune to gallantry and would sometimes seek out those pews in the chapel where inadequate gas-lighting concealed her blushes, she was anxious to reassure herself that the young shop assistant was not simply magnifying a transient affection. On 1st January, 1858, when he had inscribed her initials on the Bible Class Magazine, and looked forward to the day when bound volumes of that work would stretch along the shelves of their future home he was halted in his reflections by a reminder of some over impetuous phrase he had used in his courting on the 12th April 1857.

'I believe I have forgiveness of God,' he said. 'And I thought you, Betsy, promised you would forgive, didn't you?'

'Yes' I replied.

'And promised to love me again?'

'No,' I said, 'I don't remember that.'

'But that was included, wasn't it?'

'Perhaps it was,' I responded.

'Do trust me Betsy,' he said earnestly, 'and then I shall be a happy man. And do try to forget what I said then, will you?'

'When I forget that,' I observed, 'I shall trust you.'

'Then do try and forget it, will you Betsy?'

'Yes,' I said.

'And pray to God,' he added.

'I have,' I resumed.

'And do trust me, Betsy, for I shall be faithful.'

'I wish,' I said, 'that I did trust you.'

'When will you tell me that you do?'

'When I feel it,' I replied, 'for I cannot say what I do not feel.'

'I know, love,' he said, 'that of myself I cannot make you trust me but do try.'

He seemed desirous of entering more into it, but time would not admit of this. He left at 9.40 (Hours to-day 3, Mins. 25).

The question of complete and mutual trust had long remained a problem which she had to resolve. On 2nd January, after she had agreed to forgive his few foolish words, he took up the letter he had written to her during their seven-mile separation and read it to her aloud, continuing,

I can with truthful sincerity give utterance to the touching address of Ruth to Naomi: 'Whither thou goest I will go, where thou lodgest I will lodge, thy people shall be my people and thy God my God. Where though diest will I die and there will I be buried: the Lord do so to me and more also if aught but death part thee from me'. Such Betsy is my love for you.

His voice grew faint here: he read no further, and after further avowals of love on his part, she agreed to entrust herself to him and his promises.

At times their romance ran smoothly. She wrote out the heads of his sermons for him and they attended home missionary meetings and lectures, including one by a Mr Owen engagingly entitled 'The Faults of Thinkers'. The trust accorded to John was, however, at times withdrawn and Elizabeth wrote 'unhappy' in the margin of her diary. When her doubts and his anxieties appeared to multiply her handwriting lapsed from severe copper-plate to an inky freestyle. He worried lest a forthcoming visit to Worcester would produce temptations that would assail the unflawed trust reposed in her. To his final plea for 'trust' her reply was nothing if not measured:

After a short pause I replied: 'Yes, I have been thinking this morning and I feel my fears gradually subsiding, and giving way to thoughts and

John David Jones

Elizabeth Jones

feelings which would prompt me to believe and trust you; but – that thought which has so recently held such a sway over me is not so effectually overcome as to leave me a stranger to its effects, neither has that trust which I now begin to repose in you yet attained to that real, that perfect confidence which casteth out fear; but I doubt not that in proportion as my fears decrease my belief in you will increase so that in a short time I hope to be able to satisfy you on that point.'

It seems that, as she had forecast, her misgivings did indeed recede. Sometimes she hurt his feelings by her wish to attend church rather than chapel. He wanted only to settle down and enjoy the blessings of family life in a divinely ordered world in general and the small market town of Whitchurch in particular. She had some reservations about so complete a commitment so early in life. Yet theirs was to prove a very happy union and they created for their children a warm and cheerful family spirit that remained throughout their lives. Their first child was significantly christened Ruth, a name which symbolised the impossibility of any separation. The second, a boy, was born on 27th February 1862 and was christened German Edward..

John Jones looked forward to having a musical as well as a deeply pious home. On one of the many occasions when he spoke to his betrothed of future domestic happiness he had said, 'When we go into housekeeping Betsy we will have a piano, for I think you will soon learn.' If the young couple could have foreseen that this item of housekeeping would be the first step towards the musical fame, and the acquisition of the Gold Medal of the Royal Philharmonic Society by their elder son, they would have been astonished and felt more keenly than ever the divine watchfulness that surrounded their marriage and their home. Elizabeth did in fact take some lessons on the pianoforte and all her five children were musically gifted.

These few glimpses of the long Victorian courtship show what qualities their elder son, German, had inherited from both parents. From his father he derived a very ardent romantic nature that found expression in intense melodic writing that often surprises the listener when it bursts out of surrounding passages that seem conventional and repetitive. The greatness of Elgar, his contemporary and friend, lies so often in restraint and the feeling of immense turbulence contained. Edward German's music by comparison gives uninhibited expression to affection and sentiment. It has no darkness and seems to feel no thirst for mystery. He did not devise enigmatic titles for his works or shy away from obvious and familiar delights. From his mother however, he inherited a painstaking thoroughness that made him a perfectionist, a punctilious collaborator and a joy to theatre managements, a respected conductor and a man of precise and well-ordered ways. He checked and re-checked his scores until the end months of his life with the same thoroughness that she had timed John David's visits. From her too he may well have inherited a certain diffidence and distrust of the unknown which would ultimately curb the sense of adventure which is a necessary part of every composer's development. The strong religious feelings that motivated his parents played no part in his own later life, though he never displayed any reaction against his upbringing. From some unknown forebear he inherited a great sense of humour which does not seem to be characteristic of either parent to judge from the dialogues recorded in his mother's journal.

They began married life at The Vaults in St Mary's Street at the centre of the little town. Whitchurch takes its name from a church of white stone built by command of the Norman, William de Warenne, in 1087. In the various tongues that competed for precedence in medieval England, we find it called Album Monasterium, Blancminster and variants upon Whitchurch or Whytchurche.

The men of Shropshire, whose descendants were many centuries later to raise their voices often in praise of 'The Yeomen of England', were indeed noted for their swiftness in loyalty. King John had enjoyed one of the few military successes of his reign when he assembled an army at Whitchurch and then conducted a successful foray into Wales. During the civil wars the town raised a force for 'King Charles the Unfortunate' and guarded the royal line of communications between Shrewsbury and Chester. Its most famous soldier was Sir John Talbot, who had in his youth accompanied King Henry V to France and at the great age of eighty was forced to combat the French resurgence under Joan of Arc. In 1453 he was killed at Castillon near Bordeaux along with one of his sons. When young German Jones was a boy of twelve, the monument to John Talbot in the parish church was restored, and, on the removal of the slab of stone on which his figure was carved, the actual bones of the warrior were found in a strong box, which crumbled into dust on exposure to the air. The monument was restored and the bones re-deposited within the tomb. His heart, however, rests below a stone in the south porch, placed there so that the descendants of whose who had fought so bravely for the English flag should walk out over it to the ends of the earth.

At the time of the wedding of John Jones and Elizabeth Cox Whitchurch had a population of between six and seven thousand, of which about 3,500 lived in the town itself. Its position as a post for stagecoaches had declined;

but the Ellesmere Canal passed by the town, the railway had opened in 1852 and there were lime and chemical works – the nocturnal strolls of the young lovers were frequently taken round a building known as 'The Chemistry'. There was a cotton mill, and some trade in malt and hops. The family connection with brewing was one of the few things that German had in common with Richard Strauss, whose composing life was much vaster and so very different. The town was noted as having two banks, a savings bank and a free grammar school. Some years earlier, in 1837, a *History of Shropshire* had observed that 'the streets of the town of Whitchurch are far from manifesting great beauty or spaciousness: they are notwithstanding clean and respectable. The inns, tradesmen's shops and private dwellings bespeak the presence of moderate wealth, good trade, quiet and contentment.'

At first glance there is not a great deal in the town with its chemical works and malting industries, to suggest the happy rustic music of Edward German or bands of merry-making peasants ready to drop into a jig or morris dance at any moment. Rachel later recalled the tanyards where the pungent smell of decaying hides filled the air and savage-looking workmen stripped to the waist gave the scene the appearance of an 'underworld'. It was in one of these that Rachel, going too near the edge of the pit out of bravado, slipped almost into the machinery below and had to be dragged out covered in slime and scum. Mr Evans, the owner, had her washed and sweetened, and gave her some of his own childrens' clothes so that she would not arrive home at The Vaults too clearly a target for punishment. Even in the countryside with its meres and pastures, agricultural workers had passed through hard and stormy times. In the 1830s when there were fires caused by incendiaries protesting against the new agricultural machinery in many parts of England, the richer landowners and farmers around Whitchurch suffered attacks. In a period of ten months in 1830–31 there were sixteen fires in the district. As the government of landowners struck back, four men were put on trial at the Shropshire Assizes. Two were sentenced to death, one to transportation for life. In the 1860s a cattle plague, steppe murrain or linderspest reached the area resulting in the decimation of local herds through disease and slaughtering. In the 1870s the great agricultural depression gripped the country, when storm and frost wreaked havoc and the suffering of labourers and their families reached scarcely bearable levels. 'Merrie England' must have seemed a distant memory.

Yet on closer examination we find that a great deal of lively activity occurred even in the most unpropitious settings. The town itself was small enough to have its characters and its Dickensian intimacy. Mr John Speed, the barber, was a man of immense importance in his own eyes and spoke condescendingly in the longest words possible. He had a daughter, Lizzie, whom he extolled as a musical prodigy. 'Mount the rostrum, Lizzie!' he would say, and Lizzie forthwith gave a pianoforte recital to admiring patrons under their barber's shrouds. Mr Bradbury, the butcher, was a great Wesleyan, given to quoting the scriptures and spending much thought upon the destinations of his customers in the next world. Yet he was generally reckoned by the Jones children to be a humbug as he belaboured the butcher boys in the slaughter yard that backed onto The Vaults and was obsequious towards the visiting gentry. When Lord Combermere drew up in his carriage to give an order, Mr Bradbury would go out at the salute saying, 'Good morning, My Lord Combermere, Sir'. German and his younger brother, Clifford, were frequent visitors to Mrs Thelwell's toy shop in the High Street which was a storehouse of delights, though the owner herself was an ill-tempered old lady with a strong bias against children. The superior drapers, Walmsley & Pearson, would occasionally give two-day displays of London Fashions and German's sisters were fitted with coats trimmed with fox fur and toques styled after the fashion sealed with approval by Lily Langtry. There were rougher characters also, like Henry Smith who shuffled about the town on his toes, selling boot blacking, matches and copies of *Old Moore's Almanac*, or 'Cakey' Joe, the idiot grave digger, who for a copper would swallow worms to the horror of the children who watched him. 'Birdie' Wilkins, of gypsy origin, was an authority on the wild life of the area, and would accompany the boys on their fishing expeditions. German's lifelong passion for fishing was learnt from Birdie and his son 'Young Birdie'.

In the years 1859–60 there was a revival of the volunteer movement dormant since the time of the Napoleonic wars. The marchers of the Volunteer Third Shropshire Rifle Corps and their band proved one of the first inducements to the young German to interest himself in music. He would slip out of the house and follow its martial steps through the town. At the age of six, he decided to emulate it and from his infant contemporaries he formed a band which practised in a disused warehouse by the canal. Unfortunately his own ensemble lacked certain essential items, namely a trumpet, drums and a cymbal. As German later confessed polysyllabically to an American reporter, 'The surreptitious acquisition of these necessary instruments was the cause of the collapse of the juvenile organisation.'

When court sessions were held in the adjacent Town Hall, the Jones children could catch glimpses of the unhappy proceedings from their windows. One of the justices who came on circuit was Thomas Hughes, an acquaintance of the family, and they would be introduced to the distinguished-looking gentleman, famed as the author of *Tom Brown's Schooldays.*

There were markets and festivities. Each year in June the 'Whitchurch Clubs' were held with circus and menagerie processions through the town by day and fairground booths crowded with excited revellers and lit by napthalene lights at night.

German was the second of five children. In his young days the name was pronounced with a hard 'g'. It is believed to derive from South Montgomeryshire where a number of Christian names – Jervis, Francis, Tibbot, that is Gervaise, François, Thibault, and of course Germain – suggest a settlement with French origins. Gallic sympathies have a curious habit of re-asserting themselves in later generations. German's favourite composers were Bizet, Gounod and Franck. In addition to his elder sister Ruth, there were two younger sisters, Rachel and Mabel, and a younger brother Clifford. Within the family he was always known as 'Jim' and Rachel as 'Dick'. They were the closest in spirits, and Rachel, who had gifts as a musician and writer herself, guarded his career jealously right into old age, when using both her own name and fictitious inventions (Mrs Scott-Meynell was a favourite as likely to impress the BBC) she would pursue the musical staff at Broadcasting House with requests for performances of his works. She wrote for her own children a vivid account of life at The Vaults which not only gives us glimpses of her brother as a very lively and entertaining child but tells us a great deal about German's family and life in a Victorian market town.

Elizabeth before her marriage lived in a long old-fashioned house down by the wharf. Her father, Joseph, was a timber merchant and for his Jones grandchildren he made splendid swings and seesaws. A steep garden and orchard rose behind the house where the children would fill their pockets with orange pomaine apples after the games were ended. His wife, Grandmother Cox, was a little woman who suffered from a bad heart and had very blue lips. To the children she was a shadowy figure sitting by the fire in a cotton hood. Grandfather Cox played the cello and sang, and it was he who had introduced John Jones, a fellow member of Mr Bird's singing class, to her. Elizabeth herself joined this aptly named group, so it was in a musical atmosphere that German's parents met. When they had acquired the piano she did indeed teach herself to play, took some instruction and also gave herself lessons on the violin, in which she was emulated by her son. John's artistic interests and his affectionate nature appear to have come from his mother, who wrote poetry and had a kind and gentle disposition. When

John was only twelve, she had died suddenly from a heart condition and the boy was summoned back from boarding school to live with a stern and reserved father who took little interest in his family. Her grave rests in a sad little corner of the Congregational burial ground, along with those of several children who died in infancy. It lies some distance from that of her husband and his vivacious second wife. It was Grandfather Jones, however, who built The Vaults, and when John David married Elizabeth Cox, he vacated the house in his son's favour and moved out of the town to a place called Brownsbank with his new spouse, a spritely schoolfriend of his daughter Eliza, and much younger than himself. 'Step-grandmother Jones' was a great contrast to her serious and romantic stepson. She was a large fat genial lady who shook all over when she walked. After her husband's death she was left a comparatively wealthy woman. She kept open house at Brownsbank and invited friends from Manchester who went to race meetings, played cards and indulged in other 'fast' amusements. John's sister, Eliza, had married an Uncle Robinson of Summer Hill, Staffordshire, but often came to visit German and his brothers and sisters. She had a taste for composing short poems and acrostics, a habit which the composer and his sister learnt and kept up well into old age. She must however, have been a strange visitor for she would never sleep alone and the children had to take it in turns to sleep with her. From time to time during the night she would imbibe from a bottle of peppermint cordial kept under the pillow in order to help 'the wind'. She was highly nervous and her hands trembled so violently she could hardly hold a cup of tea. But she contrived to spend many hours copying out songs for her musical daughter, Lizzie, a popular practice at the time, though not one which would have earned the approval of her nephew, in later years a doyen of the Performing Right Society.

There was plenty of music in the family home. They played and sang pieces by Mendelssohn, Sullivan and Sterndale Bennett just as later generations of amateurs were to spend hours with *Glorious Devon, O Peaceful England* and German's own Piano-Duet arrangements of his dances. Probably no composer has sustained so many hours of amateur music-making as Edward German, both on the operatic stage and in the drawing-rooms and front parlours of untrained singers and pianists. It was a form of home entertainment in which he himself was noted. At The Vaults, oyster suppers were given on Saturday evenings and Hal Robinson, a jolly clerk from the brewery came in to share the bright fire in the parlour and the music. Here stood the piano with pictures above it, one of the Prince of Wales in his wedding clothes and another of the local dignitary, Lord Combermere. The family cat, Topsy, was wont to drape itself along the piano top during performances, though much to the children's distress she came to a sudden end by falling through the big stairwell in the centre of the building.

At a certain hour the grandfather clock would strike in the kitchen and the younger members of the family would be dispatched to the care of the nursemaid: in very early days a grim lady called Jane Savage, who chastised the children regularly in her drab little bedroom. Later her successor, Sarah Dutton, came into the household, a kindly older person who told funny stories, gave impersonations and fed the children on strange concoctions of scalded bread, pepper and salt. Jane Savage long remained a figure of family folklore. In 1895, writing to Rachel ('Dick') German, in one of the many poems that passed between them, discussing a lady called Henrietta included the stanza:

Henrietta! Henrietta!
You must never fume or fret her
For, if you do, you'll surely find
A 'savage' of the fiercest kind
Now having got this off my mind
I feel distinctly better.

German's mother ensured that life at The Vaults was well-ordered and comfortable. Above the parlour on the first floor was the drawing room, which seemed something of a royal apartment to the children, with a crystal chandelier, a fine tablecloth bought at a sale but embroidered by the Misses Poole of Marbury Hall, gold and silver shavings in the grate in summertime and coverings of white linen over the chairs and sofa. By contrast, below the house lay the cellar, a weird place of barrels and pipes and dusty racks of wine in remote, cobwebbed recesses into which the children were afraid to enter. Another setting which aroused mysterious apprehensions was the house of a distant Jones relative, The Wych, where a lunatic sister was hidden away during their visits but would make appearances and grimace from the windows.

Jim was much more lively and mischievous than his polished and outwardly restrained bachelor demeanour in later year suggested. Together he and Rachel would climb into a large bath that stood on a dais in the dressing room and there play games with penny packets of cards, an activity that would have been heavily punished if discovered. Sometimes their crimes did come to light. On one occasion the two children sought refuge in an upstairs closet only to discover that the door could not be unfastened. All efforts to open it from either side failed and the two children, imagining they were walled up for life gave loud and piteous vent to their grief. Eventually an employee from the brewery had to climb on to the roof, pull them from the window and set them on a ladder down to safety. Although Elizabeth relinquished her music lessons after Rachel's birth, when owing to the effects of rheumatic fever her hands became painful and swollen, the talents of her children soon began to manifest themselves. When still very small children, Ruth and Jim had been able to make up duets on the pianoforte and were asked to play at a concert. The principle of the 'encore' having been explained to them, Jim in black velvet suit rushed back to the piano stool before the applause had even time to commence.

There was no heavy seriousness about the family entertainments. Elizabeth Jones had trained as a teacher and taught at the church school in Bargates before her marriage. She had a great gift for captivating the interests of her children. She spent many hours cutting out figures to be used in 'shadow shows', the shapes thrown onto a white sheet stretched across the landing while the audience sat and marvelled. As the children grew older and could devise their own entertainments, family shows took place above the grocer's shop owned by John Jones's brother, Edward, at the Bank Buildings close by in the High Street. The Bank Buildings had once been a private school for the daughters of the several curates who served at the parish church. After housing a bank it had been acquired by Ted Jones for his grocery business. German spent a great deal of time with his uncle and cousins. It was Ted Jones who found German and another cousin, Jack Robinson, when both were lost one evening after an unauthorised visit to their step-grandmother's at Brownsbank, when he was about eight. As night fell and snow began to fall there was no sign of the missing children, who, for reasons which German could never remember, had been set down at a point some distance away to walk home. His mother and father became frantic with anxiety and plans were made to call out the town crier. It was Ted who strode off into the dark, discovered the exhausted infants and carried them back in triumph. Rachel surmised that the thankful parents probably remitted the punishment deserved. German, writing to Ted's daughter, Lizzie, sixty years later, remembered the evening vividly.

Although after their relinquising of the wine and spirit trade, Uncle Edward and Aunt Mary could not compete with some of the other branches of the family in material luxury, they provided the venue for happy and uninhibited jollifications by the two groups of cousins. Rules about bedtime went overboard, games were noisy and punctuated by the consumption of some of the novelties there were creeping into the general stores at that time.

Here the children tasted corned beef for the first time and various chocolate products. Sometimes Jim had to be restrained from leaning out of the upstairs window to play tricks upon passers-by in the High Street below, but it was on these premises that the 'G. and E. Jones Annual Entertainments' began. G and E. Jones were Jim and his cousin Eddie. They shared a very strong physical resemblance and the concerts became quite popular events with tickets costing sixpence each. Jim would attend all the visiting comedians and variety shows at Whitchurch Town Hall – the Christie Minstrels, Pepper's Ghost, Harry Lister and other forgotten names – and would memorise songs and sketches which he could later reproduce.

In his last term at the Academy German wrote an execrably rhymed but affectionate poem, 'Dim Visions', relating how Ted Jones and his wife watched, worried but indulgent, while the children drove nails into their best drawing room walls for the stage curtains from which they would appear in exotic disguises such as 'The Shah who came over the Sea':

> For never perhaps was I happier than
> When making these shows at 'the shop'
> (But stay I've forgotten to mention the May-
> Fields, and beautiful stone-bottled pop)
>
> Dim visions I have (coming now to the town)
> Of glue pots and cardboard and paste
> Which were used for construction of models and shows
> These visions will ne'er be effaced.

Cousin Eddie took part but was something of a hindrance as he was a wooden actor and could not control his own laughter at Jim's mimicry and vaudeville style. Brother Clifford was scene shifter and curtain operator and Rachel a partner and accompanist. Mab, the youngest member of the family, sat in the front and applauded. The fame of Jim's comic songs soon spread and he was often invited to surrounding villages for charitable entertainments. He dressed in character and his repertoire included a song called The Beautiful Boy and another, I'm in Mourning for Jemima, for which he appeared in shabby black, reddened his nose and used six soaked handkerchiefs as props. The favourite item was Old Mother Gum in which he dressed as a peppery old school dame. It included the lines:

> She had a great tussle
> When she felt all the sawdust coming out of her bustle

and a chorus, during which he danced around the stage, which ran:

> Then hurrah for Old Mother Gum
> Who keeps the infants' school.

It is difficult to visualise the composer of fastidious and delicate music who so often deplored the influences of jazz and musical comedy, leaping about the stage in these rollicking numbers and one wonders by what stages his animal vitality subsided into the quieter routine of the 'Hermit of Maida Vale.' Yet his sister agreed that he gained more pleasure and pride from the applause and the encores at these concerts than at any of his later successes in the concert hall.

One of Jim's most exact impersonations, which caused great hilarity, was of the family physician, Dr Brown, who would settle into a chair after one of the children had been visited and examined and then relate tall stories of his angling days in Scotland. Even when 'his man' called to summon him to an urgent case he would continue to sit, taking snuff, and permitting one rambling anecdote to merge into another. With the Brown family, the Jones brothers and sisters would go skating on Brown Moss in the winter and take picnics into the countryside in summer. Elizabeth Jones gave one huge Christmas party in the Browns' house which for some reason was empty at the time; the Jones family held the freehold. The place was said to be haunted which added to the excitement of the revels.

The two sets of cousins also appear to have culled examples of wild life from the countryside and put them on show:

> Dim visions I have of the hunting of rats
> Of watching the ducks, fowl and geese
> And a Grand Exhibition which we proudly called
> One of living curi-os-it-ies.

The patience of the Jones parents was certainly exemplary.

Among the numerous branches of relations the brewery people were the grandest. Once a year Aunts Anne and Jane in their crinolines and silk dresses came to inspect the Jones' home and the family. The house was spring cleaned and refurbished by specially imported retainers and no doubt the children were also. The local pianoforte teacher was Mr Charles Muller, who receives a brief but respectful mention in Scott's biography, for which German himself provided much of the material. Elizabeth had taken lessons from him but when rheumatic fever had affected her hands, she restricted her talents to singing songs by Sullivan and others. The sad ballads of

Victorian days caused the children to lie awake troubled and tristful as the unhappy tales of blighted love unfolded, in the parlour below. Muller was in fact a rather uncouth character who had been a bandmaster and settled down to teach the piano in Prees. He smelt heavily of beer and terrified many of his pupils. He would bark in withering tones: 'Do you know a crotchet when you see it?, then dab his finger on one and boom, 'Them's them.' He once knocked a girl pupil off her stool in a fit of temper and there was much general admiration for her response as she marched from the room saying, 'I'll come back when you are a gentleman.' Clifford Jones also took his departure during a stormy lesson, substituting some self-instruction on the flute instead. Jim, perhaps because of his remarkable skill at the flowery piano pieces to be found in Victorian albums, such as The Soldier's Return, seems to have weathered the storms more amiably. At a concert in January 1875 in aid of the Congregational Sabbath Schools Ruth and Jim appeared as 'Miss and Master Jones' with Diabelli's Duet in D, a bouncy piece from the old Star Folio albums and Rossini's Overture L'Italiana in Algeri. Jim was then twelve and both items call for some dexterity. In later years when he came down to Whitchurch to accompany the distinguished singer, Mary Davies, at a concert, 'Monkey' Muller rather the worse for drink, came into the back of the hall, hailing his old pupil with pride and having to be silenced by his neighbours. When Walter Hay from Shrewsbury became Jim's teacher he impressed greatly, not only because of his superior musicianship but because of his much more gentlemanly manner.

Christmas, as might be expected, was always a great occasion. Jim gave special performances on a toy theatre which had been brought specially from London. At the house of a friend, John Elliott, nearby in St Mary's Street, the Christmas season always brought a round of charades and homemade plays such as 'The Baron's Revenge' in which Jim had the principal roles. He was also very deft with his hands and with any mechanical contrivance. He may well have acquired this interest in the mechanics' institute under his uncle's guidance. Soon he added conjuring to his accomplishments.

When the family had moved to another home, the Laurels, in Alkington Road, the town band would come at Christmas time and play in the relatively small kitchen, nearly blowing the roof off. Harry the Ragman, would annually contribute to the programme a carol known only to himself with neither time nor metre, Where Jaisus Lay. Jim in his later years always looked back in his letters written around Christmas time to the happiness of the old days at Whitchurch.

Two more aspects of his childhood must be mentioned. One was the frequent excursions into the countryside. Because The Vaults had no garden and adjoined the butcher's yard with its noise and smells, Mrs Jones was anxious that the children should be taken by their nurse into the fields each day. Since their father, as supplier, knew many of the butlers and gardeners at large houses in the neighbourhood they were often invited into the parks and gardens and allowed to taste the fruits in the hothouses and orchards. Cloverley Hall, one such haven, gave its name to a suite of orchestrated pieces reminiscent of the Shropshire countryside. There were also visits to Hawkstone by horse and trap where Mr and Mrs Williams, host and hostess of the inn, presided over a rambling old world tavern that might have served as a model for the Second Act of *Tom Jones*. The park at Hawkstone had landscaped hills and dales, hundreds of scuttling rabbits, an obelisk, a grotto and a real live hermit with a long white beard, wracking cough and a skull on the table of his rough and simple dwelling, from which he would emerge to make prophecies in a thin quavering voice. Once when Jim was in his 'teens he decided to break the rule that drink should not be brought into Hawkstone Park and smuggled a bottle into the folds of an umbrella. The Jones family arrived accoutred in their Worcester fashions and Jim gallantly stepped forward to hand down the ladies into the welcoming arms of Landlord Williams. Unfortunately in doing so he overturned his umbrella, the bottle hit the steps of the Inn and its contents flew in all directions. As his mother's cousin, Harriet Mason, a very prim lady, was one of the party and was not amused, a definite gloom pervaded the rest of the day. A happier memory especially to Rachel, was of hearing a part-song by Mendelssohn, *Oh Hills and Dales of Pleasure*, sung by a choir in the grotto. Such moments were arcadian memories which Edward German had the gift of invoking.

No description of his childhood would be complete without reference to Dodington Chapel which played such a large part in the children's lives. In 1797 a portion of the Presbyterian congregation left their chapel in Dodington and met for worship, somewhat provocatively, in a shop immediately across the street. Eventually a chapel arose on this site and was opened late in 1846. Grandfather Jones was a deacon and a highly respected benefactor. When some years later a grander organ than that presented by John Jones was acquired the original instrument was removed to The Laurels, then the family home. Many years later it was sold at auction for five shillings. It deserved a better fate, for his father's playing of that organ – he used to sustain the bottom note of each 'Amen' chord and then remove his hand with a flourish – was another source of musical inspiration in the young son who sat by in the organ loft. The Jones children in their early years helped Bernie Botwood, the blower, and later played for the services themselves. Perhaps still feeling some proprietary interest in the new instrument, Jim, Rachel and two friends scratched their initials on the wooden case where they remain to this day. John Jones also trained the choir, mostly small tradesmen and labourers and Elizabeth was the principal contralto. The new organ with its handsome gilt pipes was an impressive feature in the services and it was certainly not permitted to lie idle. It was quite usual for four chapel attendances to be required for the young people each Sunday including a session at the Sunday School. This was a department of the chapel instituted in 1813 and was not at all the jolly effort at religious advertising which some modern equivalents suggest. Grandfather Jones was superintendent for a number of years. Parents were required to send their children clean, washed, combed, regularly and in good time. They were to give their children a thrashing if the superintendent desired them to do so. The children were never to speak except to their teachers and were not to tell tales of each other. If five minutes late, male teachers were to be fined twopence, if half an hour late, sixpence, female teachers fourpence. As iniquity knows no upper limits there was even provision in the rules to fine the superintendent for unpunctuality also. At the Sunday School itself there were biblical details to be memorised, canings for misbehaviour and even expulsions for the incorrigible. Surprisingly, the infant appetite for religion was not dulled and on certain evenings when chapel could not be held, Jim would mount a service of his own at home making a solemn entry into the nursery as the preaching divine and addressing his brothers and sister from a makeshift pulpit. In a gentler spirit, Elizabeth Jones took a bible class for young women in the district who came to depend on her kindness and wisdom in all manner of circumstances, and who would come to visit The Laurels to confide their troubles. Indeed the Jones's family home was the centre for all the chapel functions. When children's concerts and the Sunday School anniversaries were approaching dozens of children, washed and unwashed, would crowd into the parlour to be drilled in specially selected hymns and solos. In June, there came the Sunday School treat, when it was announced that some local farmer had agreed to lend his fields for a summer outing. Then the carts and traps were piled first with children, then with the skipping ropes, bats and balls, that Elizabeth Jones had purchased from the Thelwell toy shop. Old Testament texts and geneaologies gave way to round games, such as 'Jolly Miller' and races, and then tea followed with buns, currant bread and barrels of ginger beer, followed by oranges and nuts. Finally, the carts decked with laburnum and wild flowers made their way back through the Shropshire lanes which resounded to juvenile choruses.

Such scenes have now vanished for ever. They did not epitomise the whole way of life of a people who had to face many sombre challenges. Their farms and businesses were still often at the mercy of the elements and their homes vulnerable to all manner of sudden illnesses and disease. Yet each season of the year had its excitements and pleasures and there was no lack of resourcefulness in planning and embellishing the domestic and communal rites that were handed down from generation to generation. It is in this world of young courtship, childhood innocence and festive celebration that the music of Edward German is firmly set. He was not destined to depict in music subconscious shadows of the mind, no woes and sorrows, nor the tragic themes that haunted other composers. Yet we cannot, by confronting his music with economic and political data, dismiss the nostalgic content of his work as pure invention. The 'Merrie England' which his music conjures up is fleeting and fitful but it was there to be sought by those fortunate in the affection of their homes and the traditions of their community.

★　　★　　★

The first school Jim attended was Miss Hindmarsh's establishment in Dodington. There were many Hindmarsh sisters sharply divided into the plain and pretty. The day began with the singing of rounds and Moody and Sankey Hymns. A Mr Balshaw, the minister who lived next door and visited the school through a convenient gap in the hedge, would then give an improving talk. The gap acquired greater significance when it was learnt that Mr Balshaw had become engaged to Miss Mary, prettiest and gentlest of the sisters. This was not entirely a popular move as Miss Mary receded into the background as parson's wife and the school was left to the mercies of Miss Jane, representative of the plain faction. The curriculum was restricted and elementary, but at Christmas a pantomime was produced in which Jim played Prince Charming to a Cinderella who was regarded as the cleverest girl in the school and had long golden tresses.

Jim and his brother soon left the school to attend Mr Robert Furber's preparatory school in Bark Hill. After the early years of domestic happiness this was a period of intense anxiety and sadness for his parents.

In 1875 his eldest sister Ruth died after a long illness. Her death certificate refers to the symptoms rather than the specific cause, but these are consonant with tuberculosis, a common cause of death in young persons in those days. Six months before, John Jones had purchased The Laurels, a brick house in Alkington Road, sufficiently spacious, with a garden, and we may safely conjecture that one reason for the move was the hope that some improvement in Ruth's health would ensue from more salubrious air in the outskirts of the town. Ruth had the serene piety which her parents wished for all their children. She wrote farewells to her school friends in the last weeks and died as her mother read to her from the New Testament. Rachel too fell ill. Diabetes was suspected and the special physician summoned from Shrewsbury ordered her removal from school and a regime of rest and fresh air.

Fortunately for Jim happiness and stability were restored by the cheerful and enlightened atmosphere of Mr Furber's school. It was early in 1870 that Mr Robert Furber placed a notice in the local paper 'respectfully' announcing that he would be opening a PUBLIC DAY SCHOOL FOR BOYS in the detatched house, and would be happy to communicate with 'parents seeking for their children a complete and practical education on sound principles and moderate terms'. He added that this system would 'embrace the higher branches of education without extra charge'. Furber was a stalwart member of the Dodington Chapel and thus regarded as a safe recipient of the young pupil. His school, like many at the time, began as a small venture and Jim was one of about eight pupils. Fortunately, Mr Furber was himself a keen musician and on Friday afternoons he instructed the boys in tonic sol fa and later in staff notation. Jim and another pupil, Henry Williams, were particularly promising pupils and Mr Furber in later years recalled that they both seemed able to read anything at sight. They played a duet in public at an entertainment provided for parents and friends. One of the sons of German's partner, Victor Williams, became conductor of the Ealing Choral Society and gave many concert versions of the operas. With his old mentor, Jim appears to have had the happiest of relationships which extended over many years and took on his side the form of a teasing correspondence that complied with the eccentricities of the preparatory school world. In 1901, much preoccupied with the composition of 'Merrie England' he wrote to Mr Furber to apologise for not having been to see him during a visit: 'I have hovering around me a kind of guilt conscience; the cause thereof methinks is that I did not give you a call when I was down at Whitchurch recently'.

He appended two verses recalling the Latinical training of his youth:

Tune: 'God Save the King'

My dear Furberious
Your word imperious
Reached me from home

Thanks for invitius
But I am quiteius
Grieved to writius
'I cannot come'

Sad that the datius
Was just too latius
Otherwise I –
Would have had smokius
Cracked little jokius
At your own locius
And thus comply

Contemplating the poor quality of many of the lyrics which circumstances forced him to set, one is sometimes regretful that Edward German did not develop his own talents in this direction. Another most elaborate joking letter survives in which German refers to some sporting challenge by Furber, who was editing *The Whitchurch Herald* at the time. It shows the same fondness for the Olde English style as his music:

> To the most noble Knight, Sir Robert Furber
> Ye 'Herald' of ye Ancient Town
> of Blancminster Greeting!
>   It behoveth my proud knight to respond in part to ye haughty challenge with which thou hast favoured the noble Germanicus of Alkington and thine unworthy servant who inditeth this same. By St Alkmund! fair said thou and lusting for the fray. And right comely forsooth is the gentle sport for lordly champions.

But the writer it seems has given up sport for more simple pleasures: 'A simple diet with perchance a horn of water and a manuscript (perused upon an ambling palfrey) are the meet revelations of one whose beads are often counted and whose feet cleave in chilly midnight nakedness unto the alter steps, and yet I would not chide.' The script changes as an anxious amanuensis is forced to complete the manuscript while Germanicus travels 'to do penance' at Prees Heath, but it concludes: "But harkee!!!!! bearing his holy body the prancing steed doth near. Yes! 'tis he! He hath returned from the wilderness his penance done, and doth now stoop to inscribe his own holy name.' Then follows a signature in medieval style, which refers to Edwin Tongue, congregational minister and Jim's future brother-in-law: 'Edwinus Lingua, Ye Prior of Handsworth'.

No doubt many middle-aged gentlemen have kept up with old preparatory schoolmasters in joking tones which recall some unique episode or enthusiasm. This particular letter surprises not so much by its elaborate pastiche style which we might expect, but the buoyant irreverence which we find often in Sullivan's music but seldom in German's.

On another occasion, Jim issued some sort of medieval challenge to the champions of the Furbers on behalf of his 'reverend and valiant friend' Tongue. The letter suggests some romantic imbroglio in which Miss Furber was also involved into which Jim entered with great relish and amusement. No doubt an unmarried young minister was something of a quarry in Whitchurch circles before he was safely married to Mabel.

As well as running his school Mr Furber was a man of many parts. He helped local tradesmen with their accounts and offered his services for a number of things from land measurement to collection of debts. In 1891 he switched careers completely and he became Editor of *The Whitchurch Herald*. This journal followed the career of his old pupil with great interest. As a pillar of the Dodington Congregational church he was a friend of the family. In 1920 Jim wrote to Rachel:

I don't know if you have heard that dear old Robert Furber passed away! Cliff sent me a wire so I asked him to get a wreath for me and sent a funeral card: 'In affectionate remembrance from his old pupil.' He was a noble character. Cliff writes that he rode in the second carriage with Hettie and Jessie and there was a large following, as indeed was fitting so splendid a townsman. And so snaps another link.

Hettie and Jessie were Furber's daughters; Hettie became a keen advocate of Esperanto and gave lessons in the town.

Mr Furber's school had breaking-up concerts. Tom Lucas, an old school friend wrote at the announcement of Jim's knighthood in 1928:

Although I left school in the month of July 1875 my mind frequently goes back to those days and to our dear schoolmaster, Mr Furber, whose heart would be full of joy to-day if he were alive. I often think of the Breaking Up concerts of the days long ago and his pride in us when he had trained us as performers on those great occasions.

From Mr Furber's school Jim proceeded to Bridge House School in Chester as a boarder. The headmaster, Mr H A Ruinet, was assisted by a 'resident graduate of Cambridge and other qualified masters'. This school had been established in 1835 and was principally intended for pupils who wished to follow commercial careers. English grammar, literature and composition, geography and history (ancient and modern), arithmetic and book-keeping 'are made subjects of the most careful study,' said the prospectus. Music was bracketed with drawing and Spanish and Italian languages as among 'other accomplishments taught at this establishment' but Jim had the benefit of some enthusiastic teaching from a Welsh musician, John Owen, organist of St Mary's Church, who wrote under the name of Owain Alaw. He was the composer of a cantata, The Fall of Babylon, and other choral battlefields regularly fought over by choirs at the National Eisteddfords. German also entertained his fellow pupils with conjuring feats and with rechauffés of his music hall turns from earlier days. As well as taking a prominent part in the organising of school entertainments, he became interested in the preparation of séances. Unfortunately in his seventeenth year he, like his sisters, fell victim to severe illness and had to leave Bridge House, returning home for a long convalescence. One report published after his death records that he was a pupil at Whitchurch Grammer School. He may have spent a short time there if his parents decided against a resumption at boarding school.

The only trace we have of his time at Bridge House is a letter written by a friend, Henry Smith, to the family at the time of German's death. Although two years younger than German, Smith remembered the alarm at the school when he fell ill and his mother's hasty journey to Chester to nurse him. He also recalled that German had not seemed an exceptional musical prodigy.

It was when he returned to Whitchurch to convalesce that these talents began to develop more strongly and music became a consuming interest. We have already seen that he had given some solo performances on the pianoforte and learnt to deputise for his father on the organ. He had also taken some lessons from W. E. Rogers, organist of St Alkmund's, the parish church. The use of music in stage productions had also caught his imagination and he later recalled his excitement at the use of a small string orchestra by a travelling theatre company he seems to have visited without his parents' knowledge. By his fifteenth year he had, by his own efforts, reached a reasonable standard on the violin and sang in the alto section of the Whitchurch Choral Society. After the rehearsals he and Rogers would retire to the Working Men's Institute and play violin duets, including extracts from Sterndale Bennett's *The May Queen*. If visiting soloists wished to rehearse their items before the concerts, German would be summoned to the Victoria Hotel to accompany them. Several commented on his ability. He had even formed a small ensemble which according to the Scott biography

A family portrait

Edward German age 15

consisted of himself playing first violin, the curate second violin, a watchmaker the flute, a bricklayer the cornet and one of his sisters, probably Rachel, as pianist. In an interview given in 1915, he referred also to a local photographer who supported the second violin section and gave a special commendation to the creditable playing of the bricklayer. The group was sufficiently proficient to perform in the village halls, and he himself had to arrange the items for this little orchestra over which he, almost its youngest member, held sway.

Away from the pressures of boarding school he devoted much more time to studying and arranging music. It is hard to imagine now the conditions under which a provincial youth would have to strive to acquire the knowledge of musical history and the works of great composers. In the 1870s even a wealthy and sophisticated connoisseur might have the opportunity to hear a particular symphony or opera once in a lifetime. Through pianoforte reductions and miscellaneous albums one might become acquainted with the major composers but there were few biographers and music critics to guide and interest the young enthusiasts who wished to know more about the development of the art of music generally. To enjoy even the fragments that came to hand, one had to develop the power of imagination to make orchestral and choral music spring to life from the printed page and that is what the young musician taught himself to do.

Not surprisingly his parents anticipated that he would seek employment in some sphere more closely linked with the commercial background of his family and the local industries of the neighbourhood. He had always taken an interest in gadgets and mechanical devices and it was suggested that he should seek an apprenticeship as an engineer in Laird's shipbuilding yard in Birkenhead. He was taken there for interview but, according to tradition, it transpired that he was just too old to be accepted and the family was obliged to reflect again on his future.

An energetic and gifted ally came to the cause of music as a career. Walter Cecil Hay lived at Shrewsbury but came to Whitchurch to conduct the Choral Society. He had been particularly impressed by German's prowess on the violin and had encouraged him to persevere with his playing to the point where he was able to lead the Society's orchestra. More than once his clear and decisive playing had brought back wandering sopranos to the melodic fold. Hay now put forward the idea that the boy should try for a place at the Royal Academy of Music.

Hay is described as 'professor' in the Scott biography but this was a courtesy title. If fact he was not only a fine practical musician but also an urbane and courteous gentleman who was able to personify the profession in a manner which assuaged any doubts that the Jones parents may have had. He had a military background. Born in Shrewsbury and a pupil of the Royal Academy 1848–1851, he had been appointed bandmaster of the 12th Lancers, then stationed in Dublin. When the regiment was ordered further afield he decided to settle back in his native town and in 1852 he was called upon to form a brass band to replace the old drums and pipes of the Shropshire Militia. On the introduction of the Volunteer Movement in 1860, Mr Hay was in great demand for the forming and training of Volunteer Bands. Indeed, as bandmaster of the 2nd Battalion Rifle Volunteers at Whitchurch he had, as we have seen, already done something to stimulate the musical enthusiasm of his future pupil. It is said that he was once offered the post of bandmaster in one of the most distinguished regiments in the land but did not wish to leave his native Shropshire. The picture given in Scott is of a scholarly musician and it is certainly true that Hay had an academic training, that he had a love of chamber music and a good library of scores, and that he was the Choirmaster of many churches including Holy Trinity, St Giles, the Abbey, and St Chad's. He was the Choir Visitor for the Salopian section of the Lichfield diocese. But he also arranged the music for Hunt Balls and composed quadrilles and waltzes for parties in great houses. In his student days he had overcome academic objections to the cornet as a musical instrument and composed and played a piece for it at one of the Academy concerts. When in 1865 Shrewsbury School decided to hold an annual concert Mr Hay was appointed as trainer and conductor.

For forty years, without intermission or a hint of sabbatical leave, he trained the school choir, selected the music, wrote out instrumental parts for young players, however ineffective, coached soloists and chorus and conducted the concerts. He had a serene good nature. One Salopian remembered going to Hay's room to have his voice tested for a small boy's solo and after running up and down sundry scales being rejected in the most complimentary terms by the old gentleman who cried out, 'Capital, Capital!' when his examinee made gallant but vain efforts to reach the top note. He became very proud of his young pupil, German Jones, and prophesied to his daughter that the boy would become 'a second Sullivan'. It is strange that Hay made no attempt to introduce his private pupil into the musical life of Shrewsbury School and even stranger that in his final concert when he was presented by the Old Salopians with a silver salver and a purse of gold that he should not have included any works by his most esteemed pupil. For this was in 1904 after the success of the *Henry VIII* music and

Merrie England. Instead he chose Auber's overture *Le Philtre* and a hunting chorus by Alfred Cellier. Having, moreover, selected a Glee from *The Emerald Isle* for the choir he accorded the honours in the programme solely to Sullivan. Yet there is no doubt of his great pride in German's later success or his influence on the young man. He was an urbane and distinguished character who passed through his time at Shrewsbury, a period when many public school music masters were submitted to merciless horseplay, without the slightest worries over discipline or control. He is described as 'a striking old world figure, with his trimmed white beard, his black velvet coat and red tie, and for the school concert, brass buttons on his evening dress'. The training which he gave to the young German was intense but it greatly widened the boy's range of musical experience.

'The nine months that I passed under Mr Hay's roof were perhaps the happiest of my life,' wrote German later.

Mr Hay was an enthusiast in music. He conducted an excellent orchestra, conducted concerts, taught one harmony and instrumentation and I made music the whole day long beginning at six o'clock in the morning. Mr Hay had a splendid library of music, especially full scores. We played no end of trio and violin duets (Pleyel and Viotti). I also practised the organ a good deal and was able to play the D Major Fugue of Bach. I look upon that three quarters of a year at Shrewsbury as the most important formative period of my life.

The third member of the trio was Thomas Bratton, bandmaster of Shropshire Light Infantry. Other teachers were brought in to help prepare him for the Academy examination. A Mr Stephenson of Wrexham gave him his first professional tuition on the violin. The organist of the Abbey Church, James Warhurst, also gave him lessons for it was thought at the time that the organ would be his principal instrument. He gained further experience in his travels with Hay to advise and help rural choirs who were preparing for the Lichfield Choral Society. In 1924 writing to 'Dick' and Mab who had some news of the Warhurst's son, he said,

News about Warhurst is most interesting. I remember his father well and can see him now busy with his feet on the pedals in Bach's fugues. I used to look forward to my lessons at the Abbey Church but gracious! He must be about a hundred! It is 44 years since I was his pupil and he seemed to be a man of about fifty – but quite possibly he was younger.

In September, 1880, the time for the Royal Academy examination came.

Elizabeth Jones nervously took her son to London to play before the blind Sir George MacFarren, the principal. The test was the Beethoven Sonata in G Major and to her anxious question MacFarren was able to give the answer for which she had undoubtedly prayed.

CHAPTER TWO

The Royal Academy

The Royal Academy of Music at this date had survived almost sixty years of financial peril and suffered from the restrictions which these had caused. Founded in 1822 and opened in 1823 it owed its conception to John Fane, Lord Burghersh, later the 11th Earl of Westmoreland, and a soldier and diplomat who admired the schools of music that existed in some of the principal European cities. He was also a voluminous composer and the students in early days were kept busy performing his cantatas, operas and instrumental works as the price of his assistance. Among its first teachers were Thomas Attwood, who had been a pupil of Mozart, and Cipriani Potter, a pupil of Beethoven. It was to have the style of a naval college and uniforms were introduced with gold lettering round the hat bands, though this was soon discarded. Fanny Dickens, sister of Charles, was one of the first students and the future novelist would often be seen waiting in the vestibule to take her home. Because of shortage of funds it opened with only twenty-one students, aged between ten and fifteen instead of the anticipated eighty. For many years special appeals were necessary to prevent its closure.

It had royal patronage – Queen Victoria and Prince Albert once attended a masked ball in its aid – but no reliable subvention. The royal couple's son, the Duke of Edinburgh, was president until his death, when he was succeeded by the Duke of Connaught. But this did not pay the bills. A grant of £500, presumed to be an annual gift, was made by Mr Gladstone but it was discontinued by Disraeli and only the return of a Gladstone government in 1868 and some vigorous action by the professors saved the institution from extinction. They had agreed to forego their salaries for a period but, in exchange, had arrogated to themselves a large share of the management. The constant financial problems had other deleterious effects. The professors, although they had considerable powers, were not always of the stature or experience required. The Academy also was forced to accept fee-paying pupils to whom music was more of a graceful accomplishment than a lifetime's study.

It was not on its present site in Marylebone but in Tenterden Street,

Hanover Square, where it had absorbed a number of houses into its rambling complex, known to pupils as 'the rabbit warren'. Its original home at number 4 had been the town-house of the Earls of Carnarvon. The principal had no office to himself. Students were non-resident and German at first lodged with Walter Hay's sister in Turnham Green. Sir George MacFarren had been a student himself in the very early days. His father had been a dancing master and theatre musician but he had studied composition under Cipriani Potter, a member of a notable family of English musicians who owed his Christian name to a godmother, sister of the Italian painter and friend of J. C. Bach. MacFarren, as German was to do later, had finished a First Symphony, and heard it performed while still a student. He returned as professor in the first year of Victoria's reign. Ten years later he resigned as a result of considerable discord over the teaching of harmony. He adhered to the school of one Alfred Day, whose theories to the layman are immensely obscure but appear to imply that the notes of a chord are based upon sounds that are not heard rather than those that are. Be that as it may, the rift between MacFarren and his colleagues was a considerable one and it was some time before he was reappointed. Bernard Shaw called Dr Day's system 'a stupendous monument of ingenious folly' and declared that candidates for a Bachelor of Music degree had to find out who the examiner would be and give different answers to the same questions, 'according to whether they were put by Ouseley and MacFarren or Stainer'. Wagnerian chromaticism had enlarged the harmonic scope of writing though MacFarren continued to insist that Wagner's methods were unscientific, 'until,' said Shaw, 'at last one could not help admiring the resolute conviction with which the veteran professor, old, blind and hopelessly in the wrong, would still rise to utter his protest when there was an opening for it'. Despite his academic narrowness he was an energetic character, who conducted at Covent Garden and helped to found the Handel Society in 1844. He had written symphonies to the number of nine, that mystical bourne which so few composers cross, and operas on subjects as diverse as *Charles II, Helvellyn*, and *She Stoops to Conquer*. He had written a text-book, *MacFarren's Rudiments of Harmony*, which German studied and kept all his life. It begins uncomprisingly: 'This books presents the truth and nothing but the truth, though not the whole truth, on the boundless subject of which it treats'. It is full of densely packed information on subjects such as the proper notation of the chord of the minor 13th, which concludes with the words: 'I refer musicians for unanswerable arguments on this subject and on that of the chord of the 11th to the *Treatise on Harmony* of Alfred Day'. It concludes with progressive exercises through which German duly progressed, ticking off each of the grim-looking bass lines over which chords had to be constructed. He allowed himself only one irreverent comment during this long pilgrimage writing 'beastly ugly' against a progression of MacFarren's purporting to prove that the 'chromatic chord of the supertonic, or its inversion, may likewise be followed by a chromatic discord of the key note without disturbing the tonality'.

The debate on harmony by which the Academy was periodically riven had another result on which one may speculate: a relative absence of interest in rhythm. Much English music came to be characterised by repetitive rhythmic patterns and the absence of rhythmic experiment. German broke free from this limitation to some extent, especially in his larger orchestral works, especially by adopting melodic phrases of unusual length and interweaving the occasional irregular time signature. But the heavy drag of a monotonous pulse affects some of his writing.

Wagner described the principal as 'Mr MacFarrine (sic), a pompous melancholy Scotsman' and although he was a friendly and encouraging adviser to the pupils he was not a teacher likely to drive his pupils down new paths of thought, or even convey some of the ideas that were changing the European musical scene. In his lectures he would inveigh against 'all the iniquities covered by that blessed word "atmosphere"'. By 1860 total blindness had overtaken him although he continued to write and lecture with remarkable fortitude and still had a part of his career ahead of him as Sterndale Bennett's successor as Professor of Music at Cambridge.

When the *Musical Times* in 1903 was preparing a short sketch of German's career, German wrote a note to the editor after the corrected proofs had been returned:

Dear Mr Edwards,
'Pon my word, you will think me a nuisance – however, it can't be helped, I am really very sorry.
Well, it occurs to me that we have not even mentioned the name of Sir George MacFarren – Now if it can possibly be arranged just say a word – if only out of deference to his brother Walter [also a composer and writer on music] whom I know very well and who is equally sensitive on these points . . . Something like this: 'The Principal, Sir George MacFarren, gave him every encouragement to compose'.

He settled immediately into student life at the beginning of the Autumn Term, 1880. London in the 1880s, though it did not have the rich musical life which it enjoys today was nevertheless the swelling capital of a rich and expanding empire. There were theatres and concert halls to supersede village institutes and travelling companies that had provided the entertainment of German and his friends in Shropshire. He immediately became a Londoner and though he enjoyed country excursions, and walking and cycling holidays and found that the countryside provided inspiration for his music, his chief interests became those which only a capital city can provide. He had originally intended to spend three years at the Academy and then proceed to Germany. In the event, he remained at Tenterden Street for seven years.

His organ playing had been one of the most successful features of his examination and he had impressed Dr Stiggall, his teacher, with a performance of the Bach D Major Fugue, but soon the violin became his first instrument. He commenced lessons with Harry Weist Hill, a noted orchestral leader who became first principal of the Guildhall School of Music and was grandfather of Ralph Hill, an ebullient music critic of the *Radio Times* during the 1940s and a great champion of Delius. As the violin playing became his chief interest, he took further lessons from Alfred Burnett. He studied harmony and counterpoint under Henry Banister, another pupil of Cipriani Potter but subsequently moved to a second teacher, Ebenezer Prout, who had only recently joined the Academy staff. Prout was a self-educated but immensely industrious musical grammarian who is reputed to have once discovered and then eliminated consecutive fifths from Handel's *Messiah*. When an error was discovered in composition, his recurring phrase was, 'Fetch me down the Bible' (Bach's *Forty-Eight Preludes and Fugues*). This was then removed from the shelf and he would point his finger at the passage which accused their efforts. His own compositions are never played to-day but his two volumes on orchestration are excellent and German's skill in this field must owe much to his training.

Prout's desire to stress his own prowess as a composer – his book on orchestration frequently contains phrases such as 'the paucity of examples must excuse the writer introducing one from his own pen' – caused some amusement to German and a young colleague, Henry Wood, future doyen of the Promenade Concerts. The professor had written a triumphal march for his cantata, King Alfred, 'a truly dreadful work' in Wood's opinion. When they heard him approaching, Wood or German would strike up excerpts from the march on the piano to Prout's great delight. 'I see you know my King Alfred,' he would chuckle, unaware that the two students had some sort of private joke between them.

In kindlier vein, German received rather similar treatment later in life. On his visits to Whitchurch he would be delighted on country walks by passers-by whistling or lightly humming his popular melodies.

The ensemble class was under the guidance of Prosper Sainton, bearer of one of those strange hybrid French Christian names, Philippe-Catharine, a Frenchman from Toulouse, who had been a distinguished string performer in his younger days. His wife, Charlotte Sainton-Dolby was the singer whom Mendelssohn had in mind when writing the contralto part in *Elijah*. Sainton himself had been a court violinist to Queen Victoria and had led the orchestra in several of the theatres and opera houses in London. It was a considerable leap for a boy of eighteen to make to leave the homemade entertainments of Whitchurch and the small ensemble made up of the watch-maker, the curate and the bricklayer for a close acquaintance with those whose experience ranged from court to conservatoire. His desire to partake of the honours which the Academy bestowed and to enjoy acclaim hitherto confined to village-halls in Shropshire induced an intensely competitive attitude. At times he trained himself too hard, working for prizes and seeking distinction in not one but several disciplines.

The Academy held concerts almost every month in term time. They usually contained a choral work, and German's first appearance in the choir was on 23rd October, 1880, in a performance of a Bach motet, *Blessing, Glory, Wisdom*. Subsequently he sang in part one of Handel's Semele, Mendelssohn' settings of two psalms and a choral work by Sterndale Bennett, *Now my God*. In July, 1881, he appears for the first time in the violin section of the orchestra accompanying concertos by Kelkbrenner, Hiller and an Academy Scholar, G. T. Bennett. He made a number of appearances in both the first and second violin sections of the orchestra in Haydn's *Imperial Mass* the first movement of the *'Emperor' Concerto* and Mendelssohn's *War March of the Priests*. It was on 21st October 1882 that he first appears on the programme as a composer with a piece called *Nocturne*, himself playing solo violin with a Mr T. D. Knott at the pianoforte. In the programme he appeared under his rightful name as German Jones.

The Nocturne still exists in manuscript, its title page, unsigned, but carefully written with a quill pen, and its final bar line embellished with a flourish akin to his father's last sustained chords on the old chapel organ. Its main theme is an *andante tranquillo* in G major the violin supported by fragments of the melody in the left hand of the piano part. The middle section rises to *agitato* with several changes of tempo, and some indication of the composer's love of unexpectedly drawing out a melody. The writing for both instruments is skilful and there are numerous instructions to the players in every bar. There is an even earlier composition from his time in London a song, *Twilight*, written in 1881, a tale of tragedy in a fisherman's cottage by the sea. In later years he wrote 'Not to be Published' firmly across the front page, as it belonged to the world of gloomy Victorian ballads with pounding accompaniments.

In the following June a second composition, an orchestral piece, *Pizzicato*, was included in the programme and in July he played a violin solo, *Romance in G*, by John Svendsen, as German E. Jones. In December of 1883, in the list of first violins the name of 'Jones G' is crossed out and 'E German' substituted in handwriting. It may be that the alteration was made at a later date but it indicates the time when, probably at MacFarren's instigation, he decided to reverse his Christian names and use them as his nom-de-plume. There were at least two other Jones in the Academy concerts at this time and the change may have been made to avoid confusion. Edward German, moreover seemed a more memorable and artistic name. He continued, however, to incorporate the initial 'J'. In the first concert in 1884 Mr J. E. German was the soloist in Corelli's *Sonata in D, opus 5,* and he appeared thus in a number of chamber works in the following months.

Also in 1884 he played the viola in the Mendelssohn *Quartet in D, opus 44, No.1.* The second violinist was H. C Tonking, who had subsequently a somewhat restless career as organist and violinist which took him through churches of various denominations, the orchestra at Covent Garden and the Grosvenor Cinema, Glasgow, where he eventually became one of the first generation of cinema organists. It was the unpredictable Tonking who taught Henry Wood the organ. When on one occasion he was dismissed from his post as organist of Westminster Bridge Road he spent the evening switching around all the pipes, so that his successor started with a huge debacle the following day.

In 1882 German had returned to Whitchurch for Christmas. Apologising to his sisters for the absence of letters ('Very sorry not written but no time *honestly no time*'), he recounted the hectic schedule to which he was committed. He had already been given some work teaching and also took part in concerts at Bedford, Hereford and elsewhere in addition to his studies. 'Throughout all my work I think of nothing but coming home and seeing you all again . . . ' This was the occasion when he persuaded his sisters to write an elaborate charade, 'The Missing Wig', in which he proposed to do his ever popular impersonation of the Whitchurch doctor:

I shall buy White Whiskers for my part. It may not be very much unlike a well-known doctor in Whitchurch whose name begins with B . . . always telling anecdotes that have no meaning in them whatsoever. My great saying to be 'Ah, talking of so and so reminds me of a little story!!' Am very tired. Didn't arrive from Bedford till 3 o'clock yesterday morning. It was a fine Concert. Quartet was encored. Have no end of letters to write. It is now midnight. Glad you have written the play. I trust I have got a good and 'funny in the extreme' part! I am going to bring Mother a beautiful bit of Stilton. I sent Cliff a diary on his birthday.

German, his energy quickly recovered, played Cornelius Troddles Esq., (bald guest who wore a wig). Willie Scott, his future biographer, was August Podger (genial host). The sketch about 'The Missing Wig' had in the end a mildly ironic sequel. German's own hair receded at quite an early age and he adopted a toupée which was exchanged for grey and eventually white versions over the years. When the *Gloucester Journal* noted the 'storm of applause' which greeted his entry onto the platform at the Three Choirs Festival of 1922 and commented that 'since his last visit many winters have touched his hair', it was ascribing to nature the tribute due to art.

Within a year German had won the Tubbs Prize Bow, a bow made by a famous Soho craftsman, for his violin playing and during his seven years in Tenterden Street, he won in all six prizes and six certificates. The strain of competition and a very strong wish to justify the confidence and pride of his family drove him to bouts of excessive work and practice and at times his health appeared to be under strain once again. He was keen to win the Potter Exhibition for organ playing and would rise every morning at six a.m. in order to walk to Westminster Bridge Road Church to practise. In the competition itself he came second. 'It makes one wild to think of it . . . I would almost rather have been a mile off', he wrote. Yet it is fortunate in restrospect that his ambitions were redirected from the organ to the violin and to composition, for too early a success in what had originally been his first instrument might well have led him into the field of church music and into the life of a cathedral close where his talents for stage music would not have been given scope.

In the summer vacation of 1883, he took a group of Academy friends, all of them medallists, to give a concert at Whitchurch in aid of the cricket club funds. At this moment he was still using both names and appeared as violinist on the programme as Mr German E. Jones and as composer under the name of J. E. German. The group included the rumbustious Henry Tonking as well as a brilliant fifteen year-old pianist, Septimus Webbe, who performed a Bourrée and Tarantella by German, opus 10. Webbe, German and violin-cellist J. E. Hambleton also played a Larghetto Affanoso from a String Trio, opus 7. This work later christened Romance still exists in manuscript. The melody in A minor is shared by violin and cello with some assured interweaving of the parts, while the pianist is given some *appassionato* passages with plenty of chords sinking down in semitones. Interesting for those seeking signs of the mature musician are the copious instructions to the players. Almost every bar of every part is covered with expression marks.

German himself played movements from the De Beriot Eighth Concerto which he was later to give at an Academy concert, but which would show to his Whitchurch audience how great the progress in technique which he had made, 'The applause was simply tremendous after his violin solo,' said *The Whitchurch Herald*, 'of which he repeated the latter part.'

In 1884 as a result of his training in Sainton's class he played in Beethoven's Quartet' opus No. 1 (violin), and a Rheinberger Quartet, opus 38 (violin) at the Academy. At the same time he was made a sub-professor of the violin and thus added the teaching of younger students to his other commitments. In 1884 he also entered for the Lucas Composition Medal for which the test was a Sonata, First Movement, for pianoforte.

Many years later, in 1928, he was called upon to present the Academy prizes in the absence, through illness, of the Duke of Connaught. In his speech, he allowed himself to look back over those early struggles, referring to 'the days in our little house in Tenterden Street' and marvelling at the new premises and facilities of the 'monumental home in York Gate . . . I marvel at the difference between those days and now,' he said,

> I do not necessarily hold a brief for our little house in Tenterden Street but I never entered the doors of that Academy without feeling that I was in a temple apart and the musical friendships we made there will always be very dear to me. There is the human side to this prize giving and by the human side I mean the students who have been disappointed. I can sympathise with them because I had disappointment after disappointment in regard to bronze medals, silver medals and certificates. In the end I was happy to receive them all.
>
> In the old Academy in Tenterden Street I remember a very keen competition we had. It was for the Lucas Medal. We were all very keen on it and worked very hard for it and, of course, each one thought that he would win the prize. At last the great day came and I hurried to the Academy to look on the wall to see the name that was posted there. I arrived and I had, alas, a disappointment: but I had the satisfaction of finding that the name that was written was that of my old friend and your distinguished Professor Stuart Macpherson.

Stuart Macpherson became a teacher of Harmony, and a respected musician.

One of the last letters German received was an anxious enquiry about his health from his old rival.

In fact over thirty sonatas had been sent in and the final choice had rested between German's and Macpherson's, who won it with an *Allegro Impetuoso – Allegro Ma non Troppo* in Eb.

German's sonata in G, first movement also exists in manuscript except for the final page. After a rather heavy introduction, *larghetto maestoso*, in G minor, it proceeds to some delightful pages in a Schubertian style with neat little triplet figures worked into the melody. The judges may have thought that the second subject with its first note repeated nine times was too dull, and a good deal of the central section called for strings vibrato, rather than the piano, but the composer has a mastery of the sonata form and it is quite a big work, with harsher rhythms than are to be found in his later piano pieces. He later used the second subject in his First Impromptu in the *Album of Piano* pieces.

The rules of the Academy at this time, subsequently relaxed by the next principal, Alexander Mackenzie, kept boys and girls strictly apart in all the ensemble classes, except for purposes of musical discussion. This does not seem to have prevented social groups arising. German's friends called themselves The Party. They were assiduous in attending public concerts and listening to each other's works, finding that slender territory which exists between frankness and encouragement. The members included Moir Clark John Greenaway, Dora Bright and Ethel Boyce.

The two girls, Dora Bright and Ethel Boyce were frequent performers in the Academy concerts and themselves submitted compositions. As early as February 1882, a setting by Dora Bright of a poem by Longfellow, German's favourite poet, had been included, *I heard a brooklet gushing*, and in 1883 a sentimental song, *The Task of the Flower*, describing how a dying bloom had brought hope to a crippled boy in a garret. A romance began between German and Ethel Boyce, a talented pianist who was eventually the Lady Goldsmith Scholar.

For another student, Ellen Haas, he wrote a short song cycle setting three German poems, and these were sung at the fortnightly concerts. Many years later in writing to congratulate him on his knighthood, the singer had regretfully to report that the *lieder* had disappeared during a period of over-vigorous spring cleaning.

With another friend W. B. George, who was keen on physical fitness, the young student was drawn for a short time into a regime of 'jogging' and bouts of boxing training. "But I pray you mark the agreement" wrote

German. "He wanted to practice his guard, so I was to slash in right and left and never get a blow. I wiped his nose for him once or twice and independent of the agreement I was the happy recipient of two or three well aimed blows." Their activities were not confirmed to amateur pugilism however. Many years later German dug out of his papers an invitation to the theatre written in 1886 when George had asked him to choose the piece for a Matineé visit.

"Dear William G
(Altho' thou'rt free
to disagree)
Thou askest me
To choose for thee
What 'tis to be
That 'gether we
Shall go and see Tomorrow

One hour ere three
Hath toll-e-d
Will pay our fee
At Gall-er-ee
Of Gai-e-tee
And fervent-lee
Hope 'Haggard's' (*She'*
May give us glee
Not sorrow"

When German came to collect his reminiscences for the 1932 biography his memory played him false in some minor respects. He recalled when he was invited to play the De Beriot Eighth Concerto at a concert in St James Hall he, with some temerity, asked Sainton to lend him his treasured Guarnerius violin (one would like to call it priceless: German put the figure of £800 on it!) and that subsequently he borrowed it again for a performance of the orchestral version of his Bolero. In fact the Academy records show that he did not perform the concerto until July 1885, after five years of study, but the Bolero in an orchestrated version was performed in the July concert of 1884. Burnett had shown an interest in and had helped to arrange its publication. German later recollected that Burnett had suggested it sould be orchestrated, and although he had doubts about his capabilities, and had no previous experience, he had set to and accomplished the task. In fact a pizzicato movement subsequently called The Guitar had already been billed

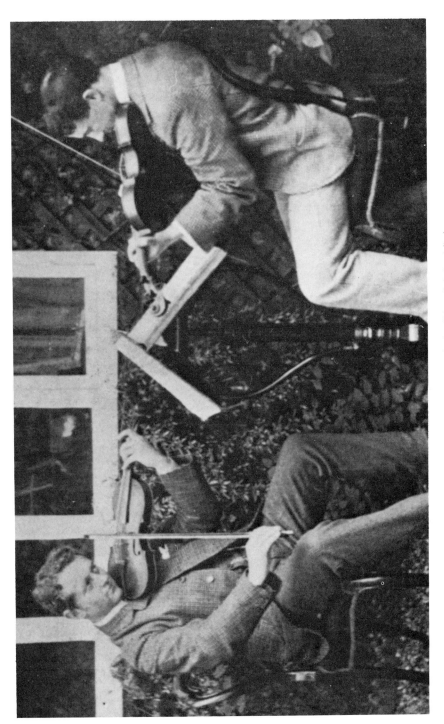

W. E. Rogers, organist of Whitchurch parish school, and his pupil playing violin duets

The Academy student

as an orchestral piece at an 1883 concert, though it may have been given principally by the strings, and it is difficult to imagine that a pupil of Prout's had not been initiated into some of the mysteries of orchestration. At all events he continued to improve as an outstanding student in a very talented group. In 1883, a fellow pupil of Burnett's, William Richardson had played his Bolero and Chanson d'Amour. The Gallicized title page of the latter is inscribed *Chanson d'amour Pour Le Violin, Par J. E. German.* It had been completed in 1882: a sentimental melody but a good sentimental melody, again with numerous dynamic markings for the players. In the July Concert in 1884, Miss Dora Bright, played *'Impromptu* and *Valse Caprice for Piano'* and in May 1885 she performed an *'Elegy'* and *'Mazurka'*.

German also recollected playing the solo part in a concerto by Viotti, a remarkable musician, whose career led him through a period of patronage by Marie Antoinette, expulsion from England as a suspected Jacobin spy during the French Revolution, and directorship of the Paris Opera, under the Restoration Monarchy when the Duke de Berri, ultra-conservative heir to the French throne, was murdered within the precincts of the opera house itself. Despite this busy life, Viotti had somehow contrived to write seventy-nine concertos, which made admirable test pieces for students. German was so impressed by his mastery of one of these that he wrote out twenty bars of his part and sent it to Walter Hay. It did indeed represent dramatic progress by the self taught boy from Whitchurch.

Ethel Boyce had many compositions performed, including a Caprice and Bolero of her own, a Gavotte for pianoforte and several of her songs. As Lady Goldsmith Scholar of the Academy she performed in 1886 an Intermezzo and Scherzo from her own Piano Sonata in G Minor. If German's Chanson d'Amour was addressed to anyone in particular it was to Ethel Boyce, as the developing romance led to an engagement. German, however, did not appear to have his father's persistent devotion, and the songs which Ethel Boyce contributed to the Academy concerts have a melancholy tinge. In May 1884 a setting of Tennyson contained the stanza:

As through the land at eve we went
And plucked the ripened ears
We fell out my wife and I
O we fell out I know not why
And kissed again with tears.

A year later she wrote a setting of a poem, *Drifting*:

So she went drifting, drifting

Day after Day
So she went shifting shifting
Further away,
O but a word would have done it
Word never spoken
So she went drifting! drifting
With her heart broken.

Ethel Mary Boyce was the daughter of George Boyce a prominent citizen of Chertsey and a county councillor. As well as possessing musical talents she shared with German an enthusiasm for cycling and fishing. For her time she was obviously emancipated. 'Please send some tobacco – I'm running short,' she wrote to a friend while staying at Bath for the season. A few years later she informed him, 'The doctor suggested smoking should be lessened with a view of leaving off altogether! I need not say I have no such view . . .' She could listen with amusement rather than fluttering consternation when a young man at a party told her how he had recently escaped from the clutches of devil-worshippers in Paris. She lived the open life of a student at a time when many young ladies were rigidly sequestered in the home. In the year before German's visit to Dresden she travelled abroad with two other members of The Party, Dora Bright and John Greenaway, and clambered among the rocky pine forests of Bohemia. ('Dora is very trying, I believe she would like to do nothing better than to get up late – dawdle about all day – and go to the opera at night.') She could be coquettish and related the success of her costume at a fancy dress ball where Dora's Carmen outfit had been somewhat overshadowed by the red uniforms of the military.

There are several versions of the story of the end of the engagement. One family tradition relates that German, desperately unhappy, walked the streets of London trying to resolve his thoughts and finally threw the ring from a London bridge into the Thames. Another, that the ring was thrown during a quarrel either into the Thames or the Severn. All appear to agree that it met a watery grave and neither young lover ever married, though Ethel maintained a long, tentatively romantic friendship with a Chertsey solicitor, Harland Chaldicott.

It is thought that German wished to pursue his career as a composer while she wished for something more sophisticated and rewarding. One only has to visit her old home, The Orchard, in Chertsey to imagine some of the problems that would have arisen for a musician with no prospects or patrons. Though now uninhabited and rather desolate, it is a huge Victorian mansion with an ornate conservatory and steps and terraces that lead down to the wide lawns, a far cry from The Vaults or the modest rooms at The Laurels.

She continued to live at The Orchard and became a prolific composer writing at least three cantatas, numerous part songs for female choirs and albums of piano pieces. She even ventured to challenge comparison with her old suitor with a setting of *Charming Chloe* written in 1924. She wrote the words of many of her songs and the score for a *Peace Pageant* produced in Chertsey during the First World War. Her letters that have survived are intelligent and amusing. It may be regretted that she did not have the opportunity to play the part in German's life which Lady Elgar was to play as a driving force in the steady advance of her husband's career. She and German continued to have a very occasional correspondence and in 1934 he sent her a copy of the Scott Biography. In her reply she said, 'I *don't* find you presented as too much of an angel. You were always liked by *everyone* and properly so.' She reminded him that he had forgotten to mention a sixth member of The Party – 'Poor old Campbell . . . Don't you remember going to his wedding?'

> I like the photograph I have of you in a light suit better than any in the book. I always wish we had seen more of each other – as life drew on you'd have realised how very 'country' I really am and that your Hermit ways were also mine when possible . . . As you know *I love* your music and the certainty that it will remain is a comfort to me in this very ugly time. And now dear boy (for so you will always be to me!) thank you again for the treasured book and please believe in the continued affection of your old friend,
>
> Ethel Boyce

It seems strange that the composer of so many romantic ballads and love songs should have grown set in his bachelor ways, though such a contradiction is far from unique. When in later year Herman Finck teased him on the absence of a wife, he replied jokingly that he had always found women had insufficient knowledge of cricket.

Although an amorous note occasionally appears in later correspondence, it was his two sisters and especially Rachel who came to supply the feminine influence in his life and he kept up a busy correspondence with them both over the years. For a time, however, The Party provided him with society, flirtations and a good deal of encouragement in his writing. In 1885 the test for the Lucas Composition Medal was the comparatively difficult one of a setting of the *Te Deum* for soloists and chorus with organ accompaniment.

The winning entry was to be published by Novello. This time he succeeded. On the day the result was to be announced he did what he could to allay his anxieties by following his old interest in conjuring and went to see a matinée performance at the Piccadilly Theatre. Looking out of the window of the bus taking him back to the Academy he saw one of the judges walking down Regent Street. His impulse was to jump off and ask for the results but nervousness held him to his seat. Avoiding other students in Tenterden Street he arrived at the doors to be greeted by the young Septimus Webbe who congratulated him on his victory.

It is an exciting moment to open German's *Te Deum* bound in as it is with over a hundred settings of the same words in Novello's *Parish Choir Book*. Almost all are now unsung, but it was his success in the Lucas Medal which determined him to seek his luck as a composer rather than an instrumentalist. In fact it does not seem to have been published for several years but German might have taken heart from the fact that when it appeared it was the most expensive *Te Deum* in the catalogue, copies priced at one shilling each. The previous year's Lucas Medal Winner had a *Te Deum* selling for fourpence only, while Sir George MacFarren and his brother Walter rated threepence each.

The anthem is of the kind that would be written by an earnest, well intentioned student for the panel of academic judges, It opens with a downward scale passage for manual and pedals on the organ, and there are plenty of fugal entry passages and strong chordal moments for the choir. The future opera composer takes his opportunities. After a big crescendo on the words 'Continually do cry,' the choir drops to a sudden unison *pianissimo* on the repeated words, 'Holy, Holy, Holy'. By contrast after quiet statements of 'The Glorious Company of the Apostles, and subsequent lines there are big shouts of 'Praise Him'. The soloists enter at the words, 'When Thou tookest upon thee to deliver Man', which is in the composer's limpid and tuneful style. The phrase 'O Lord have mercy upon us' is marked *Affrettando* and the final page dies away into a muted close with the organ solo flute, repeating the scale passage with which the anthem opened.

From the same year there is an *Andante in B♭* for organ, also unpublished and, strange for someone who had arrived at the Academy with the organ as his first instrument, one of his very rare compositions for it. It has a mild, hymn-like theme and probably was written for one of the recitals which German and his friends gave in the holidays in the churches around his home.

An Australian friend, George Herbert, organist of Ballarat Cathedral came with him to Whitchurch during one holiday. They gave recitals, played duets and extemporised on the Dodington Chapel organ. Herbert, in later years, recalled being taken to see old Muller, the piano teacher in Prees, who, having consumed a considerable quantity of gin, kept them both till a late hour, then insisted on stuffing their pockes with hazel nuts to sustain them as they tramped home through the night.

Robert Furber was quick to announce news of the Lucas Medal in *The Whitchurch Herald* adding, lest the announcement should seem egregious, 'It is at our own solicitation that these particulars are supplied for publishing.' The 'particulars' were the full record of the local boy's success at the Academy: 1881 Gold mounted bow, 1882 Two bronze medals (one for violin, one for sight singing and transposing), 1883 Three commendations, 1884 Silver Medal for Violin, Bronze for Harmony. A Silver Medal for Harmony and Certificate of Merit were also awarded at the same time as the Lucas Medal. There had been sixteen *Te Deum* entries submitted. It might be added that by the 1880s the medals were real. In earlier days the Academy was so poor that the prize-winners were solemnly presented with moroco bound cases containing symbolic pieces of chocolate, and, according to Mackenzie, even the chocolate supply ran dry on occasion.

The *Te Deum* was performed on 20th November 1885. The Party duly celebrated its success but held the opinion that better things might be done; so German resumed work on a symphony which he had contemplated some months earlier. The first movement was performed at the Academy in 1886 and earned the approval of his fellow students. There was some difficulty in persuading the Principal to allocate so large a share of the concert to the completed work but German pleaded hard and eventually consent was given. It was an ambitious project. The usual compositions by students selected for inclusion were songs such as those by Dora Bright and Ethel Boyce, or short pianoforte pieces. The symphonic form itself was not greatly in favour and larger scale works tended to be cantatas or choral pieces. In 1887 however, the completed work reached its performance. All the members of The Party attended the rehearsal in the morning, refreshed by fruit which Ethel Boyce had brought from her Orchard home in Chertsey. In the afternoon they attended a performance of *Ruddigore* at the Savoy Theatre. When they returned to St James's Hall German left his friends and listened to the performance from the seclusion of the organ loft. The conductor was Joseph Barnby, organist and composer of School Songs and Hymns at Eton College where he directed the Music. He had recently conducted the first English performance of *Parsifal* so the honour for German was a considerable one. At the close there were calls for the

Composer and he made his way down to the platform to receive enthusiastic applause. At the same concert Henry Wood gave a highly praised rendering of a movement from Ebenezer Prout's Organ Sonata. So we may well deduce that he supplied some companionship during the composer's ordeal.

No student could have thrown himself more tirelessly into the regime which the Academy imposed. He had enjoyed the London theatres and parties in his lodgings with Miss Friswell, where the girls sang his ballad songs to admiring friends, but he had shown the Academy more reverence than most institutions can hope to receive by his participation in its activities and entry into its competitions. Yet it did not seem to possess any mechanism whereby the future of a student might be safeguarded or contacts established with the wider musical scene. As he left Tenterden Street German had the list of honours behind him, but no clear path ahead in a musical world that was Europe–orientated and inclined to believe that British music apart from Sullivan, did not and could not exist. The Court of St James' was no Weimar and at no level in society did the means exist to give patronage to composers. The Academy professors, rarely successful in having their own works performed, were not rich in expertise of this sort to hand on to a pupil.

German too was an odd mixture of ambition and reticence. He enjoyed applause and slaved for it. He gradually learned the business aspects of composition, but the affectionate and warm-hearted nature of his Whitchurch home had not prepared him for the ruthless egotism that went straight for immediate recognition and rewards. When opportunity came it was to be as much through accident as design, although his achievements at the Academy, and we must now consider his lighter work there, had left a feeling of confidence in his talents.

★   ★   ★

The Rival Poets
The First Symphony is a mellifluous and quite unpretentious work displaying many of the Mendelssohnian influences prevalent at the Academy. At the same time, as he was testing his powers as a symphonist, German was engaged on another work, which, though it was conceived in a much more frivolous spirit, was destined to outlive the symphony. It had a number of revivals and even survived into the early unsophisticated days of broadcasting. This was an operetta, *The Two Poets*. In the intervals between his over-diligent and exhausting schedules of practice in London he had seized his opportunities to revisit Shropshire and indulge his passion for

walking and cycling in the countryside. In 1883 his friend, Herbert Scott, son of the Congregational minister at the Dodington Chapel, a lifelong friend, and his future biographer, had accompanied him on a walking tour of Snowdonia and the Welsh coast. At Christmas time he had returned to Whitchurch and inspired by memories of his old family theatricals they had planned a small *opéra de salon* which, it was hoped, the Academy operatic class might undertake. Much time was spent in the nursery at The Laurels weaving a plot and planning the sequence of songs and ensembles. It was originally devised as an undemanding project requiring no chorus and only a pianoforte accompaniment. It took three years to complete but the work was fitted into odd moments to alleviate the heavy routine of practice and study. It was carried on by correspondence and with a good deal of amusement within the family, much given to charades and home made entertainments. Some attempts to burlesque grand opera were included and if the original title *The Two Poets* immediately summons up memories of *Patience*, there was little desire on the part of the participants to depart from the pattern of the Savoy Operas. German came quickly to the conclusion that he held to all his days, that light music requires an effort and skill just as much as the grand and the heavy.

Fortified by his studies under Prout and MacFarren he pressed on with *The Two Poets* and was gratified to discover that Prout himself liked one of the songs. By Christmas, 1885, the *opéra de salon* was almost complete and though the finale was proving troublesome and hurried notes went to and fro with Scott, a large part of the score was ready to show to Signor Fiori, the conductor of the opera class. Fiori appeared to be pleased with the sections he had been shown and promised a performance of Act One in the following term. During the Christmas holidays, helped by Rachel and Mab, German worked at the copying out of the parts sustained by his pipe and tobacco and refreshed by country walks. If members of the opera class were normally required to concentrate their efforts on some of the operatic fare written by senior English musicians, we cannot doubt German's comments: 'They say they never took to a work so much nor so readily. We had an awful lot of fun over it and all seem highly delighted.'

The performance of Act One was given at the end of the spring term, 1886. Dora Bright and Ethel Boyce played the overture in duet form and another pianist, Albert Fox, provided the accompaniment for the six soloists. A complete performance was given in July and, as it had proved such a success, a public performance was given in the St George's Hall, Langham Place, at the end of the year.

In old age German always avowed that *The Rival Poets* (to give it its subsequent name) was a more difficult work to perform then either *Merrie England* or *Tom Jones*. Certainly without chorus, or orchestra, it throws considerable responsibility onto the six principals. It suffers from a transparently unsubtle plot that was cobbled together by students but it gave great scope to German's humorous and lighthearted nature that had been repressed by his serious intentions to excel at the Academy. Something of the old spirits of the sixpenny entertainments above Edward Jones's grocery shop seem to have revived. For a BBC production in June, 1928, the composer himself provided the outline narrative for the announcer. The scene of action is 'an imaginary Anglo-Swiss republic' although there is little in either song or story to suggest a Swiss ambiance beyond the fact that the hero is a mountaineer. The chief character is a 'village magnate and oligarch'. Paul Gervais, who fancies himself as an expert on poetry and wishes his supposed daughter, Toinette, to marry the winner of a contest of verse. The contest is preceded by a quartet invoking the muse and soliciting justice. Toinette has a decided preference for Victor Bonheur, the gallant mountaineer, and in this she is encouraged by the romantically inclined duenna-Suzanne. Paul Gervais on the other hand has a liking for the young, euphuistic and affected poet, Carol Cornay, author of a ten-act poetic drama, and awards him the prize. He lacks the manly zeal to carry off the lady and when Victor protests against the decision he is arrested for contempt by the beadle. In the second act it transpires that Victor is really the Duke of Alvarez, Toinette, the daughter of Count Verona, and as each possesses half of a divided locket, there is evidence enough to show that their families intended them for one another. The plans of the autocratic village magistrate are thwarted and the young couple, secure in their titled lineage and inherited wealth, prepare to be good Anglo-Swiss republicans.

In the original version, the duenna is called Jeanne, and another character Toinette's father, the Comte de Luron, 'an aged traveller, worn with care but wearing the marks of nobility,' is introduced, which certainly helps to explain the action.

The happy accident by which a mountaineering duke, incognito, chooses to climb the peaks so close to the residence of his lost childhood fiancée is a fair parody of the situation in many Donizetti or early Verdi plots. The contest of poetry is intended to caricature the Wagnerian contests of song. There is very little real wit in the dialogue though some of the humorous Old English touches that one finds in German's letters: 'Confound it, Sir, did I not expel you from the wapentake?' declares the outraged Paul when his prisoner reappears.

Scott produced some serviceable romantic lyrics:

The brooklet hurries down the glade
And spurns the upland with a leap
But youth, with love's resistless aid
Must slowly climb the rugged steep.

The patter songs with their obvious echoes of Gilbert lack any political or social targets but are quite fluent:

Let me introduce this gentleman as one of the fraternity
A poet from his early years, a poet to eternity
He's full of dreams on golden themes in infinite variety
And owns the fact with subtle tact and wonderful sobriety.

Although the libretto is unremarkable, the music is written with great assurance. The first eighteen bars of the two-piano introduction have a more powerful theatrical impact than some of his later overtures. They are followed by a version of the mountaineer's song, a swinging *tempo di bolero* and a lively jig that is certainly as polished as those from later compositions.

There is no chorus and the operetta opens with a duet between Suzanne and Paul who has stumbled on an amorous exchange between Toinette and the unknown Victor. Along with a recitative section it has to carry a certain amount of narrative but it has a brief lilting melody in the middle section.

Just as soon you'll drain the ocean
Freeze the sun or rend the heavens
As set lovers' warm devotion
All at sixes and at sevens.

The second duet between Suzanne and Toinette is quite elaborate and the characteristic German touch is evident in a rocking and simple 6/8 melody that ends in strong chords, as does 'If I Love Abidingly' in *Tom Jones*. Paul's patter song which outlines his plan to marry Toinette to his nephew Carol Cornay, apparently delighted Ebenezer Prout. It recalls the Lord Chancellor's song from *Iolanthe* and has a transition into the major key and a change of time from the 6/8 to 2/4 when Paul refers to his own poetic gifts:

I'm a poet. I'm a poet
I've been told so and I know it
So I do my best to show it, Every minute of the day.

The Invocation to the muse is an elegant quartet in hymn-tune style but showing already German's talent for taking an idea that seems about to reach a mediocre end and adding a final lift which gives it some distinction. The six-bar phrases show a fine sense of word-setting.

Victor's mountaineering song, already quoted in the overture, has a vigorous and chromatic accompaniment suggestive of 'the thunder peal and lightning flash'. By contrast Carol's love song has a wistful charm and shows German's fondness for the augmented fifths and drawn-out phrases. The finale to Act One, in which Paul supports Carol as the winner and the others appeal against the verdict, has a brief moment of complicated ensemble writing. What is interesting is that none of the music apart from the patter songs really emulates Sullivan, and the *Intermezzo*, a *cantabile pastorale* in the familiar 6/8 rhythm, comes from a different musical spring altogether. Again the young student foreshadows the deft touches which transform pedestrian themes with elongations of the melody, and there is a middle section which gives an unexpectedly passionate version of the theme. The Second Act opens with Paul persuading Carol to be a more ardent suitor. There are some witty arrangements to the recitatives when the two search for chairs so, that Paul may better relate the story of Toinette's fortune. The revelation of German's talent however comes in a duet for Toinette and Victor *Happy Days*, one of the very last numbers of the score. The originality of this item has never been properly appreciated. Indeed it does not even seem to have been noticed by German himself, who always speaks of the whole score as one artistic unit. In fact in this Duet,

Happy Days, when hope is twining
Round our hearts from trouble free
Happy Morn, when sun is shining
Happy light for you and me,

we encounter the heart-stirring powers of Edward German, one of the great English melodists, and although the tune is fairly simple it would be safe to say that nothing in English music written before it appeared could have led one to expect it. The throbbing accompaniment and the direct melodic thrust look forward to the sweeping theme songs of musical comedy. The voices are supported by the accompaniment in such a way that nothing detracts from the impact of the tune. If Ebenezer Prout preferred the patter song, the education of the academy students was indeed in unadventurous hands.

The success of this *opéra de salon* at the Academy prompted the students to take it on tour in the autumn of 1886 in the composer's native county. He himself set off for Shrewsbury taking with him a backcloth and the Academy stage curtains loaned by kind permission of the Principal. On arrival in the town he had to play a major part in wheeling the scenery from the station to the music hall and setting it up on stage. Further performances were given in Oswestry and Whitchurch, and in the latter town at least a crowded and friendly audience gave *The Two Poets* an enthusiastic reception. 'Should Mr German visit Whitchurch again on a similar errand,' said the *Herald* 'the Town Hall will certainly not contain all who will wish to be present.' In the following spring, further performances were given, one to an audience composed of hunting parties at Melton Mowbray, where the audience talked throughout, and another at Basingstoke. In 1901 when German had achieved greater fame after the commission to complete Sullivan's *Emerald Isle* the operetta was revived under the title *The Rival Poets* and published by Boosey & Co. At an Academy performance one of the pianists was York Bowen, later famous as a pianist, and arranger of piano music. The Musical Director was Alberto Randegger, a distinguished figure at the Academy who had been director of various Italian opera houses, conductor at the Norwich Festival, an acquaintance of Verdi, and an advocate of Wagner's Operas. He cannot have thought *The Rival Poets* beneath his notice, although it is the kind of work which gives as much pleasure to the cast during rehearsal as to the audience in performance. There is no clever theme to it such as Gilbert was able to supply in the Savoy Operas and apart from its improbabilities the plot has little to engage the attention. Yet it showed that the style of Sullivan could be adapted, varied and developed and it gave German a useful initiation into the art of vocal and ensemble writing.

CHAPTER THREE

Setting the Bard

The Two Poets had led German from violin and piano into vocal composition and he attempted songwriting. Mary Davies, the Welsh mezzo-soprano sang *Fine Feathers* at a London ballad concert, though it proved an expensive occasion for the composer who had to pay £20 for the copyright of the somewhat undistinguished words, while receiving £5 for the publication of the music. For Mary Davies he also wrote *Little Boy Blue* but his songs did not bring him fame or fortune until later in his career.

In the summer of 1887 with four other students he visited Germany. Although his music remained quite untouched by the influence of Wagner he was greatly impressed by his visit to Bayreuth. He returned through the Rhineland and, although he thought the river immensely grand, it did not provoke the musical response which it had evoked earlier in Schumann. He declared a higher contentment with the beautiful woodland and waterfall scenery of North Wales.

When supplying some notes in 1903 for *Musical Opinion* on his career he wrote, 'I went across Germany twice – first in 1887 with four Academy students (ending up this visit with the Bayreuth Festival – 'Parsifal' and 'Tristan'. What a sensation that was!), and again in 1889/90 to pay a visit to two friends who were studying there. (I find I speak of this in one of the letters I am sending).' The letter to which he referred was his philippic on the all-pervasive influence of the Kaiser's egomania in Berlin:

Every picture shop is filled with pictures of the Emperor; every photographer's with photos – all sizes and in all kinds of positions, in and out of uniform, in different uniforms, looking condescending, looking dignified, on horseback in uniform, on horseback in plain clothes, on donkeyback, head and shoulders without legs, legs without head and shoulders, helmet in hand, helmet on head, helmet on tail, flying in mid air etc. etc. All the statuary too turns on the Emperor. There are busts chiselled in all sizes and the number of different varieties to be seen in halls, houses, shop windows etc. is something

Mr Robert Furber's School, Whitchurch

Wimbledon School, view from the ridgeway

quite unbearable. The toy shops are filled with toy Emperors; when he was young the boy Emperor; then the man Emperor; in fact Berlin is saturated with the blessed Emperor as man, woman, boy, girl, soldier, sailor, tinker, tailor. The end of it all will be that the people will go stark staring mad and the Emperor himself will go off with a bang the verdict being: 'Death from explosion owing to his receiving more hero-worship than the human frame can bear!'

The most sought after photograph, private but illegally circulated, showed Wilhelm II in the costume of Frederick the Great, complete with powdered wig.

In the summer of 1887 he left the Academy where he had been for over two years a sub-professor. His compositions had enjoyed some success and praise but the routine of teaching and earning a living by playing in theatre orchestras seemed likely to postpone indefinitely the chance to realise his abilities as a composer. He recalled later that he used to earn two guineas a week playing second violin at the Savoy with seven shillings for matinées. Once when discussing his early struggles with another composer he referred to the matinée performances at Drury Lane, 'I have played in the *Ring*', said the other. 'Oh, how wonderful to have participated in Wagner's sublime masterpiece,' replied German with his old world courtesy. 'No, no,' retorted the other, 'not the opera. *The Circus Ring*. Hengler's Circus.'

He also accepted a post as music teacher at Wimbledon School. It stood on the brow of Wimbledon Hill in fine Gothic premises built in 1816. The Reverend John Brackenbury had taken over a small army school and by his energies transformed it into one of the most esteemed schools in the London region. His pupils continued to gain high places in the military examinations and it was said that it would be difficult to find in the army lists a single regiment that did not contain at least one officer who owed his early training to Brackenbury. Father of seventeen children, he nevertheless found time to devote to what prospectuses term 'the individual needs of every pupil'. His successor, the Reverend Charles Wynne, German's headmaster, was less successful and one may deduce the measure of his achievement by the fact that he eventually left for a country living in Lincolnshire. The school was sold to reappear subsequently as the present Wimbledon College, a Catholic foundation. Despite its military ambitions, and the ministrations of the Reverend Wynne, it seems to have been in the 1880s a place which gave more attention to the arts than most Victorian seminaries (as late as the 1940s the headmaster of Eton would only allow plays on condition 'they were not too well done'). As an old lady, Mabel recalled 'dear Jim taking us over to

Wimbledon to dinner once when we were just little country girls. The wonderful music room impressed me so – all parquet flooring with organ, grand piano, etc'. Jim had also taken them to the Academy where they were introduced to the great Mozkowski, whose piano duets they had learnt back at The Laurels.

His music post carried considerable prestige as his predecessor Dr McNaught, was a very successful teacher who had just become an assistant inspector of music in schools and training colleges working under the great Sir John Stainer.*

McNaught was an exponent of the tonic sol fa method. He later became editor of the *Musical Times* and was one of the rare recipients of the Lambeth musical doctorate. The two men had known each other previously as German had played the violin in a private orchestra which McNaught directed. McNaught had some misgivings about German's future as a composer and may well have thought, rightly, that his qualities of energy and cheerful sociability would be assets in a teaching career. Undoubtedly German made a strong and favourable impression on his pupils. As all teachers learn by example rather than precept he had the model of Walter Hay to guide him in the art of enthusing pupils of different degrees of skill. One of his first pupils at Wimbledon, Theodore Holland, later associated with the Academy and the Royal Philharmonic Society wrote in 1937, after German's death:

> Chance willed it that I became one of Edward German's first pupils. It happened as follows: while still a sub-professor at the Royal Academy of Music, E.G. accepted the post of teacher of violin and pianoforte at a private school in Wimbledon, where it was my good fortune to enter as a day boarder in 1887, thus becoming one of his regular pupils.
>
> As a boy my recollections of him remain vivid. We all looked forward with eagerness to Monday, his teaching day. He was enthusiastic and generous in his praise though without doubt he must have found us a dull lot. Usually patient, if things were going too badly he would break off the lesson to play to us instead. He insisted then – as

---

* Stainer's interest in music for young people led him to compose a hymn for the Band of Hope (Words by J. Compston) which contain the immortal quatrain:

To God each true heart sends a cry
And each the 'Amen' adds
As Jacob when about to die
Exclaimed 'God bless the Lads'.

so often afterwards – that music should be 'beautiful melody wedded to beautiful harmony' and we were certainly taught tuneful music such as Bach's Two Part Inventions and Hiller's Studies for the Pianoforte. The advanced pupils sooner or later had to study an arrangement of Gounod's *Faust*, the clarity and grace of which made a particular appeal to Edward German at this time. The infinite trouble he took over us boys is well shown by his unexpected appearance at one of the school concerts when he not only tuned our violins but contributed in person a part of a Beethoven Trio.

To my great excitement he once worked a little tune I had invented into the third number, 'Elegy', of his First Suite for Pianoforte.

Every Monday, Edward German lunched at my mother's home and dined there every other Monday before leading the private orchestra that met there regularly under the conductorship of the late Dr W. E. McNaught. The friendship thus formed lasted throughout his life.

Holland believed that it was through his mother's advice that Edward German adopted the name in place of Edward German Jones but as we have seen this had already occurred earlier at the Academy. The Elegy to which Holland contributed was one of the pieces played at German's funeral service, a touching link with an almost forgotten fragment of his career.

German also took some of the orchestral practices, including lighter works which the boys enjoyed, such as his own early work *The Guitar*. He inveighed against foreign influences exercising domination of English music and gave frequent vent to a favourite maxim: 'Never ape another's style'. He continued to do some teaching while he was writing for the theatre and his pupils were shown the manuscript pages of his Incidental Music for Mansfield's *Richard III* and Irving's *Henry VIII*. As his other commitments grew his teaching periods diminished but he could still be lured back to Wimbledon with promises of visits to a local shoemaker Mr Siggers by name, whose products he rated more highly than those of any other maker of shoes. Sometimes too, when he had obtained his house in Hall Road ex-pupils would be invited. Holland recalled the mysterious garden entrance and the old-world atmosphere of the house. It was German who persuaded Holland to enrol at the Academy and he maintained links with the family. When the Gold Medal of the Philharmonic Society was presented to him, old Mrs Holland, at the age of 92, attended the concert and went round to the artist's room at the Queen's Hall to congratulate him. 'The touching letter in which he expressed his joy at her presence' wrote the son, 'will always be treasured by us'.

The classical master at Wimbledon was Barry Pain who was a well-known author. He and German combined to produce the *Antigone* of Sophocles. That stern and unflinching drama is not one that immediately suggests German's musical style, and as events turned out, an epidemic among the boys led to a cancellation of the performance. One list of compositions in the German papers, not in his own hand, refers to a march and chorus from *Antigone* published by Novello. There is no copy in the British Library and Novello have no record of publication.

Though German was a favoured pupil of the Academy he had no strong champions in the musical world and no private means to give him the leisure to compose. He had not been attracted to the world of church music and despite the intense piety of his parents, he seems to have had no affinity with the strong religiosity of the Victorian age which gave abundant scope to the talents of Stanford, Parry and others. His sense of humour was too strong to allow him to set those heavy religious cantatas which figured so prominently in festival programmes. He had a great love of the English and Welsh countryside and could write impressive letters describing the waving seas on the Welsh coast, but he had no sense of the numinous which guided Elgar towards his greatest works. He was a craftsman, and like any craftsman he needed commissions. In January, 1888, after several months of frustration he wrote: 'All is patience in this world, I am beginning to believe. Goodness knows I have had and shall have to be patient'.

He approached Sir George Henschel, a German-born singer, conductor and composer who had settled in England four years earlier after three years as director with the newly established Boston Symphony Orchestra, and had recently established the London Symphony Concerts. He requested a performance of his Symphony. When Henschel disappointed him by saying that he would have to wait, German lamented that at twenty-six he was growing old and the period of waiting was too protracted.

'Call yourself old.' he said and from the sorrowful look on his face I saw he was comparing his age with my own, although he is, I should say, just in the prime of life and no need to feel ancient.'

In fact, Henschel was only thirty-seven. He had sung the treble solo in *Hear my Prayer* at the age of nine in Breslau. As a very young man he had been introduced to Brahms in the company of a dry-as-dust old Kapell-meister who said, 'Here is Henschel – he can compose, sing, play the pianoforte and conduct – while some of us poor devils can only compose', to which the gruff Brahms replied, 'Yes and some of us not even that'. German had a fondness for this somewhat graceless tale and used it when extolling Sir Landon Ronald's many talents in an after-dinner speech.

This was not the last of his frustrations. Through the help of Julia Neilson, who had been an Academy student but had turned to acting with success, he was given an introduction to W. S Gilbert, who had helped to foster her career. Her part in Gilbert's *Broken Hearts* called for a song, which, to judge from German's letter to Scott he had barely an evening to write. Known as Lady Hilda's Song it was scored *pizzicato* to give the effect of a mandolin accompaniment (not lute as he later recollected). Gilbert thought the music 'very charming and graceful', but suddenly decided that the play would be better without it. German pleaded with the actress to use her influence to reinstate the song and in this she succeeded. 'Since Mr German takes it so seriously,' wrote Gilbert with a compliance he did not often display, 'we will most certainly put back the song'.

Lady Hilda's Song is a nicely melancholic piece in which she seeks the extinguishing comfort of death 'Far from sin! Far from sorrow!' German kept the vocal line within an easy compass. Unfortunately the tribulations of the composer were not ended for Alfred Cellier, the conductor, thought the *pizzicato* effect too weak and ordered the string players to use their bows. German's dismay was, however, to some extent alleviated by a compliment from the kindly Sullivan.

He wrote several other songs at this time. The choice of words must seem sentimental and unadventurous but they reflect the taste of singers and audiences of the 1880s. As one leafs through other platform songs that appeared at the time, German's choice of lyrics and his original touches seem poetic by comparison. The Golden Jubilee of Victoria, for example, was celebrated by a song, *Light of our Nation* by a contemporary, of which the refrain ran:

> A perfect Queen
> So nobly planned
> To aid, to comfort, and command.

And the Death of General Gordon elicited the following:

> Yes the form of our brave General
> To the earth is now consigned
> But his spirit hovers o'er us
> Breathing solace to the mind.

The attitude of publishers distressed German. In July of the same year 1888 he wrote:

It is hard to get publishers to accept compositions and so make a start: they say they cannot take them until I have made a name, yet it is only through the medium of these publishers that one can make a name – that is the hard part of it.

Yet an opportunity of hearing his music without the necessity of publication was at hand. He returned in the autumn from a holiday in Hertfordshire and Scotland. According to Scott he was full of ideas for orchestral work and plans for the future but in fact, he was deeply worried about the future and his prospects seemed heavily overcast. He encountered Alberto Randegger on the steps of the Academy and poured out his tale of woe. By a most fortunate chance it happened that Randegger's advice had recently been sought over the post of musical director at the old Globe Theatre, where an American actor-manager, Richard Mansfield, was launching a season of plays. German, whose fondness for the theatre went back to his days as a child when a model theatre had been his chief amusement, and who had been a great frequenter of theatres during his student days, readily accepted.

It was not an easy task for a musician with high standards and a taste in music moulded by the Academy. He was responsible for an orchestra of twenty-nine experienced players. Within a single programme there might be very mixed dramatic offerings, serious, melodramatic and frivolous much as an evening's television viewing provides for its audience today. German was keen to improve the standard of the musical fare provided and he was supported by the elder musicians in the pit, even though the management might be suspicious of quality. Yet the press noticed his efforts and commended them. *The Sunday Times* reviewing the double bill *Prince Karl* and *Editha's Burglar* declared, 'One feature last night merited special recognition – the refined music and equally refined playing of the brilliant orchestra conducted by Mr Edward German.' The programme before and between the performances often resembled that of a popular concert. Playgoers attending *She Stoops to Conquer* at the Globe were destined to hear the Overture to Gounod's *Mireille*, *The Funeral March of a Marionette*, excerpts from Sullivan's music for *Henry VIII*, the gavotte from Thomas' *Mignon*, the *Jeux d'Enfants Suite* by Bizet, Gounod's *Serenade* and some of German's own music collected in a *Suite de ballet*. The *Musical Standard* commended the band as 'An artistic and *not* a noisy one'. One critic's final friendly recommendation deserves quotation in full:

No doubt Mr German, if properly supported, will extend his repertoire: we may point out to him that an excursion into purely classical realms will yield a harvest well worth gathering. Among the symphonies of Haydn and Mozart will be found many minuet and trio movements that cannot fail to charm even a general audience, and there are finales in Haydn full of melody, varied colour and vivacity equally delightful.

German, despite this patronising advice, continued to adhere to Gounod, Bizet and other French composers. There were items to be re-scored, and no doubt, many problems of copyright and royalties, especially for the well organised French market. Music that the public wanted to hear had to be balanced by the demands of the producer. The consciencious young director found himself plunged into another period of toil and stress.

Never was I so tossed hither and thither by overwork . . . I'm taking a lot of pains with my band – two performances, extra rehearsals etc. – and now to crown all Mr Mansfield has just decided to produce *Richard III* soon and I have to write the whole of the incidental music to it. The overture itself will take me three weeks at least; the only time I get to myself is about two hours and a half each morning, and after the theatre at night. It is truly hard work and awful worry.

The score needed for *Richard III* was a huge one. The idea of a complete score to a Shakespeare play was a major innovation in the London Theatre. Unlike modern Shakespearian productions where a few fanfares and some electronic bubblings occupy the vacant moments, the shifting of heavy realistic sets, long *entractes* between the scenes and the slow melodramatic nature of the productions called for a musical commentary that was closely akin to the days of silent films. In fact, Mansfield deserves credit for extending the idea of wedding fine verse to the best possible original music. In his press invitations he specifically asked that the critics should notice the importance of the musical score. German was not the only member of his team to be overworked and Mansfield's own doctor advised a complete rest before he undertook the role of Richard. As well as the Overture (in fact completed in *one* week), music had to be written to accompany the wooing of Lady Anne, the sorrows of the princes in the Tower, the triumph of Richmond at Bosworth Field and many other incidents.

It is interesting to note *en passant* that Mansfield, though he gave a thorough performance as Shakespearean villain, inclined to the pro-Richard School and he quoted in the programme John Stowe's description of Richard of Gloucester as 'of bodily shape comely enough' and the words of the words of the Countess of Desmond who danced with him at court and declared him 'the handsomest man in the room, his brother the king excepted'.

The production was a lavish one The *New York Times* described the opening scene:

> The pealing of bells was heard. The motley populace flocked in through the Warden's Gate, the Lieutenant and his guard appeared on the drawbridge, and Elizabeth Woodville, Queen of Edward IV, entered with her retinue of knights and ladies, priests pages, men-at-arms and court fool. In the crowd was a cloaked figure which came forward after the Queen had gone into the Tower and the populace had been dispersed. As he threw down his cloak which he had been holding on to so as to hide his features, the guards saluted the Duke of Gloucester . . .

The opening night, 16th March 1889, produced problems of its own and the music did not receive a fair hearing. A section of the audience which had been queuing for the pit, discovered on entering the auditorium that some of the best seats were already occupied by friends of the management. Attempts by German to start the overture were thrice howled down by the irate patrons. According to Scott an apology from the stage manager quietened the disturbance, but *The People's* critic reported that 'noise prevailed – during the remainder of the evening . . . the loud chattering of the audience rendered it difficult to form a fair estimate of the new music'.

Despite this inauspicious beginning, the incidental music to *Richard III* was to prove the first of German's many triumphs, and it was a score for which he preserved a special fondness. When he died his will exempted *Richard III* from his ban on publication of his other manuscript works.

At the end of the production Mansfield gave a supper. He was eager for the young composer to accompany him to America but German was delighted with his London success and wished to exploit this new talent for sub-operatic writing and his experience with an orchestra of his own. The overture reached the concert hall when the Philharmonic Society included it in a programme in defence to demands for more English music. At the same concert Dvorak in person conducted his fine Symphony in G (no. 8) though German himself with innocent pride pasted only the references to his own work in his album of cuttings.

The final evening is described in German's excited letter to Rachel, much more vividly than in the de-vitalised account he gave to Scott in old age; notable is the account of the end-of-production party, full of drama critics, theatre historians, writers and managers whom German enumerates:

My dear Dick,

Now that the season is ended and I can collect my thoughts I will drop you a line telling you "the latest". You will remember that when we parted at Euston, that Mansfield and I were not the best of friends; however, I had made up my mind to go into his room on Saturday night and say 'Goodbye' to him – after the performance. Saturday proved a very interesting day to me, as you will see.

At half past three in the afternoon a note was, to my great surprise, brought round to me from 'Mansfield the Great' which I will enclose; you will see it is to have supper with him at the Langham Hotel on Saturday night. Observe the affectionate style of his writing! My first impression was, 'All right Mr M. you want to get me to your Hotel and persuade and still persuade me about America.' On the other hand it struck me that he would have invited a lot of celebrities there to eat a farewell meal with him. This last proved to be the case. I arrived at about five mins to twelve, was shown up into a room filled with gents – there would be between twenty and thirty present; directly Mansfield (who was now in evening dress) caught sight of me, he simply *rushed* at me, caught hold of me with both hands and introduced me to no end of 'big pots' – including Beerbohm Tree, John Hare (one of Ted's favorite [sic] actors) Joseph Hatton, and one after another they came up and pushed their hands in mine and let off enough gas about the music to blow the roof off! At last we went into supper and on either side of me I found the names Mr R. Redford (the manager I told you I liked so much) and Mr Goring Thomas. (Goring Thomas did not turn up, though.) I cannot remember all who were there, but I'll tell you a few – I L Toole, Beerbohm Tree, John Hare, Joseph Hatton, Comyns Carr, Mr Gilbert ARA (the Sculptor), Joseph Bennett (Musical critic for the *Telegraph* and altogether a very 'big pot'), Joseph Knight, Max Orell, Davenport Adams, etc. etc. Henry Irving had promised to be there but didn't turn up.

Well, after supper, cigars came round and speeches began. Mansfield's health was drunk, so was Toole's and Hare's, also some of the American "guns" who were there. Then Mansfield proposed – Joseph Bennett – who is imposing looking, with white hair and whiskers. J. B. talked about the art of musical criticism and glided into the subject of 'Music wedded to the Drama'. I thought he might possibly allude, in *passing*, to my music, but I was not prepared for what he *did* say. He said that Mansfield must be complimented on having secured the services of a gentleman who was so sound a musician and whose music was so characteristic and never lost its interest and that it was perhaps *the best* example he had heard of the Art of wedding Music to the Drama etc. etc. I can't remember all he said – anyhow by the time he sat down he had paid me such a compliment as I had never had before in my life. Then up jumped Mansfield and said, 'I need hardly tell you all that the gentleman alluded to is *my very dear friend* German. I have always felt that *Richard III* would have been nothing without the music, and that just at the time when the tragedy would fall flat German's charming music always came to the rescue and pulled it through and I have the greatest pleasure in proposing the health of Mr Edward German.' They all stood up and drank 'Mr German'.

Well, of course, you know the next moment found me on my legs – I said just the following few words: 'Mr Mansfield, Gentlemen. I cannot make a speech, but I thank you all very much for your kind appreciation of my music to *Richard III*.' With this I sat down and they all clapped very heartily. Then other toasts were proposed and other healths were drunk and at about four o'clock I parted with Mansfield who was most affectionate. *There*! I think you have got a pretty good account of the supper. I have gone into it in detail because I thought you would want to know all. I have forgotten to tell you that before the performance commenced on Saturday night Mr Crooke (orchestral leader) followed by the other members of the band came into my room and presented me with a beautiful handpainted album with my monogram outside and on the front page the following was printed:

> Presented to
> Edward German
> by the Members of the orchestra. Globe Theatre. June 1st/1889

Altogether Saturday was a most interesting day with me.
Will write you again soon.
With my best love to each and all,
> I remain,
> > Your affectionate brother,
> > > Jim

Joseph Bennett had been at the opening festival at Bayreuth, though in general his criticism was anti-Wagnerian. However, Wagner need not have felt alone in his misery if *Richard III* had been proclaimed as the finest example of wedding music and drama that Bennett could recall. Shakespeare almost immediately followed him back to the pavilion, as

Mansfield spoke of the rescue work which German had carried out on his faltering play. German's letter is interesting. Beside the provincial reverence for these colourful figures feasting from midnight until four, there is an amused detachment in his tone, and his style has some of the colourful touches that were to develop as his correspondence with Rachel became so important to him in his later years. The fact that he conveyed this tale of success and flattery to her, rather than to his parents, to whom he was devoted, also argues a very strong bond between them.

What was less fortunate was that *Richard III* invoked a series of deadly skirmishes with George Bernard Shaw, in his role as music critic, from which German was eventually to retire wounded by the pen of that brilliant but unsparing writer. Writing as Corno di Bassetto in *The Star* Shaw resented that he had been urged to go to the Globe to hear German's music with its 'Wagnerian leit motivs'. He certainly found no music in Mansfield's spoken performance and deplored the omission of lines by Shakespeare and substitution of lines by Cibber in the text. He was equally critical of German's use of the *leitmotif*.

Whenever Richard enters you hear the bassoons going "Pumpum-pum-pum-pum, Paw"

It is a leit motiv certainly; but this very primitive employment of it is not 'after Wagner's plan'. The first *entr'acte* begins with a prolonged bassoon note and a slow triplet which makes you shut your eyes and ask whether the curtain is not about to rise on the tower scene from *II Trovatore*. The prelude to the last act is a reminiscence, and a very vivid one too, of the prelude and gipsy dance at the beginning of the tavern scene in *Carmen*. In short, Mr German knows his business and has come off with credit; but this music is not specially dramatic in character, and would suit *The Lady of Lyons* just as well as *Richard III*.

In fact Shaw was inaccurate about the Ricardian *leitmotif*. Quite apart from the fact that a printer's error gave four beats to the 3/4 bar, the theme is indicative of Richard's twisted character. Shaw, however, was right to imply that music can never convey the exact images of words. Even a Strauss tone-poem would be adaptable to many a different tale if the programme did not exist as a precise guide. The *Richard III* Overture does suggest tumult and knavery, and the innocent theme for the murdered princes in the Tower, with its poignant return in contrasted keys exhibits the conception of tragedy as a pre-Freudian audience would understand the term.

In his article, Corno di Bassetto referred to the orchestra of about twenty-two players and thought German had wisely omitted parts for trumpets and trombones, as well as leaving out the 'cellos. This provoked a member of the orchestra to write to *The Star*, referring to Shaw as a 'captious frolic' and asserting that he was no musician. This says more than the presentation gift for the loyalty which the young composer elicited from his seasoned players.

The player who signed himself 'The Amused One' then asserted that trumpets and trombones *had* been used, and that 'about thirty players' instead of twenty-two had been used. Shaw blamed his musical howler on the printer who had subjected 'his quavers to a course of Darwinian evolution'. But he maintained that he counted only twenty-two players. 'True. There may have been not only the trumpets and the solitary trombone 'right enough' under the stage, but also a bass clarinet in the scene dock, an English horn in the flies, third and fourth horns in the office and a harp on the roof. I can answer only for what I saw and heard.' Warming to this theme he continued, 'Besides I confess, I do not feel quite easy concerning the estimate of 'about thirty', made by one who is in a position to be exact. It suggests more than twenty-nine and less than thirty: possibly twenty-nine and a boy.'

Shaw in his review had suggested that German might have written a pastoral prelude to the scene at Bosworth Field, and the anonymous orchestral player mocked at this suggestion as the stage was filled at that moment with mail-clad warriors. 'Well, my friend,' replied Shaw, Why not? Does not the mail-clad Ratcliffe tell us that the early village cock hath thrice done salutation to the morn? Am I to be told that the village cock is not pastoral?' And again: 'Mr German has grasped the pastoral opportunity, and written a beautiful pastoral as a prelude to the road-to-Chertsey scene: a fitting place for it, I say.' Will it be believed that this more fitting place than Bosworth Field is a road full of corpses and mourners? Surely a field is more pastoral than a road!'

It is fair to say that Shaw in later life gave some praise to the Overture, and admitted that it was a more serious composition than he had allowed. He continued to dispute the relevance to the play. The piece was also played at the Crystal Palace concerts in February 1890. These concerts were given under the direction of August Manns. Despite his suspicion of 'foreign influences' German indeed had cause to be grateful to many continental musicians who helped him in his career. Manns had come from a poor German family but had worked his way up the profession by way of military bands, and spent eight years with a Prussian regiment. He had been a principal conductor at the Crystal Palace since as far back as 1855 and for almost fifty years his concerts occupied a position in English music closely akin to the Promenade Concerts to-day. The Crystal Palace performance brought forth yet another review from Shaw which deprecated the whole conception of using conventional musical forms to suggest the ramifications of drama.

> I would advise Mr German either to re-write the work or else drop 'Richard III' and simply present it as Overture in G' [Shaw was again in error: The Overture is in E minor] that is to say as a piece of 'absolute' music in overture form. For if it is to be taken as dramatic I do not see why the Richard motive should be fitted with an 'answer' as if it were a 'subject' there being nothing in the dramatic idea at all corresponding to such answer. Again, the 'fugato' is flat nonsense unless Mr German wished to suggest a troop of little Richards springing up from traps and chasing one another around the stage. I hope Mr German will, on reflection, agree with me that the man who can write a dramatic overture is the man who can invent dramatic motives and develop them dramatically in music. The oftener he falls down on this arduous task and falls back on the forms of absolute music the worse his work will be. For instance, the most entirely foolish thing in music is an overture by a Doctor of Music in orthodox form, written solely with a view to that form and then sent up for concert use with the general title of 'Portia', and 'Shylock' and 'The Caskets' written in blue ink above the first and second subjects respectively.

Having ravaged the idea of the work, Shaw conceded that German had 'proved his ability as a musician up to the hilt'. The Overture proved to be the work which brought him to the notice of the musical public. *The Morning Post* declared that the scoring was excellent and continued,

> the whole of the Overture is in perfect keeping with the subject of the drama and foreshadows in the best possible way the chief incidents of

the plot. The work was well received and Mr German was called upon the platform to acknowledge the approval of the audience, which was all the more favourable as the composer appeared then 'comparatively unknown'.

In October it was performed at the Norwich Festival, no doubt with the help of Randegger, and conducted by German himself. It had the good fortune to follow a performance of Hamish MacCunn's *Ship o' the Fiend* in which the fiendish ship had nearly gone down with all hands. The conductor had to re-start the work and the critics observed that captain and crew were frequently at cross-purposes. 'On the other hand,' said the *Norwich Chronicle*, 'Mr Edward German was happy in instituting a perfect control over the band. In securing the sympathies of the members of the orchestra he obtained an admirable reading of his very excellent work.' German certainly always seemed to pass the severe test which professional musicians or choir impose on a conductor. Sir Hugh Allen was fond of relating a story of the composer in old age conducting a choir in *O Peaceful England*. Again and again he tried to soften the final chord 'And in thy slumber *smile*' and was dissatisfied with the pianissimo. Eventually a whispered message went round the irritated singers to mouth the last chord in total silence. The effect was received by the composer with a rapturous beam and a broad gesture of affection which swept over their ranks.

The press in the 1890s appears to have written in a language all its own. The *Norwich Chronicle* urged him 'seriously' to avoid the 'temptation' of following 'the erratic and eccentric fashions' of the 'so-called advanced' school, and urged him instead to select 'the best examples of standard musicians of classical proclivities'. This advice, unnecessary and possibly harmful in German's case was swiftly followed by a misprinted line in which the writer declared it 'undesirable that our rising English composers should hold their own'.

In 1890 his Symphony in E Minor was given at a Crystal Palace Concert, with the composer as conductor. The concert also included the Emperor Concerto played by Miss Fanny Davies who, said *The Star*, 'let the piano (still black and blue from the merciless punishment inflicted on it by Mr Paderewski) down lightly'. The Symphony was in effect almost a new work though thematic material was borrowed from the Academy version. The reception was favourable and, although *The Star* remarked that 'the ability to ascend Primrose Hill does not necessarily involve the power of climbing the Matterhorn', it added that 'it would be churlish to complain of Mr German's Symphony because it is not a colossal masterpiece'.

It is regrettable that the First Symphony seems to be unknown save in the pianoforte duet arranged by the composer. It is true that the introduction is based upon a rather mundane theme that might come straight from MacFarren's exercises, and that this supplies much of the material for the development section. The imprint of the composer becomes apparent in the gentler second subject which eventually drifts in a favourite lilting 12/8 rhythm. The slow movement has a peaceful Dvorak-like theme, and the *Menuetto* provides some interesting twists and turns in the principal theme, which is treated elaborately in the mood of German's favourite French musicians. But its chief excellence is in the finale, which would justify a hearing at the close of any orchestral concert. It has a strong theme reminiscent of the Chopin B Minor Sonata (fourth movement), with syncopated rhythms and flows into a *delicato* 'tarantella' theme which is one of German's best essays in this sprightly form. When it re-appears in the bright key of E major, the effect is magical. At the close the motto theme

returns thunderously and the Symphony ends with a youthfully vigorous *presto* section.

There was praise for the scoring. *The Standard* observed that the string melodies in the *andante* movement suggested 'the methods of French composers when they wish to produce sentimental and sensuous effects'.

Shaw was again in hot pursuit. He seemed to imagine some kind of programme in the Symphony, though nowhere in his writings does German suggest that he had devised one.

Mr Edward German's Symphony shows that he is still hampered by that hesitation between two genres which spoiled his *Richard III* Overture. If Mr German wishes to follow up his academic training by writing absolute music in symmetrical periods and orderly ingenuity of variation, let him by all means do so. On the other hand if he prefers to take significant motifs and develop them through all the emotional phases of a definite poem or drama, he cannot do better. But it is useless nowadays to try to combine the two . . . and since Mr German has not made up his mind to discard one or the other the result is that his symphonic movements proceed for a while with the smoothness and regularity of a Mendelssohn scholar's exercise [the Mendelssohn Scholarship was awarded for composition], and then, without rhyme or reason, are shattered by a volcanic eruption which sounds like the last page of a very exciting opera finale, only to subside the next moment into their original decorum. I can but take a 'symphony' of this sort as a bag of samples of what Mr German can do in the operatic style, handsomely admitting that the quality of the samples is excellent and that if Mr German's intelligence and originality equal his musicianship, he can no doubt compose successfully as soon as he realises exactly what composition means.

One further orchestral work comes from this period, the Marche Solennelle in D Minor given in 1891 at one of Henschel's symphony concerts. The *Daily News* reported it as 'a creditable example of orchestral workmanship and although, perhaps from its very subject, it was hardly likely to incite much enthusiasm, the composer who conducted was accorded the usual compliment of a recall'. It is certainly difficult to imagine an audience rising vociferously to its feet at the conclusion of a funeral march.

The cessation of the season at The Globe and his reluctance to go to America left German without an orchestra and without an income. This led him into writing some instrumental music, for this was more easily saleable than orchestral scores. A Suite for Pianoforte was published in 1889, and at the same time he began the time-consuming practice of arranging his larger works as piano solos and duets. He appears to have enjoyed this seemingly laborious task, especially the writing of duet arrangements, and they did, of course, provide one of the few means of deriving an income from orchestral pieces. The latter might be played only once a year in the concert halls, and would even then be out of reach for most of the British population. The piano versions were written for the thousands of homes like that in which John Jones had endowed his new bride with a pianoforte. They were the equivalent of the videos of the late Twentieth Century which propagate versions of films into private homes now that the age of home entertainment has returned in a very different form.

In 1890 German made a selection of themes from *Richard III* for piano. It is fortunate that he did for, as well shall see, it is our only means of recapturing the incidental music. He arranged the Overture as piano duet in the same year, and also produced versions of the processional march and the

Intermezzo funebre. He produced some original piano music also: the Suite of 1889 to be followed by a Valse in A Flat, Polish Dances and a Graceful Dance. He also produced some instrumental works: Two Romances and a Saltarello for Flute, an Andante and Tarantella for Clarinet and a *Moto Perpetuo* 'Pour violin avec accompagnement de Piano'. Another French title appeared with Colombine, *Air de Ballet, pour Piano.* For two violins and piano, perhaps thinking of his duets with W E Rogers, he composed a Scotch Sketch. It cannot be said that he explored the souls of the instruments in these pieces for they were often subsequently re-written for others. A Pastorale and Bourrée for Oboe, published in 1895, was re-issued for clarinet, flute and violin. But they displayed a growing assurance compared with his Academy compositions. Songs written at this time included a ballad, *The Banks of the Bann, Little Boy Blue* and *Little Lovers.* The words are sentimental but *Little Boy Blue* at least foreshadows the dance measures of the later stage works.

At the same time he had not given up ambitions to write another large-scale work. He contemplated an opera on the theme of a Hungarian legend though the search for a suitable story was unproductive. He also wrote to Richard D'Oyly Carte, keen at this time to promote serious British opera (Sullivan's *Ivanhoe* was a result of the project) offering his services as composer, for a new work for the projected opera house 'or, if this cannot be arranged – for the Savoy'. The style of his letter is extremely engaging: 'With no wish to force myself upon you but thinking that you have had so much to take your attention [this phrase replacing 'think of'] lately that you probably may not have had the time to read much musical news in the papers – I will mention one or two of my works that have recently been performed . . . ' German enclosed the libretto of *The Two Poets* and referred to the knowledge of stage writing gleaned from *Richard III* which was 'essentially operatic'.

> I know I could write an opera (something perhaps between 'Carmen' and 'Faust') that would be successful both from an artistic and monetary point of view. It is a difficult matter to write about oneself. Not a stone should be left unturned if you should think well to give me this chance.

His letters at this stage show the persistent efforts which a composer without means had to employ to hear his work performed. He requested Randegger to help him with his approaches to the Leeds Festival Committee and also to Joseph Bennett whose words, he felt, would carry great weight in securing a performance of the Symphony. ('My Symphony is my best work. All the parts are beautifully correct and the performance would be absolutely safe.')

He was prepared to press for performance of his works but his draft letters to the Leeds Festival Committee and other such bodies show many hesitations and many erasures of the passages through which he hammered out his claims to recognition. Having crossed out several expressions such as 'I am in earnest and I mean to do whatever I am able towards helping English Art' he eventually settled on the phrasing, 'Of course, you will naturally have a great number of applications from English composers [replacing 'English-born subjects'] and it is not for me to single myself out, nor is it easy to write on one's own behalf. I must only conclude by saying *straightforwardly* [included as an afterthought] that I am an earnest composer, not a trifler and should you think to [out go 'honour' and 'encourage'] place my name in your programme I should of course, be most grateful for such an honour.' He decided against the rather gloomier 'I feel sure you would have no cause to regret it'. At this time he suggested the revised Symphony as his best work.

Fortunately, these appeals, painfully hammered out clause by clause, served as models for another more fruitful.

★　★　★

The letter that was in fact to be most productive was one sent to Henry Irving, when it was announced that the great actor was to mount a revival of Shakespeare's Henry VIII.

Even a composer who could promise D'Oyly Carte a second *Carmen* might well have been daunted at the thought of approaching the great Irving, whose personality was so powerful that he had once, as Macbeth, reduced the second murderer to a paralysed silence when requesting information about the fate of Fleance. Furthermore, Sullivan had already written some popular music for the same play. German's sister Rachel, however, was insistent that he should seek the commission and the letter to D'Oyly Carte did excellent service as a model for this second request. 'Dear Sir,' the new letter began, 'Should you require specially written music for your forthcoming production of *Henry VIII* may I offer my services as composer thereof. You will remember no doubt the music I wrote for Mr Richard Mansfield's revival of *Richard III* at The Globe. It comprised overture, *entr'actes* and all the incidental music.' He then recounted the recent performances of his work adding,

I merely mention these as showing that I am a serious composer, not a trifler. As to 'knowing the business' I think I may safely say that I understand what you would require though of course, should you entertain my offer you would want to see me and explain your views.

Asking you to be so very kind as to read through the few notices I send before coming to an absolute decision.

I beg to remain, dear sir,
Faithfully yours,
Edward German

In fact, Irving had heard and admired the *Richard III* music and invited the composer to undertake the score for *Henry VIII*. The commission involved an anecdote told rather differently by the parties involved.

Von Ranke, the great German historian and one of the founders of 'scientific history', was driven to conclusions about the fallibility of human evidence when, upon hastening to the scene of an accident on a bridge in his town of residence, he was given three differing accounts by three witnesses whom he met on his way. The story of Irving's commission to German also has several versions. That which the composer liked to relate, and which found its way into the Scott Biography runs as follows:

'As to terms,' continued Irving, 'Would you accept the same as Mackenzie received for *Ravenswood*?'

Terms! German had not given a thought to the question of payment. What could he say? He could only bow assent.

Turning then to his acting manager, Irving asked what sum was paid to Mackenzie and in reply Bram Stoker, Irving's assistant [more famous as the inventor of *Dracula*], said he believed the fee was 200 guineas together with all publishing rights.

So it was left at that. Two days later, however, when German was seated in the stalls at the Lyceum, Bram Stoker strolled across during the interval and said rather casually, 'Oh Mr German, I'm afraid there's been a mistake about the terms we mentioned the other day.'

'Ah' thought German, 'I knew it was too good to be true.'

'Yes,' Bram Stoker went on, 'I find that Mackenzie received 300 guineas, so Mr Irving hopes that you will accept the same figure . . .'

Some years earlier to an American reporter the incident had been described in slightly different form. Irving had referred to Mackenzie's fee and not knowing whether this was £5 or £50 the composer had humbly lowered his head in silent agreement. He had then received a letter from Bram Stoker saying that Mackenzie had been paid £200. Shortly afterwards Stoker had called on him and explained that a mistake had been made, adding with a smile that Mackenzie had accepted £300 and hoped German would do the same.

Nothing but the embellishments of the raconteur distinguished these accounts but in Laurence Irving's *Life* of his grandfather, commenting on the fashion in which Irving had prepared busily for the role of Wolsey by imitating the great cardinal's prodigality, he says:

> A symptom of this assumption was his treatment of a young musician, Edward German, whom he had commissioned to write the dances and incidental music. When German, whose work had given him great satisfaction, sent in his bill it was returned to him endorsed in Irving's hand, 'This account needs revising'. The next day German in dismay called on Irving and protested that for the work entailed the sum was not unreasonable. 'My dear German,' said Irving, 'I paid Sullivan double the amount for music not comparable in my opinion to yours. Please amend your account as a favour to me with that fact in mind'.

Like political leaders from the Summit Conferences both men took from a mutual encounter what they wished. German liked to emphasise his modesty and, though he developed a good business sense, he enjoyed pretending to a naïveté in such matters. Irving was able to illustrate both his magnaminity and discernment. All that the historian can say with truth is that the stories probably diverged more widely the older they grew..

Irving had meditated a production of *Henry VIII* for many years, and desired it to be a scenic as well as a dramatic feast. 'In my judgement,' he said '*Henry VIII* is a pageant or nothing. Shakespeare, I am sure, had the same idea, and it was in trying to carry it out he burned down the Globe Theatre by letting off a cannon.' Independent of ordinary working expenses the cost of the production came to £11,879.1.0d so German's share was certainly not excessive. During its first run from 5th January to 30th July, 1892, the actors' and supernumeraries salaries came to over £20,000, a huge sum for those days. It was revived from 1st October to 5th March, having run for 203 performances in all.

German quickly made notes on the musical possibilities, and themes for Wolsey, Buckingham, Queen Katherine, flourishes for the French embassy, a Coronation March for Anne Boleyn, the Vision music and, of course, the Dances. Irving was anxious to achieve complete historical accuracy and painstaking research into the buildings and the costumes of Tudor London was carried out. William Terries, who played the king, was made up to look as much like the Holbein portrait as possible. His desire for period authenticity, however, encountered a firm obstacle in German's desire to produce original music rather than arrangements of Tudor airs. German sent to Irving a cutting from the *Daily News* which touched on 'musical archaeology' but justified his rejection of it.

> If . . . you will have confidence in me, I will give you music that will have the necessary touches of old English colour and be in keeping with the play . . . only it will be without the baldness, bareness and lack of colour that music had in those days.

Interest and speculation surrounded the score even before the production opened and the press kept the public informed of the composer's progress. 'This excellent writer of "play-house" tunes,' announced the *Pall Mall Gazette* in deadly journalese, 'has found difficulty in giving musical expression to the events of the great *History* of "Bluff King Hal".'

Nevertheless a very full picture of the composer's intentions was given which corresponds to the completed score and shows how Bernard Shaw's advice had clearly gone unheeded. The *Henry VIII* Overture is a splendidly robust work that refutes any belief that German's music is too restrained.

> The Overture is written in strict form and will announce the 'motives' afterwards employed to distinguish the events and characters. The first subject may be taken to represent King Henry ['Hale and Bold' German had written in his notebook] and the second Queen Katherine ['true hearted and loving'], and the exposition ['sensual music'] ends with a few bars of the 'Coronation March'. The 'Wolsey March' will be a characteristic feature of the First Act, and in the fourth scene of this Act there is an old English dance acted by the whole company of guests, followed by a torch dance by mummers. [In fact there is music all through this Act, the characters speaking through it, and the theme that is prominent throughout is the Anne Boleyn motive, for she is the principal figure, the curtain coming down to a reprise of the King Henry motive.] An *Inter mezzo Funebre* is played before the Second Act preparing the audience for the fall and execution of Buckingham. A short allegro in G minor ushers in the Third Act and here the 'Orpheus' Trio [usually treated as a solo] will also occur. It will be sung by three ladies from the Royal Academy of Music – Miss Minnie Robson, Miss

Lancaster and Miss Kate Lewis to a harp accompaniment assisted by sustained chords for the muted strings of the orchestra. Act Four is also especially interesting from the musicians' standpoint, the extracts consisting of a short march in D major and morris dance. The coronation music is especially important with plenty of 'brass' and cymbals with a chorus. The Katharine motive is introduced into the Vision music which concludes the Act. All is joyous and happy in the concluding Act for has not King Henry obtained his heart's desire? The Thanksgiving Hymn is an elaborate number and the chorale which follows will be first of all sung by some boys from the Oratory and others, accompanied by the theatre organ and repeated as a Finale with the full strength of the orchestra. The music has been well rehearsed, and is suspected to add not a little to the general attractiveness of the revival.

When it was suggested that 'Orpheus with his Lute' should be given to Katharine's three attendants, Ellen Terry had stipulated that they must be tall and graceful, and Irving's business manager, that they must not charge high fees. To that end German explored the talent available at the Royal Academy and satisfied all three conditions as well as producing one of the world's most beautiful songs.

On 15th June, 1892, the theatre world turned its eyes on the Lyceum and Irving's realisation of the play was greeted with reverential reviews. One critic described the interweaving of music, dance and drama as 'a combined display such as Wagner may have imagined but never realised', and certainly even today the eye is stunned by pictures of the sumptuous sets which succeeded one another on the stage. 'It would take the imagination to believe what can be done on the modern stage until this splendid revival has been witnessed,' wrote one critic. 'There are fourteen complete scenes elaborately set and they change almost without descent of curtain as if by magic. The lights are turned down; there is a momentary darkness; and a gorgeously equipped scene complete with furniture is changed to another equally rich in the twinkling of an eye.' The Brussels *L'Independence* recorded how excellently the scenery had portrayed the old oak trees of Greenwich, 'ce Saint-Germain des Tudor', and thought the composer had rendered the musical atmosphere of the sixteenth century with great skill even if he had not shown the 'savant lyrisme' of Saint-Säens whose opera on the same historical subject is unjustly neglected. It was left to an American journal *'The Boston Globe'* to criticise more candidly, saying of Ellen Terry, 'Her obvious lack of physical vigour, and, for her, fairly astonishing forgetfulness

Mr. EDWARD GERMAN.

nted, and in January, 1880, he went to Shrewsbury in order to r there preparatory to entering of Music the same year he became a ution, and began his career as r. Steggall, but what with the violin and pianoforte, he found

Academy in 1887, he was elected took away with him 6 medals and His student days being over, the world, for his name was vi within the Academy walls. As is in all branches of the Art, he after disappointment both with publishers.

The promising composer age 30

Henry Irving as Cardinal Wolsey, 'Henry VIII' *(BBC Hulton Picture Library)*

of her lines corroborates the general rumour that Terry's days on the stage are nearly over'. But there was great praise for Irving as a lean and ascetic Wolsey. One MP, Sir Robert Peel, who had recently separated from his party over the Irish Question wrote to congratulate him on his fine impersonation. 'Your Grace looked just what Wilberforce once said of Manning, "the very incarnation of evil".' Several other observers noted the resemblance to that Eminent Victorian in Irving's portrayal.

Despite some of the superlatives noted above, it is rather surprising to find that in general, the tributes to the music, though it received prominent attention, were polite rather than fulsome ('The music has turned out to be both interesting and appropriate', 'Several of his pieces had high merit', etc). The reason was probably the indifference of the first-night audience. *The World* remarked that it would

> hardly tempt eminent composers specially to write incidental music for stage plays if they are treated by audiences in the manner they have recently experienced. Sir Arthur Sullivan's music for *Macbeth*, Dr A. C. Mackenzie's music for *Ravenswood* and Mr E. German's music to *Henry VIII* were on the first night, each and all inaudible owing to the chattering in the stalls. A similar fate greeted Henschel's music to *Hamlet* shortly afterwards.

The finest music from the play is contained in the G minor *Intermezzo*, with its rising *cantabile* theme but it was to be the Three Dances, during the second of which the king danced spellbound with Anne Boleyn, which became German's most familiar and popular pieces. They became part of the repertoire of every salon and promenade orchestra in the land. In the first year 30,000 copies of the music were sold, and amateur pianists performed them without respite.

It was in the popular press that the claims of the Three Dances were advanced and the fame of German spread. Some of the reviews have all the flavour of the genteel Victorian drawing-room. A correspondent for *The Gentleman*, after describing how she opened the piano arangement 'with a sense of pleasure' and advising its readers that Mr German 'is a most earnest and painstaking musician and always does his best', goes on to say "The melody of the Shepherd's Dance is deliciously catchy and yet not in the remotest degree vulgar, while the Torch Dance is full of a certain wild buffoonery. I daresay most of you remember how effectively it comes in the play".

The Country Gentleman strikes a note more jocular but equally coy: 'Do let me recommend to your favourable notice, my musical friends, the very charming dance music composed by Mr Edward German for *Henry VIII* at the Lyceum. It is published at the very moderate price of three shillings and is delightful even for the piano . . . I heard Mr August Manns and his Merry Men play these dances at the Crystal Palace the other day and *at once* determined to possess myself of a copy. Since then I have done nothing but play them over and over again. They should be arranged as pianoforte duets'. Yet we must remember that Elgar himself said that he could never listen to the Shepherd's Dance without a lump coming into his throat. When the music from the play was included at a Philharmonic Concert in April 1893, superlatives began to flow. 'As played by the Philharmonic Orchestra,' said the paper *Black and White*, 'the Overture could not but concentrate attention upon one of the most gifted of living musicians'. It described the Torch Dance as if it were a Mahler Symphony as 'glorious in its massive contruction'. When some American girls wrote to German asking him for programme notes on the Dances he replied that he had tried in the Torch Dance to give the effect of flickering flames. *The Sun* described the orchestration as displaying 'positive genius' and said boldly 'at the rate we are progressing now few will be brave enough to dare to stand forth and declare that England as a nation has no claim to call itself musical'.

Many years later such phrases seem overblown and German undoubtedly suffered disappointment from his inability to sustain the high temperature of such excited reviews. Yet the Dances remained for fifty years arguably the most popular pieces of their kind. In the early days of the gramophone a record of the Henry VIII Dances was almost as much part of the normal equipment as a set of needles. In 1900 at a concert of English music given in Naples, a rare enough event in itself, the Henry VIII Dances were the only item to be encored, and were vociferously applauded. At a Gala performance of the life and works of Charles Dickens given at the Coliseum in 1912, the Henry VIII Dances, for no ascertainable reason, were included in the programme. At the 1916 Shakespeare Tercentenary Celebrations at Drury Lane, attended by King George V, not only were the Dances in the programme but the crowds, who waited outside from dawn in the pouring rain, were entertained to frequent performances of them on the pennywhistle by a busker of taste. They ensured German's popular fame although there were times when he felt they detracted from the attention given to his serious work.

★   ★   ★

Soon after the opening of *Henry VIII* another early work the *Gipsy Suite*, was performed at the Crystal Palace. The composer had originally planned this in four movements to be called 'Lonely Life', 'The Dance', 'The Pretty Gipsy' and 'The Revel'. These last two were temporarily changed to 'Love Scene' and 'The Rejoicing'. Eventually they were published as 'Valse: Lonely Life', 'Allegro: The Dance', 'Menuetto: Love Duet', and 'Tarantella: The Revel'. The Suite is more like ballet music in the light Italian style than Bohemian and it does not have the peculiar rhythms or intervals that characterize gipsy music. It was pointed out that the *tarantella* is an Italian dance and there are few gipsies in Italy. Nor are many likely to have danced a minuet round the camp fires. Possibly some of the ideas had been set down for the projected 'Hungarian' opera. The first movement does contain suggestions of the Zigeuner tuning his instrument and as Romany is a vague and indefinable place some critics thought the *allegro* and *tarantella* were strongly tinged with gipsy character. The *Illustrated London News* declared that in his imitations of this style, 'somewhat in the manner of Bizet', German had 'succeeded to perfection'; *The Pictorial World* critic thought that the Suite was 'the most charming work of its class that I have heard from an English pen since Mr Cowen gave us Language of the Flowers . . . That is saying much,' said the writer, conclusively, 'but not *too* much.' Of the *valse melancholique* the *Musical Times* remarked, 'All waltzes nowadays are so very melancholy that Mr German has not scope for his individuality.' In the 1930s words were provided for the *valse melancholique* and the *Gipsy Dance*, and the pieces were published for use by choirs and schools.

The Suite was given a very serious review by *The Telegraph* which praised the orchestration, dismissed the *allegretto** as a 'conventional example of Gounod's influence upon a receptive mind', pleaded for a more sparing use of the cornets and trombones – 'these strident servants of the orchestral writer' – but concluded that German was not resting on his laurels but seeking distinction in other paths 'which lie open to the industrious composer'. The Suite makes full use of various percussion instruments that gipsies always appear to have lying close to hand. The *tarantella* needs every device of orchestral colour to give life to the theme which is little more than a series of running-scale triplets so a full *batterie de cuisine* was called into service. The Gipsy Suite is a work which does not require staid musical analysis but if the British paid the same degree of reverence to their light musical composers as the Viennese and displayed them through their finest orchestras on television to world-wide audiences, the *Gipsy Suite* would hold its own by comparison.

---

* 'Love Duet'.

CHAPTER FOUR

Footlights and Festivals

In the days before gramophone and radio the principal method by which a composer could become known was through commissioned works at one of the major musical festivals in the great cities. These had arisen in the eighteenth century partly out of veneration for the works of Handel, admirably suited to large choral masses, partly to help philanthropic projects and aid hospitals or charity schools. The Leeds Festival was a latecomer on the scene. Sterndale Bennett in 1858 had conducted at a Festival to celebrate the opening of the new Town Hall by the Queen. It occupied four days and included *The May Queen*, written by the conductor, which German had known and played in his Whitchurch days. Leeds medical charities had benefited to the tune of £2,000 but the subsequent festivals, confidently expected, did not take place. The idea was revived by leading citizens in 1874. Sullivan was appointed as a principal conductor in 1880 and a tradition of holding a choral and orchestral festival once every three years developed. Under the aegis of Sullivan, the Leeds Festival became an event of international importance because of the strength and splendour of the choral singing and because of commissioned works from living composers: Dvorak, Massenet, Humperdinck and other European musicians as well as Parry, Stanford and Elgar.

While working on his Second Symphony in 1892 in the comparative calm of Whitchurch, German received a letter from the secretary of the Leeds Festival saying that the committee had put down an overture of his as the last piece in one of the evening concerts. There had in fact been some criticism in the reportage of the 1892 programme for which the only new works were to be Cowen's *Egyptian Maid*, a symphony by Frederick Cliffe and a Cantata by Dr Alan Gray. Cliffe's reputation has not survived but he was a distinguished teacher at the Royal College of Music where his pupils included John Ireland and Arthur Benjamin. He had been organist at the 1886 Festival and had arranged the organ part for the first Leeds performance of Bach's B Minor Mass. Yorkshire, however, did not feel satisfied with the fare on offer and when it was announced that *in piam memoriam* a work would be included by Goring Thomas who had recently committed suicide during a period of depression, hearts were not lifted. Thomas had been, like German, a pupil of Prout's and a Lucas Medal winner at the Academy but his work was considered derivative. *The Yorkshire Post* expressed a wish that German's name should be included and remarked that his reputation 'had been winning golden opinions on all sides'. The *Richard III* Overture was selected and German himself conducted. Impressed by his musicianship and perhaps even more by his efficiency Sullivan also gave him the difficult task of making some cuts in a selection from *The Master Singers*. Orchestral musicians certainly had to work hard. The second rehearsal for the Leeds Festival concert took place in London and was virtually a public performance. Dr Alan Gray's cantata, *The Arethusa*, needed two attempts as the players had not seen the score before and errors were numerous. A rehearsal of the Bach B Minor Mass followed. After luncheon the forces reassembled for Parry's *De Profundis*, a setting of Psalm 130, the *Richard III* Overture and the *Master Singers* selection.

At the performance itself Sullivan sat on the platform and with his usual graciousness stopped the composer as he was leaving the rostrum and led him back to the front of the orchestra to shake hands with him most warmly.

The press still made frequent reference to the 'young composer' which may seem strange as he had now reached thirty, but German was slight of build and looked younger. One lady in the audience at Leeds exclaimed, 'Why, he looks like a boy. I suppose they do it to encourage young musicians.'

The Norwich Festival was much older. In 1772 the Norfolk and Norwich Hospital had been opened and an annual concert for its benefit was organised at the Cathedral with Handel's music featuring strongly. By 1824 a triennial festival had replaced these concerts. These continued throughout the nineteenth century more or less regularly and, like the Leeds Festival, Norwich was adventurous in commissioning and performing works by contemporary composers. The committee had even braved the wrath of puritanical preachers who thought Spohr's *Last Judgment* a sacrilegious work. The principal conductor, from 1881 to 1905, was Alberto Randegger, German's patron and friend at the Academy, and a new work by German was commissioned for the 1893 festival. This fact caused further acid rebukes from Shaw who disliked the festival and thought the proceeds should be devoted to encouragement of the arts and not 'to save rich East Anglicans from supporting their local charities'. He was not well disposed either to the programme for 1893, especially Parry's *Judith* – 'the East

Anglians being anxious to hear whether so famous a work can possibly be as bad as I think it is', and German incurred the blame for having 'composed expressly a work for it'. Of the sumptuous programme itself he noted 'that the committee include 25 peers or sons of peers, 19 baronets, 16 members of parliament, 4 knights, 3 mayors, a high sheriff and an ordinary sheriff, 2 judges (of law), a dean, an esquire, a colonel and not a solitary musician or artist of any degree – not even a critic to see fair play. There will therefore be no danger of having the festival spoilt by the interference of specialists!'

The first plan was that German should write a cantata and his name was now sufficiently well known for his plans and projects to be discussed in the press. When he decided against a choral work, as no inspiring text was available, *The Telegraph* felt that he had acted wisely as 'the clever young composer of the music to *Henry VIII* has something to say through the orchestra and says it with effect while his skill in choral writing has not been demonstrated on a scale of any importance'. He even had to write to the *Sunday Sun* to correct a report that his work was completed, pointing out that he had not yet even decided what it was to be.

The Whitchurch Herald thought that its readers might not be fully aware of the importance of festivals in the musical work of the country and reminded them that at Birmingham, Leeds and Norwich a selection of works by the best composers were played and all the most eminent instrumentalists and singers available gathered together. 'We cannot but feel proud' it added, 'that our gifted townsman's name will appear successively on the programmes of two of these festivals.' His arrival and departure at Llandudno for a brief holiday were noted in the local press. The *Llandudno Directory*, remarking rather oddly that he had been 'retained' to write a symphony for the Norwich Festival reported that he had enjoyed his two weeks of relaxation in the town and remarked that the popularity of the Henry VIII Dances had caused them to be put permanently into the repertoire of Mr Riviere's orchestra at the resort. His Marche Solennelle and Henry VIII Dances were given in Liverpool at a concert which included the first performance in the city of Greig's Piano Concerto and received more attention than the latter. The Dances were described in one journal as the most interesting feature in the programme.

The idea of a cantata having been abandoned, he thought first of an orchestral suite, then subsequently of a second and larger scale symphony. It was performed in 1893 in St Andrew's Hall, Norwich before an audience of 1,357. Helpful planning had put it into the same programme as Sullivan's *Golden Legend*, which involved the most eminent soloists of the Festival, so no seat was left unsold.

The 'Norwich' Symphony is the most significant English symphony to be written before Vaughan Williams' *A Sea Symphony* and Elgar's First, yet its apologists must sometimes feel that it might as well have been written on a Pacific Island and thrown into the sea in a bottle. It is one that can bear comparison with the works of Dvorak and others who still worked in the symphonic form. It aroused considerable interest when it appeared and yet it had to wait almost forty years for publication and that at the composer's own expense. It still has to receive a full professional recording. In a sense one can say that it represents an allegory of German's musical career. The first movement has the exhuberance of youth and surges along with expressions of rapture and enthusiasm. The second, an *andante con moto* in 9/8 measure is restful and melodic. In the *scherzo* we return to familiar German territory, a fanciful rustic dance in 6/8 time. The finale is proper and conventional with a chorale for full orchestra at the conclusion which recalls Brahms' First Symphony. Impetuosity and energy have been transformed into dignity and style. The work was well received at its first performance although the composer may have been disappointed by the frequent references to 'promise'. Summing up the Festival and its novelties, *The Weekly* selected two by which the 1893 festival would be remembered: *The Water Lily,* a cantata by Cowen ('future performances will be anticipated with the greatest eagerness by his myriads of admirers') and the German Symphony ('It is almost difficult at this date to say what high point in his art Mr German may not eventually reach') The applause for his work and for his conducting was thought to be enthusiastic 'as tokens of approbation are generally given very sparingly at festival morning performances'. The critics noted that there was very little academic dreariness in the development of the themes and the composer had not copied any continental school. The music is certainly not derivative and the language is German's own.

In December 1893, London audiences had an opportunity to hear it at the Crystal Palace. The audience was disappointingly small but broke into spontaneous applause at the end of the *scherzo* and appeared to be demanding an encore. The vehemence of the first movement caused some puzzlement and the orchestration seemed too heavy. A few critics pleaded for moments of repose. There was, however a devastating review from Shaw. The pit musician's defence of *Richard III* had not endeared German to him. In savage mood he deplored the practice of transfering works from provincial festivals to London. 'We never seem to get finally rid of the relics of autumn festivals. The 'specially composed' oratorio, cantata or symphony having been duly proclaimed a masterpiece is set down for its first performance in London later on: and these first performances keep dropping in all the winter and stirring up our worst passions.' Still determined to instruct German in his craft the writer averred that his talents lay in the theatre and advised him to break up the symphony and use the pieces as incidental music. 'It is dramatic music without any subject, emotional music without any mood, formal music without conspicuous beauty and symmetry of design, externally a symphony, really a fulfilment of a commission or seizure of professional opportunity, otherwise purposeless.' The criticisms are unfair. Many symphonies contain music that is dramatic without a subject, many are emotional without a persistent mood. There is nothing opportunist in a composer without patrons accepting a commission from a highly prestigious festival. The *Pall Mall Gazette* was to prove even more scornful about a performance at a Philharmonic concert in May 1894.

> Let us frankly say that Mr German should give up symphony writing for at least ten years and should take on the other hand work of a more – shall we call it? – alphabetical nature . . . The Scherzo was evidently the most popular movement of the piece – we really cannot call it symphony. There is indeed a rustic prettiness in it, a suggestion of maypoles and pink frocks interlacing in dance . . . Let it not be imagined for a moment that Mr German is not an entirely clever young man. He is entirely clever. But there cannot be the slightest doubt that if he thinks he is equipped to enter the list with the great masters of symphony he is vastly mistaken.

With unctuous concern, the reviewer concluded patronisingly, 'The mistake has been made and in all kindness we remind him of it.' In this the reviewer showed ignorance of musical history. In general the early symphonies of the great composers are not those which a writer of some renown would be terrified of challenging. The Tchaikowsky of the Second Symphony is not yet possessed of powers to write the Sixth. The Second Symphony of Schubert displays no indications of the strength of the 'Great' C Major. It is one of the great causes of dismay in English music that we do not have seven or eight symphonies of Edward German which might have shown a wider absorption of new ideas and new musical resourcefulness that could never be learned in the theatre. A composer with the temperament of a Beethoven or a Wagner on receiving such reviews would have immediately composed a Third Symphony. It is significant that German called his next Festival composition – for the Leeds Festival – 'A Symphonic Suite' and deliberately presented his work, masterpiece that it is, in a less ambitious vein. For many years he was hesitant over asserting claims for the 'Norwich'. There is no indication from his letter book that he pushed as hard for further performances as he had with his First Symphony.

It was almost forty years before it again received the mixed attentions of critics and public in the last years of German's life. By then the world had changed and though it was accorded respect the arbiters of taste were by then accustomed to a much more experimental musical language.

★   ★   ★

The success of the *Henry VIII* music led inveitably to further theatre commissions and much of German's time and energy in the 1890s were occupied in writing for the stage. While engaged on the Second Symphony, he was also writing incidental music for Beerbohm Tree's production of a play by Henry Arthur Jones, *The Tempter*. Having taken over management of the Haymarket Theatre, Tree had installed electric lighting and improved the cheaper seating. *The Tempter* followed Wilde's *A Woman of No Importance* in the gala re-opening season. Henry Arthur Jones was a successful writer of comedies though one would never guess the fact from the two sombre essays in sexual guilt which German was called upon to embellish. *The Tempter* was set in medieval times and the plot allowed generously for Tree's interest in the grotesque and his famed skill in the art of stage make-up. Jones was a playwright firmly opposed to Ibsenite social drama and exploration of contemporary themes. The prologue announces this with chilling candour:

Leave for a while
Democracy's cheap aims and sick unrest
Leave social maladies to be redressed
In nature's surgery by her wise knife
Shun the crude present with vain problems rife
Nor join the bleak Norwegian's barren guest
For deathless beauty's self and holy zest
Of rapturous martyrdom in some base strife
Of petty dullards soused in native filth.

From Norway's social and domestic problems he takes flight to the Middle Ages.

The melodrama is centred on Prince Leon of the Auvergne, a character unknown to history although we are told that his marriage to the English Lady Avis de Rougemont would prevent the Hundred Years War. This would not suit the Tempter, a Mephistophelian figure who appears in a number of disguises, and plots the disgrace of the Prince through wine, women and song. It was German's task to supply the song, particularly for some well-intentioned pilgrims to Canterbury who are led astray into bacchanalian revels. The presentation was intended to provide lavish spectacle, Prince Leon's boat being wrecked upon the Kentish shore at the outset, and sacred hymnody dispelling the powers of darkness at St Werburg Abbey, near Canterbury, in the finale.

The mood is operatic and German obliged with a very fine orchestral prelude in which a chromatic theme represented the Tempter and a theme of purer cast described the Lady Avis. The storm at sea also required music. Unfortunately, the ship bearing Prince Leon was a huge construction devised after some promising experiments with a small working model. When the actual vessel was completed and set bodily on the stage (an idea borrowed from Meyerbeer's '*L'Africane*' which occupied stage engineers at the Paris Opera for many months during the Second Empire), it would neither sail nor sink and, in the author's own words, 'instead of thrilling the spectator with terror, merely gave him a sensation of seasickness'. On the first night, when Sir Arthur Sullivan, among others, was present, the failure of the machinery and the length of time necessary to change the scene, resulted in a seven-minute pause during which the actors had to mime their final gasps as they sank repeatedly below the waves.

German had his frustrations during rehearsals. In August, 1893, he wrote to Rachel. His literary style again showed the Olde English flavour that characterised his music.

> I think I have now broken the back of my music. I have performed a remarkable feat!! which the same I will tell you. From July 6th to July 31st twenty-six days inclusive, I composed, scored and completed the overture, all three *entr'actes*, the storm music etc . . . the completed score at that day numbering 215 pages!! Ahem! and ahem. What the Billy Eccles (as Ted says) it will all be like I know not. In only know that I never wrote at such a pace in my life – I can hardly believe I have done it. It is about double the pace at which I wrote *Richard*! I have now to complete third and fourth acts, then rehearsals will commence.
>
> Henry Arthur Jones is an impossible man – musically. We have had a lot of bother over a song and nothing is settled yet. The chief points of controversy are:
> 1 Mr Tree having no voice (at least I have not discovered any) is desirous of singing a song.

2 Mr Jones and Mr Tree are both wishful that Mr Tree should be at
   liberty to do what he likes and really sing what he likes and they quite
   expect the orchestra (in a body) to follow him in these evolutions.
   Consequently (good old 'consequently' my favourite expression) I
   fail to see the use of my writing anything – !
   Really these theatrical talkers and dreamers are remarkable men!
Tree actually suggested that although he knew nothing about the guitar
he should take a few lessons on that instrument and accompany the
song himself on it – as it would *look* well!
   The worst of these idiots is they will not be told what they want is
impossible.

Despite these problems the score was completed. To give a less familiar
sound cornets were substituted for trumpets. While German was grappling
with the music Tree went down to Margate to meditate himself into his
diabolical role. The part gave him full scope. During performances he wore
a red beard and covered his eyes with flashing glass lenses that appeared to
stay on without any visible means of support. The programme notes the
overture, bacchanalian dance, berceuse and dramatic interlude. Carl
Armbruster was the conductor as German was engaged to conduct at
Norwich. The pieces were scored for full orchestra, which the Haymarket
was unable to supply, and some of the sepulchral effects were lost because
the players were submerged in an underground cavern under the stage. The
bacchanal is lively but suggests a group of excited gipsies in the cloisters at St
Werburg Abbey rather than satanic happenings.
   Max Beerbohm, step-brother of Tree, was fond of telling the story of the
Prince of Wales requesting the name of the composer because he enjoyed the
music.
   'His name, sir, is German.'
   'Yes, yes I know. Lots of Germans write music. What is he called?'
   'His name, sir, is German.'
   Whereupon a royal explosion followed and the matter was never
resolved.
   Coming so soon after his work on the Second Symphony, this task was a
heavy one. The play enjoyed some success. It has some vivid theatrical
moments as, for instance, when a flash of lightning suddenly illuminates the
helmsman of the doomed ship to reveal the Devil himself. Or when the
love-torn Lady Isobel for whom the prince has forsaken the Lady Avis seeks
spiritual guidance and the audience sees that the confessor in stainless white
robes is the same Tempter. Or when a statue on the Abbey door reveals his

features and berates the Prince for his misdeeds. The Devil is jubilant at his success and foresees with uncanny mathematical accuracy how long the impending war will last. –

> When I stand ready to unleash my hounds
> for glut and rapine of 100 years

– which is more than can be said for the monarchs who began it. The concluding scene was accompanied by three sections of music: The Devil Vanishes, The Dawn and Hymn in the Cathedral.

At the close, the Lady Avis played by Julia Neilson announces her intention of entering a convent. There is a pause. The first streaks of dawn appear in the sky and eventually spring blossoms fill the cloister garden while a burst of music from the church accompanies the consoling words of the prior of St Werburg. Just as the dramatist has covered ground already traversed by Marlowe and Goethe, the composer might have been accused of following closely in the steps of Gounod, yet the play has poetic passages and some wit. It received good reviews. *The Illustrated London News* wrote that Jones had 'enjoyed a glorious carouse with the old dramatists. The ascent of Mr Henry Arthur Jones to fame has been as rapid as it has been deserved . . . who would have thought that the author of *The Silver King* would bud into *Judah* and blossom into *The Tempter*? The play ran for 73 nights and was taken off only because the expenses of production required the highest possible receipts. It elicited an interesting letter from a friend, Harry Baldwin, who wrote partly to commiserate over the usual difficulties experienced by composers on first nights.

> They were inappreciative (sic) of your music at the Haymarket on the first night and I was very annoyed at them. I have got a ticket (a balcony stall) for tomorrow so shall be better able to hear than on Wednesday last. The public then had their heads full of the fact that it was a new play they had to applaud and had no room left in their noddles for a thought about the music. What I heard of it I liked immensely.
>
> I was talking to Colonel Arthur Collins, Princess Louise's factotum on Sunday night . . . I was talking to him about you. He took a lot of interest in what I told him and said he liked your music exceedingly. He was sitting during a performance next to Dr Joachim. Joachim said 'Who wrote this music? It is fine. It is exceptionally fine and interesting'. Colonel Collins told him who wrote it and Joachim replied 'It is the best new music I have heard for a long while and I shall expect great things from this said Mr Ed German.

Joseph Joachim was one of the most distinguished European musicians of the age. A student at the Leipzig Conservatory under Mendelssohn, and Konzertmeister at Weimar under Lizst, friend of the Schumanns and Brahms, a violinist who placed artistic integrity above mere virtuosity, his words of praise must be among the most valued which German, even at this early date, ever received. Baldwin concluded, 'there is no doubt my boy that *Henry VIII* has made you famous. It has made you known to the people of this kingdom. I am constantly coming across evidence of that. The Tempter's Song is fine but it is a fact that Tree cannot sing a d . . . m.'

In a combative preface to the published version, Jones made no mention of the music but it was later arranged as a suite and performed at the Crystal Palace. A thick London fog and a disrupted train service thinned the Saturday afternoon audience but the music was heard with proper orchestration for the first time and the Berceuse which precedes the third act was highly praised though it was marred by a mistake in the bassoon section. One critic said that it showed a measure of inspiration equal to that of Schubert and Mendelssohn in their incidental music for *Rosamunde* and *Midsummer Night's Dream*. Many years later, in 1947, Eric Coates, making an eloquent plea for the theatre music of Sullivan and German pointed out that it was written by the men themselves, masters of orchestration, while many composers of the day had to rely on professional arrangers to prepare their scores for performance.

Lurking in the shadows, waiting to sow discord with a skill worthy of the Tempter himself, was Shaw, or one of his henchmen. Early in the year 1893 the style of musical criticism in the daily *Pall Mall Gazette* underwent a sudden change. It had previously been concerned to give rather kindly advertisements to forthcoming events and mild reviews. In so far as it dealt with theatre music the paper had declared in January, 'The stage, it is generally acknowledged, is much indebted to Mr Irving and soon the musical profession will be equally so. For his magnificent production at the Lyceum he invariably selects some eminent composer to write the incidental music. Professor Villiers Stanford whose name is already associated with some of Tennyson's noblest poems will provide the music for *Becket*.' But as the year progressed the music critic's column grew larger and took the form of polemical tracts on musical subjects. The articles were not signed but they paraphrase the highly readable writings of Shaw collected from *The World* and *The Star* at this time. The prejudices of the author are certainly Shaw's: a hatred of Brahms ('For once we were permitted an evening without the solid companionship of Brahms and who shall say that this is not something for which to be grateful?'), veneration of Mozart, contempt for Saint-Saëns, and scorn for the English cantata ('We do not hold *The Golden Legend* in very high estimation because it does not appear to be by any particular composer'). Referring to a recent production of a play, *Beau Austin*, which has been preceded by the Overture to *The Magic Flute* and had employed a Handel aria as incidental music at one point, the critic elaborated his thesis that all productions should select their scores from the works of the great masters. It was a good opportunity to make a few lunges at German, whose pit musicians had dared to defend him.

> But not all music is as Mozart's or as Handel's and we receive the information that Mr Tree has engaged a certain Mr German for the special composition of the music to be performed during Mr Jones' new play with a temperate joy. Laureate compositions are never entirely successful and though Mr German's music to Mr Irving's revival of *Henry VIII* was interesting, we are still of the opinion that the careful – the very careful – choice of appropriate selections from old masters is a more desirable scheme than a novelty that may be meritorious or may be poor. But the choice should be entrusted to none but a musician of taste.

It is difficult to think which 'old master' could have provided items to accompany this tale of lust in the fourteenth century, and the sneers brought a reply in the correspondence column of the paper.

> Sir,
>   When a man seeks to ennoble art despising that which is frivolous and unworthy and ever reaching after that which is noblest and best, it is surely a little disheartening to find the *Pall Mall Gazette* – a journal usually fair-minded towards people with lofty aims – insinuating that such a man is not a musician of taste. I do not say you do this in so many words but what is one to infer from the Occasional Note in Friday's issue respecting the selection of music for theatrical performance. No one will deny you the right to give your opinion though modern musicians generally will probably differ from you as to the suitability of Mozart and Handel in this regard, and will thank Heaven that 'all music is not as Mozart's nor as Handel's'.
>   My object in troubling you immediately on reading this note is to protest respectfully and in all humility against what I fear will be regarded as a smear at one who is not only a talented musician but a true and conscientious artist. Because Mr Edward German ('a certain Mr

Edward German' you are pleased to call him) is young and comparatively unknown to fame that ought not detract from his abilities which, we have seen, have already produced work of high order and rich promise. Perhaps I may be pardoned for 'putting in my oar' for I have watched Mr German's career from his childhood and know something of the praiseworthy aims, sound musicianship and genius which have stood him in good stead where other aspirants have had little else but aristocratic influence and family connections to fall back on. The late Sir George MacFarren (himself a 'musician of taste' and no modern-school man) held golden opinions of German; and it is to such men as he that all enemies of this degenerate music (!) hall age are looking to redeem the promise of England's future as a musical country. On my own responsibility I ask the favour of your insertion of this communication as a simple act of justice to art.

A Critic

Scott's Biography does not give this letter but states merely that another critic replied. The reference to German's childhood, however, would point to Scott himself as the author. He was a journalist and critic, though not of music, and the style is his. The only other contender would be Walter Hay, but he would have been unlikely to reply so promptly to a London paper and might well have avoided the extreme feeling which soon drew sarcasm from the *Gazette*.

Our correspondent's intimacy with German's childhood and subsequent development naturally excuses some enthusiasm, even though that enthusiasm inclines a little beyond the bounds of reason. In his haste he has mis-read our note and mistakes our meaning. We passed no observations whatever on Mr German's musical taste who may be as capable as any other to select the incidental music of any given play from approved masters. Our point was rather that such a selection was likely to prove more successful as being more sure than the original (and therefore hazardous) composition of even a Mr Edward German. As to that gentleman's nobility of aim and his claims as a redeemer we have no qualifications of judging and we certainly had no intention of detracting from either possibility in a general comment on theatrical music. It is with a perfect sense of detachment that we leave our correspondent and Mr German to thank Heaven that all music is not as Mozart's or Handel's.

The musical column continued this attack a few days later, affecting to believe that the great masters had been impugned. 'Thanksgiving over the patent fact that all music is not inspired by a genius like that of Mozart or Handel is not altogether intelligible'. The arrogance of modern composers was attacked. 'It is this type, to which we are firmly convinced Mr German does not belong, which holds fast by no tradition of the past but only by the so-called aspirations of the present'. It expressed the fear that Wagner had done much to encourage 'a world of artists only too anxious to be permitted to lay aside influences which overshadowed and overwhelmed their own genius and capabilities'. There were two savage thrusts at German which Scott omits. Disclaiming any desire to injure the composer's reputation, it added, 'He assuredly has talent enough to live down even the praises of his worshipper,' and concluded:

> "The Lord Mayor of London does wisely in determining that his last banquet at the Mansion Hall shall be given in honour of music. Here there should be at least no discords, no wrong order in the toasting, nothing save harmony: but . . . the difficulty will be to draw the line in the list of invitations. We learn that Mr German (who is ever with us) has prepared a symphony for the Norwich Festival.

The tone of the *Gazette* brought the *Musical News* into the fray. It reminded its readers of the success which freshly conceived music by Sullivan, Parry and Stanford had enjoyed, declaring it strange that critic should openly announce his preference for a rechauffée of ancient viands'. When *The Tempter* was reviewed in the *Gazette*, the music, an important element, was not mentioned at all, but finally a criticism of the score appeared, which bestowed a careful measure of faint praise.

> The single word that after patient searching we are constrained to find regarding Mr German's music to *The Tempter* is that it is altogether appropriate. The dramatic action of the piece is clearly shadowed and outlined by the character of the music. The twanging chord that signals The Tempter's approach, the happy kind of seventeenth-century madrigal manner, the desired velocity of the Bacchanalian Dance and the rest – all combined to produce this appropriate effect . . . We now, therefore, are able to put it on record that Mr Edward German from his latest articulate expression, proves himself to be that which we never dreamed of denying him to be.

The writer still clung to his strange notion that the combination of *The Magic Flute* and *Beau Austin* had been one of exquisite unity.

When the controversy had run its course the music critic declared, 'That is the last word we shall utter in this world or the next, on the subject of incidental music to the drama.' Yet the hostility towards German did not disappear. Some time later Herbert Thompson, music critic of the *Yorkshire Post*, and a great admirer of German, wrote of an occasion at the Leeds Festival in his copious diary, 'Mr Vernon Blackburn of the *Pall Mall Gazette* comes and sits next to me so I vacate my seat and move to the rear.'

The dispute, however, did not dissuade the great actor managers from placing more commissions. In 1895 Forbes-Robertson, whose role as Buckingham in *Henry VIII* had been attended by some noble music, asked German to compose the score for his Lyceum production of *Romeo and Juliet*. In accepting this commission he was facing the challenge of many great works inspired by the play and was also for the first time moving away from his native land to an Italian setting and a story which called for a deeper vein of melancholy than the histories of *Richard III* or *Henry VIII*.

Unlike his contemporary, of whom one critic remarked, 'Mr Tree's *Hamlet* was no way to behave,' Forbes-Robertson was cultivated and urbane. He had originally trained as an artist at the Royal Academy and believed in beautiful verse-speaking and a measure of restraint and naturalism in the productions. *Romeo and Juliet* was a bold challenge to accept in his first venture into management, but German's music matched exactly his less strident approach.

The music was intended to convey an Italian flavour. In his notebook German jotted down his scheme for the Overture:

1 Sombre and tragic. First Subject.
2 Love theme. Second Subject. Develop same.
3 The fight in the street.
4 The death of Paris
5 Love theme
6 Sombre tragic

(Havergal Brian, the composer of many large scale symphonic works thought the Prelude showed a powerful depth of tragic feeling.)

His plans for the four interludes were:

1 Pastorale
2 Nocturne
3 Pavane
4 Dramatic interlude

On the first night Mrs Patrick Campbell was extremely ill but insisted upon playing Juliet although she was in great pain. The production enjoyed a successful run of four months at the Lyceum during Irving's absence in America.

In creating the mood for a highly romantic presentation of *Romeo and Juliet* German succeeded in producing a score that contains sufficient thematic material for an opera. The prelude grows out of a dark theme given in the bass at the outset. Portents of disaster precede the love music, and though the principal theme of this might not achieve the impossible in de-throning Tchaikowsky, it is a fine one, serving to introduce rather than swamp the music of the verse that is to follow:

The street battle with plenty of thundering brass and flying strings ensues and when it has subsided the theme of the lovers reappears.

The dramatic interlude which comes before the Final Act is another ambitious, essentially theatrical commentary. The audience is reduced to silence – or at least that is the intention of the *agitato* opening – and the theme which denotes the visit of Paris to the tomb of Juliet is played softly rising to a *maestoso* version. There are references back to the love theme, which grow more faint and hopeless; the Paris theme returns with many troubled additions in the accompaniment and the interlude dies away softly as the moment comes for the curtain to rise on the final tragedy.

There is also a fine nocturne which begins peacefully, though the night grows dark and restless, and there is a rich *appassionato* section before the music drifts into a slow dream-like waltz as the Third Act begins.

There was a great deal of inspired music in this score. German used the *allegretto* which accompanies the Capulets' reception in his pastorale, a rhythmically ingenious treatment of this much used vehicle, which has a surging and romantic refrain. The *Pavane*, which Vaughan Williams always considered the composer's most perfect piece of writing, has a delicate accompaniment that suggests soft foot-falls in the night. There is a barcarolle theme for Juliet alone, a scurrying passage for the nurse, some richly flowing marriage music, a processional episode for the duke, and a tristful accompaniment to Romeo's departure with sad, falling fifths. In the final death scene echoes of the love music return and religious chords sound at the final tableau. Although the orchestra appears to have been lacking in some respects at the start, Robertson wrote to German during the first month of the run:

> I am glad to hear that the band is now to your liking. They seem to me to play admirably. Here is a picture and let me take this opportunity to thank you heartily for all the trouble you have been at in the revival of *Romeo and Juliet* and for all the beautiful music you have given us. It has added so greatly to our success.

German was also presented with an elegant silver bowl by the company.

In 1896 he wrote some music for a second Forbes Robertson production *Michael and his Lost Angel*, another play by Henry Arthur Jones. The play does not deal with the Archangel Michael and the hero, the Reverend Michael Feversham, is an Anglican priest. No sooner had the title been announced, however, than fears were expressed in religious circles that the scriptures were being represented on the stage, even though the Archangel is not a scriptural character. One of Jones's defenders, Joseph Knight, subsequently pointed out that another recent production had presented *Paul of Tarsus* on the stage and used words from the New Testament itself against 'a background of pagan revelry and superfluous display of nudity of limb'. The refusal of Mrs Patrick Campbell to play the part of the heroine also fostered a belief that the play was in some way immoral and the inclusion of religious ceremonial for which German was required to produce the music caused offence in certain circles. The play is in fact a very heavy moral tract, a variation of the Thais legend in which an ascetic priest spends a night of passion with a worldly and wealthy woman when both (owing to a singularly unfortunate chain of coincidences) have been cast together on a lonely island. She in turn is redeemed by the force and anguish of his penitence and dies in his arms. In an early scene a village girl who had been seduced is forced by the then unsullied Reverend Michael to make a public confession of her guilt. At that point the drama calls for 'a penitential hymn with organ accompaniment sung in church outside'.

After only a week the Lyceum management announced that the play would be withdrawn three days later. When German learnt of its failure he returned the cheque which he had received for the music but Forbes Robertson, with Old Carthusian charm, refused to accept it.

★   ★   ★

Between *The Tempter* and *Romeo* German had the opportunity for further instrumental composition. For piano a berceuse was published, as well as a rather dull Concert Study, a Second Impromptu and a Minuet in G. Among vocal compositions were the Songs: *In a Northern Land, Ever Waiting* and *In the Merry May Time*. The third, as the title suggests, is to a lyric commonplace enough, but the song is quite difficult for both singer and accompanist. *'Ever Waiting'*, a pretty if sentimental song, exhibits German's gift for drawing out a melodic finish in a way which singers found grateful in performance. German also wrote part songs, *O Lovely May* and *Who is Sylvia*. At a concert given in Dewsbury by an admirer, G. H. Hirst, one of the chorus masters of the Leeds Festival, there is mention of a sextet (*andante* and *rondo*) for piano and wind instruments. This is presumably the piece which appears in the *New Grove's Dictionary* (in the vocal section as there are references to a voice part) as Serenade for V.I. Pianoforte, Flute Oboe, Clarinet, Bassoon and Horn (1890). It is not recorded as an unpublished work, but the British Library has no copy and although many woodwind groups have enquired of its whereabouts it seems to have disappeared. It may well be one of the pieces inherited by Ruth Tongue, Mabel's daughter, which went up in flames when her house was destroyed by fire.

Rachel, too, had three songs published in 1894: *The Lonely Brook, There was a Rose* and a strong setting of Elizabeth Barrett Browning's *Unless*. Though she did not have her brother's experience with the orchestra, her songs bear comparison with his at this stage in his career. Mabel, too, wrote some organ voluntaries for use in the Dodington Chapel, and piano pieces. It was rather as if some Lilac Fairy had visited the Brontes and modified the curse which produced tragic literature into one which encouraged family devotion to sweet music and light verse. Clifford contributed with performances of Cesar Franck on the Pianola, and also played the flute.

German spent some holidays at this time fishing in Scotland with friends, and hymned the expeditions in verses written on New Year's Day, 1896.

Accompanied by my Harp
Accompanied by my Harp
I fain would sing of Carp,
Of Georgie Carp and Teddy Carp, –
Of Jimmie Carp and Freddy Carp –
Accompanied by my Harp.

Oft have I tried in vain
To reach a happy strain.
I've sung both gay and sad,

I've sung both good and bad,
I've sung both flat and sharp –
Accompanied by my Harp.

But now I'll bide my time
And concentrate on rhyme.
In asking you to wait
Till I have bowed to Fate,
Till Love has conquered Hate,
Till at the Golden Gate
You'll meet your faithful Carp –
Accompanied by his Harp.

'It is really very fairly mad! Like I used to go occasionally when I was young', he wrote to Rachel, when he discovered it among his papers many years later. 'We called ourselves "The Carp Club", I don't know why, for Carp is the coarsest of fish and *we* used to go after the aristocratic Trout!'

In more serious vein, the major work on which he was engaged at this time was for the Leeds Festival of 1895. The Symphonic Suite in D minor probably betrays through its title some nervousness at not being abe to sustain the full symphonic form, after the critics' strictures of 1893 and 1894. It was originally intended that the Suite should have five movements, though the idea of an A-major march as the third section was discarded during the course of composition. Very early in his work on this commission, German sketched out the first two bars of the *valse gracieuse* which is its best-known movement. The first movement, marked prelude, *allegro moderato*, is in fact a full symphonic movement with first and second subjects, counter-themes, a sophisticated development section and a coda which works up in crescendo where the first theme is given out by the full brass section. It was the second movement, the *valse* which most quickly attained popularity. In addition to its lilting tune, its movements of subdued *pianissimo* and the flutterings of strings and woodwind, it has a fine *cantabile* theme for violas, cellos, single oboe and bassoon accompanied by slightly syncopated chords on four horns. The harp is much used; the woodwind have imitative entries of the *valse* theme, and the movement ends with the quietest of harp and *pizzicato* string chords. It is a *tour de force* of delicate and fastidious orchestration. The third movement was also ingenious. There was a solo theme for bass clarinet, and muted strings divided into several parts. It contains a graceful second subject rising in scale passages and reaches a strong and expressive climax before it too comes to a quiet conclusion. The finale is described as a saltarelle, Italian *tarantella*-style, and would serve excellently as ballet music, as in fact would the entire Suite. It is a noisy and aggressive movement with surprises, sudden *sforzandos* and a reference back to the prelude. The trombones are heavily employed and make the final entries to round off a spectacular movement as arresting to the viewer as the listener.

The Leeds Suite is a strong work in which the themes are closely interwoven. The first movement, especially, with its forceful triplet groups has moments which presage the opening of Elgar's Second Symphony.

It was helped at the 1895 festival by the comparative failure of the other novelty on the programme: A symphonic poem, *Nocturnal Vision*, by Massenet, which Herbert Thompson described in his diary as a fraud. The 'vision' was based on the unlikely event of a traveller settling down to sleep at midnight at the thundery summit of the Simplon Pass. Shrouded in mist he hears the voice of a loved one echoing over the hills. Thompson described it as being closer to the description of an over-worked music teacher trying to relax after eating an injudicious amount of cucumber, while his daughter practices sentimental ballads in the adjoining room.

Early in 1896 Stanford had tried to arrange for German to visit New York to conduct *Shamus O'Brien*, his opera which had enjoyed a successful run of fifty performances at the London Opéra Comique. German's letter on the subject shows that having accepted comparatively small sums for his early compositions he was beginning to learn a considerable amount about the business aspects of music:

Dear Professor Stanford,

Do not think that I am mercenary man before anything else for I assure you that I am *not*. The principal reason tempting me to go to America is of course the fact that I am in love with your work. Apart from the artistic side of the matter, one has to be exacting with regard to terms and I therefore wish to state straightforwardly just what my terms are.

Two first class passenger reservations there and back for myself, an attendant or friend.

That I am guaranteed £160.

That it is left to me as to the number of performances I conduct.

That I am free in my movements when not conducting.

That I receive half the sum – £80 before I start.

That although I am guaranteed £160 I need not necessarily stay the whole of the time (4 weeks), that is, if the opera is going to my satisfaction. Is this not so?

Against this I promise to use every effort to give the opera a successful production and to make it 'go'. The chorus will have been taught their part by the time I get there and the orchestra must of course be a good one. I shall then put the finishing touches and polish up the whole.

Please let me hear by wire from you as soon as possible tomorrow.

Not surprisingly the negotiations fell through. A few weeks later, he wrote to Stanford saying that as nothing definite had been heard, he had been forced to make other plans. 'I am more than sorry for I have told you of my honest enthusiasm for your opera but you will admit that everyone has to look ahead and make some kind of definite plan especially at this time of year.'

Further evidence that he was firmly set on composition came early in 1896 when he declined an offer to become a professor at the Royal Academy of Music:

Dear Sir,

I am deeply sensible of the honour conferred on me by the offer in your letter of the 29th. I have most seriously thought over the subject of becoming a professor at the Royal Academy of Music and I do not feel that I would have time to properly attend to the duties such a post would involve.

I have not come to this conclusion without a great amount of thought. I am sincerely sorry for no one has a greater affection for the institution than I have but it would, after all, be a contradiction for me to accept an important post knowing at the same time that I could not properly attend to my duties in connection with it.

These are my honest feelings in the matter and I trust you will accept my regrets in all sincerity.

Yours very faithfully,

Edward German

At the start of the year, he had been able to move from Kilburn Priory to No 5 Hall Road, off Maida Vale, an old-fashioned house but one situated very close to the West End. It was relatively secluded and possessed a garden. He lived there for nearly a quarter of a century during which time many of his most famous compositions were created. It was a bachelor establishment and gave the impression of a dwelling lifted from some country village and set down in the city. The garden was surrounded by a high stone wall, mellowed with age and overgrown with ivy. Spring flowers, apple and cherry blossom suggested the idyllic world of verdure and sweet romance that many of his songs conjure up. French windows led from the garden into a panelled study where the signs of the composer's work, his pianoforte, violin, piles of manuscript paper and printed music were to be seen. Banks of flowers were also evident inside the house.

He had no fixed hours for work but rose early and often continued writing, if the mood seized him, till two a.m. He enjoyed watching the cricket at Lord's nearby and often attended new plays. He was shy of accepting grand invitations, though he enjoyed bachelor evenings at the Savage Club and dinners with artistic friends. The impression which he liked to give was that of complete control and measured contentment.

It was in 1896, however, that he received a note from another distinguished actor, the handsome George Alexander, who* put his box at the St James Theatre at German's disposal and asked to have a chat for a few moments after the performance. Alexander wished to discuss a score for *As You Like It* which was to be produced later in the year.

German did not on this occasion produce a full programme of incidental music. The first part of the play was accompanied by the music of other composers selected by the conductor, Walter Slaughter. German contributed the music for the Masque of Hymen in Act V and some of his other music was also given between the Acts, including the inappropriate 'Tempter' Bacchanal. Julia Neilson played Rosalind to great acclaim and among the supporting caste was C. Aubrey Smith, the future portrayer of English squires and colonels in Hollywood films, who played the role of the Usurping Duke. In the Forest of Arden, German could relax into his characteristic mood and he contributed a woodland dance, children's dance and rustic dance. The song, *It Was a Lover and His Lass* was set for two trebles but, very strangely, he set no other songs from the play. During

* Alexander had waged a long campaign against patrons who came late to Matinees and ladies who wore large hats. One playgoer complained to him: 'What is the use of asking ladies to take off their hats in your theatre? I sat behind Mrs Alexander the other day and did not see a thing.'

rehearsals, it was suggested that The Cuckoo Song from *Love's Labour's Lost* should be transferred but this idea was discarded. *The Telegraph* praised the music highly:

> It will probably be found necessary to shorten some of the scenes in order to get the audience out of the theatre in canonical hours but as luck will have it, the masque at the end of the play with its beautiful new music by Mr Edward German, lovingly handled by Mr Walter Slaughter, gives to the pastoral comedy a Christmas charm which every intelligent child will appreciate. Mr German's music so tasteful, so delicate and so melodious . . . is a distinguished feature of the revival.

The production in fact ran for longer than any previous revival of the play.

As You Like It seems to have interfered with the progress of another romance. Earlier in the year we find German writing to a friend Alice Chapman: 'My dear girl, Will you come for a spin on Monday night? Turn up at Clarence Gate at 8 o'clock. If you can't come, send me a wire on Monday morning. There's a good girl. Yours E German'.

In September he wrote from Whitchurch:

> My dear Alice,
> I have been nearly 'off my thatch' since I last wrote to you. I am doing the music for Alexander and you have no idea what a lot of work it means. I had done a good deal of it and last week found he had new plans so most of it was wasted and I am hard at it on new lines. This writing for theatres is awful work. I don't quite know when I return but will let you know. I do hope you had a good time during your holiday. I only had a few days in London though. Since then I have been going about working . . .
> Bob and I did no biking: in fact I shall soon have forgotten how to stick on the saddle if I am not careful. I often think of our nights at the Princesses. Now dear girl, excuse more and hoping you are well and to see you before long.
> Believe me,
> Yours, E G

By October his schedule was even heavier.

> My dear Alice,
> I am not quite 'off my thatch' but nearly. I have to go to Norwich all next week and Bristol the week after for the Festivals. Then there is this

As You Like It stuff etc. It does seem a shame for I should really like to meet you again, shouldn't you? Still I am bound to get all my work done and you don't know what time it takes nor what a worry it all is . . . I hope you are feeling well dear girl and that we shall meet again before long. I wish I were not so busy but I nearly always am at this time of the year so there you are, you are, you are.
>   Yours ever,
>   E G"

His lady cycling friend may by now have thought he was back-pedalling. There were one or two more excursions to the theatre, but she appears to have attended *As You Like It* alone. In early December:

> My dear Alice,
>   Fancy you going to the matinée. I am so glad you were there and that you liked my contribution to the programme. There is not much of it but it took a lot of getting ready. The notice in *The Telegraph* was good but I am not puffed up and I hope I never shall be. Critics (many of them) have a nasty habit of dropping you like a red hot coal. Still, they have certainly been very kind to me up to now for which 'thank the gods'.
>   It is awfully nice of you to write to me. I do hope circs will allow us to meet again before long. It seems a generation ago since we used to go cycling – Ah well! circs are funny things and I seem to have had a lot of them the last two or three months.
>   Excuse a short note this time.
>   Yours
>   Jim

Experts in 'disengagement' might recognise this as a polished example of the genre. At all events, Alice became in time, Mrs Fareham, and the tone of the letters of his later years is strictly formal.

> Dear Mrs Fareham,
>   Unfortunately I am engaged on Monday evening so cannot come to dine with you then as you kindly proposed.
>   Please pardon a hasty note and believe me,
>   Yours sincerely,
>   Edward German

Like Ethel Boyce, Alice kept a nostalgic memory of the friendship. From retirement in Worthing, she wrote to congratulate him on his Philharmonic Gold Medal in 1934.

> Dear Mrs Fareham,
>
> It was kind of you to write me about the Philharmonic Medal. I shall of course value it greatly for the rest of my life.
>
> I was interested in what you recall of so many years ago.
>
> I seem to remember all the incidents you mention and very enjoyable they all were.
>
> Thank you for your invitation but alas! I do not travel nowadays.
>
> My eye trouble is of course unfortunate but my general health keeps fairly good.
>
> I am,
>> Yours with kind regards,
>> Edward German

The work in *As You Like It* also prevented him accepting an invitation to write a musical work for Marie Tempest, the actress–singer, who had been a student at the Academy. He wrote his regrets to her:

> Since seeing you yesterday I have taken a most careful survey of the work I have to get through during the next twelve months or so, and I find that it will really be useless for me to entertain the idea of writing the opera. I did not think I had so much that must be done until going seriously into it.
>
> You need not, however, have the slightest fear of betraying your trust in me with the plot. Not a syllable shall ever escape me.
>
> To say I am sorry does not half explain my feelings, but I am quite convinced that it would be useless for me to think of undertaking the work. I hasten to let you know of my decision so as to cause you as little delay as possible.

The score for 'As You Like It' certainly does not seem worth the forfeiture of true romance or of other lucrative commissions. It is in no sense a masque and there remain only the three dances, and the duet, '*It Was a Lover and His Lass*'. The dances are pleasant enough, but, as we shall see later, German planned them with cafe performances in mind and they have none of the poetic sense shown in *Romeo and Juliet*. Even the basic rhythms repeat the Henry VIII Dances. The duet fails to exploit the lascivious overtones which overlie the apparently innocent song sung by the two pages about the 'country copulatives,' and is simply a virginal duet of the old English variety. Nothing remains of any setting of Hymen's 'Still music':

Then there is mirth in heaven
When earthly things made even
Atone together.

or his anthem of marriage, 'Blessed Bond of Board and Bed.' It is even more strange that the opportunity to set other songs from the play, *Blow, Blow Thou Winter Wind*, or *Under the Greenwood Tree*, was not grasped.

The original list of German's manuscripts refer to *As You Like It*: *The Masque of Hymen* and 'an orchestral score'. In his last year on receiving the Honorary Freedom of the Worshipful Company of Musicians German presented them with the *As You Like It* dances. Yet there still seems to have been some MS for Mabel to take at the dividing of his papers. *As You Like It* was acquired by Mabel and passed by her to her daughter Ruth. Ruth is described as having lived in very chaotic conditions and twice her house in The Quantocks was burnt down. After the first fire she was persuaded to deposit all her manuscripts with Southampton University and it has now the original MS of *Tom Jones*, *The Emerald Isle* and sundry other works. But of other incidental music there is no trace, and it must be assumed that many pages which form a unique chapter in the history of theatre music, vanished in the first of the fires. It would be an interesting task for composers of the Carl Davis school to reconstruct German's incidental music from his own piano selections.

One has to remember of course that, save for productions like Irving's, theatre bands of the day were unfitted for any kind of complicated concerto for orchestra. There were probably one or two talented violinists for whom German wrote the jigs and the strong and regular leading melodies. The wind sections would quickly be lost in any sort of adventurous rhythms, or sophisticated part-writing. Shaw remarked that 'by simply assassinating less than a dozen men I could leave London without a single orchestral wind player of the first rank' and even at the Royal Colleges of music professional players had sometimes to be imported to sustain the woodwind parts. When Mackenzie invited German into his box for the first night of *Coriolanus* for which he had written some incidental music, they found themselves just above the trombone section whose frequent slips caused the incensed composer to lean over with audible reproofs. When German wrote for the festival orchestras his music could be as intricate and rhythmically varied as any but it would have been tempting providence to depart too far from conventional rhythms and harmonies for the average musicians in the pit.

During 1896 he also planned some incidental music for a production of *Hamlet* that Alexander contemplated. The Prelude was to be based on a theme representing the ghost and was to contain a march that would form an *entr'acte* before the Fifth Act. He was also approached to write a ballet to be staged at the Empire Theatre. There was some negotiation over the fee as he was now in a position to demand a substantial figure. He stipulated 500 guineas plus a royalty of two pounds per performance, the management offered 300 guineas and in turn he suggested 400. In May he wrote again to George Edwards, the director, to ascertain his decision. Later he set out his modified terms: £400 down an account of the fees, such fees to be at the rate of £2 per performance. 'If you will agree to this we will consider the matter settled and the subject of the ballet can be agree upon at a later date.'

When the management held out he agreed to their terms provided he kept the publishing rights because of the pleasure that the work would give him. The project was never realized, which is to be regretted as German could have provided the basis of a classic work such as *La Fille mal Gardée*, in an English idiom. Nevertheless, he had plenty of work on hand including a commission for the Birmingham Festival. He was, however, learning to be business manager as well as musician.

By May, 1897, Alexander's production of 'Hamlet' was still in doubt. German wrote to him.

I have thought over the matter of 'Hamlet' and will as you wish be quite frank with you. My object in seeing you last night was to get, if possible, some idea of when you were likely to produce it. I gather that it cannot in any case be before the end of the year, if indeed then. Now as this further postponement appears to suit my plan . . . I think it would be wiser to let *Hamlet*, his 'perturbed' father, and the public rest in peace a little longer and give me more time to complete my Birmingham Festival work I told you of last night.

During the Diamond Jubilee Celebrations of 1897 he was invited to compose a piece for the Royal Philharmonic Society and produced his English Fantasia *In Commemoration*. He was dismayed when he heard that it was to be played first on the programme.

'Although I feel very strongly on the subject,' he wrote 'of placing a novelty written specially for the Philharmonic Society first on the programme (The National Anthem counts for nothing,' he declared, somewhat out of tune with the mood of the Jubilee,)

I still ask in a friendly manner to kindly bring the matter before those whom it may concern in time to have the first announcement in the papers in proper order. I shall be quite content to be placed second after the Jubilee Overture of Weber though for contrast it would certainly be very much better to have Cowen's vocal items in between. However, that is not my business. I hope you will be kind enough to let me know what you may have been able to do for me in the matter so that I may know how to act.

The English Fantasia was not published as such, but re-emerged in 1902, as the Rhapsody on March Themes for the Brighton Festival. There are two principal themes though both are introduced in a number of different guises. The first is heralded by opening flourishes and then swings along in good style, with a lighter trio section. The composer's familiar delight in interpolating a two-beat bar in order to make his melodies interesting rule the Rhapsody out as a parade-ground piece. A long quiet movement follows with a noble ten-bar theme, and this is also used as the basis of a quick march section, which begins *pianissimo*. The first march returns and the rhapsody ends with a coda based upon its assertive rhythms. The crashing six-bar phrases, the shifting of accent from one beat of the bar to another, the sudden interpolation of the half-bars and the accompaniment of swirling strings serve to make this an exciting concert work. It was one of the composer's favourites.

1897 was a busy year for he also wrote his Symphonic Poem, *Hamlet*, using some of the ideas which he had sketched out for the projected production by George Alexander. The Birmingham Festival had begun in 1759 as a commercial venture organised by a Richard Hobbs, organist of St Martin's Church. But it too had become linked with the raising of funds for hospitals. The Festival enjoyed a period of great importance in the nineteenth century when in the august setting of the Town Hall massive choral and orchestral forces were assembled to perform works such as Mendelssohn's *Elijah* which received its first performance there. In 1885 Richter had succeeded as festival conductor and it was he who conducted *Hamlet*. The symphonic poem was much more serious than his previous pieces but in some respects 1897 was propitious for more serious work. German himself had been ill at Whitchurch early in the year and his father died shortly afterwards.

He introduced himself to Richter by letter:

Sir,

You may know perhaps that I have been asked to write an orchestral work for the forthcoming Birmingham Festival. This will be a

Symphonic Poem on the subject of Hamlet. The directors are, I believe, considering this being a commemoration year, they will also include my new English Fantasia which is to be produced at the Philharmonic on June 17th but they wait for your decision in the matter.

As you do not, I expect, know anything about me, I write to ask if I shall bring the score around for you to see, so that you may be able to give the matter your consideration and also judge if you think the work suitable.

In any case I think it would be better if you would be so kind just to look through the score before you see the directors.

I beg to remain,
    Yours faithfully
      Edward German

In Commemoration was not given at Birmingham but *Hamlet* was well received. German's Symphonic Poem is a comment on the Drama rather than an epitome of the contents. As Hamlet is the most central character of all the tragedies, so his themes dominate the music. It is a forceful reading of his character. Although he may think momentarily of Ophelia he banishes these reflections and his neglect of her ultimately brings about her death. The desire to carry out the ghost's behest and avenge his father's murder is the mainspring of action: and although the arc-shaped motif which is his begins with a reflective and melancholy version, it is developed stridently and aggressively throughout the work, and with more rhythmic freedom than German usually devised.

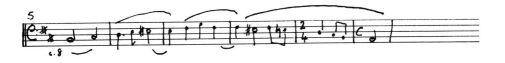

In the opening page there is a midnight bell, and muted strings give out a syncopated figure suggestive of vibrations or mysterious tremblings in the night air. When the Hamlet theme reappears it has undergone a metamorphosis into something much more athletic with octave leaps and strongly accented fifths, though restless passages intervene. The Ophelia theme is first heard prefigured through Hamlet's imagination but follows in a simple and innocent version representing her true character. By contrast, the Claudius march is intended to convey the pomp of the court, the king's ambition and love of power. German marked it *'pomposo'* in the score, but hollow splendour in music is not an easy concept to carry off successfully, and (with its echoes of the *Henry VIII* Coronation March) this passage interrupts what has been a tightly wrought work. However, the royal formalities are interrupted by an excited version of the Hamlet theme which mounts to great fury as the king's fate is determined. A portion of the Ophelia theme for solo oboe accompanied by a single horn announces her untimely death and music suggesting the obsequies and sad procession which follows. One very striking effect is the repetition of the religious passage for full orchestra, played *pianissimo*. Memories of Ophelia return but Hamlet casts them away and his theme in its resolute form undergoes several transmutations until the sharp irregular chords depicting the stabbing of the king ends the orchestral rampage. The final pages depict Hamlet's own death after the duel with Laertes. Bassoons and clarinets sustain low chords while the tympani measure out the slowly diminishing heart throbs. It is an ending which takes one back into the theatre but highly effective for all its simplicity and sparse scoring. *Hamlet* was a work greatly admired by John Ireland.

Although German himself was increasingly conscious of the need to plan musical programmes and achieve contrasts the idea was unknown to the nineteenth century festival committees. The relatively dramatic *Hamlet* had to take its place in a bill of fare which contained the closing scene of *The Valkyrie*, Beethoven's Fifth Symphony, the Overtures, to *Manfred* and '*The Master Singers*' and Brahms' *Song of Destiny*. To add to the competition Richter's commanding grasp of Wagner and his concentration on massive effect, left the audience drained of emotion after the *Master Singers* prelude. 'The wondrous tone, power and firm grip of the strings came upon the listener like the rushing of an avalanche,' said one of the Birmingham critics. In the event, *Hamlet* held its ground well.

> The favourable impression the work created at the rehearsal on Saturday was doubly enhanced by a second hearing and revealed new features of great importance . . . He handles his subject with masterly skill and shows varied and picturesque orchestration. The applause at the close of the work was so enthusiastic that the composer was called up on the platform to receive the well-earned homage of the audience. To Dr Richter and the orchestra the composer is indebted for having interpreted his work in such a masterly manner.

As always German had an exceptionally heavy work load to sustain. As well as composer, arranger and conductor he still had to act as his own business manager and seek fresh commissions.

He approached his old colleague from the Academy, Henry Wood, with a request that he might give the first concert performance of the masque music from *As You Like It*. 'I have just arranged it for concert use and it will be ready (Novello's) almost directly'. He tried to impress upon publishers the virtue of attacking the European markets by having published scores available. At the same time in December, 1897, he wrote to Richard D'Oyly Carte saying, 'For the next nine months I am free to undertake work for you (this in strict confidence). Have you a libretto ready by Gilbert or someone Gilbertian?' He also wrote about the 1898 Leeds Festival:

> Dear Mr Spark,
>   Although I am most unfortunately unable to write a new work for the next festival, I sincerely hope that I may in some way be connected with it. Would you like me to conduct my English Fantasia written for this year's Philharmonic Concerts? If so, I should feel most honoured.
>   The work lasts from 15 to 20 minutes in performance. I consider it one of the best things I have ever done.
>   Believe me,
>   Yours sincerely,
>   E. German

He suggested '*Hamlet*' for the London Philharmonic Concerts. A good deal of his energy was spent in endeavouring to interest conductors in his orchestral works. He was particularly offended that Henry Wood had refused to include *Hamlet* in his concerts because the conductor considered that a recent Crystal Palace performance had been the first in the capital. 'To come to the point at once,' he wrote, 'it is of course useless for a man who would be an orchestral composer to battle with the world alone without a conductor and an orchestra.' He hoped that Wood might instead select the Leeds Suite or the Second Symphony and offered to see that he was not charged for the score and parts.

> Will you reconsider the matter or perhaps bring it before Mr Newman? Just what you will. I should be glad of a line from you at your convenience. I may add that the Philharmonic are not going to do *Hamlet*. They decline it, I believe, on the same grounds as you did, though they have not even heard the work. It is to be done in

Manchester by the Hallé orchestra on February 3rd. There! I have liberated my soul to you and I am sure you will not take advantage of it.

To Novello's he continued to urge cheaper publications of band parts.

For orchestral purposes, very ordinary style is sufficient. Anything to cheapen orchestral music! Now all I have said will be met by the remark 'Orchestral music does not pay'. From the point of view of the publisher I can quite see it is very serious. It is certainly not reasonable to expect them after going to the expense of engraving the score and parts to give them away, yet I really fear it has come to this nowadays – that unless conductors (that is big conductors of full professional orchestras) *do* receive score and parts gratis, they will not entertain the performance of orchestral work. This is a lamentable fact. I offer no solution save that of an enthusiastic millionaire descending in our midst!

★   ★   ★

At the end of 1897, he had to cancel his Christmas at Whitchurch because of a sudden request by Alexander that he should write the music for *Much Ado About Nothing*. He agreed to write only the Overture and hoped that suitable pieces could be selected from his other stage music. Some of his previous work was in fact used but more new music than originally stipulated was provided.

Julia Neilson played Beatrice and George Alexander, Benedict. The score was dedicated to the latter. The scene in Leonato's orchard, depicted on stage with a back cloth that showed a panorama of Messina and the wide blue sweeping Bay, was accompanied by a peaceful 9/8 theme suggesting the lapping of waves. a full waltz was written for the Masque and there was a love theme for Hero and Claudio that Hollywood might well have employed in the early days of romantic films. There was some scurrying music for the Dogberry scenes and a march for the entrance of Don Pedro, that suggests a distant kinship with both Henry VIII and Hamlet's uncle. The most popular new piece was the *Bourrée*, a very fluent and jocular dance unlike any of his other music and reminiscent of the easy style of Percy Grainger. The Overture begins and ends with lively gigue music, at times combined with the Hero-Claudio theme and the Don Pedro march also makes a short appearance. It is a full concert overture, fluttering through different stages of key, and should not be completely ousted from programmes by the *Beatrice and Benedict* overture of Berlioz. The cathedral scene, played in an exact stage replica of the original, called for special music but none has survived.

A composer still had to be vigilant over the exploitation of his music. He was incensed during this year because a firm of publishers had produced a 'Suite for Orchestra' by Edward German.

'Some years ago,' he wrote to the *Musical Times*,

> I wrote some small pianoforte pieces – no connection one with the other – and at the same time parted with the copyright to the publishers. Of these pieces, three (*intermezzo, tarantella, bourrée*) have now, without my knowledge or consent, been given to a gentleman [the arranger was Henry Geehl. The publishers had already given him the Scotch Sketch to orchestrate] to score for orchestra . . . My object in writing is merely to disclaim the work whether it be good or bad, as my own . . . It seems an injustice, apart from copyright being his, that the publisher should be at liberty to tamper with one's work in such a manner.

He was particularly keen to have cheaper band parts produced for his next major work, *The Seasons*, which was written for the Norwich Festival of 1899 but composed after a summer visit to Snowdonia in the summer of 1898. This was the moment to have attempted another symphony; *The Seasons* is nevertheless an ambitious work. The only comment that appears to have survived from his mother about the music of her devoted son is concerned with the Suite. She was unwell, and could not always receive visitors to The Laurels. Despite her husband's death she had kept the establishment going. 'I quite expected the critics to say that G's Suite was too long,' she wrote to Rachel. 'I daresay he will be disappointed, but we shall hear what the musical papers say.'

It is a relatively elaborate work and he was still revising it when the summer of 1899 came round. The first movement (Spring) in A major is based on the ideas of hope and new life, and Spring arrives in a joyous rush culminating in a strong orchestral climax. As this subsides the woodwind gives out the sort of phrases that might occur to the wanderer in the fields in this season. The second subject is a love theme and German referred to a 'young man's fancy lightly turning to thoughts of love'. A section marked *tranquillo* again attempts to recreate the atmosphere of the fields and wild-life. The love theme reappears and the spring motif is given a strong version by strings in unison against chords for the brass. The movement reaches a very animated finish with strongly scored chords in syncopation.

The Harvest (Summer) is another merrymakers' dance, but shows how, released from the confines of the theatre pit, German could invest his ideas with much more colour and ingenuity. Oboe and harp intrude a minor version of the melody at one moment, and after a new figure is worked up into crashing *fff* chords for full orchestra, the principal theme returns quietly for the clarinet, this time reinforced by the 'cello section, an octave below. A sudden *diminuendo* brings the movement to a close.

'Autumn' makes a reference to the memories of summer and the cor anglais has a plaintive solo. The main theme is an expressive rising melody announced first by the second violins and taken up by other strings. There is a reference to the Spring theme but the sombre mood returns and the brass reiterate the sad cor anglais theme heard at the opening. Again there is a very quiet close.

Christmas Time (Winter) represents the two aspects of Yuletide: the first in the nature of a chorale or dirge deals with the gloom and darkness of the season. The chorale like theme shows German's fondness for alternating between 2/4 and 4/4 bars in one extended melody. The *tarantella* theme is intended to display the Christmas festivities. There is a long introduction and eventually the principal subject appears on the clarinet, though strings, piccolo and harp all contribute various figures. Towards the end, brass play the chorale, while strings and woodwind continue the *tarantella*. There is a sudden burst into the key of A major but the music resolves itself into the predominantly minor mood of the whole suite, although the rushing scales and chromatic chords at the conclusion add an energetic coda.

He conducted *The Seasons* himself at Norwich and it was well received. It has been neglected even more than some of the other works though in his lifetime German would often conduct separate movements from it. The work was extremely well received. The *Eastern Daily Press* reported:

> Mr Edward German is no stranger to Norwich, instrumental works from his pen having figured in the programmes of two previous Festivals . . . Here we have music which, though suffering somewhat from alteration, will considerably advance the composer's fame as a brilliant writer for the orchestra and which will appeal with irresistible force to hearers of every kind.

After a description of the movements concluding with,

> 'In "Winter (Christmastide)" the writer displays his full strength and employs the whole force of the orchestra with telling effect. A brisk

tarantella occurs in the middle of the piece while the chorale-like theme which runs through this movement is very haunting and the end is splendidly elaborated,'

the critic added:

Mr German both at the Royal Academy of Music and at the rehearsal at Norwich on Monday had taken the utmost care that his latest work should be thoroughly well understood by the bandsmen and he received his reward last night for the interpretation seemed to be flawless. From every part of the Hall emanated signs of approval exhibited with unbounded enthusiasm.

All who worked with German remembered *principally* his attention to every detail in the expression marks, the same precision with which his mother had recorded each step and measured moment of her courtship. George Baker, the singer, in a radio interview many years after working with the composer recalled this aspect strongly, yet much of popular comprehension of his style was based upon slipshod renderings in cafés and promenades.

A second great popular success came to him just as the century closed with the Nell Gwyn Dances written for *English Nell*, a comedy in four acts by Anthony Hope and Edward Rose, founded on the novel *Simon Dale* by the former. The play had been mounted for Marie Tempest. As soon as the actress heard that the play had been accepted for production she set off for the Hall Road and met German at his garden gate. He agreed to write the incidental music and when the dances were first played to her she wrote, 'For the pieces I wish you every success which your charming music deserves. Everything that lies in my power to do will be done: if I fail I can only ask for your forgiveness.'

The play was a very light-hearted impression of Restoration times and established Marie Tempest as a comedy actress. There was again no attempt at historicity. *Early One Morning*, a favourite melody of German's and, (according to *The Graphic*), 'a prime favourite of the servant maid's in the days of Nelson' was used.

The Overture is a very splendid theatrical curtain raiser with a romping introduction followed by a romantic theme depicting the two young lovers in the story. *Early One Morning* makes its appearance and receives elaborate treatment, being finally combined with the *Merrymakers' Dance*. Two songs for Soloists and Chorus were included in the play but never published. The three Dances, *A Country Dance*, *Pastoral Dance* and *Merrymakers' Dance* became almost as well-known and popular as the *Henry VIII Dances*. Indeed, the first and third are indistinguishable in style from their predecessors and suggest that the chorybantic arts had not progressed greatly in England between the days of the Reformation and Restoration. The second, however, with its wistful and halting theme, and mellow interlude is unlike any other piece by the composer and could easily be mistaken for a movement from an Elgar suite.

The programme noted several other compositions by German in the Intervals, which must be borrowings from his previous scores. The conductor at the Prince of Wales Theatre was Landon Ronald, German's future friend and advocate. Ronald had entered the Royal College of Music at fourteen years old and studied under Parry. He was for a time accompanist and conductor for the famous soprano, Melba. Like German he found employment in theatre orchestras but a fortunate opportunity to conduct in Europe established his reputation. In 1910 he became Principal of the Guildhall School of Music, a position he held for over a quarter of a century. The association with German was felicitous. In the *Sporting and Dramatic News* a cartoon depicted a young lady at the piano, discarding the Henry VIII Dances and pounding out the Nell Gwyn with the caption, 'Mr Edward German's admirers can rejoice that the pianoforte young lady can now vary her repertoire.'

WITH MISS MARIE TEMPEST TO ACT IT AND MR. EDWARD GERMAN TO
WRITE THE MUSIC—NO WONDER "ENGLISH NELL" IS A SUCCESS!

*A print from "The Entr'acte" of Oct.
20th 1900, at the time of the production of
"Nell Gwyn" (Marie Tempest & Edward German)*

A Nell Gwyn cartoon with German's comments

A scene from 'A Princess of Kensington' at the Savoy *(BBC Hulton Picture Library)*

CHAPTER FIVE

The Conscript Savoyard

On November 22nd 1900, Sir Arthur Sullivan died after a long and painful period of illness. He had been too sick to attend the revival of *Patience* a fortnight earlier, and Gilbert, though he had hoped his collaborator would appear to take the curtain calls, to give the appearance of friendship (at a revival of *The Sorcerer* they had taken the calls as if an invisible barrier existed between them on stage) had only D'Oyly Carte for company. Sullivan had been working on the score of an operetta *The Emerald Isle* with a libretto by Basil Hood. Hood had in the previous year produced a libretto *The Rose of Persia* for which Sullivan had provided the music and it seemed as though he might become Gilbert's successor for if he was a less talented writer, he was certainly a more amenable one. He was two years younger than German and an ex-military man who had been educated at Wellington College, where he left no trace, and the Royal Military Academy, Sandhurst. He had served in the Princess of Wales Own (Yorkshire) Regiment but retired from the army in 1898. He wrote a number of light pieces for the stage, and was later to produce English versions of the great Viennese operettas: *The Merry Widow*, *Waltz Dream* and *The Count of Luxembourg*. Like German, he appears to have been a bachelor and enjoyed the London clubs and he attracted little publicity despite his collaboration with two important composers. His libretti have some fanciful and ingenious ideas but could not provide the satirical force of Gilbert and his attempts to reproduce the Gilbertian patter-songs resulted only in pale imitations.

Sullivan had in fact advanced very little with the music for *The Emerald Isle*. In the light of subsequent events, it seems that the choice of German to produce a full score from Sullivan's themes and sketches seemed entirely natural, yet it involved some boldness on D'Oyly Carte's part for German's output both for the stage and concert hall had been mostly orchestral. He had composed no cantatas and no light opera since his student days to demonstrate skill in ensemble writing or setting of elaborate word patterns. As we have seen, a previous application for consideration by German to the Savoy management had produced no results. Yet Sullivan's admiration for

German was well known and the young composer had a strong supporter in William Boosey, director of Chappell & Co. who persuaded Carte to invite German to save the situation. Boosey wrote in his *Fifty Years of Music*:

> Arthur Sullivan always impressed upon me – not that I needed conversion – that Edward German was the one composer who was capable of carrying on the tradition he had established of a delightful new form of English light opera. What a pity therefore, that he never had a W. S. Gilbert or a libretto worthy of his setting. Basil Hood wrote admirable lyrics – witness 'Yeomen of England' – but he had not the dramatic instinct.

German described the commission in notes he compiled to help Scott with his biography:

> This brought him into contact with Basil Hood who was an indefatigable worker and he kept E. G. very busy. They used to meet at Hall Road and overcome difficulties. Many were the evenings they spent there together. Sir Arthur had actually completed only the two first numbers. He had, however, sketched fifteen other numbers including the finale to act I. There were all orchestrated and (except the choruses) harmonised by E. G. This . . . was a labour of love. EG's original contributions were eleven numbers including the Devonshire Song and chorus.

In the light of the plaudits which his work received and the fact that it led to the composition of *Merrie England* one cannot regret this sudden advancement of the composer's fortunes. Yet it precluded the completion of a violin concerto, which he had promised for the Leeds Festival of 1901 and on which he had started work. The committee released him from his contract, even though the violinist Arbos had already been engaged by Stanford, and the Overture from *Romeo and Juliet* was given instead. Yet, as German was such a very accomplished violinist himself, he might have produced a work in his truest romantic style. He never returned to the idea.

The presence of the work also prevented him from visiting his mother, whose health was rapidly failing. He wrote to Rachel,

> Oh that things should have happened like this – my distress at not being able to come and see my dear Mother is heartbreaking; I *do* feel she understands but I also feel that many will *not* understand and will

think me hard-hearted and undutiful but if they think this they will be casting a great injustice on me and will be unaware of the great love and affection I have for the very noblest and best Mother that ever man and woman had. Oh Dick, it is hard that I cannot leave. It happens that at any other moment of my life I could have come and nothing in the world would have stopped me. Ah well, I feel comfortable that *she* understands. God bless her and give her a loving kiss from me.

A few weeks before the opening of *The Emerald Isle,* Richard D'Oyly Carte died and the management of the Savoy Theatre was undertaken in the weeks before the production by his widow, Helen. German's labours on the score were greeted with great acclaim. After the breakdown of the Gilbert and Sullivan partnership and some years of revivals, it seemed as though the Savoy tradition might sparkle again and keep London supplied with delightful and entertaining pieces as in the 1880s.

'A thousand times over has Edward German justified the choice which selected him to complete Sullivan's score,' wrote *The Sunday Times.* 'Mr German's accomplishment of amazingly difficult tasks is brilliant,' said the *Westminster Gazette.* 'To Mr Edward German,' exclaimed the *Manchester Guardian,* 'let the highest praise be given.' Some of the critics gave credit for the original elements supplied by the younger musician. The *Yorkshire Post* declared,

> In two respects it may unhesitatingly be affirmed that the score marked a decided advance on previous Savoy operettas. In the first place, far more work is put into orchestration which is a beautiful finished mosaic, full of delightful details, yet never obscuring the melodic flow of the music to the extent of endangering its success with the frequenters of the Savoy. Of still greater moment, is the far higher artistic worth of the sentimental songs. The song of the heroine, Rosie, *O Setting Sun,* . . . is we think, the best thing of its kind ever heard at the Savoy.

It was now over ten years since the appearance of the *The Gondoliers,* Sullivan's most melodious score. Though there is some beautiful music in *Utopia Limited,* neither of the final G & S operas had contained any popular tunes. German's skill seemed to bring new ingenuity and refinement to a pattern that had become outmoded.

Like most of Hood's work, the plot of *The Emerald Isle* has strengths and very evident weaknesses. It is set in Ireland around the year 1800, where the

Earl of Newton, Lord Lieutenant, is trying to anglicise the peasantry and force them to speak with English accents. He has hired Professor Bunn, a Shakespearean reciter and elocutionist to teach correct English speech in the schools. A rebellion against the plan is led by Terence O'Brien, who although educated at Eton and Oxford University is strongly nationalist. Inevitably he is in love with the Lord Lieutenant's daughter, Lady Rosie Pippin. In an elaborate charade, the Irish characters persuade one of their number, Molly O'Grady, to impersonate the fairy of the caves of Carrig Cleena, who according to legend can lure men to immolation in her bewitched realm. To add colour to the tale Bunn is disguised to come forth as an old man who has passed decades under her spell. Not surprisingly, the English troops when called upon to arrest the rebels in the caves refuse to move. When, finally, Terence is captured, Rosie pleads with her father to release him and Ireland's problems are solved with enviable ease.

The story gives scope for one excellent ensemble in which the Lord Lieutenant and his Countess urge the troops, men of the Devonshire Regiment, forward, with martial strains, to be met by murmurs in the bass line, 'We don't intend to go to Carrig-Cleena,' which increase in volume:

Lord Lieut:	The bugle's joyful note May prove an antidote To such a scare.
His Chaplain:	They do not move at all In answer to its call
LL.Countess	
Chaplain:	What does it mean?
Soldiers (ff):	We don't intend to go to Carrig-Cleena.

The musical humour has the stamp of Sullivan and historically the scene is interesting as the last in which British troops could be comically portrayed as nervous of danger. It was Sullivan's idea, too, to insert God Save the Queen as the bass line of the music which introduces the Lord Lieutenant. Despite the praise heaped upon German for his brilliant matching of the unfinished score the warp and the weft are not particularly difficult to detect. Sullivan's melodies are sharp and rhythmic. His accompaniments remain distinct from the melodic line as in the delicate opening chorus of Act II where a *pizzicato* dance accompanies the stealthy Irish rebels. He also wrote the beautiful Irish air, *Come Away Sighs the Fairy Voice*, as affecting as anything in the Savoy operas.

German's hand is discernible in some of the opening numbers but his entry is unmistakable when we come to the introduction to the Countess's song, *When Alfred's Friends their King Forsook*:.

The lyrics of his song, dealing with Alfred and the Cakes, and Charles II in the Royal Oak would not gain acceptance by a school magazine, but, by switching the accents from one beat of the bar to another and interpolating unexpected additional bars *pomposo* into the accompaniment, he does his best to make it humorous. He had two qualities which he brought to the score. In romantic solos he could far outdistance Sullivan, and Rosie's aria, *Oh Setting Sun*, in which the two melancholy verses lead into the passionate third stanza, had no predecessor in the Savoy canon. He also had the gift of adding subtleties to a melodic line. He achieved the first rapturous encore of the evening with the *Song of the Devonshire Men*. Here his delight in long lilting sequences was ideally suited to the list of courting girls left behind in the west country:

There was Mary Hooper and Mary Cooper
And Jane Tucker and Emily Snugg
And Susan Wickens and Hepzibah Lugg
And pretty Polly Potter and the rest o'them.

and his quick fire close to each line was one of his happiest operatic strokes. He showed himself as adept as Sullivan in the combination of cross rhythms between soloists and chorus in the waltz song '*I cannot play at love*'. This was wrongly printed in the vocal score, and Rosie's part was given to Murphy. The composer's copy has some rather irritated looking emendations in his own hands. German rose to an operatic style that was to reappear in *Tom Jones* in the scene *Nought Shall Divide and Tear our Souls Asunder*'. The great Savoyard, Henry Lytton, always considered that 'Blind' Pat Murphy was the most difficult role he had to play, for his eyes had to be fixed upon one spot no matter who was speaking or how disturbing the action. He recalled an occasion in Dublin when the dancers in the jig were thought to be kicking their heels too high in an unauthentic manner and booing commenced. This was quelled by a voice from the pit. 'Shame on ye. Can't you be aisy out of respect for the dead?' followed by another, 'An Sullivan an Oirishman too he was!' (Sullivan's Irish father was bandmaster at Sandhurst and professor of brass instruments at Kneller Hall.) The atmosphere of a wake having been happily established the audience sat back contented.

There are two main weaknesses in *The Emerald Isle*. Although Hood had amusing ideas, his patter songs lack humour, the tone is snobbish, the targets are feeble, and there are no memorable catch lines. German endeavoured to sugar them with his favourite titillating consecutive sevenths and other devices, but it is astonishing that they were accepted by a management such as the Savoy. Terence's Song,

> There once was a little soldier
> Who was made of wood

with its 'Rat-a-plan' chorus must be one of the worst lyrics to be thrust on any musician, and unperformable without acute embarrassment on both sides of the proscenium arch.

The other weakness, even within an Irish scenario, is the incessant use of jig 6/8 rhythms. Of the twenty-eight numbers at least fourteen are in 6/8 time, and several of the others are Sullivan's. In later operas, German rationed himself more severely, but the score of *The Emerald Isle* displayed a certain insensitivity to the overall effect on the musical design.

After *The Emerald Isle* the hope was expressed that German would be given the opportunity to write an operetta of his own, unfettered. The wish was very soon answered for within a year, in April 1902, *Merrie England* was produced at the Savoy, a work that was entirely in his own idiom and gave him an opportunity which he seized with great ardour.

The joyous nature of the music belies the sad circumstances in which it was written, for his mother died at this time. Distressed though he was, the occasion brought him back to Whitchurch, the meadows of Shropshire and the memorable happiness of childhood. It is said that much of the score was sketched while he was staying at The Laurels walking by the meres and resting on a particular stile outside the town. These rambles produced the great melodies but the actual scoring had to be completed in London and fitted in with a busy round of appearances to conduct at concerts.

Merrie England seems so natural a growth in English music that it is difficult to imagine the world without it. It seems to bear out Schumann's observation that composing consists of recalling those tunes which exist already. Although Hood must take the credit for devising a vehicle that would give full scope to the composer's talents, the plot is not a strong one and compounds an odd mixture of history and fiction whereby the Earl of Essex and Sir Walter Raleigh are seen as rivals for the affection of Elizabeth I. Essex appears variously as patriot. ('The Yeoman of England'), villain (he tries to disgrace Raleigh by exposing the latter's romance with a lady-in-waiting, Bessie Throckmorton) and finally the reconciler since he appreciates that the marriage of Raleigh and Bessie will leave his way to the Queen's heart more open. The scheme whereby the Queen seeks to poison her rival is bizarre and conflicts with the whole image of Good Queen Bess which pervades the opera. Yet in performance, logic melts before the vitality of the score. It is astonishing that so many memorable arias were written in so short a space of time. The magic of the work rests entirely with German.

Hood's libretto deals at length with the antics of Walter Wilkins, a player in Shakespeare's troupe, comedy is the foremost intention and the script at first sight suggests little of the enchantment of the forest glades. Even the lyric, *My Troth is Plighted to This Gentle Maid*, the kernel of arguably the finest and certainly the most romantic Act Finale in English opera relapsed originally into the dampening parlance of the Senior Common Room:

> Blow high, blow low
> Now coram publico
> I let the whole world know
> My heart is Bessie's.

It is easy to forget too that *The English Rose*, does not appear in the play as a love song, but a flattering device whereby Raleigh seeks to enter the Castle at Windsor among the May Queen's morris men. The music of *Come to Arcadie* far transcends the lyric. The introduction to Act II with its horn calls and tensely driven strings, followed by the off-stage chorus, *The Month of May*, has no need to bow before Verdi as a prelude to the mysteries of Herne's Oak. Yet along with the comedy the stirring allusions to the Elizabethan Age set within the maytime revels at Windsor and embellished with frequent references to the Robin Hood legends, seem to leave out nothing that could evoke memories of England's greenwood heritage. It was German who seized upon these and the element of pageantry. The elegant March which leads into the first entrance of Elizabeth is a great theatrical moment.

All this of course, was interspersed with passages of lower degree and German had to do the best he could with some of the matter. With Wilkin's song, *King Neptune Sat on His Lonely Throne* a happy device of Hood's to make the ducked and bedraggled comedian pass off his watery arrival as an embassy from the Sea-god, he succeeded admirably, again with carefully placed and essential subtleties in the markings. Where Hood relies on archaisms, the phraseology of old madrigals and references to Dame Nature, Dan Cupid and coy figures of mythology, the jarring phrases are more often than not swallowed up in the gaiety of the score. He also interpolated the dances into the comic as well as the pastoral episodes and thus created a greater unity than the original script possessed.

It was of this work that Ethel Smyth said she had 'gone quite wild with joy over it. It is an immortal masterpiece. Anybody and everybody today would, I should say, give the rest of their lives to have written it. Anyway I would.' Millions of other music lovers, especially those gathered around the choral societies and operatic societies of the provinces, have given an affection to *Merrie England* that can only be paralleled by the Viennese devotion to *Fledermaus* (It might be added that *Fledermaus* has a much sillier plot, a bunch of unattractive characters and a much narrower range of musical feeling.) In Coronation Year, 1953, over 500 amateur operatic societies put on *Merrie England* and such was the demand made upon theatrical costumiers that the societies at the end of the queue found themselves performing in any clothes that could be scraped together from the Wars of the Roses to the time of Oliver Cromwell. The work's strengths set it apart from the Savoy operas. The characters possess a warmth and reality that the puppets in Gilbert's carefully contrived plots lack. Jill-all-Alone, the supposed young witch, who is outlawed by the jealous May Queen and her revellers, if played by a first-rate actress, provides one of the few great mezzo parts in English light opera. Though his frolics loom overlarge in the action the idea of introducing a comedian from Shakespeare's company who feels that the bard gives too much attention to tragedy shows Hood in inventive mood. The details of the historical romance may be partly fictitious but the picture of the Virgin Queen guarding 'peaceful England' from foreign foes but regretting bitterly the absence of unselfish love in her own life, and indulging in caprices, is near enough in spirit to history.

1902, the year of the first production, which saw the beginnings of the Entente with France, was a good moment for patriotic nostalgia. After the imperialist celebrations of the Diamond Jubilee in 1897 and the satisfied contemplation of the splendours of Empire, had come the difficulties and isolation of the Boer War. As the new century opened, Britian was aware that there were threats to its Empire, not least from the ambitions of Germany with its unpredictable Emperor, its strong young industries and its naval challenge on the seas. *Merrie England* combined an expression of patriotic fervour with sentimental reminiscence of the time when a smaller England girt in by 'the ever-hungry sea' had been contented in its own island freedoms. In German's centenary year, 1962, Martin Cooper in a thoughtful article in *The Telegraph* expressed the view that the libretto reflected a more serious jingoism of the period. Whereas in *Pinafore*, Gilbert's song, *He Is an Englishman*, is wholly humorous, *The Yeomen of England* is wholly serious. *O Peaceful England* refers to waves of war beating around our shores and prays that the period of peace may be extended a little longer. The libretto was also freed from the mordant satire expressed against the Victorian court that clouded Gilbert's last two collaborations with Sullivan and which had caused the audiences some uneasiness and worry.

The critics who witnessed the first night were clearly unaware that this opera would become a unique part of England's musical heritage. They could not be expected to see that its power to stir the heart would be massively enhanced by the perils and dangers that beset their native land in two World Wars. The first impressions were certainly friendly. 'The work is pure *opéra comique* and that too of a high order,' said *The Times*, adding in headmasterly terms: 'Mr German has given of his best and we all know how delightful his best is.' The *Pall Mall Gazette*, old enemy turned ally, talked of his 'inexhaustible talent for melody' and 'bubbling inspiration' and claimed that 'Sullivan's place seemed to be vacant no more . . . He has drunk deep at the fount of English folk music,' it continued, 'and his music is permeated with the characteristics of our national songs.' This last comment was not at all true. German took little or no part in the exploration and collection of genuine folk songs and invented rather than imitated a folk-song style.

Within a year numerous songs from the score had been published: *The English Rose, O Peaceful England, The Yeomen of England, The Waltz Song* (a very unfolk-like interpolation), The duet *Come to Arcadie*, arguably the jewel in the whole work, the quintet, *Love Is Meant to Make Us Glad* and others. German himself arranged the four Dances for violin and piano, and there was a version for military band. A Fantasia on Edward German's opera was written by an F. Griffiths, a Waltz sequence on the melodies by a C. Kniefert, and a 'Set of Lancers' by an N. Williams. Kniefert also produced swiftly a selection for orchestras, and there were versions for military band and pianoforte.

But the strength of the work lay not only in the ceaseless flow of tunes, this time in a more varied pattern than *The Emerald Isle*, but in the rich operatic style achieved in the First Act Finale in which there is characterisation in the music – heroic for Raleigh, turbulent for the Queen, mysterious for Jill and in which an unforgettable reprise sweeps over the music of the Morris Dance as the curtain falls. These are among the finest pages which the composer wrote and one can only lament that there seemed in England no librettist or poet at the time who could force German's attention upon the great riches of the English novel, so that his imagination could be stretched to ever wider horizons. He himself wrote later that 'the press at once recognised it as a gay little piece – style popular yet scholarly'. 'Scholarly' seems a curious word for the composer to apply to this particular work. Over the years he came to appreciate the widespread devotion which *Merrie England* engendered but at the start he certainly considered it a 'light' work when compared to his Symphonies and *Hamlet*.

Writing to the editor of the *Musical Times* who was seeking material for an article about him he said, 'I should like you to say a goodish deal about *Merrie England* because it is in its own way a little masterpiece (this is my private opinion).' He also felt it was worth quoting the remark of Hamish MacCunn who conducted the provincial tour, despatched when the Opera with the full Savoy company and orchestra sold out in the Edinburgh theatre for the whole week. 'Whether it be haggis or harmony, "mountain dew" or melody, the land o'cakes kens fine when it meets with a good thing. Hock aye.'

★   ★   ★

Merrie England enjoyed a long run at the Savoy, had a successful tour of the provinces and returned for a second run in London. The management, rubbing its hands gleefully arranged for three new operas to be written by the same team and, within a year, *A Princess of Kensington* had been put on. It might be argued that if German had had the temper of a Puccini he would have thrown the libretto out of the window when it was first presented to him. The story involved a mixture of fairies and mortals which all too readily suggested an attempt to imitate *Iolanthe*. Instead German's only weapon appeared to be gentlemanly puzzlement. 'I doubt if anyone will know what this is all about: I don't,' he said when he first saw the draft. When Basil Hood replied that the audience would return to try and find out, German, instead of pointing out forcibly that few patrons go to the trouble and expense of revisiting a theatre to see a work that has mystified them once, set to work to produce a score. At one point in the Second Act he declared, 'This plot seems to me to be getting more complex and unintelligible,' but by then a great deal of the music had been composed and the easy personalities of the two men sorted out some kind of compromise. German did not have the genius of a composer such as Richard Strauss who could select from a libretto the ideas which gave inspiration and send back the sterile suggestions to be improved or cut. He provided music for all the librettist's efforts, good, bad and indifferent.

The story is certainly involved and would tax the memories of the audience through a long evening. An Englishman, Prince Albion, had fallen in love with Princess Kenna, the daughter of Oberon and Titania, and the immortal who has given her name to Kensington. Kenna's *immortal* lover, Azuriel, will not be convinced that Albion is long dead, so Puck, the sprite, decides that someone impersonating Albion must be seen clearly and decisively marrying a mortal to get him out of the way. Just at that moment, four sailors from H.M.S. *Albion* arrive in Kensington Gardens, from

Waterloo Station. They are on leave from Portsmouth and they have the name *Albion* distinctly written on their hat bands. One of the sailors, Jeff (played in the original production by Henry Lytton) is selected as Prince Albion, and the mortal bride chosen to be seen marrying him is Joy Jellicoe, daughter of a rich London banker. Jeff is, however, betrothed to the formidable Nell Reddish, niece of the proprietor of a tavern, The Jolly Tar, at Winklemouth-on-Sea, whose family are in hot pursuit of her claims . . .

Hood certainly bubbled over with ideas. *A Princess of Kensington* is the only opera of German's to be set in his own time and as such it might have benefited from a more racy musical comedy score. Prince Albion, we learn, was carried off in a London smog, Joy's father, Sir James Jellicoe, goes bathing in the Serpentine each morning leaving his clothes to be snatched by Puck and used as disguises, Nell is anxious to find a really wanton husband whom she can reform and changes the name of The Jolly Tar under her management to The Jolly Teapot. The old inn slate is put outside for her wedding list subscriptions. Joy Jellicoe's suitor, a young bank clerk called Brook Green, follows Joy down the Winklemouth after a quarrel and takes a job as a boatman under the pseudonym 'Pierhead Morgan'. Jeff tries to persuade Nell that there is a more urgent task of reform needed on his shipmate Bill Blake, and paints such a picture of his wickedness that Nell declares she will never marry, whereupon he tries hard to keep her to her word.

What surprises the modern reader is not so much the confusion, which is an element of modern farce, as the extent to which the nostalgic patriotism has changed to a crude jingoism. There is an echo, but a raucous one, of 'The Yeomen' in a song about the Volunteer Movement:

And what of the Londoner
Who now lives in London
Who carries a rifle
And camps on the Down?
English the seed of him
And London the breed of him

When his country has need of him
He'll fight for the Crown.

When Puck seeks to get Brook out of the way he conjures up a band of The Red Marines in which Brook can enlist, so there is clear scope for a recruiting song:

Do you always want to travel
On a tube or on a bus
Or a battleship or cruiser
Like the likes of us?

and

Then don't stand dumb
For the drum says 'Come'
And you know what the Music means.
Don't you be a Molly Colly,
Say 'Goodbye Polly'
And Join the Red Marines.

The growing German naval threat is explicitly referred to:

Geography – here's E.F.G.
You'll recognise perhaps
They're England, France and Germany
According to the maps.
And HMS a British ship
A cruisin' round our coast
And givin' foreigners the tip
But there we mustn't boast.

And when all the fairy and mortal misunderstandings are sorted out the problem of the birth-rate which concerned major European nations at the time is focussed upon in the final chorus:

And here's to the Maids of Britain
And may they all be wed
And from their stock may others
As sweet as they be bred.
To give their sons for fighting men
Upon the land or sea
For England, Scotland, Ireland, Wales
Each for the other three.

There is no reason, of course, why an operetta should not have a political bias, but the libretto of *A Princess* epitomises some of the brasher features of Edwardian society. Puck's patter song refers to strikes ruining mining industry in the face of foreign competitors, laments the undermanning of the navy and the disunity created by the troublesome Irish. Yet Hood could also produce some inspiring lyrics which called forth some of German's most moving music. The lines which come in the bridal chorus –

> Ye silver chimes of fall and fountain
> Ring out from mountain unto mountain
> O West Wind, spread thy rushing wings
> To hear the Anthem Nature sings!

– produced from German one of the most haunting pages in the whole of British operatic music.

A romantic lyric, *My Heart a Ship at Anchor Lies*, also elicited German's finest aria. If this melody were a setting of a German poem it would be reckoned the gem in any Lieder recital.

Fuller Maitland a scholarly critic of *The Times* who had already devoted a long and serious article to the *Henry VIII* music, had been admitted to the Dress Rehearsal and afterwards he sent German a note: 'I cannot refrain from a word of heartiest congratulation on the delicious new opera which I enjoyed immensely today although I had to leave after the First Act. Its success is absolutely a certainty and the fact must delight all who care for what is good in music.' Yet there were some banal patter songs to be accompanied and too little variety in the duets and trios that constituted the bulk of the score. At some point in the proceedings, there was a rift between German and Hood and the composer penned a note in his usual worried fashion: 'My dear Hood, I have felt for some time past there has been a misunderstanding between you and me. I have an idea in my mind that it was started by some well-meaning but tactless friend. I kept silent thinking that you would see that I was in reality sound through it all . . . '

The rift centred upon someone called 'Fred' who may have reported back to the writer German's misgivings over the libretto, There is no one in the cast called 'Fred' but clearly he was a friend of Hood's and a problem to others. The break was healed but the series hoped-for never materialised, German set a number of Hood's lyrics in subsequent years and discussions over a future opera were always amicable, if unprofitable. Some years later Hood endeavoured to interest German in a stage work on the life of Sir Francis Drake, but the idea did not appeal.

Despite a holiday in Whitchurch, his activity at this time was very considerable. He produced the *Just So Songs*, settings of the poems by Rudyard Kipling. German always rose to the level of his lyrics, and in these songs he was able to give expression to his sense of humour: the effects of a bumpy storm at sea 'when trunks begin to slide', the leaps of the kangaroo and dingo, the sly innocence that matches the double-entendre, and the hymn-like sounds that accompany parental comments. 'Rolling down to Rio' became the favourite song with its sea-shanty style laced with memories of Handel in the nursery. It was subsequently issued in many versions for soloists, duettists and chorus.

Kipling wrote, 'Will you please accept my belated thanks for the keen pleasure that your settings of *Tegumai* and *Merry Down* have given me. They are the ones that I like the best in the *Just So* Book, though the *Camel's Hump* runs them very close. Our children sing them zealously.'

In 1903 German was elected president of the Royal Academy Music Club, an association of former students and teachers, and in 1904 he had to give the presidential address. To public speaking, he gave the same care that he did to composing, noting down the main themes, 'orchestrating' them with numerous erasures and substitutions, then recapitulating his ideas boldly underlined in headings. He also continued to work on the arrangements of his music for home performances, particularly the pianoforte duet version of his E Minor Symphony.

The title of Fletcher's play *The Faithful Shepherdess* attracted him as the possible subject for a cantata, but the projected text did not prove inspiring, and even the composer may have felt that a fresh succession of Shepherds' Dances and *Pastorelles* would be something of a self-parody. Various subjects were suggested to him. We must be thankful that he did not tackle one which lies in his papers: 'A Dramatic Cantata: The Knight of Shuna' in which Richard the Lion-Heart is greeted on his return to England in the following fashion:

Chorus of Knights:	Magnificent! Magnanimous!
Chorus of Soldiers:	Beneficent! Illustrious!

Chorus of People: Glory to our gracious King
                              Glory give
                              As we do live
                              He doth excel in everything

German had to wade through much matter of this kind.

In 1904 it was the turn of the Cardiff Festival to request a work from the new famous composer. The resulting *Welsh Rhapsody* is a great tour de force and one of the finest examples of his powers of orchestration. The Cardiff Festival was comparatively recent having been inaugurated in 1892. It is strange that the idea of the Violin Concerto abandoned for *The Emerald Isle* did not recur to German when this commission was given for he had great difficulty in deciding what form the new piece should take and described how he used to take evening walks pacing to and fro across Maida Vale, tossing ideas about in his mind. It was over breakfast and a pipe of tobacco that he thought of a suite based upon Welsh folk songs. He had just started to develop his thoughts when Sackville Evans, the closest of his friends, called and gave eager support to the idea. Evans happened to possess two large volumes of Welsh songs and he returned home to collect them. The rest of the morning was spent leafing through the pages, German at the pianoforte and Sackville Evans singing. Before lunchtime the theme for the slow movement and finale had been decided upon.

The *Welsh Rhapsody* is something much grander than a mere setting of folk songs. Though the four movements are linked, each is distinct in character. In the first – '*Loudly proclaim o'er land and sea, This is the home of liberty*' – the composer derives two subsidiary themes from the song, one a strongly flowing Wagnerian melody, and the other a softly treading march. After a repetition of the opening phrases, by full brass and reeds, the aggressive mood subsides, and the songs which form the basis of the scherzo are introduced. These are the jig-like figure of *Hunting the Hare* and the more staid *Bells of Aberdovey*. During a long crescendo flute and piccolo play in half-time the melody given out by brass and strings below. German keeps on changing his orchestral colours and pizzicato strings play counter subjects when the Hare reappears across the scene. Some minor chords eventually intrude and prepare the listener for the memorable third movement: *David of the White Rock* given out by oboe and 'cellos in octaves to an accompaniment of muted strings. One phrase particularly is drawn out to be used as the basis of the development of the theme and a counter-theme on the violins joins in with the final entry of the song. The movement fades to the merest whisper (pppp) at which level of volume the side drum enters and, as if distant over the Welsh hills, snatches of *Men of Harlech* begin to be heard. As with the famous March in Tchaikowsky's Sixth Symphony, fragments of the song are thrown about from one section of the orchestra to another and the March itself is played quietly at first, leading into combinations of various component bars of that seemingly intractable tune. Much play is made with the rhythm of the final bars.

The sounds again descend to whisperings so that the composer can build up a huge sixty-seven bar crescendo culminating in an *sfff* roll on the tympani followed by a clash on the cymbals and a massive declaration of the March itself. Hearing the work for the first time without score any listener must wonder how the conclusion is going to come and, obvious though it may be, German's device of leading into a great chord of the seventh is one of music's exciting moments. From this point the pace becomes faster, the brass gives out fanfares and the final bars keep up suspense to the last.

The *Rhapsody* was written in the first part of 1904 and performed in September, the only novelty in the Festival. Its reception was tumultuous. The Welsh audience rose to its feet the men shouted and the women waved their handkerchiefs. It would be difficult to think of another piece of music whose first reception in the concert hall could bear comparison. One writer thought that the only parallel was the Hungarian excitement which greeted the Rackoczsky March from Berlioz's *Damnation of Faust*.

In 1905 he made a return to the theatre to write the incidental music for *The Conqueror*, his last essay in this genre, for the fashion was declining. *The Conqueror* was a play by Millicent, wife of the fourth Duke of Sutherland. She was a lady of great beauty and ability who not only gave time and energy to a variety of worthy causes. She had aspirations to enjoy literary success also and in order to avoid the accusation of using her title to woo acclaim wrote under the pseudonym R. E. Fyffe. She sought James Barrie's advice on the first two Acts of *The Conqueror*, a play in blank verse, and he replied that he found it strangely masculine and thought she should practice more regular daily writing so that the feminine gifts she possessed would emerge with less constraint. Undeterred she submitted the completed work to Forbes Robertson who was sufficiently impressed to choose it as the inaugural piece for the Scala Theatre, as he had great preference for plays that afforded opportunities for spectacle. The Scala Theatre was unusual in having been planned by a medical man interested in the theatre, Dr Distin-Maddock, a surgeon at the Italian Hospital in London. The *British Medical Journal* praised its attention to matters of health: the lightness and airiness, and noted that it marked a great advance in theatre sanitation. It was certainly an improvement on former places of entertainment that had occupied the site once known as the Queen's Dustbowl. When for a while the theatre was named the Prince of Wales it had enjoyed high esteem under the management of the Bancrofts but it had been cramped and uncomfortable.

In its new form, with the large staircase that gave it its name, it was hailed as one of the finest theatres in the world and the possible home for a national theatre. Much greater provision was made for rapid escape in case of fire and presumably boredom also.

The story of *The Conqueror* centres upon Morven, Lord of Abivard, who is world conqueror, slaying his thousands and riding roughshod over tribes and peoples. The girl, Amoranza, whom he had saved to be his bride, prefers another young version of himself. For the greater part of the play which is set vaguely in the Dark Ages – 'a mixture of Malory and Maeterlinck,' as one critic put it – the lovers pass the time waiting for the return of the dreaded conqueror. This may have reflected some of the Duchess's own anxieties concerning the reactions of the Duke to a similar romance of her own, but it did not make for strong drama and the intervals of waiting had to be filled with rustic dances, war songs and processions of conquered kings. This was why German's talents were required.

It cannot be said that the Duchess's work inspired him to anything novel or distinguished. The Conqueror theme was meant to epitomise the marauding bands of warriors sweeping over the wide plains of Europe and Asia:

O Rhapsody of Conquest,
O cry of valiant blood,
We press the purple wine press,
Let loose the crimson flood.
Break down the hedge of weaklings,
Build up the walls of strong,
And shout, shout, SHOUT
To scattered nations
The Conqueror's Triumph Song

A modern Russian composer in barbaric mood might just succeed in setting the words in a welter of pagan discord. German accepted the style as the same genre as a school song so the final effect, despite the fur skins and Scythian helmets, must have been very like an Old Boy's Re-union. In Evadne's Song it was surely tempting providence to adorn a lyric that began *'Daisy Daisy'*, though in this case the words were addressed to the flower and not the occupant of a 'bicycle made for two'. There is a Children's Dance and a Satyr's Dance. The titles are almost interchangeable though the former has a good melodic interlude. The most successful piece was a setting of a Herrick poem for male voices, the *Watchman's Song*, a chorale which shows how much German's music benefits from words that rise above the mundane. Music in the intervals was taken from his previous scores.

According to Scott, the production was 'notable' but the play had less than a dozen performances and must have been a costly failure. The Duchess received a brief telegram from Forbes Robertson: 'Sorry; must come off Saturday'. She wrote to her friend, Lord Esher, 'The last three weeks have been so tempestuous and I am very tired. I had no idea actors could be so stupid. Forbes Robertson to my thinking has no talent, courage or money!' German appears to have escaped unscathed though he made little reference to *The Conqueror* in later years. He certainly maintained a more cordial relationship with Forbes Robertson than did the Duchess, for we find him in 1908 saying that he has been approached in regard to the possibility of his *Romeo and Juliet* music being used for the Lyceum revival.

> I have no objection. May I ask if you have any? There will be no question of fees: I take it to be a compliment to my music and considering the opportunities of having one's orchestral works performed are so very rare, I feel that you may perhaps kindly acquiesce in the matter. Will you? I wrote to you about three years ago when Martin Harvey *thought* of reviving it and you replied that you were quite agreeable. I wish I had known of this when we met the other night.

At about the same time he asked the singer, Ruth Vincent, to help him with a concert to be given 'by a friend of mine' at Stafford House by permission of the Duchess. 'The only inducement I can offer, if inducement it be, is that you would be conferring a personal favour on me. I send you a list of patrons and the audience is expected to be a brilliant one.'

Despite the collapse of *The Conqueror* who had been unable to add a London audience to his tributary peoples, German was now the most esteemed figure writing for the musical theatre. Other British operettas came and went but the vocal scores of *Merrie England* and *A Princess* kept the music before the public as did the selections and piano versions. Yet in one respect he was restricted for he had established his fame as a melodist and of all the elements in his art this is the hardest to sustain in effortless flow. Richard Strauss and others were able to use technique and the new resources of harmony to make their melodic gifts cover yards of manuscript. The needs of light opera demanded a constant stream of inspiration, which it was not within any musician's capacity to supply. Nor would English managements have been interested in stage-works that employed more serious development and metamorphosis of themes. The fact that German was soon once again to write a work that overflowed with melody is an indication of his extraordinary gifts.

CHAPTER SIX

Tom Jones

During a long sea-voyage from Australia to San Francisco, the impresario, Robert Courtneidge, passed the time by reading Fielding's great novel *Tom Jones* and was impressed by its suitability for a musical play. There had already been a spoken play *Sophia* produced in the late Victorian period, in which the actress, Kate O'Rorke, had enjoyed great popular success. It is surprising that German or indeed the Savoy management should not have considered more carefully the great possibilities for music in the spacious treasury of English literature. The fact that the Fielding bi-centenary fell in 1907 bestirred the plans and a libretto was put together by Courtneidge and A. M. Thompson. Charles H. Taylor was commissioned to provide the lyrics.

A team of four might suggest frequent conferences and cumbersome cobbling-together of ideas but in fact the final libretto suited German's talents perfectly. The sexual temperature of the original had to be reduced, but there remained a love story with just sufficient strength to weave its way through three Acts, while Sophia Western and Lady Bellaston urge their separate claims upon the hero. The original earthy story contained no fairies or supernatural elements and allowed the composer, who could never have fanned the flames of wild tribal camp fires, as demanded by *The Conqueror*, to write to his own taste. As always, when he had to depict human figures rather than grotesques, German was stirred to write genuinely romantic music. When, in the Finale of Act II, Lady Bellaston makes her feline approaches to Tom Jones they elicited a theme of shivering sinuosity. The humorous passages in a long picaresque novel were telescoped into a series of diversions which, at least, represented a welcome change from imitations of Gilbert. Benjamin Partridge, the village barber, who plays a part in the story, is eminently human and this too suited German better than bizarre inventions. Even so there was some difficulty at rehearsals as, odd though it may seem, Dan Rolyat, the comedian who played Partridge had to be restrained from interposing a topical joke about tram-cars into the script, and the conductor had sometimes to wait patiently in the pit while impromptu slapstick occupied the stage.

Tom Jones is German's most operatic conception. He was keen that the work should show a move towards a grander style on the musical stage. On 12th March, 1906, he wrote to Courtneidge:

> I have refrained from worrying you knowing full well what that will mean and you have certainly had your share. I am awaiting a draft of the lyrics of Act III. Perhaps you could see Taylor and get something drawn out for me. I somehow have a lurking fear that going in for so-called 'musical plays' may possibly dull your sympathy for the more serious art trend of *Tom Jones*. I look upon this opera as an experiment and I wonder whether a new syndicate – quite independent of your present one – which seems to be solely and wholly mercenary – could be formed for the purposes of producing it. If it is not successful – well – then a higher form of entertainment is not wanted. But I am sure these are your views too!

Later he had some hesitation and struck out this passage, writing instead to Courtneidge that he was awaiting the lyrics for Act III, and that there were one or two matters which he wished to talk over. But the draft letter is evidence of his ambitious approach.

German also wrote to Courtneidge over the question of the conductor as Hamish MacCunn, who had been musical director for *A Princess*, had asked to be considered. 'In the event of my choice falling on him, would it meet with your approval, or is there anyone else you care to suggest?' MacCunn, the son of a Clydeside shipowner was a young composer also. He had studied under Parry and Stanford at the Royal College of Music and later taught harmony both at the Academy and privately. Liza Lehmann was one of his pupils. There was no doubt about his ability for he had directed *Siegfried* for the Carl Rosa Opera Company and had conducted the first performance in English of *Tristan*. His opera, *Jeannie Deans*, based upon Scott's *Heart of Midlothian*, was to achieve some success before 1914. There had been a measure of coolness between German and MacCunn as the latter's career as composer had suffered some setbacks. *Golden Girl*, with a libretto by Basil Hood, had not enjoyed the éclat of his colleague's operas. In June 1906 German wrote to his rival:

> There are certain difficulties which I cannot very well explain. I am wondering if you think we should work together comfortably. The

last time you were kind, very kind and helpful – indeed almost invaluable! but there came a time when I could not but feel that something had happened. Something *wrong* had happened. I have kept this to myself all these years and had your last letter not forced my hand I should have been still silent. (In the ordinary course of events there is not in all common sense any reason why you should not write operas and with whomever you may choose.) As it is, I think it best to me to tell you what is on my mind and if I am wrong you must forgive me. You will remember that evening in Dec. 1901, in my room here, when I told you that I had signed to write three more comic operas to follow *M.E.* and I said to you when Greer's wire, 'On your advice will engage MacCunn', came, that the only difficulty I saw in our being associated was that you yourself were a composer. You assured me, however, that you only wished to conduct and help me with the production; we shook hands on this and you thanked me.

Your kindness and the pains you took at rehearsal I shall never forget. While wishing to have your able assistance I am wondering if it would be better for me to engage someone who is merely a conductor and not a composer.

Such rivalries are frequent and inevitable in the theatre and were smoothed over. Courtneidge in his autobiography paid tribute to the benevolent effect which, by and large, German and other musical directors had during rehearsals. German's emollient tactics are well illustrated in his next letter:

My dear MacCunn,

I certainly apologise to you for not having written you sooner but there were difficulties which were not easily explained and I kept putting off until I really didn't realise how time was going.

As to my manners I accept your rebuke too, but I fear they have always been erratic, and I can assure you that I have not meant [he erased 'any ill-will'] to be rude. Each time you called it has happened that I have been out.

Well, if after this you care to come round on Saturday morning, I should be glad and will try to explain. If not I will certainly come round to you.

Yours ever,
E. German

It is good to know that this bout of ill-feeling between old friends had a happy conclusion. On the first night when German was suffering from the effects of overwork, MacCunn was beside him to take over the conducting if necessary. Some years later when MacCunn died, German was instrumental in helping his widow to realise some royalties on his music. To mark her gratitude she presented him with the manuscript score of one Act of MacCunn's opera, *Diarmid*, with a libretto by the Duke of Argyll, which is now with the MS of *Tom Jones* in Southampton University Library.

The opera opened in Manchester on 3rd April 1907 at Princes' Theatre, and two weeks later it began a very successful run at the Apollo Theatre in London. Robert Courtneidge, a stern and protective father, allowed his talented daughter Cicely to play a minor role as Rosie Lucas, friend of Sophia. The *Play Pictorial* devoted a long article to it, complete with photographs of the three Acts and extracts from the music. It referred to the opera 'taking London by storm' and nightly 'playing to packed houses'. Of German it said, 'Outside the sphere of abstract music he has done nothing better.' To the end of their days German's two sisters championed the respective merits of his two light operas: Rachel preferring *Merrie England* and Mab awarding the palm to *Tom Jones*. When the composer was asked which he preferred he replied, '*Merrie England* is older but I was younger; *Tom Jones* is younger but I was older.'

Sometimes the libretto falters, especially in the lyrics, where Latin tags obtrude and a certain coyness prevails. There is a strange abundance of songs about third parties, who have nothing to do with the plot, '*On a January morning in Somersetshire*', for example. Of course this is in the well-worn tradition of English folk songs which rely upon the eavesdropper. The genius of the score lies in the way the music for each Act sets the scene and brings to life the setting. Neville Cardus, writing twenty years later about the work declared:

> German, with a single stroke of his orchestra, at the outset of each Act creates the right atmosphere, and before the opera is over the music has passed through three different habitations. The chorus at the beginning of Act I ('*Don't you find the weather charming?*') is not only full of west country air; it is afternoon air: the music tells us at what time of the day and year the opera begins, for the orchestration beautifully suggests the low note of mellow monotony which belongs to October. Immediately Act II opens, the music loses its smack of the open country: it is antique, quaint: (for example, the Dance to Partridge's Song) and matches to a nicety the Inn's old world furniture and away-from-the-highroad quietness. Then for Act III, the lovely *gavotte* which is heard as the curtain rises lets us know by its stately movement and

nocturnal tonalities that we are now among the aristocratic graces of Ranelagh, as the place stands poised in the moonlight. Take any stretch of music from its proper act in *Tom Jones* and play it in another Act, and the effect would be incongruous. The *Barcarolle* has the perfume of Ranelagh: the *Madrigal* in Act I tells us of Somersetshire.

Unfortunately the merits which Cardus had so shrewdly and correctly assessed seem to have been partially hidden from the composer. For the concert version he condensed and mixed up the music of the three Acts, leaving the plot and this brilliant differentiation of mood in total disarray.

The finesse of the orchestration, however, was a matter in which German took pride. In 1908 when a fresh production was envisaged he had to combat both the threat of a reduced orchestra, and the desire of Courtneidge, who was an impresario and not a musical connoisseur, to alter the score.

Even so *Tom Jones* underwent changes during its first years. One song, *The Foundling Boy*, was excessively maudlin and the critics remarked that the hero gritted his teeth and went through it with the best grace he could. It was later removed and when an amateur society wished to re-instate it in 1915 German was adamant that the decision had been correct, and all the parts had been destroyed. There is, however, a copy in Southampton University Library. In February 1908 he wrote:

My dear Courtneidge,

I am sorry to have been long in answering your last letter. I have read it several times and of course there is much in it that is of great importance. The question of extra numbers has always been a difficult one. They are much harder to write than ordinary numbers when, after all the worry and anxiety concerning them, they may be taken out. Of course, I agree with you that one ought not to rest until we get it right, but I doubt very much if I could write any better numbers than those you mention. I'll tell you, however, of an idea that has occurred to me. It is to make the Laughing Trio itself an ensemble number – or for full chorus – everybody laughing. It would be a novelty. The three laughers are nearly 'pumped out' by the time the Trio comes. They have no breath to sing, but the number itself is good. Could not the chorus gradually come in and catch the infection of the laugh? Anyway, I believe I could arrange it in such a manner as to make it very effective. I will do this with pleasure but before starting I should like to know how it strikes you. [His idea was ignored: as usual, he was insufficiently assertive.] Then, I would take out Derry Down altogether and rush to the entrance of Squire Western. In America it was certainly better dramatically without it. As to the number for the 3rd Act in place of Saws, Saws I don't know what to say, but in view of the autumn tour and if you are prepared to give it another trial of which I am delighted to hear, I'll try, if you'll let me have a good lyric, to write something. As to the length of the piece, I only know that in order to get through in time some of the numbers are just rushed through and spoiled, particularly the Madrigal and Festina Lente – at least this was so on the big tour.

Yours sincerely,
Edward German

Later in the year he wrote again to Courtneidge with great acumen:

To my mind *Tom* is now almost as right as we can make him. Of course it is impossible to please everybody – the only improvements I can think of are the knocking off of some of the dialogue before the trio Saws, Saws in Act III and some of the time in the the waits between each Act, but I don't know if all this is possible.

Of course, the question of the orchestra – the inadequacy of the travelling orchestra – is a constant trouble and hurts me some: the fact is my music is simply 'bungled' through. I feel sure that people are more influenced by the quality of the orchestra than you may think, or they may vote a thing bad – without knowing exactly why – *I* know why, when I think of the shocking little handful of 'raggy' players in the band, and the sounds they sometimes produce. It is generally considered that, give the audience good principals, chorus, dances, scenery, plenty of laughter and all is well, whereas musically, the orchestra is the backbone of the whole performance. If you could come along and pioneer a better state of things in this regard – the full recognition of the importance of the orchestra in comic opera – real comic opera – you would be a real benefactor.

I do not know if you could or would wish to interfere with your present tour but *you might give the question a thought for sometime in the future*. It is genuine grievance and a considerable difference would be made if it were possible to travel – say five musicians. Never misunderstand me about laughter and fun – it is of course most important – if not all-important. I only want to see every element as near perfection as possible, but that is not my department.

It is interesting to note that in this same letter he suggests that

Courtneidge should see Hood and discuss the possibility of a new comic opera, which suggests that after *Tom Jones* German felt in a creative vein. His emphasis on the importance of the orchestra in light opera is crucial but with his customary shyness he retreats almost immediately. 'What a long letter!! however, you need not trouble to answer its details.'

As well as giving importance to the orchestra German attached much more significance to the chorus than any contemporary writer of operetta. A very full and important role is allotted it in *Tom Jones*. The opera opens with an elaborate ensembly of country gentry, the ladies gossiping and the men discussing the hunting field. In Act III there is a choral *gavotte*, one of German's most inspired pages and a *Barcarolle* for semi-chorus and chorus. The finales to Acts I and II are long concerted pieces filled with action and varied in key and mood though both extremely well wrought. The first ends with a grandiose reprise of the duet between Tom and Sophia Western, *For Aye my Love*, and the second returns to the march, *A Soldier's Life*, rising to a strong climax. Of the solos, Sophia's *Waltz Song* is the most well-known though in style it is somewhat out of keeping with a remarkable unified score. A more ambitious aria is *Today My Spinet Closed and Idly Still*, which she sings in Act I and more in harmony with the general mood is the *Dream-aDay Jill* in Act II. Tom's song, *If Love's Content Lie in the Spoken Word* with its excellent lyric shows the mature talent of the composer of *Happy Days* in *The Rival Poets*. The swashbuckling *We Red Coat Soldiers Serve the King*, if it does not rival the spaciousness of *The Yeomen* is full of deft touches which seem to be inexhaustible, with German hovering over the same harmonic patterns. The Madrigal, *Here's a Paradox for Lovers*, its delicate introduction oddly echoing that to Fauré's *Agnus Dei* in the Requiem, is more ambitious than anything in the Savoy operas in this genre. Indeed the whole work calls for musicianship of a high order and it is sad that despite some dated aspects the resources of a great national company have not been called upon to give a worthy representation of its many remarkable merits. It would at least be an occasion for chorus work to shine, undimmed by excessive critical interest in the principals.

He was still writing ballads and was very much his own business manager. He sent William Boosey at Chappell's his song, *My Memories*:

> You will observe that the words are by the redoubtable Boulton! This in all probability will be my *last* with him. He worries me. As to terms I am more or less open. I suggest you pay me ten guineas down and a royalty and 3d after the first 300. In any case I should like to give you

the refusal of the song. It is, I think, one of the best I have ever done but its popularity is, of course, uncertain.

Re *The Drummer Boy*, I have just heard from Boulton that he will not accept the 1d royalty from *me*, but he will if it is paid through you. May I therefore request that you will be so kind as to deduct 1d from my royalty and send it direct to him. This request of mine may make it possible for you to do this.

I feel this is the only way to 'clear the decks' with B. and it is a pity the song should be kept back any longer.

In the course of this letter he refers again to publishing *My Memories*. I fancy if you offer him 3 guineas for the words the matter would be ended. I am tired of negotiating with Boulton and I should like you to publish both songs.

He had in fact had quite a long association with Sir Harold Boulton, Bt, who wrote lyrics for many famous composers of the time. The association went back to *Three Spring Songs* written in 1898, and *Four Lyrics* of 1900. Despite Boulton's avowed intention of restoring the prestige of English song-writing his lyrics are rather tepid, though German set them pleasantly enough. The first of the four lyrics, *Sea Lullaby*, has a strong romantic mood that foreshadows *O setting Sun*. In 1904, together they produced a patriotic hymn for Canada. *Canada, Land of my Heart's Adoration*, registered strangely for copyright with the Canadian Department of Agriculture, was an anthem altogether too conventional to make any impact against similar contenders. It was Boulton, however, whose poem *Glorious Devon* was set with matchless style in 1905. This instantly became a baritone vehicle second only to *The Yeoman* in popularity. As a result German was frequently sent lyrics by the laureates of many countries on *Sweet Somerset, Sylvan Surrey* and the like, all of which he returned with his customary modest recommendation that he felt sure another musician was waiting to be inspired by the offering.

It is clear that he did not find Boulton easy in matters of business, but they resumed their friendship when German rushed to offer sympathy when Boulton's son had a narrow escape from death during World War I. In old age they would dine together at the Bath Club.

Along with *Glorious Devon* German also published *My Lady*, words by F. E. Weatherly, the finest of his songs, and one of the greatest of English melodies, moving between 2/4 and 3/4 rhythms with an effortless flow and matching the words with great simplicity. Fred Weatherly was a King's Counsel and had a fund of courtroom stories. He once defended a very rough looking ex-burglar and won his acquittal. Passing along the street he heard the conversation between the newly released man and his wife. 'Bill, the bloke wot spouted for you is the bloke wot wrote The Star of Bethlehem!' 'I don't care wot he wrote. He got me 'orf.'

Writing lyrics for the drawing-room was quite an industry. Clifton Bingham was the author of several German songs. A friend once found him in a Soho restaurant pencil in hand, and a picture of misery uttering profanities as he was having great difficulty with his verses for Christmas cards.

★   ★   ★

An American production swiftly followed the success of *Tom Jones*. Henry Savage was a New York impresario who specialised in importing European successes. In the autumn of 1907 he mounted *Madam Butterfly* 'Puccini's Fascinating Japanese Grand Opera', and Lehar's *The Merry Widow*. The press announced that on 11th November at the Astor Theatre Savage would offer 'the reigning London comic opera success *Tom Jones*'.

Although *The Emerald Isle* had been given in New York shortly after its London presentation German had not been directly involved. Several transatlantic visits had been mooted but never materialised. On this occasion he took the opportunity to go and superintended the rehearsals. The advertisements referred to a chorus of fifty and an orchestra of thirty-five. The orchestra proved too large for the pit of the Astor, and spilled over into the aisles, where the woodwind section sat on camp stools. He had also received an invitation from Walter Damrosch to conduct the New York Symphony Orchestra at a concert in Carnegie Hall. Damrosch came from a notable family of musicians. His father, Leopold, had been born in Posen and was a violinist appointed by Lizst to lead the orchestra at Weimar. Like many European musicians he and his family had ventured to the New World. One son, Walter, founded the New York Symphony Society, and another Frank, was for a time chorus master of the Metropolitan Opera. The Damrosch family did much to extol the merits of Wagner and Brahms to American audiences and the invitation to German was a just source of pride. In World War I despite his origins Walter Damrosch came over to Europe with the American Expeditionary Forces and founded a Bandmasters' Training School.

On 5th October 1907, together with Courtneidge and Thompson, German sailed on the *Lusitania*. This was the new turbine ship of the Cunard Line and by reaching the Sandy Hook Lightship from Queenstown in four days and twenty hours, it snatched the blue riband from German rivals amid great jubilation. Colonel Kowalski, chairman of the celebratory concert declared, 'Although we applaud the *Deutschland* as the pace-maker, yet we cheer the *Lusitania* for beating her in this heroic struggle to wrest from the German giant the blue riband for speed. The Lion is again master of the ocean highway and this English victory is one in which the whole world joins' German himself wrote, 'Everybody was excited and delighted and seemed to feel that they personally had had something to do with this record-breaking. I know I did and Thompson said he did too.' Thompson was a keen socialist and a friend of Robert Blatchford, a well-known left-wing publicist. He no doubt applauded the comments of George Croydon Marks M.P., who declared: 'I desire to pay a tribute to the stokers stripped to the waist, those sturdy men shovelling in coal as never before in order that this vessel may fly the blue riband of the Atlantic.' The record had been achieved despite some rough seas at the outset. On 6th October German took only light refreshments and limited himself to a solitary cigar at ten p.m. On the 7th he awoke to find all the appurtenances in his cabin swaying at strange angles with a 'most weird and Maskelyne-like look'. The main deck was closed because of the waves sweeping over it and the fate of Prince Leon in *The Tempter* must have occurred to him. By daylight he found the experience of the storm an exhilarating one. 'A beautifully clear morning, huge waves of darkest blue, white-capped, came like a tireless army and hurled themselves against the boat.' The autumn gales were strong and the authors of *Tom Jones* fared better than many travellers. The opera stars who set off for the Metropolitan season in the *Kronprinzen Wilhelm* shortly afterward arrived in a heavily battered condition and were unable to participate in the ship's concert. When the *Kaiser Wilhelm* tried to win back the blue riband the rudder came off and the passengers were subjected to great anxieties. The German press published reports that the Lusitania was designed as a troopship which could speedily land a British Expeditionary Force in Europe and was being crewed by Navy Reservists.

The Anglo-German competition was evident in many spheres. The Lusitania also carried Claud Brabazon and the team competing for Britain in the great St Louis Balloon Race, in which Germany triumphed. The only musician referred to in the list of distinguished passengers was Mark Hambourg, the pianist. German greatly enjoyed the later stages of the voyage. Of the vessel he wrote, 'She is like a superior Hotel Cecil that moves through the water at about 200 miles a day'. He was confused by the multitude of stewards, amused by the bugler calling passengers to meals and fascinated by the luxurious arrangements on board. Thompson made some effort to convert him to his socialist views, especially when, in the smoking room the discussion turned to the sagas of the American millionaires and the ostentatious wealth of New York society, It was a forlorn crusade, however for German's political views were well to the right of centre and reflected the self-help philosophy of the Victorians. In the troubled 1920s he was wont to set down on paper his mordant thoughts on socialism, trades unionists and the necessity of capitalism. In practice he was always the most kind-hearted of men. When the *Lusitania* put in at Queenstown he was much distressed by the fate of the poor and helpless middle -aged woman who had tried to secure a place in the steerage section but had been refused admission on medical grounds and thus lost the opportunity of joining husband or son in the United States. Hoping that the authorities had relented he searched the steerage quarters of the ship but in vain.

He took a great interest in his fellow passengers, especially one gentleman 'in a blue serge suit and commodore hat' who told stories of his innumerable journeys over the seven seas, to which, polite as ever but unable to compete, he could only utter, 'Extra-ordinary' from time to time. The wanderer confessed to sea-sickness each time he set off on his adventures. 'I looked on him as a kind of Vanderdecken doomed to roam the seas for ever, and again ejaculated, "Extraordinary"!! Funny kind of man,' he noted.

A further antidote to socialist feelings was supplied by elements of rowdyism in the Second Class which he toured on the final evening. He preferred the refinements of the First Class such as the selection of old English sea songs played by the ship's orchestra during dinner. 'I always like our old sea-songs and tonight was no exception; they are so breezy, melodious and refreshing.' He noted some ideas for a *Nautical Rhapsody*.

The *Lusitania* docked in New York on 11th October. Unlike Caruso who startled the ship's company of a rival vessel by serenading Manhattan with scales and trills on his approach, German slipped quietly ashore and went to the theatre where the cast of *Tom Jones* was waiting to rehearse. He was impressed by the training which the chorus had received from the conductor, Herman Perlet, and in the evening he himself took the first of many rehearsals which extended over a month. 'I found they were very good, especially the girls; they were quick and intelligent in taking hints, Perlet has taught them splendidly.' We have seen already the importance which he attached to the place of the theatre orchestra in light opera and he was equally delighted with the musicians at rehearsal. 'Very fine players who read music wonderfully well: I found them most painstaking and obliging.' The principals may have provided more problems. Louise Gunning (Sophia) had recently enjoyed success in *The Paradise of Mohammed* but the audiences were surprised by her vocal accomplishments in German's work.

Tom Jones faced some severe competition for interest. It was due to open only a few days before the Metropolitan season with Caruso in *Adriana Lecouvreur*, followed by Chaliapin in *Mefistofele*. The Met, 'founded on the rock of social tradition' attracted huge press coverage of both singers and audience. The display of jewellery in the boxes was so glittering it was referred to as 'The Diamond Horseshoe'. In addition to *Madam Butterfly* and *The Merry Widow* a rival season of opera was being simultaneously given by Oscar Hammerstein's Manhattan Company and interest in this was heightened when an over-intense Don José actually stabbed Carmen and she fell to the ground in a swoon, blood gushing from her arm. This sort of thing seems to have been endemic on the Yew York stage. While *Tom Jones* was being given Mrs Patrick Campbell at another theatre in *Hedda Gabler* attacked Mrs Elvsted so forcibly the latter screamed and had to be soothed on stage before action could re-commence.

In addition to singers, many European concert artists swarmed to America to perform during the season. Paderewski and Pachmann, Kriesler and the even more esteemed violinist, the Czech Jan Kubelik, were all in New York giving concerts during German's stay. Indeed the *New York Times* carried a long and woeful article about the estimated $6,000,000 which foreign musicians at the lowest estimate carried away from American shores each year. It was suggested that both Paderewski and Caruso would leave $160,000 richer. Richard Strauss was reported to have received $30,000 for a tour, Saint-Saëns $15,000. Even Elgar was said to have been overpaid at the Cincinnati Festival the previous year.

Before the opening night there was considerable interest in the extent to which the shocking nature of the original tale would be on view. Some of the critics were hoping that German's treatment would be more robust than rumour predicted. According to *The Herald*:

Theatregoers are to hear a musical version of *Tom Jones* at the Astor Theatre to-morrow and we are told that we need not prepare to be shocked. The comic opera in question has been composed by Mr Edward German, who is not very well-known in this country despite the fact that he has composed some excellent music, so this raises one's hopes.

Has he taken advantage of the original novel and has he made his music tell what the librettists did not dare to? Has Mr German translated into music Squire Western's language – language that was ruddy in its frank glow. If so he must have employed some of the batteries of one Richard Strauss. All all events we shall see to-morrow night what we shall hear. Glees, madrigals and rollicking dances are said to prevail, forms of music in which this composer excels. The plot as described, is almost above reproach, it is said, and at least we can introduce our sisters to *Tom Jones* without apology.

If anyone hoped for the sensualities of *Salome* in this rendering of the novel they were to be disappointed. Though the opera was certainly not in tune with the advancing forces of Prohibition it was unlikely to offend other elements of puritan opinion. The composer's own youthful and essentially English looks also caused some surprise. One woman journalist described him:

> In appearance Mr German is trim and businesslike. There is no affectation in his manner and he is as far as it is possible to imagine from the dreamy long-haired eccentric which we were accustomed to recognise as the ordinary type of artist. His hair-cut is quite the same as though he were a banker or stockbroker.

He expressed some distaste for an American musical comedy he was taken to see and which he left after the first interval, remarking that 'In places it almost rose to pantomime level, but never quite'. It would be interesting to know which of the many Broadway shows had been selected for his delectation. Probably it was *A Yankee Tourist*, 'the dancing, prancing musical farce. Girls! Laughter!! Music!!! Starring Wallace Beery', which was playing at the Astor while the country dances and stately gavottes of *Tom Jones* were in rehearsal. The sedate comment was of the kind that Scott liked to quote though it comes oddly from the erst-while rogue-player of the six-penny entertainments. In any case by the time it reached its apogee in *Chorus Line* American musical comedy was to prove healthier stock than the enfeebled descendants of Edwardian operetta.

In view of the competition *Tom* succeeded remarkably well. The elegance and craftsmanship of the music and the orchestration were duly praised though the critics noted the essential disparity of styles which affects a piece that at one moment aspires to a grander operatic form and at another becomes traditional comedy.

'It has been heard and seen in London for months and now it has come to this city of noise to try its tuneful fortunes,' said *The Herald*.

The music sparkles in its quaintness and it rings true for it is written by a musician. But despite its charm is it "light" and "catchy" enough to win popularity? Does the native audience care enough for skilfully written and delightfully sung numbers from which it departs without a 'whistling' tune in its memory? These are tests which *Tom Jones* will have to face: and let it be hoped that it will win for it has grace and exquisite delicacy enough to ensure everlasting success – provided there is a public for such serious melodious charm . . .

The book is founded on Henry Fielding's story but the burrs of that late gentleman's language have been removed with utmost care. Especially does this apply to the impetuous vocal explosions of one Squire Western.

It is hardly fair however, to call *Tom Jones* a comic opera. It is really a romantic opera. It is true there is comedy in it, and good comedy too, purveyed by the inimitable Mr Walter Norris, he of the nervous wink and eloquent feet who plays most admirably the role of a village barber. He loses a leech named Lizzie and this loss wins for him the audience's sympathy and laughter. But he is legitimately funny in a hundred other ways and he is allowed to prattle even in Latin, which is a defiance to a Broadway audience.

The *New York Times* gave space to mentioning German's serious compositions, found the Old English style a shade monotonous but decided that it consisted of 'well written, well scored melody, the most of it, and the greatest sort of relief after the average American – or English for that matter 'musical comedy. There is a morris dance as a prelude to the Third Act which should rival in popularity the other morris dance in *Henry VIII*. There are several concerted items written with much grace and flow of melody, among them *The Barley Mow, Here's a Paradox for Lovers* and the Finale of the Second Act.' The *Times* objected even so to the intrusion of modernisms such as 'O look who's here'.

Within a fortnight Savage was able to take a larger section of the theatre pages to display the tributes of the majority of the papers. 'Tom Jones is a real treat,' 'Music of a high order'; 'Ought to fill the theatre for a long time'; 'Pulsating Music'; 'The various waltzes, marches and glees follow in quick succession and captured many an honest plaudit'. Bookings were opened for four weeks ahead.

On the 17th November, German conducted the *Welsh Rhapsody* in Carnegie Hall. As the programme had a nationalistic flavour and included Stanford's *Irish Symphony* and works by Grieg, some critics concluded that German must indubitably be Welsh. 'Mr German also speaks with native authority when he is concerned with the Welsh national utterance' (wrote the *New York Times*, compounding the error). 'His Rhapsody is a less highly organised development of national tunes than Stanford's Symphony, his treatment is more obvious . . . There is good work in it and some stirring passages and it is a composition well worth hearing. Mr German conducted it with finesse and skill.'

The audience for the New York Symphony Orchestra was one of the largest for the season.

'It is not so many years,' said *The Herald* 'since the makers of classical music were Germans and Germans only but Mr Damrosch has recruited his men from no less than fourteen nationalities . . . The most interesting feature of yesterday's programme and a novelty here was a *Welsh Rhapsody* by Mr Edward German, an English musician whose opera *Tom Jones* received a welcome here last week. This *Rhapsody*, which dates from 1904, is by no means great music but the composer makes good use of Welsh melodies, notably of the famous Men of Harlech which he weaves into the imposing finale.'

German made a strong friendship with Damrosch and others in musical circles. He wrote, 'We spent a charming time together. I found the Americans delightful and kind hearted and I cannot understand that anyone could do otherwise.' He greatly enjoyed the sightseeing although a return journey from Philadelphia to New York was made in a cloudburst and the ferry crossing had to be endured in the worst weather he could remember.

His one American journey was very brief. On 20th November he boarded the *Oceanic* alone, for Courtneidge and Thompson travelled independently. There was an initial delay when an Italian passenger complained about the food and attacked the unfortunate cooks with a knife. When he and some compatriots had been bundled ashore, the ship set sail. As a lone bachelor German had only the conversation of the elderly trio who shared his table to entertain him. One neighbour, 'a benevolent-looking old man with a highly polished voice that suggested the pulpit' asked if he were Mr Edward German, the violinist. 'Now a composer,' said German with the correct degree of modest diffidence. The old gentleman dismissed the difference and recollected his own efforts on the violin. It appears that German had much sanctimonious conversation to endure during the trip. Although sharing a First Class table his fellow passenger put forward 'self-sacrifice' as the key to happiness, and dwelt periodically on his certainty of the after-life. German's outlook was one of scepticism. The piety of John and Elizabeth Jones had not held any influence over his middle and later years. He had a mildly fatalistic attitude. In his last years when correspondents urged him to resume composition he would refer to the measure of inspiration which had been meted out to him and with which he had to be content.

CHAPTER SEVEN

This Wicked World

Although *Iolanthe* was Gilbert's most famous and delightful excursion into fairyland it was by no means his first visit. In the 1870s he had written a number of plays in blank verse that dealt with fairies and mortals: *The Palace of Truth, Pygmalion and Galatea* and, in 1873, *The Wicked World*. The plays were financially successful but were punctuated by a series of arguments and contests of will between the irascible dramatist and his players, especially Mrs Madge Kendall, a leading actress whose performance Gilbert would on occasion criticise audibly from his box at the Haymarket. He also wrote a parody of *The Wicked World* called *The Happy Land* under the double pseudonym of Gilbert à Beckett and F. Latour Tomline, and incorporated some heavy political satire. Three of the characters were made up to resemble contemporary politicans, including Mr Gladstone, prime minister of the day, and *The Happy Land* came under the ban of the Lord Chamberlain until changes were made.

The Wicked World was also the cause of one of the many law suits brought by the contentious Gilbert. In the Court of Common Pleas, he brought an action against 'Enoch' a critic from *The Pall Mall Gazette* who had described the play as indecent and offensive. In fact the lines complained of were couched in such Victorian circumlocution that a modern audience would fail to spot any prurient matter at all. The jury, however, found for the defendant after a trial characterised by great hilarity, and Gilbert had to pay £60 in costs. At about this time his uncertain temper was displayed in an incident when he came to blows with an actor who was just about to enter through a trap door, knocked him down, negotiated the trap door himself and played the part for the rest of the evening. Towards the end of the year he had a violent and wordy quarrel with Buckstone, Manager of the Haymarket about a fourth play, *Charity*. It was a heavy and serious piece about a woman who atones for a sinful relationship by a lifetime of good works, having, like the gentleman of the *Oceanic* arrived at the conclusion that self-sacrifice was the highest virtue, though presumably by a different route.

Gilbert long retained a particular affection for these blank verse plays written when he was still under forty. He had also in 1906 renewed his associations with the Savoy Theatre, when he agreed to come out of retirement and re-stage a series of the Savoy operas. The productions were highly successful so far as the public were concerned, but his association with Helen D'Oyly Carte suffered the volcanic course of most of his professional associations.

Helen D'Oyly Carte who had before marriage been her husband's secretary, was an excellent business woman and quite an expert in theatrical matters. She appears to have assured her Manager, Boulton and the Musical Director, François 'Honest Frank' Cellier ('brother of the composer of *Dorothy*) that Gilbert would not have sole control of the casting. Gilbert for his part, was very keen that a young singer, Nancy McIntosh, should play the leading soprano part in the first revival, *The Yeomen of the Guard*. Although happily married and sometimes given to ostentatious prudery, Gilbert had a driving wish to further the careers of certain young actresses in whom he felt he had divined some unique quality. Many years before, in 1893, he had met Miss McIntosh, an American, who was a pupil of George Henschel. He immediately took charge of her career, to the ultimate detriment of the plot and the dramatic balance of the opera he was at that time writing with Sullivan, *Utopia Ltd.* He re-wrote the libretto increasing the importance of the part that he had in mind for her, introduced a new character to sing duets with her and re-designed several musical numbers to build the scenario around her. His obsession was one of the causes of the relative failure of this penultimate Savoy opera. Sullivan recorded that he was 'disappointed with her voice' but, bowing to the inevitable, had not objected to her playing Princess Zara.

When the management was less than enthusiastic about Nancy McIntosh as heroine of *Yeomen of the Guard*, Helen D'Oyly Carte endured a series of letters that referred to the great insults the author had suffered, the pain given by contempt for his opinions, and threats that he would take no responsibility for any weaknesses in the production. The quarrel worsened when Mrs D'Oyly Carte expressed fears the he intended to prejudice reviewers against the chosen cast of *The Gondoliers*, an inference which Gilbert described as 'a gross and gratuitous insult'. 'I regard with dismay, he wrote of the revivals, 'the fact that they are being produced in a manner calculated to do them an irreparable injury.'

This was mild compared with the correspondence that developed as the series continued. In 1909 he wrote of 'the gross insolence and black ingratitudes which have characterised the Savoy methods during the last two and a quarter years . . . the operas have been insulted, degraded and dragged through the mire.' Not even the Lord Chamberlain's veto on a performance of *The Mikado* in 1907 because of a visit by a prince of Japan, Britain's new far eastern ally could deflect him from his principal quarrel. He continued his accusations that Mrs D'Oyly Carte was throwing away the ladder by which she had risen to fortune.

In happier days he had once suggested to Helen Carte that he might turn *The Wicked World* into an opera libretto but her husband (this was in 1897) had not been enthusiastic about the musical work that had a female chorus only. It is said that many composers, Sullivan, Elgar, Messager, Massenet, Liza Lehman, and Alexander Mackenzie had all at one time or another been approached but rejected the idea. According to Mackenzie, Sullivan 'would not hear of it'. Elgar 'gave no reason for his refusal'. Massenet had written some remarkable fairy music for *Cendrillon*, though the opera was not produced until 1899, and as a practical man of business he wanted to attempt a different type of subject.

In December 1908, Gilbert turned his attention to German:

Dear Mr German,

I have conceived the idea of a 3-act fairy opera, but the story involves a peculiarity which *may* stand in the way of its accomplishment. The peculiarity is that the chorus *must all be ladies.* You will be able to judge whether this would be a delightful novelty or an insuperable difficulty. As I see the piece in my mind's eye it might be productive of exquisitely beautiful effects – but your mind's *ear* may be altogether opposed to the notion. The story is eminently fanciful – in parts strongly dramatic with a view of playful humour running through it. There would be only three men's parts – a dramatic tenor, a vigorous baritone or bass, and a buffo who would be probably a light baritone.

If the idea commends itself to you and if your engagements would permit you to collaborate, I shall be very pleased to go into details.

Yours very truly
W S Gilbert

A further letter assured German that the *tone* of the piece would strike him admirably.

A few weeks earlier German had had a meeting with Basil Hood to try and find a subject for a cantata, but no workable ideas emerged. Gilbert's proposal was courteous enough and the opportunity to collaborate with the greatest English librettist would obviously have its attractions. It is clear that

German was flattered by the idea of an association. In January, 1909, he wrote to Rachel:

> Just a line to say that altho' I have had two interviews with WSG *I have not written* a note of music yet. He is at work on the 1st Act and seems inclined to wait until he has *finished* it: he will then send it to me.
>
> I don't think there is any 'run' in the thing: but I shall of course go through with it, if only for the *advt*. Of course, nothing must be said about it yet. I'll write you again soon.

The rapid agreement which he gave to the plan was, however, to prove doubly unfortunate. On the one hand it led to his involvement with the litigious Gilbert, a series of embarrassing situations and ultimately to his retirement from the theatre altogether. On the other hand, it gave him no opportunities to develop and strengthen the bolder operatic style of *Tom Jones*. With *The Wicked World* retitled *Fallen Fairies*, he was manacled once more to the outworn Savoy tradition, setting a fantastic story about fairies and mortals, instead of exploring other English novels which might have inspired him. One would have expected that someone in his position with so many acquaintances in the theatres and clubs would have had some inkling of the librettist's uncertain temper and frequent descents into acrimonious wars of words. If warnings were issued German did not heed them and agreed to provide the score.

For some time relations with the great man were cordial. Gilbert wrote early in February to say that he had completed the First Act and German was invited to Eaton Square to hear it. Gilbert hoped that Curzon, manager of the Prince of Wales Theatre, would produce the piece but asked German's advice as there was some uncertainty over the expected run of the production already playing there, 'S. Hicks is anxious to deal,' he added. 'So is Vedrenne, but I doubt whether Vedrenne is a capitalist.' 'Gilbert is delightful to work with and he seems to have great faith in me,' wrote German. 'He treats what I say with respect and often acts on it. The fact is that he is such a giant he can afford to be doubly polite and nice.' German gave himself to his task with his customary conscientiousness. In mid-February 1909, he wrote, 'Dear Sir William, Just a line to let you know that I am getting along with the 1st Act and I think it should come out (ultimately) very well . . . When I have sufficient of the Act done I will hope to bring it round to you, there are several little points which we might discuss.' In March he asked Gilbert to alter the second verse of a song for Lutin, the fairy messenger, to the same rhythm and shape as the first. On March 15th, 1909, he thanked Gilbert for the Second Act, and added,

I am sticking a little over the remaining numbers of Act I, though no more than I always do when trying to get a thing right. For Selene's song, Poor Purblind Wayward Youth I have conceived a kind of alluring waltz rhythm (not of the commonest, of course, I hope you will never have any fears of me in this regard). I want to keep the numbers as well contrasted as possible and not be heavy except when necessary. When I get a little more done I will hope to bring it round for half an hour one morning, when perhaps Miss McIntosh will help me to convey my meaning. I think it is *most* kind of her to have offered to do so. I am so sorry to know that you have been seedy but you are, I trust, better now.

Helen Carte, though also offered the new work had no desire to work with the author of so many of the insults heaped upon her. Curzon was unable to promise a definite opening date, but in April another producer, C. H. Workman, had appeared. He was a singer, who specialised in light comic roles.

In April, Gilbert wrote:

I have received the enclosed from Curzon from which it appears the matter is definitely at an end. I have introduced a song (a good one, I think) for Lutin, which much improves his part in Act 2. I am going to re-write the verses you wanted re-written and I mean to try my hand at a song for Darine at the opening of Act 2. But this I am not sure about. Workman, a singer who specialises in light comic roles, is likely to take the Savoy, and if he should do so, is anxious to arrange for our piece. I have asked him to come here on Wednesday to lunch. Will you come too? The 12.40 Euston to Harrow would bring you here in time and my car would meet you at the station.

When German entrusted the first batch of manuscript to the mail Gilbert went personally to the station to ensure their safe collection. In May he wrote, "Sir William" be d——d. Please call me Gilbert.' German was consulted over the singers:

There is a young lady, a friend of a friend of ours, who has a glorious contralto voice. She would be an ideal Darine provided that she is vocally equal to the music – and I think it would be worth your while to hear her. She is singing at a concert given by Miss Bateman at the Aeolian Hall next Tuesday at three. Perhaps you could find time to go and hear her? She is a handsome girl six feet high, with a very fine stage presence. She sings under the name of Miss Sara Nattier, but her real name is Grett.

For a time negotiations hovered between Workman and Malone, manager of the Adelphi Theatre. Lacking a theatre of his own it was necessary for Workman to enlist financial support from those backers known in the profession as 'angels', a species which, like the fairies, divides into the fallen and un-fallen varieties. On 10th May 1909, Gilbert wrote uneasily to German of Workman's delay in getting his people together'.

When Workman had finally put together his syndicate, German was invited to Grim's Dyke to meet him and play some of the music. He was still an uncertain supporter, however, and Malone was again approached. 'I am relieved,' wrote Gilbert, 'that you take my view of Workman's conduct.' The talks with Malone were to have the additional purpose of putting pressure on Workman and his backers who provided problems from the outset. 'I suggest a day that is a week ahead in order to give Workman time to see his syndicate and if possible, bring them to reason.' Tripartite discussions went on between the author, composer and impresario, and Gilbert wrote on 10th June: 'Workman has written imploring me to give him a few days grace in order that he may arrange matters with his syndicate which he feels confident he can do. So I have written to Malone explaining matters and asking him to postpone his visit until some day next week, say Wednesday . . . Did you *gather* anything from your interview with Workman?' By 28th June, everything appeared to be settled and it was agreed that *Fallen Fairies* would be produced by Workman at The Savoy.

Gilbert was well satisfied on all counts. On 14th July he informed German: 'I have drafted an agreement in which I have stipulated (*inter alia*) that you should have absolute control of everything relating to vocal and orchestral matters and that no engagement for principals or chorus should be made without our joint approval.'

It was on this point that portents of the oncoming storm made themselves felt.

Nancy McIntosh, who helped German to run through his score with the author, had been selected for the leading part of Selene, the Fairy Queen, and German had not objected. The financial syndicate, however, wanted a Miss Spain as the leading lady after Gilbert imagined the matter settled. Only after the words and music had been read and sung through, did the syndicate prevail upon Workman to object to Nancy McIntosh.

'A week after the Reading,' wrote Gilbert wrathfully,

> you wrote to us and offered us ridiculous and insulting terms and inform us that you were bound to Miss Spain for your first three productions . . . some gentleman who is interested in her having contributed £1000 to your syndicate. With regard to the terms, I never haggle. They are immutable and must be accepted or rejected en bloc. I have not a word to use against Miss Spain for parts to which she is suited but she is wholly unsuited to Selene. Moreover, I decline to have my libretto cast by a syndicate.
>
> You have caused us to lose two months in idle negotiations and you have lured us into confiding to you details of the music and libretto on distinctly false pretences. I decline to have dealings with a man who is capable of such conduct.

Workman was a comedian, and not a professional diplomat. He had assured the syndicate that Miss Spain would triumph, but now quailed before Gilbert's epistolary onslaught. German was at this stage firmly caught in Gilbert's chariot wheels.

'I do not press Miss MacIntosh on you,' wrote Gilbert.

> I only say that German and I are completely satisfied with her, that *I* wrote the part for her and German the soprano music. If you can find a better at her salary, £25 per week, we will accept her but Miss Spain, an excellent *soubrette* would be quite out of place in a stately part calling for scenes of passion and denunciation. Miss McIntosh is an admirable singer and accomplished Shakespearean actress with an individuality and appearance which are exactly what the part calls for. Please let me have your decision at once as another manager is coming on Friday to hear the piece and music unless I stop him.

For the moment Miss McIntosh remained as Selene.

There must have been some relief when Gilbert departed for Wiesbaden in July. François Cellier who had been a thorn in Gilbert's side during rehearsals, had been removed as music director at the Savoy. Modifications to lines and verses passed to and fro with friendly ease. 'Play with the lines as much as you please and let me know whether you like them,' wrote Gilbert to German. Relations between Gilbert and Workman, however, plunged from one hazard to another.

Miss Nacy McIntosh as Selene the Fairy Queen in 'Fallen Faries'

Gilbert, Workman and German discussing 'Fallen Faries'

Dear Mr German,

We shall be very glad to see you on Monday by the 12.40 from Euston.

The difficulty is that Workman asks us to read the piece and play the music to the syndicate that they may determine whether they will or will not produce the piece. To this I have replied that the piece has already been accepted by Workman – that he is under contract to produce it at the Savoy on withdrawal of *Mountaineers* and that we shall most certainly enforce the terms of that contract.

Unfortunately I have accidently destroyed the letter in which he accepted the terms embodied in my letter of 6th July. Have you a copy of that letter? If so will you please bring it with you on Monday. Workman says that he can find no such letter among his papers, but that I take to be a clumsy evasion. It is of no great consequence as there is no end of secondary evidence to prove that he has accepted the opera. Anyway it is clear that we can compel him to produce our piece immediately after the *Mountaineers*. I decline altogether to recognise the existence of the syndicate – who are merely his bankers.

Yours truly,

W S Gilbert

In his next letter the same mixture of courtesy to German and rumblings against Workman continued.

Gilbert had pressed German to make a cut in the Finale because of the difficulty of inventing stage business to fill the time. German, in reply, emphasised the thought which he had given to the work which had occupied him for several months.

In the Finale, I cannot see, if it is to get home, where I can cut it further. This also goes quite fast and to my mind will be most effective. However, I'll still think it over. Speaking generally I think you will find when you come to rehearsal that I have thought out everything very carefully.

The cuts, however, came.

Dear Mr German,

Many thanks for the 'cut' which was suggested, I need hardly say, wholly in reference to the difficulty of filling up the time with appropriate business.

I have not yet been able to elicit a distinct avowal from Workman that he unreservedly accepted the terms contained in my letter of 6th July. I have now written to him to say that I will entertain no other matter connected with the piece until I have received a definite yes or no answer to my question.

>   Yours truly,
>   W S Gilbert

German privately had doubts about the length of the run that could be expected. 'It is all artistic,' he wrote to Rachel, 'and the idea is pure Gilbertian, but it is a fairy opera not a comic opera.' He had refused to accept less than five per cent of the gross takings, the original offer, but at one moment he withdrew his request for a guaranteed £250. As usual he was overworking, simultaneously preparing an edition of *Tom Jones* for use by amateur societies, and matching the final version with the conductor's score. He had been forced by pressure of work to turn down an invitation to write special music for the Welsh National Pageant. A letter from Gilbert on 24th October informed him,

> I can get nothing but evasive replies from Workman, – but our case is so clear and so cogent that I have placed the matters in my solicitor's hands as the only means of bringing him to book.
>
> I must tell you that the oftener I hear your music the more impressed I am with what appears to be its high technical qualities, its fund of delicate melody and its great variety.

At long last a satisfactory response was elicited from Workman and rehearsals proceeded.

In addition to the scoring and supervision of parts for the Savoy, auditions for principals and chorus, delayed by recriminations over the contract, had to be fitted in. The elderly Gilbert had not lost his relish for selecting lively young lady aspirants.

> Dear Mr German,
>
> There is a young lady – pretty and with distinct acting ability, the daughter of a colonel in the army, who is disposed to join our chorus. I know nothing of her singing ability but she tells me that she is regarded as a good singer, and, as she expresses it, 'the best in Surbiton' where she lives. She has not practised of late, as she is occupied in town all day and is too tired to practise when she gets home. She may be a 'find' *but* even if her voice is not all that it should be, her brightness and

attractiveness would be valuable on the stage, and on that account you might be disposed to take a lenient view of her vocal qualifications. Of course, if she *can't* sing, there's an end to the matter.

She can't get away from her business (manicuring) on Thursday so I thought that perhaps you would be good enough to hear her at your house on Saturday at four.

I am strongly disposed in favour of Miss Maidie Hope, if you are satisfied that she could sing the music. With her as Darine, C. Fleming as Ethais and Wilson as Phyllon I should consider we had (from my point of view) an excellent cast.

Very truly yours
W S Gilbert

A few days later, returning to problems of casting and raising modifications to the music, Gilbert addressed his collaborator, for the first time, merely as

Dear German,

I have told Workman your views about Mr Herbert and he is *off.* — is, I am told given to drink. I don't think we could risk him, if that is true. He smelt very strongly of spirits yesterday.

I hope most earnestly that you will see your way to allowing 'Poor purblind souls' to be taken in a slower and more *lovesick* manner. Selene is dying with love for Ethais as she is singing it.

Yours truly,
W S Gilbert

Casting problems are well captured in a letter of 10th December:

Dear German,

Miss Venning (the suggested understudy for Selene) will call on you on Friday at eleven. Also Miss Caldecott (for chorus) concerning whom we hesitated but did not engage. You kindly said you would give her an indulgent hearing as I understand from three quarters that she would be a valuable accession to the chorus. Perhaps she did not do herself justice when we heard her – I have asked her to call on you on Friday at 11.30.

I think Mr Herbert would do for Phyllon. The other man, as I understand, is not to be relied on – and he smelt of spirits very strongly this morning.

Yours truly,
W S Gilbert

While Gilbert sharpened his nostrils at the Savoy, and the procession of young women made their way to Hall Road, excisions and alterations continued to flow from the author.

> 'It has occurred to me that it is a pity that Ethais has nothing to sing in Act 2, except a part in a duet. How would it be to delete Selene's song, Oh Love that Rulest in Our Land, and restore Ethais' song, The Tocsin Tolls for Two, treating Ethais' song somewhat in madrigal form – finishing each verse with 'The Tocsin Tolls for Two' and following this with a semi-humorous, semi-solemn 'Ding Dong! – Ding Dong! Ding Ding Ding Ding Dong!' for both. Of course, I should have to re-write the present lines – either in the existing metre or in another metre as you may decide. I think the effect will be good. I have a suggestion to make which I hope you will see your way to act upon. It seems to me that Darine's opening music about 'Fierie wild barbaric shapes, all head and tail' is taken so fast that it gives her no chance of making any *acting* effect with it. I got Miss McIntosh to play it and sing it more deliberately – so as to give Darine the chance to *act* through it and the effect seemed to me to be particularly impressive. I earnestly hope that you will see your way to allowing it to be sung so as to give a *strong dramatic effect* to it. The words are important as conveying to the audience the impression that the fairies have formed of the condition of the world and its inhabitants.

What was banished one day was quite liable to be restored the next.
7th December, 1909 (one week before the opening night):

> I'm very much afraid Workman will be able to make nothing of his song, Suppose You Take with Open Mind, and that the best way will be to omit it altogether. He will have plenty left and he is quite willing (as I am) to dispense with it. What do you say?

8th December 1909:

> I am having another try at Workman's song Suppose You Take. Leave the first verse as it is – that's all right. The second verse I've recast as over. The variety in the metre will help you and suggest the variety in the features described.

It has to be remembered that at this late hour every bar of music that was changed involved the alteration to music and to rest bars in over thirty orchestral parts. German seems to have borne with it all patiently, though even changes in tempi had their effect on the impact of orchestration by which he set such store. The evolution of a work during rehearsal is not, of course, uncommon. The MS Scores of *Merrie England* and *Tom Jones* contained many cancelled bars and obliterations. But the burden of such revision inevitably fell on the composer. Those who were less tractable, however, met with overflowing vials of wrath. The designer, Joseph Harker, was visited by the author, who found some of the scenery not to his liking and demanded changes. Harker replied that he had worked to designs already approved, and changes would involve further repayments for his services as well as delays in production. At this rebuff Gilbert plunged into a furious diatribe which lasted ten minutes and outshone any examples of violent abuse which the artist could recall. When Harker refused to be intimidated Gilbert stormed from the theatre and at the final dress rehearsal, at which an audience was present, made a point of saying that everyone but the scene painter had supported him loyally. Workman, for whom the main comedy part had been designed, had a number of minor illnesses, probably feigned, and kept out of the author's way as much as possible.

Nancy McIntosh was still in possession of the part of Selene. She was a member of Gilbert's family circle at Harrow, as well as being his favourite artiste. When German was invited to lunch at Grim's Dyke it was she who penned the letter on behalf of Lady Gilbert. The first night took place on 15th December and *Fallen Fairies* received a favourable reception from the fashionable audience. Gilbert dined at the Beefsteak Club and then spent the evening in Nancy's dressing room as he had an aversion to sitting through his own first nights, but he took the stage for applause at the close saying in the course of his speech 'I hope you will agree there is life in the old dog yet.'

In an interview given to the *Daily Sketch* the same day, he said of the music: 'It is extraordinarily beautiful – equal to anything I have ever heard – and quaint when quaintness is necessary.'

'That must mean,' observed the reporter,

> that the mantle of Sullivan has fallen upon German, and that the new composer, like the old, sees humour with the same eyes as the author. Granting this we may expect the people to demand more and we may picture Sir William in his great library at Grim's Dyke lying back in his favourite old arm chair to think out fresh fancies and frolics of phrases for the entertainment of countless thousands.

This idyllic scene was not to be realised. The critics were not so kind the following day, and a week later Gilbert wrote to his collaborator: 'The notices have been rather cruel but I think the piece is more affected by this cursed [Scott omits this word] Christmas season and the coming election than by them. My own opinion as to your music is worth nothing. I can only say that I am delighted with it, throughout, as we all are.'

The critics were divided into those who thought Gilbert's talents were flagging and those who thought the master was still incomparable in the realm of light opera. To modern taste the piece must seem fatally flawed. The heavy accent on the 'vile' nature of mankind grows tedious and has no dramatic strength. German's music too, despite its artistry and thoughtful craftsmanship is not really a vehicle for satire. It has not the swashbuckling vigour of Sullivan, and his characteristic touches of harmony, and rhythmic change, the modulations and extended phrases argue a restraint and delicacy of feeling, at variance with Gilbert's bludgeoning attacks on everything and everyone. There are a few delightful tunes in *Fallen Fairies* but apart from the Finale to Act I the audience would not have found it easy to go home whistling them. The Overture is definitely sub-standard with a wooden march tune, and throughout the work there is too great reliance upon the old 6/8 jig rhythms.

The truth is that Gilbert's libretto failed to inspire, and also gave his collaborator little chance to develop his potential skills in ensemble writing displayed so finely in the three previous operas, The sweeping melody, *Oh Gallant Gentlemen* is extended to a broad climax at the end of Act I and there is some highly seductive music for three-part female chorus in Act II.

> For many an hour
> Within her bower
> With Ethais philandering
> Our excellent Queen
> No doubt has been
> In roseate dreams meandering.

But elsewhere, solos and duets follow one another at length and in Act II Lutin, has three songs in quick unvaried succession. The fairy music is certainly quite full blooded especially Selene's 'Viennese' waltz *Poor Purblind Wayward Youth*, and skilfully avoids comparison with the daintiness of *Iolanthe* (though no doubt the chorus was divided along the lines unkindly observed some years ago by the critics of Dvorak's *Rusalka* into 'fat nymphs who sing and thin nymphs who dance'). Yet the score shows no great advance in technique. *Go Then Fair Rose* and the aria for Selene, reintroduced later to bolster up the production, '*Love that Rulest in Our Land*, are rich and romantic but in the style of earlier work. Moreover, the association with Gilbert appears to have led to some echoes of the Savoy operas which steal upon the ear; snatches of *Is Life a Boon* from *The Yeomen of the Guard* and *Our Great Mikardo Virtuous Man*. Nor would it have been possible to set lyrics such as *When a Knight Loves Ladye* without evoking memories of half a dozen settings of similar lines by Sullivan. Although before the opening the press gave great attention to Gilbert's inexhaustible vigour ('the brightest brained man of his day,' said *The Sketch*) and prophesied a new series from the partnership, not only were their talents less complementary than those of the old partnership, the dreamy softness of German's music cloaking rather than accentuating the satire, but the composer's cultivated self-effacement precluded demands for the concerted romantic situations in which he excelled. Though, as he had said to Rachel, he had accepted the invitation for reasons of prestige, the experience seemed to congeal, temporarily at least, his musical powers and even his personality.

The collapse of *Fallen Fairies* was made infintely more disastrous by the quarrels over Nancy McIntosh, in which both sides tried to enlist German's support.

On 22nd December when the show had been open only a week, Gilbert wrote to say that he had been informed that the management wanted another Selene. Although angry, his respect for German modified the tone.

Dear German,

I have just received the enclosed astounding letter from Workman. What it means I cannot guess – but I expect it is actuated by an intention on the part of the directors to strike at me through Miss McIntosh. Is it your opinion – tell me quite frankly – that their act in inflicting this unparalleled outrage on her reputation as an artist is in any way justified? To take her out of the part and place another lady in it would inflict infinite damage on the piece – for it would be at least ten days before another lady could be got ready. I am practically in your hands. If you think Miss McIntosh should give up the part *she shall do so* – and pray believe that, if you so decide, both she and I will accept your decision without the smallest feeling of resentment, as I know you are absolutely fair minded and the best possible judge of what is best, really, for the piece. Pray be quite frank as I am most anxious that she should not be placed in a false position – and no one – not even an amateur board of directors – can decide this point as authoritatively as yourself.

    Very truly yours,
      W S Gilbert

It would not have been in German's nature to desert Nancy at this stage and, despite his long experience of the theatre, he was profoundly distressed by the turn which events had taken.

> Dear Sir William,
>   I return Workman's letter: it has much upset me.
>   You know quite well the admiration I have had throughout for Miss McIntosh and I still doubt, considering all points, if we could get a more *artistic* exponent of the part. I am not going to pretend that her singing latterly has been quite what I expected – her voice seems of less volume than when she sang at Grim's dyke [sic], but I put it down to overwork or nervousness.
>   I have now told you quite frankly – as you wished me to do – all I feel. I was so upset when the letter came that I felt I could not reply right away.
>   Yours very truly,
>   Edward German
> P.S. I know nothing of the syndicate but as to their wishing to insult you through the medium of Miss McIntosh – surely this could not be!

In fact at one point the syndicate *had* summoned German and endeavoured to persuade him that the audiences were not satisfied with Nancy and a replacement must be found. The letter he wrote to Gilbert is full of erasures and amendments though he declares that he refused to hear anything against her and would not see or hear another lady. Finally it was crossed out in his copy-book and was presumably never sent, though it shows his hesitations over acquainting Gilbert with the strength of the opposition. Gilbert was sufficiently pleased, however, with the letter he received.

> Dear German,
>   Your very kind letter is just such a letter as my experience of you led me to expect. I quite agree that, owing to the fatigue of rehearsals and also to her being somewhat out of condition, Nancy's voice has not been as full and round as it was before her long and fatiguing rehearsals – but that it is a voice which keeps people out of the theatre is a charge as preposterous as it is insulting. My firm belief is that there are wheels within wheels and that, for some reason unknown to me, the syndicate intend if possible to place a nominee of their own (a Miss Evans, I believe) [Miss Spain was no longer mentioned and Miss Amy Evans

was the new candidate of the syndicate] in Nancy's place. Workman actually stated that Nancy sang out of tune – a thing that I believe she never did in her life – and this by itself is sufficient to show the animus by which they are actuated.

She is staying in town and knows nothing about the syndicate's intention. I shall see her tomorrow and shall have to break the news to her. I am desperately afraid of the effect that it will have on her sensitive temperament and I expect she will be quite unable to play and sing on Monday. She will do so if she can but I have warned Workman to get her understudy ready. What course she will eventually take – whether she will insist on the terms of her engagement (which is for the 'run') or whether she will save her face by a plea of ill health and necessity for rest I do not know.

Very sincerely yours,
W S Gilbert

This was the first time Gilbert has signed 'very sincerely'. The old man's emotions were heavily engaged.

He demanded an interview with the hapless Workman, who had become entangled in promises to all parties; though the impresario bent before the storm on this occasion he did not break and Gilbert was forced to tell Nancy that her part in *Fallen Fairies* was ended. She appears to have departed with dignity but for her protector the matter was not at an end. When Workman asserted during the highly charged interview that nine people had left the theatre because they did not enjoy her performance, the author accused him of having planted them there in the first place, and threatened legal action.

Sir,

This is to give you notice that I intend to apply to a judge in Chambers for an ex-parte injunction restraining you from playing *Fallen Fairies* this evening except with Miss McIntosh or her accredited understudy Miss Venning in the part of Selene. I give you this notice that you may be in a position to face the contingency.

I am yours, etc.

On the same day he wrote to German:

Dear German,

I have consulted my solicitor and he strongly advises us to apply to a judge in Chambers, next Wednesday, for an injunction to prevent

Workman from allowing anyone but Miss McIntosh or her understudy to play Selene in accordance with the terms of his agreement with us and with her.

It will be necessary that you and I should make a joint affadavit to the effect that by our respective agreements, no one is to play in the opera without our joint approval and that we are quite satisfied that Miss McIntosh and no other should play the part.

If you will join me in this I shall be much obliged. I propose, unless I hear from you to the contrary, to call for you at Hall Rd at eleven on Wednesday – that we may proceed together to my solicitor's office in Lincoln's Inn.

 Yours truly,
 W S Gilbert

At first German hoped that Nancy could resume her role but Gilbert next day swept this suggestion aside:

I find it would be useless to apply for an order compelling the Savoy management to re-instate Nancy McIntosh as she is so sadly affected by her infamous treatment she would be physically unable to take her part again, even though the court decided in her favour. Nevertheless, I will call upon you tomorrow at eleven to talk over the state of affairs and will take my chance of finding you at home.

German was duly collected into the taxi and taken to see Norman Birkett, the dramatist's solicitor. He was most unhappy to be embroiled in this backstage warfare, and shrank from the thought of court appearances. His situation was an unenviable one. As he had been so keen to have the association with Gilbert, and as he had help and co-operation from Nancy McIntosh he should probably have lent his weight to their cause. On the other hand, he had always had reservations about the singer's prowess, he was aware of Gilbert's power to stir up animosities, he hated any unconventional publicity, he did not live in the rich baronial style that Gilbert adopted at Grim's Dyke, and he might well have feared that a lawsuit could be lost, for the courts might decide that the management had been deceived as to the adequacy of the performer. That would be an expensive matter and would frighten off London managements from putting on his work in the future. His irresolution offended his partner. 'German joue le fainéant,' wrote Gilbert, who kept his diary in French, immune to the prying eyes of servants, 'et ne désire pas se mêler avec un procès. Alas, l'affaire est terminée.'

Relations were not helped by an erroneous report in the press that the Savoy were planning to follow *Fallen Fairies* with *The Emerald Isle*. German denied the rumour and Gilbert accepted his statement, with grace.

Dear German,
   Thank you very much for your kind and explicit reply to my rather impertinent question. The fact is that the syndicate seem to think that they have the right to revive *Ruddigore* after *Fallen Fairies* – a position which I dispute and I am indeed negotiating with another management for its production. If they had contemplated the production of one of your operas, it would have shown me that they had abandoned their claim on *Ruddigore*. As it is I am sorry that the report is erroneous and I hope for your sake they may decide to follow *FF* with the piece of yours.
   Yours truly,
   W S Gilbert

Fresh difficulties arose over the inclusion of Selene's aria, *Oh Love that Rulest in Our Land* as Gilbert had no wish to enhance the role of new Selene.
   'I would much rather (it) were not re-instated,' he wrote.

It was cut out not because Miss McIntosh couldn't sing it (for in those days you expressed the highest opinion of her vocal abilities) but because it was redundant and stopped the progress of the piece – and also because I did not like the words. As a substitute I wrote the duet for Selene and Ethais . . . I am sure you will see the matter from my point of view. Moreover, both Miss McIntosh and I are bringing actions against the company for breach of contract (my case is now with counsel) and the fact that a song was cut out when Miss McIntosh was to have sung it and re-instated for Miss Evans would be an [word blotted out – imputation?] against Miss McIntosh that an unscrupulous syndicate would not hesitate to employ.

German's reply was conciliatory, not to say apologetic:

Dear Sir W,
   I have read your letter and as to the song in Act II the idea was suggested to me by Mr MacCunn and I agreed that it might be desirable. I had not thought of it from your point of view. Therefore I shall now do nothing further.

As you know my aversion to all legal contentions I am very sorry to hear of probable trouble of that kind.

> Yours sincerely,
> EG

It is true that Gilbert had made further efforts to persuade German to join him in legal proceedings but he had not succeeded, and the composer's soothing comments were now turned against him.

> I am sorry you disapproved of my resorting to law proceedings. I must tell you frankly that I have no alternative but to pin you down to the terms of the two letters I have quoted . . . You will no doubt remember that when we were on our way to Birkett's you said to me, 'Miss McIntosh sang magnificently on the first night,' I replied, 'You really think that' and you answered, 'Yes, she sang magnificently.'

To complicate matters further, German now had Hamish MacCunn, the conductor, urging him to stand firm over the integrity of his score, without regard to Gilbert's wishes. As for the latter, the onset of the legal case had begun to stir his pugnacious feelings and his letters were more violent in tone. His recollections of the taxi conversation were preceded by a passage of rich invective:

> I am sorry you disapprove of my resorting to law proceedings but I think if *you* had been subjected to a similar outrage to that which has been inflicted upon *me* – that is to say, if some lady without the ghost of a voice and who had never even attempted to sing a note, had been told off in defiance of all contracts to sing your excellent music, even your dislike of legal proceedings would have yielded to indignation. *You* bear it quietly because you get a more powerful and full voiced (though not a more artistic) singer than Miss McIntosh – I indignantly resent the syndicate's action in employing a lady to deal with my most carefully written and most difficult libretto who has never spoken a word on the stage before and who is utterly incompetent even to deliver a message – whose acting, in short, is beneath contempt.

German endeavoured to defend himself but his misery is evident in his letters as this, by now daily, exchange, proceeded.

Dear Sir William,

I am very grieved to receive your letter. I don't know that I can say anything more except that I *never* said that Miss McIntosh *sang* 'magnificently' on the first night. As far as I remember it was *you* who used the words.

I have said all along that her performance was splendid, and it *was*, considering the nervous strain through which she was going. This is all very distressing to me and nothing would make me happier than to be able to give her singing unqualified praise.

Yours sincerely,
Edward German

Gilbert, however, had only so far been using the lighter weapons in his armoury. A heavier bombardment came when he received a suggestion from German that he should audition a particular singer as Darine, for Maidie Hope had also left the company.

Dear German,

No I will not concern myself in any way with the Savoy. If you had supported me, we could easily have swept the floor with that gang of ruffians – as it is I am left to fight alone. I wish to God that the piece were finally withdrawn. Nothing would give me great pleasure than to know that its last hour had come.

Let Miss Hilda Morris or anyone else play Darine; the librettist doesn't count.

Yours truly,
W S Gilbert

German was now coping with two difficult issues. The first was the inclusion of Selene's aria which Gilbert wished to remain unheard. On receipt of the latter's demand German had obligingly wired MacCunn, who was rehearsing it, to stop the performance, and had also informed Workman by telephone that he acquiesced in the author's wishes. As could have been foreseen this brought a vehement counter-attack from the outspoken MacCunn. He had already sought to make German defend his own interests in a letter of the 13th January.

My dear Edward,

Workman has shown me a telegram from Gilbert prohibiting the use of the song in Act 2. That is, he prohibits it unless it be 'authorised' by him. *Now* what *must* be done in the matter is this. You can quite reasonably suggest to Gilbert that he revert to his original construction, re-instate the song and omit the duet!

He told you that the duet was written in place of the song didn't he? Well, the duet isn't much of a success with the public; whereas last night the house not only applauded but *cheered* the song, and double encored it – I didn't take the second encore, as Miss Evans was evidently and quite naturally, pretty excited and tired.

I am convinced that the retention of this song in the piece is, as things now stand, our *only* chance of avoiding an untimely closure. Therefore, dear boy *do see* the man, and if necessary 'entreat' him, as the Scripture says.

Surely he must have more regard for your interests than deliberately to allow the piece to peter out.

> Thine,
> Hamish

At 11.30 the same evening, MacCunn again penned a note:

My dear Edward,

I have just heard from Ward, per phone, that the song *was done* tonight – and that it again secured a *double encore*. It is our *last hope*. I left the theatre about 9.30. Harry conducted as I am feeling rather seedy.

Indeed, if all this damned nonsense continues I am afraid I can be of no further active use in the matter.

I would do anything I possibly could for your sake old boy, but all this *agitato* business is getting on my nerves;

> In haste,
> Thine,
> H

Marginally emboldened by this German did approach 'the old man' with a request that the song be included. 'Considering the many months work I have put into the opera, and that every little is a help to the possibility of making the piece run I wonder if you would reconsider your decision and allow it to be re-instated?'

Gilbert's first reaction was entirely negative:

Dear German,

No consideration will induce me to consent to any alteration whatsoever in the libretto. I am now engaged in applying for an injunction.

Later on the following actions will be brought against Workman *personally*:

Gilbert v Workman – Breach of Contract
McIntosh v Workman – Slander and Wrongful dismissal
    Yours truly
        W S Gilbert

At the same time as he was making efforts to salvage the song, German also had to contend with efforts made by Gilbert to embroil him in the impending actions over Nancy's capabilities. He had written another letter on the 13th.

Dear Sir William,
    I shall not feel comfortable until I have told you that one thing in your last letter hurt me. It is that you do not seem to realise the admiration I have for your libretto. From the moment you approached me in regard to giving it a musical setting I have been quite ingenuous. I have tried to show you the pleasure – indeed the honour – I felt at being associated with you.
    On one point only have we come into conflict. When you pressed me to pronounce on Miss McIntosh's singing in the theatre (and you added that you would have not the least resentment to my plain speaking) I could not conscientiously give it unqualified praise. Much as I admired her artistic attributes I was placed in a very delicate position as our correspondence will show.
    For the rest time will prove all things and whatever happens I shall always feel proud at having been associated with your fine libretto.
    Yours very truly,
        Edward German
P.S. You say you are going to pin me to my letter of December 22nd and 28th. I think it will be better for me to show the whole of our correspondence since Dec 22nd (when you wrote enclosing the letter from Workman). This will give you some idea of the delicate position in which I was placed when sending my replies to you.

By the time *Fallen Fairies* was a doomed enterprise. MacCunn wrote again to German three days later on 16th January, 1910 with some venom:

My dear Edward,
    I suppose that you have heard that the 'notice' is up on the call board terminating the run of *Fallen Fairies* in a fortnight. My sympathies are with you in the whole wretched and unhappy history of the piece up to now.

And I can't help saying that I think Gilbert has acted or is acting in a manner so contemptuous of you and the deservedly high place you occupy in the musical world of this country.

On the occasion of his speech after the first night he spoke of there being 'life in the old dog yet'. The sort of life he exhibits as an unwholesome old hound is not edifying. Why don't you put your foot down and insist upon your song being sung and so secure to the piece a sporting chance?

As ever,

H. Mc.

When Gilbert heard of the threatened closure, and the management's desire to attribute failure to his suppression of the most applauded song, he relented to a small degree, declared that he would be distressed at being the means of throwing eighty people out of work and agreed to the inclusion of the inaptly named *Oh Love that Rulest in Our Land* if Workman would apologise for using it without permission and pay certain costs. German thanked him for his 'kind and considerate' letter and urged Workman to accept the terms, which he did. Gilbert replied civilly that he had been guided by consideration for the composer's interests which he would be sorry to imperil. 'At the same time I cannot allow Workman and his precious syndicate to twist my tail with impunity.'

The production closed on the 29th Jan. The receipts were low according to Workman, there were only £16 of bookings spread over several weeks, and the only life-line that Workman could offer was a promise to continue if Gilbert and German would guarantee him against loss. It appears that German did make some gesture of assistance but there was little chance of the begging bowl being replenished in Eaton Square, from where Gilbert wrote on the 30th:

Dear German,

As I wired to you I will most certainly not guarantee that syndicate of rogues and fools against loss. They have paid me nothing since Jan. 1 and of course will pay nothing. A piece treated as that piece has been must necessarily go to pieces and from my point of view the sooner the better, for, as it is, my libretto is held up to ridicule and contempt every time it is played.

I have today commenced my action against Workman for breach of contract.

Yours truly,

W S Gilbert

P.S. If you had joined with me in applying for an injunction to restrain them from substituting Miss Evans for Miss McIntosh, I believe the piece would now be running to £200 houses. The libretto really counts for something.

German's unhappiness was the more intense as his critics had a measure of justice in their case, however intemperately Gilbert may have expressed himself. If he had had doubts about Nancy McIntosh the moment to stress them was during the audition period when he was allowed a large share in the musical decisions. No doubt her closeness to the Gilbert household would have made this embarrassing, but she deserved the support of those who had selected her. A touch of the scrupulous exactitude of his mother comes into the correspondence where he qualifies his praise and makes reservations. If the soprano were in truth ruining the production however, then better methods of making a change could have been employed than those which the syndicate chose. MacCunn's position was the correct one. German was a composer of national renown, and should have defended the retention of Selene's aria which had been with considerable labour scored and rehearsed and proved popular. The truth was that any rupture in friendships and trust threw him into agonies of indecision and examinations of motives which extended his sympathies to all parties. With both Hood and MacCunn in times past he had worried himself unnecessarily over supposed breakdowns in trust. A letter of 1896 to a friend who he thought had been in some way leagued against him began, 'Of late my feelings have been played upon to such an extent and my whole nature has become so dismayed that I have lost confidence in myself, in you and in everybody.' As he found his main happiness in the company of good friends and had no domestic hearth to which he could retreat for consolation or championship these altercations were deeply grievous. But the pain of *Fallen Fairies* lay not only in its intensity but its prolongation.

Neither space nor probably the reader's patience would admit a complete record of the long rumblings and explosions that followed the failure at the Savoy. Gilbert demanded another affidavit to the effect that both men had contracted with Workman and not with the syndicate. 'Although Workman is a man of straw he can nevertheless command a salary upon which, or a portion of which, we can make a claim.' German's refusal, led to re-iterated attacks in which he was by now saddled with responsibility for the full debacle: 'If you had joined with me in applying for an injunction against putting a lady in the part who had never spoken a line upon the stage the piece would have been running merrily at the present moment – but your abstention caused the bottom to be knocked out of the opera and it sunk at once.'

Eventually proceedings came to a close. Nancy McIntosh, too, was appalled at the prospect of facing cross-examination in court and German wrote with some firmness to say that he would have to state in evidence that he knew of the existence of the syndicate and believed Workman to be acting for them rather than in his own private capacity. Nancy had engagements in Vienna and Budapest which she could not cancel and would therefore not be present when her case was heard. Although he rebuked German for accepting a lower royalty to help out the management ('I am sorry you consented to reduce your very moderate royalty. He knew better than to ask me to do anything of the kind') Gilbert stopped the actions, leaving Workman and his backers to pay the costs. He did not forgive the actor and refused to let him touch the Savoy operas in the future: 'Mr Herbert Sullivan [the composer's nephew and legatee] has shown me your letter re the Savoy Operas. I do not intend to waste any epithets on you – you can easily supply them yourself. It is enough to say that no consideration of any kind would induce me to have dealings with a man of your stamp.

The re-burgeoning of the Savoy tradition was not to be. In February, 1910, German had written to Rachel, 'Gilbert's actions may come on at any time. He is an awful old warrior and I have quite done with him so far as writing another opera is concerned.' Before his death Gilbert wrote only one dramatic piece. *The Hooligan* produced in 1911 on the joyless theme of a prisoner in the condemned cell who dies of heart failure when he learns of his reprieve. He did not follow up his acquaintance with German and continued to hold him responsible for the doom which had befallen *Fallen Fairies*.

Perhaps the most surprising feature of the story is the indulgent treatment which the episode received in Scott's 1932 Biography. It says of Gilbert, 'He was well served too by the company who entered thoroughly into the spirit of his fancy and he found an admirable exponent of the fairy queen's part in Miss Nancy McIntosh'. In the face of all the evidence it asserted, 'Neither he nor German had written with an eye to a popular success, and both accepted the situation philosophically, satisfied that they had, at any rate, achieved a work of art. For German there remained the memory of delightful associations with the famous dramatist.'

At the time of publication Lady Gilbert was still alive, and German, only very moderately favourable to the idea of his life being recounted, avoided carefully any criticisms of those past figures who had played a part in his career. By 1932 he had so far developed the persona of the 'verray parfit gentil knight' that he was unlikely to prompt the author with memories of all this turbulence. As for Scott, he wished to set down a tale of uninterrupted progress from humble beginnings to crowning honours. The result was a major distortion of a highly painful experience, which left its mark on the composer's career. Just as the attacks of Shaw had driven him to retreat from symphonic expression, the experiences he suffered as a result of his association with Gilbert and the signal failure of the work terminated his involvement with opera. He never again wrote a new work for the stage.

CHAPTER EIGHT

The Fall of Arcadie

1910 was a year of recuperation. In the spring German took a holiday in the Loire district of France though he always preferred the beauties of the English and Welsh countryside to any other. In the summer he revisited Whitchurch and was able to indulge his love of fishing. He continued to reject poems proffered as lyrics for his music, with his customary politeness. 'I do feel it is very much more effective as a poem,' he would conclude. He also kept a close watch upon performances of his music. A lady who had sung one of his arias at The Alhambra found the following numbing epistle in her post-bag.

> I do not know if there was any misunderstanding between you and the conductor but the song was certainly taken at far too slow a pace with the result that instead of being passionate it became dull and tedious. The conductor started at too slow a tempo and it seemed impossible to recover.
>
> There is another point which is all important – it is that, should you sing the song again I must ask you to kindly keep to what I have written in the separate song publication and not make the ending as at the Savoy, as it does not tally with the score and band parts . . . Besides I do not like it, and the effect on Sunday night was bad in the extreme.
>
> All this of course has nothing to do with my appreciation of your beautiful voice . . . but if it is your wish to sing the song again there are certain points which need clearing up. If you would like me to try over the song with you I should be delighted to do so. I could be here any morning this week.

In the summer he was approached by Beerbohm Tree for the use of the *Henry VIII* music. He agreed to adapt the score wherever possible to the new production but the incidental music rights rested with Irving and his heirs and time was short. He was disappointed that the notices made little or no reference to his contribution. 'Music not really *heard* because Tree having closed-in the orchestra so much,' he wrote to Rachel. 'It is after all only incidental music and is used to help colour the play. Still it is there for those who wish to listen.' Although he did not charge for the music, 'It is only for the *new* music I write that I should make a charge,' he gave thought to its use in the new version.

Dear Herbert,

In the midst of all, this is perplexing as to the dances in Act I. I think the following should be a practical solution. Will you think it over?

Let the Graceful Dance come where it is down – *first* then at the end burst right in the Children's Morris Dance *instead* of the leaping one. This latter I am convinced will never be satisfactory unless you have a troupe of professional dancers.

The Children's Dance coming immediately on the Graceful Dance would be in splendid contrast and would take off the harshness it would have if it stood alone in the middle of the Banquet Scene . . . I am only anxious to get it shapely from a musical and contrasted point of view and what I suggest would be quite correct and I fancy would please everyone. I hope for your approval but perhaps the idea has already struck you! In haste I am,

Yours sincerely,

Edward German

Reports of this production, lavish after the fashion of Irving, suggested that he had composed several new pieces of music and the correspondence over copyright suggests that there was more than the sung Grace which has survived. He had to share the musical honours with the King himself as Henry's air, *Pastime and Good Company*, was included.

He also agreed to an arrangement of his music for *Richard III* being used for a condensed version of the play at the Coliseum given by Seymour Hicks.

This was given in May, 1910, and was a section of a very mixed set of offerings. Hicks gave scenes from Acts IV and V: they were preceded by a tableau showing the fate of the Princes in the Tower, to the accompaniment of German's music. Interest then switched to the Battle of Bosworth which was enacted by a large cast magnificently accoutred in medieval armour and in full heraldic colour. German conducted for the Premiere. The Bill was shared by a troupe of performing ponies, Japanese jugglers and a picture-show through the 'Bioscope'. He had a great fondness for his *Richard III* music and welcomed the chance to have the Overture and the 'Earl of

Richmond' March included, but the production was not a success. German wrote to Hicks in December:

> I have read your letter and I was wondering why *Richard III* had been withdrawn for when I was at the theatre and from what I hear from friends it was a pronounced success. It seems, however, that you were compelled to take it off! I call it absurd and unjust. Absurd because the people liked it and unjust because it will throw so many out of employment. Beyond this I know nothing and can say nothing. I am one of those men who never enter into controversies but I shall certainly speak my views to anybody whom I may meet on the subject. The great point in my mind is that it was an artistic production.

He seems to have erased from the letter his regrets that cuts had been thought necessary. Early in the year he was asked to write some new music for a Hicks production but felt unable to undertake the work. The days of the expensive and pageant-like productions appeared to be over. There were, however, more developments in the entertainment world and German was soon involved in problems concerning the use of his music in picture palaces.

Many of his dealings with publishers at this time concerned either his songs or arrangements of the operas in concert versions. He wrote to Boosey at Chappell's in July:

> 'Since my chat with you yesterday over the telephone, I have been thinking. You do not like An Old English Valentine (I am not sure that *I* do quite). On the other hand you do like Love in All Seasons. Now I have no wish that you shall publish what you do not like: I therefore propose the following: You take Love in All Seasons in lieu of An Old English Valentine and consider the terms settled.

He contrived to reject various libretti. 'I think it is very fanciful, original and the tone of it is high, yet to be quite candid the subject in general does not strike me as one that would attract present-day managers,' he informed a would-be author. 'It seems perhaps, to lack human interest and strength . . . of course my decision has nothing to do with the merits of the book . . . it may appeal to another composer quite differently . . . I should like to add that I appreciate the compliment paid me in that I have been the first permitted to read it.'

Of 1910 he wrote, 'The year just departed has been a doleful affair and I don't think many will be sorry to see the last of it. To me personally it has been quite uninspiring though perhaps it is not fair to blame it for that.' He was uncertain about the future of composition and aware that his own manner of writing was beginning to seem old-fashioned and unadventurous. He deplored the efforts of the Viennese school of Schonberg and others to break with established tonal structures and discard the ideas of melody as they had been paramount for over two hundred years. He criticised the readiness with which younger composers followed the styles of Richard Strauss and Debussy and the break with old-established symphonic forms.

'I do not advocate stringent laws in regard to composition,' he declared. 'From a master hand everything must naturally be shapely, however modern and advanced it may be, but into students, while they are students, I think it would be wiser to instil a little more of the ethics of form.' He had his own fears that his particular methods of composition might well seem archaic to a younger generation.

I seem petrified by the modern trend of Art. If you heard some of the ultra-modern works you would understand what I mean. There is a fashion at present, and that fashion is to pretend you enjoy what is incomprehensible. Of course, I ought to be strong enough to disregard it believing as I do that beauty, shapeliness and sanity will prevail in the end. What I begin to feel thankful for is that I have been able to work for thirty years in a more congenial atmosphere.

Beneath his attacks on avant-garde composers lay the fear that even along his own chosen path inspiration did not lead him as lightly as before. He spent many hours sketching out ideas and discarding them but he seemed unable to break into new realms. It is significant that when he was invited to compose music for the Coronation of King George V and Queen Mary he did not produce an entirely new work but resuscitated some of the incidental music from *Henry VIII* and developed two of the themes into a Coronation March and Hymn. No one seems to have noticed any incongruity in employing for the occasion themes connected in the original with the crowning, not of Henry, but of his ill-fated wife. Few consorts have had more different careers than Anne Boleyn and Queen Mary. It was far from being the only coronation march at the Abbey ceremony. Marches by Tchaikowsky and Frederick Cliffe were also included for the processions, and an odd addition was Wagner's Huldigungs March written for Ludwig II of Bavaria. The closing piece was Elgar's dark and brooding Coronation

March which appears to portend the passing of an Age. Elgar could certainly not be accused of having embraced atonal music or broken the conventions, and yet his stature as a musician had grown hugely in the Edwardian period. In 1900 a German newspaper had hailed Edward German as the most outstanding composer in England, yet by the end of the first decade, he must have been aware that another now occupied this high place and this too may have contributed to his melancholy. Yet in public he maintained his lively and efficient demeanour. He enjoyed discussing details of the service with Sir Frederick Bridge, organist of the Abbey (known as 'Westminster' Bridge to distinguish him from his brother, the organist of Chester).

Sir Frederick's own anthem, written to accompany the acts of homage proved much too short and in 1937 at the Coronation of King George VI the Director of Music held a collection of anthems in reserve while keeping a careful eye on the mobility of the peerage. It was at the Coronation of 1937 that German's own composition was given a more prominent role for it accompanied the entrance of Queen Mary, and followed the lighter music of Grieg which had been thought appropriate for the arrival of the young Princesses, Elizabeth and Margaret. 'A short pause,' stated *The Times*

> and the more demonstrative melody of Edward German's Coronation March burst out as the procession of Queen Mary preceded by the Queen of Norway passed through the West Door. But it could be no blame to the composer if his music hardly seemed adequate to express the feelings released by the sight of the revered Queen Mother, facing with quiet dignity the ordeal of what could only be for her a poignant if proud moment.

German sent Scott a typically entertaining and graphic account of his struggles to reach the Abbey in time for the 1911 Service. He had to abandon his taxi near Trafalgar Square and penetrate the crowds. Eventually he was plucked from the multitude by a policeman and made a solitary journey from Whitehall between the ranks of troops that lined the streets. He wrote subsequently to Rachel, 'The King has sent me a medal to be worn in remembrance of their Majesties' Coronation . . . I expect others have had one too, still it is very nice of him isn't it?'

He also kept, I hope with some amusement, the programme of music submitted some time later for King George's approval at a Command Concert. His own Coronation March was given a very firm royal tick and so were Sullivan's *Overture Di Ballo*, a selection from Tchaikovsky's *Swan Lake*, Elgar's *Sevillana* and selection from Lehar's *Count of Luxembourg*.

Rejected were a *Grand* selection from *Das Rheingold*, the Prelude to *Tristan*, and *Parade of the Tin Soldiers* and a piece of Japonaiserie, *Ke-Sa-Ko'*. A programme that embraced *Das Rheingold* and the Parade of the Tin Soldiers would have been a most unusual one.

The most magnificent performance of his Coronation March and Hymn *Veni Creator Spiritus* was that played by massed bands at the Indian Durbar, when King George V appeared before the Vice regal staff, the massed retinues of the Indian princes and the peoples and regiments of the Empire. It was played while the King Emperor and Queen Empress processed from the Royal Pavilion to the thrones.

A very different representation of the music occurred when some kind of sequence of scenes from *Henry VIII* were projected in primitive form at the newly established cinemas. Under the impression that Irving's rights to the music did not include cinematograph or picture rights, German accepted a £10.10.0d fee for the use of *Veni Creator Spiritus* at Vernon's Picture Palace. He also received a small royalty from the Palace Theatre management, but he allowed the free use of the Grace he had composed for the Tree production of *Henry VIII*.

The 'pictures' on view at the Palace Theatre called forth objections from Mr H. B. Irving, the actor's son. German wrote to ask him to waive these, saying that he had charged nothing for the 'new' music in order that it could be heard. ('To get music heard at *all* these days is difficult enough and I imagine that at most the exhibition will only go on for a week or two.') Further correspondence ensued, German claiming that he had assumed the acting rights to the new music were not the cinematograph picture rights.

> I therefore told him that he was at liberty to use the Coronation Hymn at the various picture palaces by payment to me of a nominal fee, (as a matter of fact it was ten guineas but it might have been one or a hundred for all I care).
>
> If (as I also told you) I am under a misapprehension and the acting rights *do* cover the picture rights, I shall return the fee to Mr Barker and ask him to make his arrangements with you. So much for the *new* music – none of which – with the exception of the little Grace – is published.
>
> As regards the 'old' music, it is correct that I told Mr Barker that by purchasing the parts of the published music he could play that when and where he liked, the purchase of the parts carrying with it the right of public performance – except for acting and stage purposes. The point to be settled is *do* acting rights cover cinematograph rights?

On 11th March the lawyers decided that acting rights did cover this new mode of entertainment and German promptly returned his ten guineas though he gave vent to his irritation in a letter to Tree's agents. 'It seems to me that the one likely to suffer most in this miserable business is myself in that it will probably stop my music being heard. What is the use of writing music if it is not heard?'

Simultaneously he advised Barker (Will G. Barker) to continue using the new music until he heard from Tree's manager, though he did not think there would be any ban placed on it.

As regards the original music, the Shepherd's Dance and Coronation March is I think all that is used in the picture palaces. That is of course for you to settle with Mr H. B. Irving. In any case if you are doing wrong in using the numbers you can easily substitute something else. The present uncertainty is very unsatisfactory for all concerned.

In March 1911 a rather unusual arrangement was made. He accepted with pleasure a proposal of Novello's that he should compose six part songs in the next twelve months and give Novello the copyright of the same. In return for this Novello agreed to publish the orchestral scores of *The Seasons* and *Rhapsody on March Themes*. In June, German sent them the first part-song, *The Three Knights*. He requested that they should send three guineas to the author but added that he hoped the other songs to follow would have non-copyright words. He requested Novello 'for the last time' to keep the scores marked at as low a price as possible so as not to prevent performance. Finally he asked for the five guineas owing for the *Henry VIII* Grace.

At about this time there was further pressure from Tree for him to collaborate with Basil Hood on a musical play, *Drake* to be produced at His Majesty's Theatre. He declined, because he thought the notice too short, and believed that the Elizabethan setting would challenge *Merrie England* too closely. These were the years of the naval race between Britain and Imperial Germany. *Drake* might have had some topical apeal but the atmosphere of those years – darkened by the House of Lords crisis with its overtones of class conflict, the Irish troubles and the tensions between the great powers of Europe – did not seem propitions for the frivolous world of operetta. The antics of the Four Jolly Sailormen and the quayside festivities outside the Jolly Teapot at Winklemouth-on-Sea which had characterised *A Princess of Kensington* had little place in the age of Dreadnoughts. A more topical note was sounded in his setting of Rudyard Kipling's *Big Steamers* (1911) which reminded the population that their daily bread could be cut off by blockade.

Send our your big warships
That no one may stop us from bringing you food.

In fact as all minds were turned to the question of sea-power German himself had considered a nautical rhapsody as his next orchestral work. 'The work I proposed to write for the Philharmonic Centenary was . . . *Nautical Rhapsody* but I found as I proceeded that I could not get it to my liking. I further felt that, MacKenzies [Britannia] has said practically all that is necessary in nautical music and I decided to lay it aside.' No further ideas suggested themselves and he was obliged to write to the Philharmonic Society,

Considering the fact that I have not been able to satisfy myself so far, I am sure there is small chance of my doing so now, therefore to be honourable and to give another composer the opportunity of providing a new work while there is yet time I beg to ask you with all possible regret to allow me to retire.

If I should at some future time write anything that I myself consider worthy of the Philharmonic Society I will hope to honour myself by giving you the first refusal of it.

There have been occasions in the past when I have failed to please myself with my work and have thought proper to retire but that it should be so in the case of the Philharmonic is a disappointment I feel to the utmost.

I can only offer my sincere apologies to the Directors and express a hope that they will not think me unmindful of the obligation I am under to them.

This is an important letter. Having sought opportunities to have his orchestral works performed in the face of a great deal of difficulty and indifference, he was now forced to abandon a rare opportunity of writing a major piece that had been commissioned for a great musical occasion. Pressures of work in the theatre, the painstaking preparation of scores, piano scores and selections, the necessity of conducting his business affairs, had not left the resources of energy needed to produce the inspiration required. Moreover he was conservative in his travels. He might well have sought out some new ideas by travelling to new cities and landscapes. Even the abandoned *Nautical Rhapsody* does not sound a very original idea. Instead of seeking new horizons he celebrated his fiftieth birthday, Shrove Tuesday, 1912, by conducting the Whitchurch Choral Society in the concert version of *Merrie England*. Writing to one of the soloists (Gladys Roberts) he told her that

> a very small choral society are doing *Merrie England* on 20th February. They are making an effort to revive the fortunes of the old society and have asked me if I will go down and conduct the performances. Of course, I would not dream of doing so except that Whitchurch is my native town and it comes to more or less a personal matter. Naturally I should like you to sing the parts of Jill and the Queen but I think your professional fee would be out of the question. All they could possibly afford would be £3.5.0d. I should be pleased to add another two guineas to this myself. You could leave London in the morning of the 20th, rehearse in the afternoon, then after the performance, at night, some friends of mine would put you up and you could return the following morning. Now, should you be free do you feel inclined to come down and oblige me? [He erased the phrase 'sacrifice yourself for this particular occasion!'] Please be frank and whatever you say I shall perfectly understand.

If German was anxious not to attach too great an importance to the acclaim of Whitchurch, the same was not true of the townspeople themselves. 'It is only natural,' said the *Musical Times*, 'that the inhabitants should have followed his uniformly successful career with a measure of pride and affection only to be appreciated by those who were present in the Town Hall and joined in his warm reception and endeavoured to sing Auld Lang Syne in too high a key.'

This was German's first public appearance in Whitchurch since he had sung alto at the old Choral Society's concerts, given his student performances and occasionally conducted the band in one of his early compositions. Seats for the 1912 *Merrie England* were at a premium and 'the audience included representations of every class not only in the town but also from the countryside far and near'.

'The Whitchurch Amateur Orchestral Society,' said the *Musical News*, 'had shown a true sportsmanlike spirit in standing down in favour of a professional orchestra of twenty-one.' The chorus of sixty-nine voices has been trained by W. E. Rogers, organist of the Parish Church, German's old friend and teacher. In the Interval the Rector of Whitchurch made a presentation of a gold sovereign purse from members of the Society, and begged the composer 'as the only great man Whitchurch had so far produced to take great care of himself'. At the end of the evening he was given three rousing cheers. A month later, writing to Rachel, he said:

I recently heard from Edith (Clifford's wife) and she said that the enthusiasm over the concert was *still going on*. But it undoubtedly was an extraordinary occasion. Everything seemed to conspire to make it a complete success, and I shall always look back on it as one of the happiest events – perhaps *the* happiest event in my life.

The *Musical Times*, noting that the concert recalled memories of his early prowess on the organ and violin asked: 'Is it therefore too much to hope that German may one day turn his attention to writing a violin concerto, and perchance an organ sonata?'

It was during these years immediately prior to the First World War that he ceased the prolific and varied composing which had continued almost unabated since *Richard III*. Instead, he accepted numerous engagements to conduct and even overcame his previous reluctance to adjudicate. Nevertheless, Whitchurch ensured that he did not cease to compose altogether.

In 1912 a Girls' High School had opened. For a time it was in the old building where he had himself been a pupil of the Misses Hindmarsh, and his brother Clifford sent him an account of the event. The Headmistress, Miss Keightly, had with great enterprise pressed him into service to compose a school hymn. Such works are generally of very ordinary quality and there can be few schools which have had the honour of a work from such a musician as busy and distinguished as German was at that time. The original MS copied with the neatness and care that headmistresses command is in the possession of the School, now Sir John Talbot's School.

In 1913 he had a narrow escape from serious injury when a taxi in which he was journeying skidded and crashed into a bus in Edgware Road. The impact caused him to be thrown forward against the screen and he suffered facial cuts and bruises. It was the second taxi accident in his career in Edgware Road for in 1908 when he was in a taxi travelling at a speed he estimated at nine mph a boy suddenly appeared from nowhere in front of the vehicle. On this occasion, in his answers to police questions, he had defended his driver most emphatically. Perhaps that is one reason why a group of London taxi drivers sent a splendid wreath to his funeral.

He took an interest in the Guildhall School of Music over which Landon Ronald now presided, and his letter of 10th December, 1913, when the Principal had expressed some fears about a student production of *Merrie England* give some indication of the reason why Ronald was such a staunch champion.

My dear Landon,

It is a little awkward to reply to your letter. I quite understand your difficulties – they are undoubtedly great and so great indeed that I really don't know if I ought to come to one of the performances or not. I, of course realise that the school theatre is quite inadequate but I have no doubt things will be much better than you anticipate especially when you get the orchestra going. So here's to you and success! I am quite sure you have done everything. All the same I fancy you would not like me *not* to come at all, so I propose coming on the Saturday afternoon – of course in a private capacity – and let us hope for the best.

As ever,
Edward German

If he could be tactful and encouraging he could also be sharp. During the pre-war years he did a great deal of work on the preparation of scores and band parts for the operas. Some underling in Chappell & Co. had failed to recognise the extent of the work involved and received a reproof, written with an asperity that one wishes would creep more frequently into his music:

Dear –

Reverting to your call this morning, I would ask you to kindly have* all the parts of *Tom Jones* you have in the establishment corrected according to the set I brought in. This should be commenced at once as it will take some time. I will call in one morning to see how things are progressing.

I may add that I could wish that you would show (as I am in the habit of being shown) a little more courtesy in helping me in a very difficult task: it is quite impossible to launch these thousands of notes without certain errors creeping in even to the last; and after the enormous amount of work I have had it is not for you to complain – indeed for the future I feel much inclined to go direct to Mr William Boosey and tell my wishes to him.

Yours faithfully,
Edward German

In 1910 an album of several of his pianoforte compositions was published and in subsequent years some of his earlier works were re-issued.

---

* Whatever other learning Mr Robert Furber imparted, he did not explain the misuse of the split infinitives. German continued to split them throughout life with the joy of Siegfried at the anvil.

Ashdown's published his student Bolero for Violin and Pianoforte in 1912, as well as the Berceuse of 1894 and the Melody in E^b of 1895. He continued to write the part songs for Novello including *Beauteous Morn* and *In praise of Neptune*. Individual songs too made their appearance and in 1914 the *Three Songs of Childhood* – with their piano interludes connecting the cycle – to words by Margery Lawrence. With their suggestion in the music of the nursery sewing machine, the chinoiserie of the tea-cups and the gently rocking cradle, go some very haunting and pretty sequential tunes, though the type of singer who carried off these demure 'action songs' is probably an extinct species.

As one leafs through the old and faded copies of German's songs one might well be forgiven, knowing how many are old fashioned and sentimental, for passing over a copy of *When We Grow Old*, words by Hilda Hammond Spencer. Yet it is one of his supremely beautiful songs, where the last line of the introduction becomes the first line of the poem and the strong phrases for both voice and piano carry the poignant harmonies forward without any cloying effect. Had it been included in one of the operas it could well have rivalled his most famous songs in popularity. Yet it seems to have remained virtually unknown. It is sentimental but the sentiment is uplifting, a testimony to his parent's mutual trust, and a musical farewell to the world of peace, quiet faith and optimism.

In May, 1914, just before the European storm was about to break, the Bournemouth Symphony Orchestra reached its twenty-first season and held a dinner to celebrate. A galaxy of British composers assembled and Parry, Vaughan Williams, Mackenzie and German himself all took part in the concerts. It was German's duty, flanked by an enormous model of the Bournemouth Pavilion in sugar, made by the hotel chef, to propose the health of Dan Godfrey, the musical director who had fought manfully for British music. German acknowledged that in such a time and place Godfrey had had to cater for all manner of musical tastes, but complimented the orchestra on having continuously educated and elevated the public mind:

'Mr Godfrey,' he declared, 'was always on the look-out for novelty.' He was inclined to call him

a high musical chief scout . . . His motto was not only 'who goes there' but 'what goes there'. The very moment a new symphony or overture or concerto was talked about, whether modern or ultra-modern, difficult or super difficult, Mr Godfrey literally swooped down on it and carried it to Bournemouth and presented it forthwith. What we are coming to with all this modern ultra-modern music is not for me to decide but I feel that whatever happens Mr Dan Godfrey will be in at the death.

He concluded a graceful speech by assuring the conductor that British composers felt a great debt of gratitude for the excellent way he had treated their works.

To Rachel he wrote of a concert given by the Incorporated Society of Musicians, clearly a less lively movement than it is today. He was taken by William Shakespeare, the Professor of Singing, and remarked, 'Nature seems to have a mould for turning out these dry-as-dust old doctors, who meet every year, read papers and decide whether in the future crotchets shall have their stems turned upward or downward.'

Soon, however, even the broader questions which hovered over the direction of the arts were to be waived aside by the clash of arms and the entry of Britain into the European War.

★   ★   ★

The War of 1914–18 wreaked devastation on every aspect of the Old European order. Ancient sovereignties were swept away along with religious certainties, and a fixed social order. The careers of composers who might have proceeded from the Royal Schools of Music to continue their traditions were abruptly broken and inexorably altered. Arthur Bliss served throughout the war in the Royal Fusiliers and Grenadier Guards; Ralph Vaughan Williams in the Royal Army Medical Corps and later as an artillery officer. Many such as George Butterworth and Denis Browne, a promising young composer and critic from Rugby, friend of Rupert Brooke, never returned. One of German's Harrison counsins, related through his grandmother who died young, and from whom he seems to have inherited his disposition and aesthetic tastes, was a remarkably gifted pianist who was giving recitals in the years immediately before the War: both he and his younger brother were killed in France, thus robbing the family of someone who seemed likely to sustain the musical tradition.

The performing arts suffered as players and singers were drawn off to the trenches, and the ranks of the orchestras and choral societies were correspondingly thinned. The links with continental music, and the presence of mid-European musicians, many of whom such as Henschel, Randegger, Damrosch, Richter and Manns, had helped German in his career were temporarily ended. The infiltration of ideas from Vienna which enjoyed an extraordinary ferment of artistic experiment in the pre-war years was halted. Even familiar music by German composers, highly appreciated before the War, suffered from a moral censorship, and Edward German himself was fortunate that the fame and popularity of his music protected him from the obvious criticisms.

He wrote little during the War, though he worked on the *Theme and Six Diversions* which was first performed in 1919. The losses and bereavements of the years were beyond the consolations of romantic operetta and only the lightest of musical comedies were able to survive in the theatre. One composition owed its origins to a relief organisation for Belgian refugees and a *Daily Telegraph* Fund launched on their behalf. Under the editorship of Sir Hall Caine *King Albert's Book: a Tribute to the Belgian King and People from Representative Men and Women throughout the World* was published , and German wrote a hymn tune, entitled Homage to Belgium 1914. Its solemnity matched the mood of the time and many felt that words should be added so that it could be sung in choral services. A number of people sent in verses of their own devising for consideration but none was felt to be suitable. The idea did not rest, however, and German sought out his old friend, Scott, and invited him to supply some words. Together in a quiet village in Westmorland they composed an intercessory hymn, *Father Omnipotent Protect Us, We Pray Thee,* which was first performed in Westminster Abbey in 1915. It was sung in many churches and chapels through the War but a new version was necessary 'Dear Mr Littleton,' wrote German to the publisher,

> I am really sorry to bother you but so many people have told me (and I admit that I ought to have known) that for congregational use the high F is fatal.
>
> I have thought over the matter for weeks and have at last decided to ask if you would be willing to publish a new arangement I have in D^b to take the place of the present one in E^b.
>
> It will I feel involve difficulties but I do feel strongly that what I have done is *right* and will be for all times. Will you give it your consideration?
>
> As to the financial side I would give up my royalties up-to-date and start afresh with the new arrangement.
>
> This is merely a suggestion.
>> Yours sincerely,
>> Edward German

A Welsh version of the words was composed, and there was even a suggestion that Lord Curzon should produce a version in French. He declined, however, and wrote to German with the customary appreciation of his own worth, 'Alas, I am so overwhelmed with work that I no longer have any time for translation. But I hope you may secure someone worthy of your setting.'

The hymn has a solemn introduction and there are three verses. The second, marked to be sung quietly, shows how the mood of the nation had changed since Edwardian audiences applauded *A Princess of Kensington*:

Judge Thou our Cause O Lord,
In Mercy befriend us.
Thou, only Thou art righteous.
By Thy Grace defend us.
Bind up the hearts that Bleed,
Guard us in time of need,
Hear us we humbly plead,
In Thee we trust.

In 1917 Ethel Boyce also contributed to *Hymns for Use in Time of War* the words and music of a similar hymn: God of our Fathers, and Lord of the Deep.

Germans' hymn was one of the very few religious works which he wrote, and even it had not been expressly religious when first included in *King Albert's Book*. He treated its use with reverence, and recalled that once when he had heard it sung in the City Temple, he had been too moved to sing a note.

He also made a setting of Rudyard Kipling's poem, *Have you news of my boy Jack?* Three days after Kitchener's public appeal for volunteers, Kipling's son, John, had offered himself for a commission although he had not reached his seventeenth birthday. When he failed to gain acceptance because of his youth and poor sight, his father had persuaded Lord Roberts to secure him a nomination in the Irish Guards. This was the son of whom Kipling had written years before to say that he was singing the '*Just So*' Songs with zeal.

In August, 1915, after months of impatient waiting, John went with the Second Battalion Irish Guards to France and within a few weeks was reported wounded and missing at the Battle of Loos. *Have you news of my boy Jack?*, though it is cast in a timeless ballad form, reflects the anxious searches that the Kipling family made through the Americas, the Swiss Red Cross and the Vatican, in addition to exhaustive enquiries from the wounded men of John's own battalion. It was two years before they heard from a Sergeant Farrell of the Irish Guards that John had been shot when a company of the Guards had been leading an attack. He had been laid under cover in a shell hole in Chalk Pit Wood by the sergeant. More than ten thousand British soldiers in the battle had been reported missing and never seen again. The hopes that the Kipling parents had maintained for so long a time that he might be a German prisoner yielded slowly to the knowledge that he was lost.

German's setting of the poem was written and orchestrated for Dame Clara Butt, and was first heard at a Royal Philharmonic Concert, with the composer conducting. Within German's restrained emotional range in his songs, this shows a fine sense of word setting. The heavy chords in the unsung bars emphasise the absence of news and the one passionate outburst, 'What comfort can I find?' stands in relief out of the generally stoic treatment. The setting is not mentioned in Charles Carrington's excellent *Life of Kipling* but the author himself admired it and later requested another work from German. He had in 1917 written a *History of the Irish Guards*. It brought him into contact with many of the officers and men who had fought in the war, and he sought out especially those who had served under his son. In his loyalist Ulster days Kipling had written slightingly of the southern Irish, and to express his new admiration for those brought by personal tragedy into friendship he wrote The Irish Guards, a poem which prefaced the regimental history. This too German very speedily set to music.

The poem recalled the days of the Irish Brigade when the English faced it at Fontenoy under the Marshals of Louis XV.

> Ah France, and did we stand by you
> When life was made splendid with gifts and rewards
> Ah France, and will we deny you
> In the hour of your agony, Mother of Swords.

German gave the words an elaborate setting, and his Erin style employed so often from *The Emerald Isle* onwards had no difficulty in matching Kipling's poignant bravado:

> Old days, the wild geese are flighting
> Head to the storm as they faced it before
> For where there are Irish, there's loving and fighting
> And when you stop either, it's Ireland no more.

The Irish Guards March is not one of German's large scale works, but it is certainly one of his finest and most stirring compositions. Kipling approved tremendously.

> Dear Mr German,
>
> I've heard The Irish Guards several times and I hasten to send you my congratulations! It's wonderful and it goes with a dash and a devil that can't be beat.
>
> I note in the copy you sent that the line in the first and last chorus runs 'the wild geese are fighting' It should of course, be 'flighting', and Pilken Ridge ought to be 'Pilkern', but I expect these were only errors of the copyist.
>
> I foresee a great success for the song and I send you my best thanks.
> > Most sincerely,
> > > RK

In July 1918 shortly afterwards, the author wrote from his rooms in Brown's Hotel:

> Dear Mr German,
>
> I have seen Mr Hassall, bandmaster of the Irish Guards, today and he is very keen on having your Irish Guards set for a march for the regiment, and I have suggested to him that he make an appointment and talk the matter over with you.
>
> I'm sure you will agree that everything that can be done in any direction to cheer and inspirit our men just now is most important and that if you can see your way to help in this you will. Personally too I should be very grateful.
> > Very sincerely yours,
> > > Rudyard Kipling

In October German approached him for his signature on the MS, in all probability to be sold for war charities. Kipling replied:

> Dear Mr German,
>
> Of course I have signed it for you to whom my verse owes so much and get all the money you can from the assurance that I have never signed a music MS before and never will again.
>
> It is not necessary to tell you that this is an act of self-preservation against the legions.
> > Ever sincerely
> > > RK

German made at least four versions before he was satisfied and the result was one of the finest military marches. He amplified the strain of Irish folk song in a fine *cantabile* middle section. Kipling was delighted and wrote saying that he looked forward to hearing it in the Green Park with the full band.

His dealings with Kipling, though amicable, had not always run so smoothly. In 1915 he made a version of *Rolling down to Rio* for male voice choir, but the terms which Kipling demanded were a barrier to publication. As always German was more anxious to have his work available and sung than to squabble over royalties and fresh negotiations were made with Kipling. He offered to accept half a guinea per thousand copies sold, and make no charge at all for the arrangement. In the event he was fortunate for the publishers secured a division whereby twenty-five per cent was divided equally between the author and himself.

He was at the same time asked for patriotic reasons, to consider settings of Kipling's naval ballads. He did not – to quote his customary phrase – feel he could 'set them with the success they ought to have'. He did set the poem *Be Well Assured* but could not decide on the title. In sending it to Boosey at Chappells he said that he had been asked by another firm to set the whole *Fringe O' the Fleet* poems, 'but when I came to lines like

With his shining black belly half blacking the sky

and

We move in the belly of Death

I felt that these at least did not cry aloud for musical help! So I proposed to set just this particular one.'

German also set two other poems that did not spring so directly from the war but struck the patriotic note: *The Countryman's Chorus* by Helen Taylor and *All Friends Round the Wrekin* written by his friend Scott. It was also during the war that he made his first contact with the recording studios. The band of the Coldstream Guards under his great friend Colonel Mackenzie Rogan, had recorded a selection from *The Emerald Isle* in 1915. In the summer of 1916 German himself made recordings of the *As You Like It* Suite, the two dances from *Much Ado* and the *Henry VIII* and *Nell Gwynn* dances.

In 1918 in aid of the Red Cross and the Order of St John, he participated in a concert organised by Landon Ronald at Queen's Hall. The programme contained a Toy Symphony in which many distinguished musicians took part. It was composed by Richard Blagrove, a professor of viola at the Academy and that rather rare being, a serious student of the concertina.

German had asked to be allotted the triangle, but found himself at a desk in the second violins along with the brilliant Albert Sammons. Elgar played the cymbals, Myra Hess and the Misses Scharrer were the nightingales, the two Sir Fredericks, Cowen and Bridge, played the rattles, and the pianist Moisewitch, the coveted triangle; C. Haydn Coffin, the original Tom Jones and pianist Mark Hambourg played the castanets. When the nightingales began to blow into the mugs of water the second violins received a shower and Sir Alexander Mackenzie provided himself with an umbrella for the performance.

Landon Ronald with a nine-foot baton was the conductor at the start but after a while he was pushed off the rostrum by Mackenzie. Mackenzie was displaced by Cowen who in turn was displaced by German. All four musicians conducted the last movement in fraternal accord. During the interval the charitable funds were swelled by an auction of MS donated by Elgar, German, Cowen and Ronald. George Robey was the auctioneer. Many years later German found himself next to Robey at a dinner, which he felt to be a great honour.

Unconnected with the War, but an occasion in which he figured prominently was the Shakespeare Tercentenary celebration at Drury Lane in 1916. Asquith, the Prime Minister, was President of the organising committee and the selection of music inspired by Shakespeare was given to Mackenzie and Parry. 'The selection is not a large one,' wrote Mackenzie, an odd remark as a great deal of music had been inspired by or written for the plays. In fact the celebrations caused many to realise how much music among contemporary British composers Shakespeare had inspired. Berlioz, Tchaikowsky, Mendelssohn, Verdi and other foreigners were excluded but even so a mass of Shakespearean music remained. To German, Mackenzie wrote, rather condescendingly one might think, 'As you, among other reasons, have written more music to the bard's plays than anyone else it follows that you're included.' Because a marathon of spoken drama was to follow, the concert was limited to an hour, and German's *Henry VIII* Dances were chosen in preference to *Hamlet* or *Richard III*. The conductors were Beecham, Wood, Harty, Mackenzie, German himself and Norman O'Neill, whose *Hamlet Overture* opened the programme. German also figured in the programme as responsible for the music for an excerpt from *Coriolanus*, though no subsequent reference exists to this, and it may just have been a few trumpet flourishes: perhaps his name was put in the programme for Mackenzie's by mistake. *The Daily Telegraph*, referring to incidental music used later in the spoken extracts referred to the excellence of German's music for *Romeo and Juliet* and *Much Ado* in comparison with his more famous Dances and averred, with a degree of over-enthusiasm perhaps, that they 'should be heard continuously in our concert halls'. Of the composer it said, 'He is so modest and retiring that he succeeds entirely in hiding his light'.

The Tercentenary celebration was attended by King George and Queen Mary, and several members of the Royal Family, and raised £5,000 for the Red Cross. The throng outside the theatre was so great and the weather so bad that the public were admitted considerably before the advertised hour. All the great actors and actresses of the day took part, and the theatre was packed, though space in the Pit was cramped owing to the presence of projection equipment for *The Birth of a Nation*. The programme contained some fascinating rarities: Elgar's incidental music for *The Merry Wives* and *Twelfth Night*, and Roger Quilter's music for *A Winter's Tale*. The Telegraph urged those conductors who had permanent orchestras at their command to see that this treasury of riches was searched again. 'If that be the case, then something in the way of a permanent memorial to Shakespeare's influence on this country's music will have been erected.'

Elgar could not be present but wrote a few days later:

My dear German,
Your kind note gave me the greatest pleasure. I had no idea you would go to the concert but you would have found me here alone afterwards smoking a pipe and listening to your 6/8 *Henry VIII* with all the exquisite pleasure I have always derived from it. It gave me a real personal thrill to hear of your triumphal appearance at Drury Lane. For the occasion I would have preferred *Hamlet* but with a somewhat holiday audience (it must have been this I gather) the dances were the better choice – only I don't forget your serious works too.
Ever yours,
Edward Elgar

Hamlet had also received a signal mark of approbation from Parry and Stanford when it was selected as a test piece for the orchestra at the Royal College of Music in 1915. German conducted the students in a performance at the start of the course. Although the choice was an accolade for his skill in interesting orchestral writing he continued to revise and amend earlier works. At about the same time he wrote to Henry Wood:

My dear Wood,
In view of your doing the Valse Gracieuse on Friday next I am sending you the conductor's copy (carefully marked) which I used at

the recent De Lara concerts. I am also sending your librarian the special parts to agree with same.

I hope you will be so kind as to use these: they are complete and in perfect order. The fact is I saw a way of making extensive improvements since the original score was published – hence my writing you.

My regret is I cannot offer you a full score up to date. Of course I could alter the original for you in ink but it would be a big business and I hope you will not mind using the one I send. Naturally all I have sent is *private*.

With best regards,
Edward German

He began to be more aware of the long gap in creativity that had occurred since his last orchestral compositions. Writing to Rose Newmarch, about the programme notes for the Henry Wood Concert he was at first anxious to leave out the dates of publication for the March Rhapsody (1902) and the Valse Gracieuse (1895). 'They seem so long ago I would prefer they were not mentioned.' There were many hesitations in this letter: 'After all, if the work is good, what does it matter when it was written!' He wrote twice on the subject and finally apologised for troubling her about 'nothing in particular'. He nevertheless seemed anxious lest the public and critics should point at the long silence.

In 1915 when writing to Hood he added, 'I wish we could do another comic opera together but there! I am you know such a very hopeless person.'

He suffered from continuing to act as his own business agent, and his notebook is filled with discussions of royalties and performing fees, arranging for band parts to go to professional conductors as well as operatic societies, and discussing the details of conducting engagements. When Julian Clifford proposed a performance of *Hamlet* he was told not only to make sure that each band part was initialled E.G. (as various alterations had been made) but also of the necessity of providing a deep-toned bell or gong for the occasion.

Sometimes his correspondence has its lighter moments, as when in 1916 he wrote to the editor of *The Era*:

To the Editor,

May I ask you (privately) to kindly contradict the paragraph in your issue of the 19th to the effect that my full name is Edward German Smith.

Since it is thought necessary to state a real surname at all may I say that it is *Jones* not Smith. We may as well be correct in these things!

I should not like people to think that I have written personally on the subject and I am sure I can trust you to say nothing more than that you have received the information 'on the highest authority'!

His correspondence shows him working hard on behalf of others, raising contributions from friends for a performer struck down by illness, or approaching publishers on behalf of the widow of Hamish MacCunn, who had died of throat cancer and whose son was at that time on the western front. He also endeavoured to help his niece, Ruth Tongue, Mabel's daughter, to have her illustrated children's stories published and endeavoured to interest O'Neill in providing music for her children's plays.

The War did not dim his spirits entirely and one of his unknown compositions of 1916 marked 'Private: For Christmas use only' is a ridiculous song, '*The Arrow that Went Wrong*', words by 'Edward Balfe' though this may well be a pseudonym for one of the Williams Brothers of Whitchurch:

I shot a rabbit
To start the day.
My cursed luck –
It got away.
I shot a partridge
Up in the air –
It fell to earth
I know not where.
I shot a pheasant
'Twas flying high
Yet off it ran –
I wonder why!
In fact I hit things
Each time I aim
But never Kill them
B—y shame!

Sequel (spoken)
Long long afterwards
In a wood
I found that self-same
Little brood.
There was the rabbit

Looking healthy and trim
(No shot of mine
Had affected him!)
There was the partridge
– the pheasant too
(Both seemed delighted
To be on view!)
All sang their song
With might and main:–
Oh Johnie dear
Do try – do try again!

The old stomper of the Bank Buildings Sixpenny Concerts re-appears momentarily, and the advocate of 'beautiful melody, wedded to beautiful harmony' let himself go with a good bar-room thump that must have made for a *pièce de résistance* in Christmas festivities.

Another song in the same vein, *The Blooming Sparrow*, was written out for Rachel in the composer's old age:

There was a b – sparrow
She had a b – nest
'Twas built inside a – spout
Because she thought it best
There came a – tempest
It rained so – hard
That nest and sparrow both were washed
Into the – yard.

And on it goes for sixteen stanzas, the expletives politely expunged but suggesting themselves without difficulty. Within the private circles of family and friends German could still be prevailed upon to perform his party pieces though they lay some way along the spectrum of taste from his hymn for the Whitchurch girls.

Of the War itself he had some bad experiences when the Zeppelin raids on London began.

At about 11 at night I heard terrific and earth-shaking booms and looking up, saw a shiny thing with searchlights fixed on it from all sides. Guns fired and shells burst around: then one seemed to burst right under it and I thought hit it; anyway it rose to an angle of forty five degrees and gradually clouds enveloped it and I saw no more. But that was a quarter of an hour of real inferno, and I confess my knees knocked!

In November 1917 he reported further raids:

On Wednesday night I was sitting in my room here expecting every second to receive a bomb on my head. The whistling of the shells and the bursting of the shrapnel and the ominous hum of the engines overhead all made an Inferno for something like two hours.

In March 1918 he was fortunate to escape injury. 'Oh, what times we are living in! Eleven people were killed within 300 yards of this house on Thursday night. And yet I go on living in London.'

He still walked a mile each morning before breakfast and when he began to take in interest in 'gramophoning' he had to rise early to attend the studios.

He was forced to console and encourage Rachel and his brother-in-law, Will, when their elder son joined the Royal Army Medical Corps in 1915.

I sympathise *most* deeply with you – he is a dear boy and like many others, ought never to have been called upon for this but he has done his *duty* to his country – he and you will always have that fact to console you . . . As it is we love him, respect him and honour him. These are no cheap words. His letters are *fine*; God bless him. I feel proud of him.

The young German to whom his uncle was very deeply attached was eventually posted to Palestine and he shared Rachel's anxieties.

'I have been thinking a lot about German,' he wrote on 25th November, 1917.

You must know I feel awfully anxious: have you heard from him lately? You might let me have a line. Allenby is not giving the Turks much rest in Palestine – we are all waiting to hear of the fall of Jerusalem. I suppose German is in that neighbourhood and I am sure doing his duty nobly; it is all very terrible to think of.'

Coming after a period when German had been wrestling with fears of a decline of creativity, it might have been expected that the War would halt his output completely. It certainly interposed a barrier between the romantic fictions of light opera and the era of the syncopated American musicals that were soon to usurp the stage. By temperament he was patriotic and had only a peripheral interest in politics though given to a forceful expression of uncomplicated opinions. He was now in his fifties. Where he felt that his talents could be used he had assisted with charity performances and answered requests for music that might inspire the public. But the War wrought no revolution in his musical language or style. The cessation of concerts and difficulties of travelling had enjoined a period of recuperation, and intermittently he worked on an orchestral piece that showed his technical powers undiminished, while at the same time showing no trace of the Armageddon through which the nation had passed.

CHAPTER NINE

The Hermit of Maida Vale

Two major compositions were given their first performance in the years after 1918, and then German abandoned original work almost completely. The onset of health problems came early to him. A severe attack of rheumatism in the summer of 1917 had driven him to a cure at Llandrindod Wells, one of his few absences from the capital. In the years which followed the War his letters to Rachel constantly allude to the weather, and he and his sisters posted regular bulletins on their fragile health to one another. Yet his immense industry had re-asserted itself. He completed the major orchestral work, *Theme and Six Diversions* on which he had been working. It was ready for performance at a Philharmonic Society Concert in March 1919.

The theme was original ('very original,' German used to say). It has a plainsong character and is different in character from his more typical mellifluous themes. It is said that the inspiration came from a suggestion made by Elgar as far back as 1905, when both composers were at the Norwich Festival, that German should write a tone poem based upon the story of King Canute, one of England's lesser known royal composers. Canute was reputed to have invented a melody as he was rowed across the Fens near Ely and became inspired by the distant chanting of the monks. Elgar certainly kept the idea in mind and in 1911 he again endeavoured to urge his colleague to composition referring to his music 'which you know I love', and adding, 'I wish you would write that 'Canute' for me. Why not for the Philharmonic?' At that time German was contemplating his *Nautical Rhapsody* and the idea, though it might have been considered to have a nautical aspect, hardly fitted into the scheme of things. If the monks of Ely provided the initial impression for the theme, the work as a whole is abstract and the diversions, which include a scherzo, gipsy dance and waltz do not suggest life in the cloisters in the age of St Dunstan. But the theme itself could well correspond with Elgar's vision of the Fens and the distant sounds of worship.

The dignified but rather elusive theme is given out forcibly by the brass and an extended version is played by woodwind and strings. It ends in a minor and grave march, but returns with elaborate rushing passages for the strings in counterpoint. A lighter scherzo movement leads into the *Gipsy Dance*, with many piquant woodwind solos. It is the romantic middle section of this diversion which touches the heights of German's genius for melody and suggests what a classic ballet score he might have written if times had been propitious. The slow movement for nine-part strings is a dreamy and restrained section, followed by the most masterly of waltzes. This is a full concert waltz, superior to any in his operas and more delicate than any from the Viennese composers. Indeed, if some mischievous conductor on April Fool's Day slipped it into the Second Act of *Arabella* it would pass as an example of Straussian wizardry to any who did not know the score, and be acclaimed as one of the high spots of the evening. The final diversion is announced by the brass and becomes a marching section over a *pizzicato* base and harp chords. The brass give the theme staccato and there is the air of the operatic finale about the impassioned conclusion, which must again cause one to regret that no inspiring serious libretto had ever been put in German's hands. We must be grateful for the work itself, but the thematic material is beautiful enough to sustain a more more extended composition.

It flows with an ease that belies its halting construction and the composer's melancholy doubts about the fading of his inspiration.

Soon afterwards he produced one of the most popular of his songs; the rollicking part song, *London Town*, to words by John Masefield, describing the yearnings of the Londoner for scenes close to those of German's own boyhood, 'the croft and hopyard, and hill and field and pond'. It was swiftly arranged as a solo and German himself made a version for male chorus which required a transposition at one moment into a key signature with seven flats.

For the 1922 Centenary celebrations of the Royal Academy of Music, he was invited to contribute another orchestral work, for he was at this time the most famous and certainly the most popular composer among its alumni. In April 1921 he went to a performance of *Othello* at the Court Theatre and his imagination returned to the Shakespearean music he had written in the 1890s. His reply to Mackenzie's invitation is dated October 6th, 1921,

> In reply to your kind letter I write to say it is my present intention to call the work I hope to do for the R.A.M. Centenary; English Rhapsody: an orchestral impression on the Willow Song from *Othello*. You know the old melody, 'a poor soul sat sighing' – I can hear you saying, 'A poor cat sat dying' – especially after what has happened.
>
> About a month ago the mother of two live kittens was gassed and

apparently dead, the vet sent for etc. Everything all right now, however.

I propose to do as a (b) to the Willow Song, the Harvest Dance from *The Seasons* just to show the audience what the old man did when he was young!

The work was dedicated to Mackenzie. The mood is elegaic and there are no lively dance rhythms as in the diversions.

In his own notes for a gramophone catalogue German wrote:

This work, written for last year's R.A.M. Centenary, is founded on the traditional melody, *A Poor Soul Sat Sighing*, sung by Desdemona in

Othello. As Mr German has treated it, it becomes symphonic and careful listeners will note the recurrence and development of parts of the melody, and in the end a complete reprise with counterpoint for the celli and bassoon. It is moulded in more serious vein than is usual with this composer.

In fact, although in its harmonies and key structure, *The Willow Song* represents German's furthest step into the shallows of the sea of modernism its mood harks back to the great dramatic Interlude in *Romeo and Juliet*. As the soft string *pizzicato* leads into the final chords we expect the curtain to rise on Desdemona's chamber and the moods recalled by the music to reach their climax in the stage passions. Although *The Willow Song* comes in Act IV of *Othello*, German sets the atmosphere as Desdemona rests between that scene and the final catastrophe.. The metamorphosis of the two main themes of the long melody have been turned into memories of Othello, proud and splendid, and of the moments of love that have dwindled into apprehensive fears.

The counterpoints to which German referred are given to woodwind and soft brass, interpositions that do not allow the melody to rest, reflecting Desdemona's words: 'That song to-night, will not go from my mind'. It was fitting that the spirit of Shakespeare, the impulse of more ardent days should have accompanied him in this reflective work that suggests in its very nature renunciation and the closing of a career. It has the atmosphere of a final work, although German had not consciously decided against writing again.

The Willow Song was the prelude to catastrophe in more senses than one.

The Centenary concert is an impressive landmark in the history of mismanagement. Between 500-700 extra tickets had been issued beyond the actual capacity of Queen's Hall. As a result the packed building was besieged by angry crowds and the scene before the arrival of King George V and the Royal Party had an alarming resemblance to the fall of the Bastille. Percy Scholes, the musicologist and critic related how he fought his way in and remarked: 'They have classes in stage fencing at the Academy. They must start a course of concert room boxing and the critics shall attend it. Ernest Newman certainly relished the opportunity to 'dip his pen in acid ink'.

Until Tuesday I have never suspected the Royal Academy of Music of Music of having a sense of humour, but on that evening I, in common with other people had to admit that I had done it an injustice. It was a really brilliant idea on the Academy's part to issue for its orchestral concert at Queen's Hall many more tickets than there are seats in the Hall – nothing funnier has been seen for a long time than crowds of disappointed people, among them several musical critics – being turned away from the doors. I cannot imagine a more humorous way of wasting a busy man's evening. So highly appreciated was the joke that its perpetrators kept it up the next day also, but after this second experience of academic humour, my time being limited, I could not try again on Thursday. I was sorry not to hear any of these concerts but I shall hope for better luck at the next centenary of the Royal Academy.

Worse than this, various changes had been made to the programme since it was first planned which had reduced its length without anyone noting the fact. German was most scrupulous in informing concert promoters of the exact timing of his work. He arrived at the artists' entrance where many of his former fellow students had gathered to hail him. It was five-and-twenty minutes to ten, so he had ten minutes to spare before going to the rostrum. He was told that he was too late, for the programme had expired musically long before the anticipated time and, after some piano solos by Myra Hess despairingly filled the void, the Royal Party had departed. Both King George V and Queen Mary noted in their Diaries they returned at 9.45 although the Concert had been scheduled to finish at 10.00. It might be added that they had had a very full programme with the wedding of Lord

Louis Mounbatten to Miss Edwina Ashley earlier in the day. George V in any case was not a man to wait around. Sir Henry Wood, on one occasion when the mezzo soprano Conchita Supervia had interpolated some encores, had to rush the orchestra through the 'Rackowsky March' at a speed it had never been taken before as the King had sent a message to say he did not intend to spend a minute longer at the concert over the appointed hour.

The Willow Song was included in the next evening's programme, but the same scrimmage for places ensued. 'At the advertised time of starting,' said the Morning Post, 'a great number of ticket holders were lined up outside the closed doors of Queen's Hall.'

When German sent in his account for expenses he added with some magnanimity, 'What a triumph the Centenary has been!' though one might divine a certain irony in the postcript. 'Would you be so kind as to send me a souvenir or two: I was unable to get one.'

★　★　★

His decision to cease major composition was not a conscious one, nor did he accept it readily.

In 1927 writing to his sisters about the illness of his friend Scott he said how much he envied 'The Poet' his facile pen.

> I wish mine were nowadays. What I say is: if you can't do anything as good as or even better than what you have already done, than don't do it. It sounds a bit Irishified or something funny. Ah well, it is not from the want of trying and don't think I am happy in my silence. All I am happy in is that what I have done seems to live and give pleasure and after all that is something. For 35 or 40 years I kept my 'nose to the grindstone' It is interesting, though a little sad to read the enclosed letter written when I was at work on *The Tempter* (1893) then in the flush of energy, youth and ambition.

The *Theme* and *The Willow Song* are works of such skill and maturity that we must regret that German had 'drowned his book' and no longer sought to conjure up the masque and the pastoral scene in sound. We cannot doubt his own diagnosis that the struggles and the overwork of early years had taxed his energies, though in his conducting and his social life, and in his letters he seemed anything but fatigued. He was certainly hostile to any of the new experiments made in music, although he was rarely very specific about the composers or the schools which he detested.

Herman Finck liked to relate the story of the second loudspeaker which

German had fitted to his radio so that his housekeeper could listen to broadcasts in her own room. One evening she rushed in to him and said, 'Oh, Sir Edward, has your wireless gone wrong because mine has. It's making the most dreadful noises.' German was delighted to discover that she had been listening to Stravinsky's *Rite of Spring* and assured her that her ordeal was only temporary.

He did not enjoy all the works he had to examine for the Mendelssohn (Composition) scholarship.

'Today the Mendelssohn Scholarship has occupied my mind,' he wrote later in the 1920's. 'There was a full assembly and in the end the prize went to a boy called Sampson – he is terrifically modern and I think his work may be buried forthwith. I really can't see what we are coming to!!' He found many aspects of the post-war world uncongenial. 'Modernity is doing away with all nice feeling and quality does not seem to matter much nowadays . . . Tonight we are being invaded by airplanes and the noise upstairs is really terrible. Modernity again!'

In 1921 the lease on his Hall Road house came to an end and he moved to 5, Biddulph Road on western side of Maida Vale. He wrote to Rachel that he had 'a little tiny house in which to end my days. I hardly know if I have done right but something had to be done . . . from what I see in the papers the world seems to be growing steadily worse.' He greatly missed the restful and leafy glade he had created at Hall Road during his creative years. But the success of the *Diversions* seems to have improved his morale and one particularly happy event took place in 1921 to cheer him. He presided at the Savoy Orchestral Dinner, a re-union of members of the orchestra associated with the Gilbert and Sullivan operas. One, Ellis Roberts, had actually played in *The Sorcerer* as long ago as 1877. He enjoyed making the speech, and described the party as being 'like a large family reunion'. It was more congenial than his dinner with the Critics Circle:

> To have made a speech with Ernest Newman gazing at me from the opposite table – this was my experience on Friday night. To think I would have lived to do such a thing! It was at a Dinner given by the Critics' Circle (of which E.N. is a member – fearfully exclusive lot). Pinero responded for the drama and I for music. E.N. is quite simple and charming to meet – told me there was little culture in Brum [where Newman had worked before joining *The Sunday Times*] etc. – but Oh! his pen! he will doubtless ever dip it in acid ink!

To some extent he seemed to live his life in separate compartments and the characters who frequented one had little relationship with those in another.

As he had more time and leisure, his letter-writing to his sisters became a regular task and letters went forth from Biddulph Road every few days. It is certain that a good deal of financial help went also which enabled them to maintain more comfortable standards than would otherwise have been possible.

There was no income to be gained from the Whitchurch Wine and Spirits Firm. It must be doubted whether his father, John David, was a good man of business. Certainly between the time of his death and that of his wife, Betsy, German had been forced to lend £500 or more to help the firm to continue. The money could not be repaid and in exchange he accepted The Laurels although this brought no profit as his brother Clifford was permitted to lease it at a very low rent. When Clifford, who played some part in the management of the firm died, his will and the ledgers, examined by German's friends in London, revealed that others had appropriated much of the capital. There were dependents apart from the immediate family who had some stake in the trade and German was forced to see that they did not go unpaid. It was his music and the income from it which had to be utilised to compensate for the collapse of the firm.

Clifford figures infrequently in the family correspondence. To the end of their days, Rachel and Mabel recalled the happy times they had enjoyed with 'Dear Jim', but the younger brother remains a shadowy figure. He stayed outside the constant circulation of letters on music, health and London life which passed between the other three. His wife, Edith, died young and he had no family, and he appears to have been affected by melancholy as a result. As a child he had been a first prize winner in the proclamations of school results which Mr Furber placed in the local press and may well have found it hard to live in the shade of his brother's fame. Yet his early death in 1922 left German inexplicably ill and confined to his room for weeks. He appears to have had some kind of nervous breakdown and, given his temperament, this may well have been the result of self-reproach at his failure to look after and protect his younger brother from melancholia. He certainly gave his remaining years to ensuring the financial security and, so far as he could, the happiness of his sisters.

Rachel had married Will Jones, chemist, and had two sons, German and Arthur. The nephew German had composing gifts, and married Dorothy, daughter of a well-known Birmingham Singing Teacher, Madame Minidew. The uncle was fond of his namesake and wife, and enjoyed their visits. There is an amusing cartoon drawn by Dorothy, which shows the women of the family genuflecting before him in thankfulness for his seasonal gifts. But the younger German found it hard to settle to any steady routine of work, and the family letters indicate that he tried several avenues without any great achievement.

'Hope German is being given a fair chance,' wrote his Uncle in 1924. 'If so I am sure he will make good. As dear old Dad used to say: 'That your strength may be equal to the day – or was it the other way round?' Arthur, Rachel's second son, had a larger share of his uncle's business instincts and had a career in banking. In later years he was very zealous in supervising the work of the Performing Rights Society and the publishers, and kept the family records with care.

Mabel had married the minister at the Congregational Church at Dodington, the Reverend Edwin Tongue, and moved with him from one place of ministry to another. One of her sons had died in childhood but she had two other children. Her other son, Eric, became a colonial official in East Africa. Her daughter, Ruth, though she was later to prove a very self-willed and intractable daughter had inherited a measure of the family talent, became a school teacher in Harrow, produced plays with young people (attracting the patronage of German and Sir Ralph Richardson), wrote and illustrated books and eventually made some collections of west country folk songs. Her uncle had quite an admiration for her sharp intellect: 'Tomorrow Ruth comes to have lunch with me,' (he wrote June 22, 1923), 'and we go to [Drinkwater's play] *Oliver Cromwell* afterwards. I think it may be fairly prosaic but certainly high class and with two such brains as Ruth's and mine we shall no doubt enjoy it!' The gift of a clock from Edwin and Mabel produced a letter in his best Whitchurch vein:

My dear Edwin,

I am getting anxious about the anatomy of my new clock! Will you kindly ask the vendors how often it requires winding – whether once a year, twice a year, once a month, once a week or what! I have tried to make some impression on it during the four days I have had it but it refused to budge a notch. In the meantime it goes on ticking and chiming placidly and beautifully. It is a great success and quite a companion, but there must come a time when it requires *winding*! I have decided not touch it again for a week and I'll see what happens. All this is, of course, only my fun, yet it is strange that it won't take the key even for a single notch.

The Barometer baromets perfectly and the Thermometer thermometed 67 in the shade today.

Yours with love to all
EG

For the Christmas of 1924, German wrote another of his odes:

> We meet again to eat again
> And let the bottle pass.
> We'll all forgive each other
> If we take another glass.

The old Nannie of The Vaults and Laurels days was still alive:

> To Nannie of the eighties,
> Born in eighteen forty-four,
> We give congratulations
> And our love for evermore.

All the members of the family were toasted including the dog:

> The dog that boasts his blood of blue
> And likes to bark and shout it
> Is sometimes just a nuisance
> But we'll say no more about it.

He kept his sisters informed of his conducting engagements and in the early 1920s these were numerous. *The Theme and Six Diversions* were given many performances. Of one he wrote, 'I was recalled three times and the orchestra had to stand up. In the parlance of Arthur's young friend I was "frightfully bucked".' Rachel had suggested that he should seek a more colourful title for the work, but he found alternative suggestions too wordy. 'Besides it is all published now.' In April 1923 he conducted a concert of his works including the *Theme*, *The Willow Song* and *Winter* from *The Seasons* at Bournemouth.

Gramophone and broadcasting revolutionised the world of music, especially in the dissemination of pieces that had a popular appeal. German had taken an early interest in the first. In 1917 he had written to Rachel, 'I still go gramophoning. I have a session on Friday next and shall have to be up by 6.45 – cold work these mornings.' His music was well suited to the tastes for which both new industries catered. In time almost every middle–class musical family in the land would have its record of the *Henry VIII* Dances. When broadcasting began in 1922, he inspected the announcements keenly each week, to see if his name were present. More than that he listened to every performance he could on his headphones and he and Rachel exchanged their views about its merits.

'By the way I do *not* conduct for the wireless people but no one may see what it may develop into,' he wrote in March 1923. 'At present they have but an inadequate orchestra. They seem to do a great deal of my stuff.' In July, 1924, he wrote, 'I am told there is an "Hour with German" at Newcastle soon, and that the programme is 'unhackneyed' – but perhaps you may not be able to be switched on to it.' One of the unexpected fruits of Radio was the easier opportunity to detect supposed borrowings from works which one had hitherto regarded as one's own. To Rachel, on 4th January, 1925, was this complaint.

> I should like to shake Eric Coates but I won't. When I meet him he says, 'I just love every note you have written.' and I believe he does – but – as you say – well! As to M.E. on the wireless I shall do nothing. Chappell's have taken their stand (wrongly as I think). All the same there can be no harm in your writing again requesting that it shall be done. It all helps in these revolutionary days . . .
>
> The so-called 'Solway' Symphony by McEwen is simply boredom. But the César Franck Symphony in D Minor and the same composer's Symphonic Variations are really beautiful things.

A fortnight later he continued, 'Yes I agree with you that Eric Coates is very, very naughty. I heard (wireless) the other night a Suite of his called *From the Countryside* – well, well, well! I'll say no more – simply *naughty boy!!*'This must have been the first time that German had heard *From the Countryside* but as early as 1916 *The Sunday Times* had made the cutting comment on its Promenade premiere, 'The work would have made a stronger impression but for its obvious flattery of Edward German and that the indebtedness should not be overlooked the management had unkindly included the *Henry VIII* Dances in the same programme.' If Coates was guilty of imitation it was a sincere form of flattery. He was always a most enthusiastic champion of German's music.

He himself conducted the *Theme and Diversions* in 1925, when part of the Three Choirs Festival was broadcast from Gloucester. After the rehearsal he wrote: 'I think it will go very well at Gloucester – Unfortunately it comes later in the programme and may therefore be cut out by the BBC by the words "Ten O'Clock Time Signal".' On the evening of the concert however, the timing did not cause problems 'I have heard from many people that the *Theme* came through beautifully. This doesn't lessen *your* word of judgement. The brass was a bit noisy, but it really is very difficult to get everything as it ought to be. Of this occasion the *Gloucester Journal* remarked, 'He received a tremendous ovation. The orchestra played with a keen sense of enjoyment which was shared by the audience.'

It was at this time he made the acquaintance of Joseph Lewis, orchestral conductor, and later Head of Music at the BBC's Birmingham studio. He was a vigorous supporter of German's orchestral music, and would visit him with scores to discuss points on interpretation. He soon became 'Faithful Joe' in the brother-sister correspondence.

Lewis first encountered German before the First World War, when the latter came to Birmingham to conduct the first perfomance there of the *Welsh Rhapsody*. 'My two most vivid impressions,' he wrote many years later,

> were the thrill of his music and his modest, almost frightened, demeanour after a brilliant triumph. Since that most unforgettable performance I suppose I have conducted the work some fifty or more times and the joy of it increases with the years. One performance stands out in my memory – at the famous Three Valleys Festival at Mountain Ash. I shall never forget it for the choir of over a thousand voices and about four times that number in the audience rose and sang the Men of Harlech theme with astonishing volume.

During the years, especially when Lewis was at Birmingham, he presented most of German's work. He gives an engaging glimpse of him in old age, when some lesser known work was to be performed and 'Faithful Joe' visited him at Biddulph Road to hear his views on interpretation.

> I would sit at the table with the score and he would sit beside me with his own original manuscript. He would then conduct an imaginery orchestra and give a running commentary on the various phases of the music. Whenever there were difficulties he would point with unerring finger to the exact spot in my score although he could not see a single note"

Both men suffered acutely from rheumatism and when their correspondence was not concerned with tempi and dynamics they would digress into strange remedies – from having a potato or nutmeg in the pocket, to a silken thread around the wrist..

German also approved strongly of the young conductor John Ansell. 'I missed the *Welsh Rhapsody* on Empire Day but Lella says it was finely played under John Ansell who is, by the way, of the best musical calibre, other conductors sometimes gave cause for concern. 'I wonder what D.G. (Dan Godfrey) will make of my things tonight,' he wrote in December. 'I did not 'phone him as it might have unsettled him – so let us hope for the best – but his *tempi* are very erratic.'

His sisters continued to help with efforts to have *Merrie England* broadcast, despite the reluctance of Chappell's, who may have felt that a professional performance would deter amateurs. In November German himself wrote to Willian Boosey:

So far as I can see you can do me a great service (incidentally Chappell also). Could you allow M.E. to be broadcast from 2 Savoy Hill? Hundreds and hundreds of people would hear it and it would I believe be the occasion for still further stimulating operatic and choral societies to do the work.'

Chappell's eventually gave permission. *Merrie England* was broadcast the following year on the eve of the composer's accolade.

Another compartment of his life was centred upon the ACM Club. It had been founded in 1909 and took its initials from Sir Alexander Mackenzie, Principal of the Royal Academy. German in his biographical notes described it an 'probably the smallest club in existence' for there were only four members: Mackenzie, German, Col. J. Mackenzie Rogan, CVO (Director of Music of the Coldstream Guards), and Herman Finck, conductor and composer. They had intended to meet on their respective birthdays for convivial musical discussion, but at times when they felt the need for a gathering, additional 'birthdays' would be invented. Several musicians endeavoured to gain admission to the group but the original membership was never enlarged.

They appropriated to themselves the following descriptions:

Mackenzie	–	The Sage of Bloomsbury
Rogan	–	The Doyen of the Guards
Finck	–	The Sprite of Drury Lane
German	–	The Hermit of Maida Vale

If further abbreviation were needed they became: 'Merry Mac', 'Regal Rogan' 'Fatted Finck' and 'Gentle German'. 'Gentle German' wrote the musical toast 'with acknowledgements to Henry VIII'.

Here's to the Merry Mac. Here's to the Merry Mac. Here's to the Merry Mac. And his Men.

The Toast of course derives from the *Henry VIII* Dances.

Mackenzie and German were very great friends. Mackenzie's music today receives even scanter recognition than German's but he was a prolific composer with several operas and oratorios to his credit. His opera, *Colomba*, had been visited by Mr Gladstone, who, in the interval had informed him in resonant tones that he was himself 'three parts Mackenzie'. At the conclusion of his Cantata, *Rose of Sharon*, at a Norwich Festival he had been pelted with rose petals by the admiring throng. His *Ode on the Golden Jubilee* in 1887 was written for performance at the Crystal Palace, and simultaneously in major cities throughout the dominions. For the Crystal Palace performance the conductor had electric buttons beside the score to detonate cannon in the grounds, though not all came in on cue. Like German he had served his apprenticeship in theatre orchestras and had played *Champagne Charlie* and other popular numbers as accompanist at the Strand Music Hall. He had appeared on stage in the bands required for Mozart's *Don Giovanni* and Verdi's *Ballo in Maschera* and like German he had written Incidental Music for Irving. A trombone blast which was intended to accompany Edgar's shooting of a bull in '*Ravenswood*', had produced unseemly mirth at the first performance. His training after the Royal Academy had, however, been more extensive than German's and he had studied in Germany, where as orchestral violinist he had learnt the works of the German masters. He recalled having played Liszt's 'Faust' Symphony from the proof sheets. After MacFarren's departure he had succeeded as Prinicpal of the Royal Academy, and it was during his time that the move from the premises in Tenterden Street to York Gate took place. He held office for thirty-six years, instituted many reforms, helped to form the Associated Board and also conducted Philharmonic Concerts, giving the first British performance of Tchaikovsky's 'Pathetique' Symphony. His friendship gave a strong ballast to German's more nervous and delicate temperament and the latter's admiration for him was unreserved.

Herman Finck was also a graduate of theatre orchestras and had actually played for German in *Richard III* at the age of sixteen. He was the son of a Dutch violinist and composer who had come to London and he himself conducted many musical entertainments at the Palace Theatre of Varieties and Drury Lane. He composed popular pieces of light music such as *In the Shadows* but must bear the blame for enhancing the deplorable recruiting song of the 1914-18 War. *On Sunday, I walk out with a Soldier*, with a very catchy melody.

Finck was a great raconteur and a jovial companion. One evening he invited German to the Savage Club, where he was made an honorary member for the occasion. The duo – 'Herman and German' entertained the members with their music, and the artist, George Stamp, who had a fine tenor voice sang some of the German songs.

'Regal Rogan' came from a military family and joined his first regiment as a drummer boy setting himself the challenge of learning every instrument in the military band. He became in time bandmaster of the Coldstream Guards and ultimately of the Brigade. During the First World War he had conducted the Band while under fire from the enemy. In uniform, he had the reputation of being the handsomest man in London.

Sometimes other guests were invited. On one occasion, Finck's birthday, the group was joined for lunch by E. V. Lucas, the writer, and Cedric Hardwicke ('An actor now appearing in The Apple Cart' as German explained to his sisters. In his forgiving way German had overlooked the castigations of Corno di Bassetto and *The Apple Cart* was one of his favourite plays.) On another occasion Anthony Hope, the novelist, was a guest when they lunched at the Garrick Club 'where portraits of all the great actors and actresses of our time and before adorn the walls', and he thought nostalgically of those whose appearances on stage had been heralded by his music. He greatly missed this element in post-war productions. In 1930 he wrote of Henry Ainley's *Hamlet*:

> As to *Hamlet* – well frankly I was disappointed – cold and somehow didn't smack of Shakespeare, except now and then. I missed music. No overture, no *Entractes* only a few fanfares on trumpets and drums etc. But, of course, those scratch performances are never – *can* never be properly rehearsed. Ainley as Hamlet was on the whole *fine* . . . for the rest they were out of it – especially Ophelia. Visions of Ellen Terry.

Quite separate from the ACM Group was a circle of friends which formed the very centre of his social existence. They were his constant companions on visits to the theatre, restaurants, and cricket matches at the Oval and Lords. Hardly a week went by without their visits to Biddulph Road, or German's visits to them. Sackville Evans has already been mentioned, Bert Thomas, a cartoonist, was a frequent visitor throughout the 1920s and sometimes called two or three times a week. F. W. Hagelman (Hagey) was another member of the group. Edward Ayton, a fellow enthusiast for both fishing and cricket was also a great theatregoer, and with one or other German visited most of the notable productions in the West End, including many of Shakespeare. Lella Davies, a pianist, who lived close by at 36 Biddulph Mansions was also a very close friend. Like many bachelors German did not like to lunch or dine alone. The figure '185' which appears frequently at lunch time in his diary, was the number of the Evans home in Maida Vale, and he would often dine with Bert or Hagey at Frascati's, the

Café Royal, Simpson's in the Strand or (before cricket matches) at Jack Straw's Castle in Hampstead. They made visits to the Empire Exhibition at Wembley, the Royal Tournaments, the Zoo, Whipsnade, and even the Ideal Home Exhibition. These were not friends in the public eye, and, at this distance of time it is not easy to sense the basis of camaraderie. They all certainly visited German during his illnesses and kept up his morale when the afflictions of blindness threatened. Sackville Evans was married, and indeed German was a generous godfather to members of his family. There are references to meeting Bert and family on occasions. Ayton was married, though in later years he went to live in the Channel Islands, while his wife continued to live at Cheltenham. Many references to entertaining the 'D's and 'E's in his papers refer to the Davies and Evans entourages. The impression is given that in the 1920s German enjoyed a rather 'undergraduate' existence as far as health allowed, convivial, eventful and relatively carefree, something that his over-strained ambitions and limited means had precluded in his years at the Academy.

A certain affectionate flamboyance prevailed reflected in the long and colourful letters Ayton sent during German's final illness:

> I listened in to the commentary of the All India – England match at Lords, which was unfortunately broken into by the weather, and apart from the weather, thoroughly enjoyed it – I wonder if you ventured so far and had your favourite seat in your favourite corner on the pub balcony. I thought of you there and I thought of lots more of which the name 'Lord's' stirred the store of rich memories . . . Turn to Cricket when you have the blues or feel that things are wrong. You have then visions of green swards, white flannels, the bright sun overhead, the staid umpires (Farrant and West), the black scoring board opposite which seems to be endowed with life and get into motion the moment a batsman hits a ball for a single or boundary. These things, and the reigning peace overall will clear away the cobwebs, clog and cloud and leave in their place the serenity of a new dawn.

It was unfortunately not an intellectual world and not one to inspire new creative efforts. With Bert he exchanged aphorisms and cures for the world's ills, but there was no forward search for ideas. The circle was a happy re-creation of more youthful friendships and days of shared merriment at Whitchurch. He travelled frequently to conduct but always seems to have returned to London as quickly as possible. That he had overworked in earlier days is evident and he had earned the right to relax.

But it is significant that serious work on transcription and arrangements began more earnestly when the illness of 1927 brought home all too cruelly the quick passing of time.

One task he did begin was his Second Selection from *Merrie England*. 'I have little musical news.' he told Rachel in January 1927. 'The 2nd Selection proceeds.' Later in the year he wrote, 'The Second Selection from *Merrie England* is soon out and should gradually become well known but these things take time. I am now at work on the military band arrangements. It is an awful job with instruments in about six different keys but wait until you hear it on a M.B. – I think it will be a little bit of "all right".' Then came the news: 'I tried out the 2nd Selection, M.E. with the Coldstream and it came out splendidly, and yet it has not been performed although a special set of parts was sent to the conductor. Nor have I heard a single performance by orchestras: Well, I suppose we must have patience. The fact is the world is *overstacked* and *bursting* with compositions and it is almost a physical impossibility to get through.'

There are not many light operas which could sustain two distinct selections of popular melodies. German sometimes joked that he would like to make a Third Selection, so that he could include *The Sun in the Heavens is High* which had never attracted notice, and needed some consolation. The military band selection was arranged in part by Dan Godfrey, Junior, who had done many such selections from his works. 'Yes, the military band arrangement was half Godfrey and half German,' he told Rachel. 'But I decided I would keep my name out. Sullivan would not have appeared to have had time to touch M.B. arrangements.'

During the 1920s, there were still 'Edward German Concerts' given at Bournemouth, Eastbourne and elsewhere. It would be tedious to describe all these, but some deserve mention. In March 1927 he conducted at Manchester and described the concert to Mab:

> Well. I had a most 'marvellous do' at Manchester. The reception was – well – extraordinary! The Manchesters (sic) love melody. I enclose a notice from *the* highbrow *Manchester Guardian*. It is really very nice but, of course, he doesn't stoop to describe the scene at the end. Three of the Cox family (bringing with them early photos of dear Mother) – appeared in the artists' room. Pleased to see them. Think *male* Cox was a son of Uncle Joseph – the other two were mother and daughter, cousins of mother's uncle's sister – or something like that. Anyway, they were all very nice.

Later that year he was invited to Aberystwyth. The programme included the Coronation March, *Hamlet* and, of course, the *Welsh Rhapsody*. The young soprano, Elsie Suddaby sang *It Was a Lover and His Lass, The Dew upon the Lily* and *In Summer Time*. Of the *Rhapsody*, he assured Rachel, 'You need have no fear about the first movement – whenever I have heard it played under different conductors it has been something approaching a jig!! No I will see to that: it must be dignified. The concert was an enormous success.

> I had a great time at Aber. The Welsh enthusiasm was tremendous over *Hamlet* and the *Welsh Rhapsody* and they would not let me go over the latter; and as to the second part of the performance (Beethoven's Mass in D) to which I sat in the stalls and listened. I never heard such magnificent soprano singing in my life. There is no getting away from it – the Welsh voices are unique – fresh, silvery, true and telling. As you know I'm an 'orchestral' rather than a 'choral' man, but I take off my hat to the choral singing I heard on Tuesday night.

In the autumn of the same year he conducted *Tom Jones* at Bournemouth.

> Godfrey writes that he has put down the Symphony in A minor for concert in January. He says he hardly likes to ask me to conduct it so soon after *Tom* but that, if I would, he would be delighted and so would everybody else – he assures me in a second letter that I cannot go too often – but my dear Dick – I think I *can*. That is strongly my present feeling.

In the same year 1927, he engaged a new housekeeper.

> I have just seen my proposed new housekeeper. She is a huge creature from Sussex – 51 years of age – has been married twice – both husbands dead – has one son who is musical – is a bit weak on her feet but not much – has a nice kindly face and has been described as 'homely and motherly' which the same I should say she is – I have an idea she will suit.

With his liking for nicknames, the new addition, Alice, became 'My Sussex Dumpling' but proved excellent in her role. 'She is as broad as she is long – that is nearing 6 ft – is an excellent cook and keeps the house as clean as a new pin.

It was fortunate that he had strengthened his domestic arrangements for problems of health multiplied as the years proceeded.

As we have seen in February, 1922, on the day after funeral of his brother Clifford he had a completely unexplained illness and took to his bed for some weeks. In September 1924 he had a severe attack of pleurisy.

He was very conscious of the passing years though he affected to make light of the matter. 'I have sometimes thought,' he wrote to Mab,

'since two years ago that I was getting old – this was when a kind-hearted Cockney sitting in a bus said to me (I was *standing*) 'Come on Dad, here's a seat for you!' But now I have really got it! See notice of Crystal Palace Concert: 'The wonderful old gentleman who bears the hallowed name of Edward German'. I suppose he thought I was about 88. No matter, I shall survive, but it sounds really funny to me.

In December 1925, he had sciatica in his left leg, and also found he preferred a lower rostrum for conducting.

As I get older I find I cannot stand heights. For *Tom Jones* I had the rostrum on a level with the platform and was perfectly happy. If I come to Birmingham for that long postponed concert I shall want the same. Honestly, I would like to blot the whole thing out – they keep me hanging on so – I wrote Lewis some time ago asking to be let off but he 'kept me to it'. I shall certainly not go unless I have a low rostrum.

The problems were more serious than he intimated to his sisters. When he was called upon for jury service early in 1925 he requested the help of his doctors to excuse him and a Harley Street specialist wrote to confirm that he was suffering from myocardial degeneration with complications which would 'contra-indicate' jury duty.

Early in1926 he had rheumatic gout in his right leg. 'I really don't know when I shall be able to get out and do a bit of walking . . . it is of course very painful.' For a time he found his right leg useless and this affected his conducting. He conducted at Bournemouth in 1926 and wrote, "the concerts were splendid, but it was a strain on me – bronchitis – never had it before – beastly thing!!" The gout persisted through January 1927. 'I am still in the house with gout – *my* gout, my own special brew – robs me of powers of locomotion but I am better and, as I say, hoping to get out early next week.' He found the winter 'cruel and searching' and went to Jaeger's to purchase heavy woollen garments on Rachel's advice. By March he was fit again to conduct at the Manchester concert and to attend rehearsals.

He would have liked to conduct the Symphony in A Minor at

Bournemouth but that and other plans were dashed by a much more serious blow. On 11th November 1927, Sackville Evans wrote to Rachel:

Dear Mrs Jones,

I am very sorry to convey to you poor news of Jim.

Yesterday afternoon about six o'clock he suddenly became quite blind in his right eye. An eye specialist from Harley Street saw him this morning and ordered him to bed and keep quiet. He is not allowed to read, write or even talk for at least 2/3 weeks. This of course cuts into his engagement at Bournemouth on the 22-23rd. He almost feels like taking the risk of going but was strongly held back not only by the specialist and his doctor but also by his friends.

The left eye is in good condition and he is suffering no pain. It is most essential that he shall have perfect rest and lie placid. That is the only condition in which there may in time be some improvement in the right eye . . . His eyesight has been troubling him for some time past.

A month later after a period of rest in semi-darkness and despite further worries his spirits were equal to the event. He wrote to Rachel with the old use of nicknames. 'The right eye is a thing of the past. The left, however, has an astigmatism which 'the Bishop' [one of his specialists] possibly overlooked. Therefore I am getting new glasses. These will no doubt help me. Anyway I am glad I have been. It is a relief. *Now* my toast is instead of "All friends round the Wrekin" – "Here's to making the best of things!"

As the BBC and the recording companies spread his music more widely his fame in Whitchurch was correspondingly enhanced. When his cousin, Mrs Johnson, received a letter, silence would be ordained in the Grocery Stores, and there beneath the rooms where he had given the Sixpenny Concerts, the customers, mute among the tinned foods, would listen to the reading of the Epistle. As well as making private visits he conducted two performances, in 1924 and 1927, and one cannot close this chapter of his life without describing them, though they were not on the scale of concerts at the Crystal Palace and Queen's Hall. Whatever his private thoughts – and these as we shall see were sometimes restive, he played the role of local celebrity with the utmost generosity.

On St George's Day, 1924, the Whitchurch Choral Society celebrated its fiftieth anniversary and a choice fell inevitably and proudly on *Merrie England* with the composer in person to conduct. 'One of the works of the greatest living Whitchurchian,' as the Herald put it, 'a old member of the Society who took his share in its earlier activities and has since become one of the greatest of living musical Englishmen.' The Assembly Hall was crowded and so many applications for tickets were disappointed that the public were admitted to the final rehearsal and the Hall was filled for that also. The evening brought to the town one of its first experiences with traffic problems as people came in from the neighbouring villages and cars were ranged up the main thoroughfare 'from the Church to Mr Arrowsmith's Shop'. The reception was tremendous, and the tale of the evening performance lost nothing in the *Herald's* lapidary style. German was cheered as he entered the hall, his 'magic wand' directed the orchestra, largely his own selection of instrumentalists, in the *Henry VIII* Dances which were also included, and subsequently in the Opera. The harpist, Charles Collier, was reported as being 'the finest in the world'. After the final chorus, the composer was given a standing ovation.

The Rev J.W. Vincent, Vicar of Marbury and Secretary of the Society, promptly invited him again for the following year, but German declined, though he did give Vincent some help in finding soloists for *A Tale of Old Japan*. 'I must regret to say my word "farewell" meant "farewell". It really is with regret for, as you know, I have only the warmest feelings for the choral society and I appreciate more than I can say your invitation to come yet once again.' The Rev. Vincent, however, was not to be put off lightly. He pleaded that the Choral Society had been suffering competition from other musical organisations. After the 1926 Concert, although Stanford's *Revenge* had been musically a great success, he lamented that the competition of a Point-to-Point Meeting, and a Masonic Lodge gathering had depleted the audience. 'The result being many of the best seats were vacant and we lost money.' He held up the new 'Palladium' building as an inducement, as it was more commodious and had better acoustics than the Town Hall. 'We can honestly say we are continually being told what a treat it would be to hear one of your works in it.'

German again put pen to paper:

Dear Mr Vincent,

This is perhaps the most difficult letter I have ever had to write for it is to say that, after very careful thought and deliberation I have come to the conclusion that I cannot break my word as to my farewell visit – this alas! took place two years ago and was publicly announced and published.

Apart from this, however, I do not feel I could stand the strain of another performance. As you know, I am getting old – I shall soon be sixty five! and, of late, I have been conducting very little.

Now will you please tell every member of the society, with my affection, of my regret – and at the same time of my great appreciation.
Believe me to be,
    Yours very sincerely,
    Edward German

Needless to say Vincent won, and the announcements went forth that Mr Edward German would be conducting the concert version of *Tom Jones* in 1927. To Rachel he wrote:

I agree with you that Vincent of Whitchurch is a 'terror'! I simply could not escape another visit but this will be *the* final, for apart from the immense worry it gives me to get my principals together and rehearse them, I have to get them at reduced fees and pay for their accommodation at the Victoria Hotel.

  It is all very well
  For Vincent and Lee [Chairman of the Society]
  But what about, what about
  What about me!

No, this really will be the Finale

The seats of the Palladium were quickly sold and again the rehearsal took place before a full audience. Cars came from the adjoining counties, and as far away as the Potteries. The *Herald* again recorded the magnificence of the occasion and the ovations.

'When at length he gained a hearing' German thanked the principals (who included Roy Henderson as *Tom*) the chorus and orchestra. 'All has been everything I could have desired,' he said, 'and I thank you, ladies and gentlemen, for your kind reception of the work and me.' He wished success for the Society 'in spite of other attractions that have come to the town.' [These included 'Eve's Leaves, The Lure of the East', also announced for the following week on the Palladium boards.] With in inward smile, no doubt, he referred to the longsuffering patience of the Rev. Vincent 'which was so important a factor in making the evening possible.

Despite his parting words, 'I won't say that horrible word "Goodbye" – I will simply say 'from the bottom of my heart "Fare you well",' This was not to be his last visit, though he did not conduct again. In 1931 he visited the Society. Whatever his misgivings, he confided them only to Rachel.

Am so glad you and Arthur are coming to Whitchurch and you will sit with me. It will no doubt be a big event – *the* social event of the season! So we shall have to dress like dukes and duchesses. I would fain be out of it all. You are well out of staying with friends: it is never satisfactory.

As to the performance, I don't know anything – not even the conductor's name.

The 'orchestra' will no doubt be heart-rending but we must keep smiling – that is the great thing. We must let them think it is all just first class. Heaven only knows – perhaps it *may* be!

Lest anyone should think that this implied anything other than deep affection for his native town, let us read further, 'Coming from the gay to the grave I would rather leave the choice of my little plot to you, as you will fix it up and let me know particulars as to cost etc. Mr Lee is a kind man and I am sure he will help you.'

He had already decided that his ashes should rest at Whitchurch.

CHAPTER TEN

The Accolade and After

The sudden affliction to his sight was mitigated by a major step in public recognition and in 1928 the New Year opened with the announcement of his knighthood. A few months earlier the *Musical Times* had made a strong demand for this.

> We doubt if any other English composer has so constantly captured both general and musical public. How many of Sullivan's orchestral works are heard today? Is there one to rank with the *Welsh Rhapsody*, *The Seasons* and *Theme with Six Diversions*? When we reflect on the destinations of some knighthoods in recent years (not musical ones we hasten to add) and see German still passed over, we have difficulty in maintaining a proper attitude of respect towards the fountain of honour. Is there nobody in or near the cabinet with knowledge of English musical life?

Before Christmas 1927 he had been able to pass on to Dick the news that the honour would be granted. 'Dearest J,' she wrote,

> Have just received Lella's note with the great news. You may depend on all of us keeping it a dead *secret*. You have suffered a great loss with your eye but this is a great compensation and will make all our Xmas's very happy ones!
>
> It could not have happened at a better time because any social obligations can so easily be got out of on account of your disability and you can just go on quietly as before. The whole country will be rejoiced – especially Chappell & Co.!
>
> Rest assured dear Jim, nothing will leak out in this quarter – we can all keep a secret.

Many congratulations flowed in from all parts of the country. Naturally one of the first came from Whitchurch.

The *Herald* stated that

> it was with feeling of supreme satisfaction that the people of
> Whitchurch learnt on Monday morning that a knighthood had been
> conferred upon Mr Edward German in the New Year Honours List
> and the message of congratulations despatched by the Chairman of the
> Urban District Council expressed the sincere sentiments of every one
> of the inhabitants.

So too did the girls of Edward German House at the Whitchurch High
School.

The magazine of the National Union of Organists congratulated those in
high places who had discovered – albeit somewhat tardily – the merits of
Edward German. 'His music has attained outstanding popularity,' it
declared. 'When we hear so much about the low standard of public taste,
which I do not believe to be so universal as is assumed, it is well to
remember that this appreciation has not been won by 'playing to the
gallery'. All German's work is distinguished by fine taste and his lighter
music is wrought with as much care as the more serious.'

Ethel Boyce wrote affectionately from Chertsey:

> It was a real pleasure to open my paper this morning! I am as glad as
> if it had been something nice for myself. You have for many years
> deserved whatever honour England could give you as a composer and
> now at last, the honour is yours. It is delightful to think (and of this I
> am always sure!) that your music will continue long after you and I
> have gone. It is so musical, so direct and so *truly* English!

To Sir Edward German (I like to write it)

H. W. Richardson of the Academy condensed his feelings into a couple of
bars:

Mr Byrne, timpanist of the Bournemouth Symphony Orchestra for
twenty-eight years wrote in to record the great pleasure he had always
enjoyed in playing German's music. An old student friend sent a

photograph of 'The Bayreuth Pilgrims of 1886'*, A fellow lodger from his early days in London in Bartholomew Villas congratulated 'Sir Edward German – unbowled, uncaught-not out'. His relative Arthur Whittingham began 'Arise Sir Edward. I was delighted to see your name in the Honours List. None of the others mattered after that . . . All *Whitchurch*, not to say the World will join in the chorus of congratulation'. Laurence Kellie, who had played Carol Cornay in the student tour of *The Rival Poets* and (rather more immediately successful in love than that character), had married immediately afterwards, also recalled student gatherings in the same lodgings.

German himself said, 'They still keep coming in and the number of lies I have told to get out of invitations is appalling.'

He received the accolade almost on the eve of his 66th birthday on the 16th February 1928. On the 13th and 15th of the month he had conducted *Merrie England* for the BBC Studios. The immediate result of his new honour was a grand dinner given by the Music Club and the Royal Academy Music Club combined at which Mackenzie presided. Afterwards he wrote to Rachel who had been present with her sister. 'Yes, the occasion will want a bit of getting over but of course it *will* vanish in time: not, however, to you, Mab and me.' Three hundred guests joined in the testimony to what *The Star* called 'the white-haired modest genius, whose scholarly orchestration has been so familiar to us all for so many ears.' Sir Thomas Beecham should have replied to the toast 'British Music', but according to press reports 'left before the soup' (Consommé au fumet du tortue, Paillettes au Chester, Crème divine) and Dr McEwen had to take his place. The main toasts of the evening, however, were made by Mackenzie and Elgar. Although Mackenzie seems to have classed *Henry VIII* as one of German's light operas, 'the titles of which were as familiar in their mouths as their tunes were to their ears', he paid tribute to him as one of the Royal Academy's 'most distinguished sons'. Elgar's tribute was plain and sincere. *The Evening Standard* commented on his speech: 'A rare event – for few have heard Elgar save in the musical sense.'

'Everything that has come from his pen I have received with the greatest joy and pleasure,' said Elgar. 'I have the deepest appreciation for his genius.' He described German's works as 'the highest and most beautiful of the lighter forms of music.' He could not refrain from a swipe at those who devoted too much time to the resuscitation of folk songs: 'Folk songs are all very well,' he declared, 'for those who cannot invent their own tunes.'

* German recorded 1887 as the date. See page 48.

German's speech is worth quoting in full for the press extracts do not do it justice. He took great trouble over it and there are two versions: one written out in full which he learnt, and the second, to assist his failing eyesight, in red and green capitals heavily underlined giving the main headings to guide him through:

Chairman, Ladies and Gentlemen:

Thank you for your kind reception of me.

I also thank those kind friends who have just spoken so flatteringly of my work and of me. I fear they have spoken all too flatteringly – and yet – I know them both to be honourable men – men of integrity – therefore I accept their kind words and I offer them my sincere gratitude.

I am particularly gratified (this despite the fact that he has associated me with those questionable monarchs, Richard III and Henry VIII) and I rejoice to find in the chair tonight my dear old friend Sir Alexander Mackenzie. He has always been sympathetic. If the world went merrily and happily he was sympathetic. If it went all awry he was equally sympathetic and, as to advice and discussions on various subjects, well he never sent me empty away. I take it as a great compliment, a great honour, that he should occupy the chair tonight.

What shall I say – what can I say of that other great musician and friend – Sir Edward Elgar? His music has gone forth into all lands and has shed distinction there. His words tonight were gracious. My reply will be simplicity itself. I would ask Sir Edward to accept from my heart my sincere thanks for his sincere words. I would also offer him my congratulations on the honour recently conferred on him.*

You all know Sir Edward is a great composer: but few I imagine know him as the Good Samaritan. The little incident I am about to relate will show him in that light. It occurred at a Bournemouth Festival some four or five years ago. We were staying at the same hotel close to the Pavilion where the Festival was held. I had gone down with an acute attack of lumbago. I could scarcely walk, much less conduct.

Just before dinner on the night of the concert I was to conduct, Sir Edward suggested we should eat at the same table. With what appetite I had I said I would be delighted. We sat down and he startled me with, 'German, I am going to give you a pint of the best champagne they have in the hotel.' 'Champagne and lumbago!' I said, 'Yes,' was the

---

* Elgar had been awarded the k.c.v.o. in the same Honours List.

rejoinder. Sir Edward was loyal to the last, he took my score in his left
arm, and placed his right arm in my left and so we walked to the
Pavilion. After I had conducted my programme the lumbago seemed
to vanish as though by magic.

It is hardly necessary to add that the reason Sir Edward took my arm
was my lumbago!

When I look round this room and see so many distinguished and
brilliant people and so many of my old friends I feel I would like to
mention each individually. I must however say how very proud I feel
by the presence of the three principals of the three great institutions of
music in London. My friends, Dr John B McEwen, Sir Hugh Allan and
Sir Landon Ronald. It is difficult for me to adequately express my
appreciation.

I would not forget those directors of music and military bandmasters
who have done such splendid work in popularising good British music
all over the Kingdom and throughout the Empire. In this connection
there is one I would mention who has done so much probably more
than any other man, in raising the tone and status of military music in
this country. He is with us tonight – Colonel Mackenzie Rogan.

There is someone here, one with whom I have been associated in
days gone by in several productions – principally *Henry VIII* and
Romeo and Juliet. Who can ever forget his portrayal of Buckingham in
the first named play! By his presence tonight he bestows honour not
only on myself but I feel on the whole world of music: I refer to that
great actor and artist – Sir Johnston Forbes-Robertson.

Coming to myself, I fear the inevitable has happened! I have to make
a speech! – the kind of thing I have avoided for years. But for some
weeks past – from the time our friend Mr Alfred Kalisch extended to
me the kind invitation of the Music Club (here I would pause for a
moment to assure them that I fully appreciate the great honour they
have done me) I have been dimly concerned that tonight I should be
expected to say a few words.

Well to my mind music is more eloquent than words, I do not mean
by that that my own music is eloquent, but, whatever it may be, I feel it
would respond to this trust far more satisfactorily than my words.

Now that is all I am going to say about my own music.

As to modern music, ultra-modern music, super-ultra-modern
music, I have the greatest respect and love for most of it – that is – some
of it. The other some of it seems to me to be most fearfully and
wonderfully made – this comes under the category of the super-ultra-

modern! I sometimes wonder what music was meant to be. Is it not possible that it was meant to make us happy rather than miserable: to give us pleasure rather than pain.

But here comes the great gulf that divides light good music from light bad music.

I once heard it said that before a composer launched on a light work he should have to his credit four fugues – or was it five? Yes, I think it was five: five fugues and two completely developed and orchestrated symphonies. I quite agree, for then he would be fully equipped to enter the arena of light good music.

I am, of course, taking for granted that the five fugues were good ones!

Happily we have in this country and in the room tonight many delightful and distinguished composers of light good music. On the other hand – and I hasten to add *not* in this room – we have a veritable army of men and, alas , women too, who write light bad music. They are all insincere, they are all ill-equipped – indeed, they are not equipped at all and they poison the very atmosphere of healthy English music. If I had my way they would all be burnt at the stake – or another place equally fiery.

However, Nemesis comes along: and Time, immovable Time decides in the end what shall live and what shall die. I would put it in a more homely phrase and say: the good will swim and the bad will sink.

With that happy reflection I think we may perhaps leave the subject.

And now, Mr Chairman, Ladies and Gentlemen, it is only for me to again thank you from my heart for this splendid reception you have given in my honour.

I can assure you that as long as my life may last it will remain with me a most grateful memory.

His attack on modern music, and 'bad' light music was light-hearted in the context and was punctuated with laughter and applause. The press, however, scented a controversy and gave prominence to these remarks, occasioning a cool reception in some of the more fastidious journals.

The Evening News approached for a rare favour of an interview, declaring that he was certainly the mildest mannered man that had ever expressed a wish to obliterate fellow human beings. The interview is interesting as an example of rendering answers answerless:

'Who are some of the composers you think should be burnt at the stake?' asked the Evening News representative.

'The composers of light bad music,' said Sir Edward, with the gentlest of smiles.

'What is light bad music?' persisted the Evening News Representative.

'I can tell you what *good* light music is' said Sir Edward. 'I regard *Carmen* as the standard of good light music. *Carmen* is champagne, Bizet himself wrote nothing else nearly as good.'

'Is jazz what you mean by bad light music?'

'I would rather not discuss jazz. What I mean by bad light music,' said Sir Edward, 'is music written without scholarship, without knowledge, without feeling – written, I imagine, purely for money. I am afraid such music constitutes the bulk of what is listened to in England at the present time.'

Although he returned to the theme of 'bad' music from time to time, he kept his opinions on fellow composers, and musicians of the past to his private discussions or his letters to 'Dick'.

'Blow Delius and his meandering work!' he expostulated when one of his own works had had to be hurried in the remaining radio time. The idea of the Delius Festival did not inspire him either: 'Soon we shall be having a boom fashion in Delius. Tommy B[eecham] has spoken! Tommy B hath told us so! and Tommy B can do it! We shall be told to read into his music something that is not there. Personally, his music bores me, and it is so drawn out.' Typically, however, he soon corrected any jealous impulse: 'Poor Delius, I fear he bores me, but he is at least *serious*. What a joy to him to hear his works performed under such ideal conditions.' He was particularly delighted by a review of a concert of works by himself and Delius in the *Birmingham Mail* in which 'Fred comes off second best.'

There was an amusing occasion in 1929 when he failed to hear a 'Mackenzie Programme' on the wireless and relied on Dick to provide him with matter for his note of congratulation.

The fact is I told him I was much looking forward to listening in to it. Well I put on the earphones at eight o'clock and heard some pianoforte stuff going on. I looked again at the *Radio Times* and found this programme was 5 G.B.

I have heard all the items on his programme. I just want you to say which of them came out specially well. It would vex him if he thought I had *not* heard them and after all it is a simple 'way out' – for me.

His music to me is very refreshing and he need never know that I did not hear it tonight.

A few days later he wrote, 'I am getting a 5 G.B. set.'

When he heard that a popular song, '*The Fishermen of England*', had made its appearance, his note to Dick contained the comment, 'The Yeomen will be jealous!' Later they compared their impressions: 'I quite agree,' wrote German, 'The Fishermen of England. No class!!'

★ ★ ★

Of Elgar's Second Symphony he wrote, 'Yes, I agree that Elgar's Second Symphony is too diffuse. His First (in A♭) has a great theme. Now he is writing a Third. Wonderful man.' His verdict on one of the great symphonies of the century is odd and reminds us that even for those at the pinnacle of their profession, opportunities to hear works performed were rare enough to hinder true appreciation. Elgar's Third Symphony was of course not completed. Both composers suffered from the inability to absorb the new features of composition that had appeared in the post-war period. This is most probably the moment to dwell for a moment on their friendship and sympathy.

It is remarkable that England should have produced at the same time two musicians whose early lives had so many similarities. Both came from the Marcher regions and retained a lifelong love of the scenes of boyhood. Both derived inspiration from the reverberations of old Celtic culture that seemed to waft across the countryside. Both had their first experiences in music making in self-taught groups of family and friends. Their fathers were both organists in local churches, and their mothers women with artistic taste and discernment. Both began their careers with a few lessons on the violin and became members of local ensembles, though to German the opportunity for high academic training came at the age of eighteen and his career at one time appeared to progress more rapidly.

Their friendship began in 1905 when the two men, German aged forty-two and Elgar five years senior conducted at the Norwich Festival. German attended the first London performance of Elgar's First Symphony in 1908, and may well have felt from that moment that his own work in light opera was to be overshadowed by the astonishing growth in Elgar's confidence and depth of expression that took place in the first decade of the century. Both composed Marches for the 1911 Coronation Service and these were recorded together by Landon Ronald at the time of King George V's Silver Jubilee.

Even so it was not until 1914 that a closer association came about, and this

German having tea with Elgar

The A.C.M. Club. Col. J. Mackenzie, Mr Herman Finck, Edward German and Sir A.C. Mackenzie (seated)

was at Landon Ronald's instigation. He had been to visit Elgar at Severn House and wrote:

> A week ago I spent the afternoon with Elgar and the conversation turned on you. I feel that you ought to know what an ardent admirer you have in him. When I tell you that he loves your music as much as I do there is nothing more to be said. I am quite certain that it would have pleased you, could you have been behind the scenes and heard me play a lot of your stuff to him. He was walking about the room, and kept declaiming that it brought a lump into his throat.
>
> He is anxious to know you personally better, and as you are both friends of mine I want to be the means of bringing you together.

A lunch was arranged at the Savage Club, and a strong friendship developed. Both men had enjoyed a liking for fishing, cycling, walking. German did not share his colleague's interest in the turf, and was forced to call in the opinions of his friends when the Derby came round. But both enjoyed watching cricket.

Both, during the Great War, had contributed to *King Albert's Book*. German, as we have seen, composed his *Homage to Belgium* and Elgar submitted his *Carillon*. Both took part in the various charity concerts that took place as the War drew on.

Of course there were many differences. Elgar sometimes affected to despise the mechanics of composition and did not enjoy discussing it. German's letters are filled with comments on music and the information he provided for programme notes is not hesitant about calling attention to features of the composition and unusual effects in the orchestration. German was capable of writing to order music such as the score for *The Conquerer* that filled a need but scarcely aspired to immortality. There were limitations in his style which the creative impulse was unable to break, and repetitions in the mannerisms which he could not discard. Despite his adoption of the role of 'Hermit of Maida Vale' he was a clubbable companion who never knew genuine loneliness. Something of a fatalist and agnostic he never endured the spiritual searchings which led Elgar to compose *The Kingdom* but falter before *The Last Judgement*. Yet there was something in each which the other envied: an inner strength in Elgar, a sense of light hearted mockery and a soothing acceptance in German. It is said that when Lady Elgar died, German's was the only music to which the bereaved genius would listen.

In 1919, German was one of the privileged audience allowed to hear the rehearsal of Elgar's 'Cello Concert'. On the following day they met at a reception arranged by a gramophone company when the quality of serious recording was exhibited by some records made by the violinist, Jascha Heifetz.

The two men continued to meet at the Bournemouth Concerts. On one occasion, Elgar arrived towards the end of a concert, but hearing that a piece by German came at the end of the programme, paid the full cost of the ticket and went in.

In May 1924 German wrote to congratulate Elgar on his appointment as Master of the King's Musick and on Elgar's seventieth birthday there was a princely exchange of compliments:

> My dear Elgar,
>   I suppose 70 is an 'occasion' – ! and so I send you my greeting – also my thanks for the pleasure your music have given me these many years.
>   I need not say more.
>   Yours ever sincerely,
>   Edward German
> P.S. I listened in on your Birthday

> My dear German,
>   Thank you: but my music cannot possibly have given you one hundredth part of the joy your music has given me
>   Yours ever,
>   Edward Elgar

German refers to the Birthday Concert in his letters to Rachel: 'Yes, Elgar is a great man. I listened in on his Birthday (the 2nd) and was greatly impressed both with his wonderful idiom and his own wonderful vitality in conducting the whole of the long programme.' When German received his knighthood in 1928 Elgar telegraphed on the 2nd January, 'Warmest and loving congratulations from your affectionate friend'. Elgar also hoped to accompany German to the Palace for the Investiture as he too was to receive a further decoration, but unfortunately he was called for the 14th February and German for the 16th. Nevertheless he took over the responsibility for the insignia. 'Please accept it with my love: may you live many years to wear it.'

On 30th January 1930 Elgar conducted a concert of his own works at the Queen's Hall which included the Violin Concerto and the First Symphony.

German attended and managed to catch his friend for a few words at the close 'What wonderful music!' he exclaimed in an additional brief note of appreciation.

> 'It was nice to see you again if only for a few minutes. Do you remember the last time we met in the Queen's Hall Artists' Room? The rehearsal of your 'Cello Concerto to be produced the same night was held up by Coates' until nearly 1 o'clock. I have never quite forgiven him for that. However, all things find their level.
>
> Of course, don't reply to this: I only wanted to tell you of my appreciation.
> Yours as always,
> Edward German.

Elgar was deeply sympathetic to German's health problems and the loss of sight which afflicted his friend, and he did take the opportunity of sending the reply that German's note had expressly disclaimed:

> It was the greatest pleasure to see you on Thursday and I was very proud to know you were there. I wish you had a better account of your health to give me. I was greatly concerned to learn of your sight and, without knowledge of such things but with deep affection for you and your work, I cannot but hope I can see you very soon and that things will have improved. My love to you dear German.

In 1933 when Elgar was awarded the GCVO, German again wrote to congratulate him:

> My dear Elgar,
> I did not think you would care to be bothered with my congratulations on your new honour: but I saw our mutual friend Mackenzie and he said he had sent you a message. So I decided I would do likewise. Therefore my dear Elgar will you accept my heartfelt congratulations.
> That is all!
> Yours as ever,
> Edward German

Elgar's scribbled reply was sent two days later: 'All thanks for your very kind letter. I am very glad to hear – excuse P.C. – I am snowed under! My love to you.'

The most perfect letter which passed between them and not, I believe, hitherto recorded as it was buried deep in the German papers, was one sent by Elgar on June 6th, 1932, when the latter's elevation as Companion of Honour released correspondents from using his title: 'No my dear German. No. Not Sir Edward. *You* are the Sir Edward. My envelope should simply bear my name and the letters C.H. afterwards.'

For 1928 there were a few more public occasions. On 31st March he made his last public appearance as conductor at Bournemouth with the *Theme and Diversions*. 'The next event will be the Levée on June 1st. I shall appear in all my war paint – sword, buckler, cocked hat, shoes with silver buckles etc. Dear old Mac is going to present me and we may have a photo taken together afterwards.' He felt 'uncommonly well' for the occasion and both musicians donned their *School for Scandal* costumes as Mackenzie called them. His housekeeper, Alice, was ill in bed at the time, with suspected appendicitis, but her sister-in-law ('another of the Sussex Yeoman Stock') came to take charge of his domestic affairs, and the hot mustard baths with which he staved off the 'gout and rheum etc.'

On the 19th July he was invited to deputise for the Duke of Connaught at the Summer Prize giving ceremony of the Royal Academy. Philip Agnew, who introduced him, said:

> We feel it an honour that this duty falls to one of our own old students, to one who has gained a very high place too in the esteem and affection of his fellow musicians. His music has an universal appeal. It is ever popular and has given pleasure to countless people in every corner of *Merrie England* – that *Merrie England* that he knows so well how to portray – and among the long roll of students who have carried distinction there is none of whom the Academy is more proud and justifiably proud than Sir Edward German.

It was on this occasion that he recalled the old days in Tenterden Street, and his competition for the Lucas Medal, which was won by Stuart Machperson. His words of consolation to the runners-up were like the gentle effects in his music. The theme is common enough and one has heard it expressed in a hundred different ways from Speech Day platforms. German expresses the idea in words with the same deceptive simplicity he displayed in musical sounds. 'There is the human side to this prize giving – and by the human side I mean the students who have been disappointed.' No one could improve on that and no doubt his speech heartened many in their efforts.

The performance of his works brought some criticsms which Rachel took very much to heart and she may have threatened to use the press correspondence columns. Some comments on a concert performance of *Merrie England* under Henry Wood led to the following words to 'Dick'.

Don't be upset about the Manchester Guardian notice – I read it and thought – for that super-brained critic, it was excellent. [Neville Cardus, who was in fact a considerable admirer of German to whom he ascribed his first interest in music.] The M.G. and Birmingham Post both have super-brained critics – that is – musically. From the literary point of view they are of a very high order – especially the former.

It was from the M.G. I had this illuminating account of my distributing the awards at the RAM Prize Giving:

"A frail figure with white hair ascended the platform with a stick and when he spoke his voice was so weak that one could scarcely hear what he said of his old Academy Days." (That was all!)

I have become hardened to these disappointed wasps!

They live to criticise and find fault – nothing else.

As to the same singer taking both Jill and Queen Elizabeth, this was thoroughly thought out some twenty years ago, and has proved to be the *right thing*.

In numberless choral societies all over the country, the payment of an extra £10.10s for another singer (for a small part) would have prevented the aforesaid numberless choral societies from doing the work, for most of them have to think in guineas. Nothing will ever be *just* as it ought to be.

As a matter of fact it gives one singer a great chance for change of voice and dramatic sentiment but I fancy Henry J. W. put the pace on so much that he skittled all the poor principals. Anyway I have had a letter from him. He 'just loved directing the work' and he called it a 'bright and gay little masterpiece' . . . please return it as it might be useful for W.H.S[cott] for the appendix [of the projected biography] – perhaps not!

'Thanksgiving Hymn' the other night was abysmal.

Don't suppose the M.G. man has ever heard the Concert Version of *M.E.* with an adequate orchestra before. Nor do I think he has heard my big orchestral works.

Never mind. *Say nothing.* Time will prove all things, especially in music which has a language of its own and should not be subjected to mere words.

A year later Malcolm Sargent was innocently fending off a Mr Meynall Scott (Rachel of course)* who was seeking to establish an English light opera season with Edward German's works prominently included.

In November he conducted some of his part-songs at Windsor, at a concert given by the Gentlemen of St George's Chapel, at the invitation of Sir Walford Davies. The activity of the ever-present Walford Davies (German and Rachel referred to him as 'The Reverend') furnished material for one of his best letters:

My dearest Dick,

Well, Windsor is over. It was a great success and I have come to the conclusion that Walford is a truly remarkable man, he has a capacity for work that is almost terrifying. He had been 'at it' all day with conferences, correspondence, rehearsals, etc. They met me with the car at 4.00 and Lady W. drove us to The Cloisters.** What a house! Staircases corridors, recesses – some of the house was built in the time of Henry III and when I looked at it, it made me think and wonder.

We had no sooner arrived than Walford was off again to give the final touch to the boys and make final arrangements at the Hall which the same was in the Town not the Castle. Lady W. Miss Piggott (a cellist who had come to play Sonatas with him) and I had some tea and cakes. Walford returned and almost immediately started rehearsing with Miss Piggott.

At 5.45 the Choir came to the house for me to rehearse them (Walford, of course, at the piano). At 7.00 we had supper (a very good pheasant) after which we went up to dress. We arrived at the Hall about 8.10. Crowded out – and the concert could not commence till nearly 8.30.

The Dean, Chapter and Vergers were all there in their war-paint – and I was introduced as 'Our Guest' – but we said nothing – what was there to say!

Then W had been bustling about the whole time mounted the platform, spoke, played the piano and conducted. I was sitting with Lady W in the front row waiting for my turn. W made some nice remarks about me and I ascended and had a real fine reception.

* She contributed several variations on the name. See page 9.
** Lady Walford Davies after her husband's death became Mrs Margaret Lambart, wife of the Lower Master of Eton College, Julian Lambart. She was a great organiser and a generous and cheerful if somewhat daunting hostess to young masters, who will recognise the bemused sense of fatigue induced in German.

I conducted the 1st group of my part-songs – the choir (all picked voices) sang most sympathetically and beautifully. I felt quite touched.

Then I returned to my seat and the programme went on to the end of Part I.

Interval for talk and introductions (for which I don't care).

Then Part II. In due course I went on again and conducted a group of 3 Part-Songs. Then some charming nursery rhymes (humorous) by W. and we ended with a stirring performance of Rolling Down to Rio. 'Three Cheers' for EG from the choir, followed by ditto for Sir W. We both shook hands warmly in front of the audience and that was the end–

W had taken part in every blessed item in the programme besides making many little speeches, before each item (some of them very humorous) and besides playing the great G Minor Fugue of Bach on the *piano* at lightning speed. Yes, he is a bit of a superman!

When we returned to The Cloisters, we had some refreshments – He had some light fare with China tea, also some hot milk. I had the light fare and a glass of port. Lady W is really very nice and homely and I am bound to say so is he. Of course, he was called away to interview some people in the middle of his China tea!

This morning (he was up at 7) I met him in his study and he was writing. Two men from the choir came to see him, he had to answer a telephone call: at 9 o'clock I bade him farewell. Lady W drove me to the station and saw me into my carriage and I arrived (owing to fog) a good half hour late.

Today he is giving two lectures at the BBC!!! How does he do it?

My fondest love dear Dick,

    As always,

     Jim"

But German himself was hardly idle. The following week he conducted *Tom Jones* on the radio having celebrated Finck's birthday by a lunch at the Curzon Hotel where Robert Courtneidge and Edward Gwenn, the actor, were among the seven guests of the ACM Club.

On the 22nd of that month, as a Vice-President of the Gilbert and Sullivan Society he laid a wreath on the Sullivan Memorial in Temple Gardens. It was in the year of his own birth, 1862, that Sullivan had first achieved fame with his music for *The Tempest* and their careers had enjoyed many similarities. Both had written a considerable quantity of incidental music for the theatre and had achieved popular fame with their light operas. Both regretted the precedence given to these in the public mind over their serious compositions. German, however, did not take his comic opera work so lightly or feel it the encumbrance that it sometimes seemed to Sullivan. His tribute to his predecessor was generous in the extreme:

> The genius of Arthur Sullivan was unique . It may well be questioned if attributes of such rare quality and a versatility so outstanding will ever again be found in combination. Especially memorable was the eternal spring of melody of which he was the creator. Another gift was his almost uncanny sense of rhythm – it enabled him, when he willed, to turn into a swinging melody a lyric, the march or complex rhythm of which would have driven many another composer to despair. This unquestionably is one of the secrets connected with the living success of the great Gilbert and Sullivan series. The relationship may be summarised thus:

> Without Gilbert there would have been no 'Birth'.
> Without Sullivan there would have been no 'Life'.
> With both there can be no 'Death'

If his tribute to Sullivan was generous, his desire for Gilbert's immortality, after the saga of *Fallen Fairies*, was saintly. Many another musician on the slopes of Parnassus would have pushed the librettist over a convenient cliff, and used the occasion to compare Sullivan's tribulations with his own. A pot-pourri of gems by Sullivan and German, played on the radio, caused some family guess-work between the sisters. 'The enclosed letter will amuse you,' German wrote to Dick. 'She got wrong on that charming number – *Sing a Rhyme of Once Upon a Time*' – that is Arthur's. Mab got wrong on the overture (she said it was one of Sullivan's best) – that is *mine* not Arthur's. Well it all adds interest to the work.'

One other unrecorded composition must be mentioned which relates to a strange experience in the old Hotel Cecil. Certain promoters of music-hall acts invited William Boosey of Chappell's to a matinée at the Hotel and put on display a lady who was blindfolded, as testified by well known doctors, but could nevertheless play any piece of music put in front her. Boosey had brought with him an overture by a French composer, not well known in this country, and the pianist performed it perfectly. On the next occasion Boosey asked German if he would accompany him and bring some new music specially composed. German, with memories of his own conjuring days, was extremely sceptical but eventually wrote out a theme in the very smallest handwriting, which was hardly legible, and added some intricate harmonies.

The master of ceremonies said that the task would be difficult but the lady would do her best. The music was placed in front of her and, blindfolded, she mechanically but correctly produced every note. German was astonished, and unable to explain. It seems strange that such a gift should never have brought fame to its owner but he presumed that the performance would not have been suited to large audiences in theatres.

The loss of eyesight does not seem to have dimmed his enjoyment of life. As the list of engagements shows he was able to delight in his appearances as Sir Edward. He also resumed a testing programme of work as in his younger days though the checking of scores was now a slower and more painful process. There was no further original composition but he gave much thought to new arrangements and re-editions.

He agreed to the setting of the *Just So Songs* for chorus and orchestra and chose a younger musician, John West, to carry this out under his own supervision. Unfortunately West died and he had difficulty in finding a collaborator who reached his exacting standards. The project was eventually realised in 1947, when a version for chorus and orchestra was made by Dr Gordon Jacob. Victor Hely Hutchinson, who had been impressed by *The Rival Poets* and had orchestrated the overture and several of the numbers, was the keenest of the assistants and he began a selection of German's songs. A young Etonian, he had joined the musical staff of the BBC and was later to be its Director of Music. He was skilled in the arrangement of sequences of songs, and set verses by Lear and Lewis Carroll. He was in fact one of the very few who carried on German's particular style though in this genre only. Eric Coates and other followers were soon drawn towards the bolder and more modern idioms of the large-scale concert orchestras. The union between mastery of serious and light music which Sullivan and German had exemplified ended with the advent of mass radio listening and the projection of programmes at particular audiences. German would have been as mystified as, say Mozart, by the insidious progress of the much abused term: Classical Music.

For his part he began a heavy schedule of work once again and found the energy and powers of concentration to supervise arrangements of his music until the last months of his life.

★ ★ ★

The three projects that occupied him in the years following his knighthood were the publication of the 'Norwich' Symphony, the hesitant acquiescence in Scott's plea for a biography, and the defence of composer's rights under the Copyright Law.

As far back as 7th March 1925 ('was this not dear Mother's birthday?') he wrote to Rachel that he intended to have the score of his Symphony in A Minor published by Novello at his own expense. Work and illness had held up his plans but he continued preparations. In 1929 he told her, 'I am slowly getting on with the Second Symphony (the Norwich) in preparation for publication. It will, I fear take me a long time as I cannot use my sight too much. I am not altering a note but just improving marks of expression and phrasing.' To Novello he wrote:

> I note the cost of publishing the score and orchestral parts of my Norwich Symphony. Well, altho' it is more than I anticipated I am prepared to meet the payment. I will of course, read *all* the proofs (with my eye trouble it will naturally be slow work) Will not your own reader look them through before sending them on to me? I should greatly appreciate this. I must, however, abide by your custom.

'I fear it will be, if done, a very long and expensive matter,' he confided to Rachel. 'But I do feel it should be available for conductors and orchestras.' When the Symphony was published, *The Times*, in an article entitled 'A Forgotten Symphony' took great exception to the fact that the event received so little publicity.

> It seems a little odd that the full score of a Symphony written nearly forty years ago and long forgotten should arrive by post for review without explanation of any kind. This is what has lately happened with Edward German's Symphony No. 2 in A Minor, produced at the Norwich Festival on August 4th, 1893. Our first thought on receiving it was to scan the scheme for Promenade Concerts Season to see whether a revival was in prospect. But no: as a matter of fact the name of Edward German appears nowhere in the scheme: even the *Nell Gwyn* Dances and the *Welsh Rhapsody*, long the delight of promenaders, have vanished. Next, since the score is one of the most beautifully engraved productions of Messrs. Novello (price one guinea), we sought enlightenment in that firm's monthly publication, the *Musical Times*. In the column headed 'During the last month', we found the Symphony listed in a three-line advertisement between a new harvest anthem (price 1½d) and an organ piece. We searched the

editorial columns of July and August for some account of so important a publication but drew a blank. Evidently Messrs Novello are not interested in the Symphony and do not expect anyone else to be. Their columns are filled with a controversy over musical appreciation, they have no space for the appreciation of what is by far their most important production during many months. This suggests that there is still something seriously amiss, not in the music publisher's conduct of his business, about which Messrs Novello have nothing to learn, but in the attitude of English people (those for whom the publisher caters) towards English music. Their advance during the past forty years or so in the attitude to their own composers is constantly acclaimed and to some extent is real. Are not whole programmes in this year's Promenade Concerts devoted to Elgar, Delius, and Vaughan Williams? But nothing of orchestral music written before the dawn of the enlightened twentieth century is allowed to count. A conductor who would revive a nineteenth-century symphony does so at his peril and if a publisher is induced to engrave the score of one, well, the less said about it the better, even in his own advertisements.

The Times contrasted the apathy accorded to native composers with the ardent championship of Russian orchestral music undertaken by Belaiev, the Leipzig publishers, which established many popular works in the repertory. It acknowledged that many advances had been made in symphonic writing since 1893, but nevertheless considered the 'Norwich' an original work, free from direct influences of dominant composers of the time, Brahms, Dvorak and Tchaikovsky. 'Save for one episode in the Finale which does rather suggest that he composer had lately fallen in love with *Die Meistersinger* (and who had not at that date?) it is delightfully independent in style and fresh in invention. How long will the English people go on pretending that their music stopped with Purcell and began again with Elgar?'

Reprimanded by *The Times*, Novello did include late in the day a short piece on the 'Norwich' in their September issue. The *Musical Times* acknowledged that if it had come as a new work it would have had a run of performances. Indeed it considered that the symphony could well delight modern audiences sated with the impassioned outcries and the shoutings in romantic jargon that German's contemporaries had used the symphonic form to express. It talked of 'the calm and clear outlines' of the Symphony, 'the controlled emotional pace' and the steady development of themes 'under a quieter rein'. It concluded that a performance would 'conduce more to the greatest happiness of the greatest number than nine out of ten of the novelties of recent years have done.' German's own comment was, 'The austere and "touch me not" *Musical Times* is interesting re the symphony. On the whole I think it will do good.' Although German as a composer had always enjoyed affection he did not receive reverence, and irreverent comments did not escape him. 'Nasty old man Montgomery in the *Radio Times* ("What the other listener thinks") Never mind. It will all come right in the end. I agree that The Yeoman has been rather overdone. But he is a B.F. to say that of all I have written he cannot tell "'tother from which".'

Although it had not been included in the Promenade Concerts a performance was scheduled for 27th November at Queen's Hall. 'I expect I shall catch it from young modern students. Never mind.' On the 28th he wrote to Rachel. 'The performance of The Norwich . . . was so far as I can judge a success. I had to go the platform and bow. I hear the *Daily Mail* describes me as an old dotard helped on and off and altogether a kind of wreck. Well, we can't help what we look like.' (I would *like* to look like say – Sir Oliver Lodge on this occasion). Suggestions that he looked old and frail could usually be reckoned to inspire rumblings of displeasure. 'After all the *work* is the thing. *This* may live on when I have gone into smithereens but the critics might leave personalities out of it.' He continued to be irked for several days. 'The *Daily Mail* had evidently cut the part I wrote you about. *The Evening News*, however, gets pretty near to it. As a matter of fact everything was really *all right*. I merely asked the attendant to give me his hand as I went on the platform. Lord – these critics – at least *some* of 'em.' The reception of the music divorced from the image of the frail old gentleman appears to have been good. For a moment of virtues of restraint and delicacy seemed to be popular 'This music possesses a quality even rarer and more valuable to-day than it was in the past – sanity,' said the *Musical Times*. 'This symphony is a micocosm as a symphony should be, where we meet all manners of moods. But the adventures we meet are entirely those of the art of music. The composer does not substitute a crossword puzzle for a modulation, nor does he halt the orchestra in its course to introduce a quartet of pneumatic drills. That is why he gains our confidence from the first and having aroused our interest keeps it alive to the end.'

Henry Wood did give a performance at the Promenade Concerts in 1932. This was not greeted with unmixed delight. 'Booked seats for Proms. Alas, the blessed symphony came blessed *last*! *and* after all the blessed extremist modern! Well, well, here's to making the best of things.'

Of the reviews he wrote to Rachel:

Now we have three 'orrid ones re the Norwich! Of course, they had to come, but we have to keep a level head in these days of modern thought. I could have wished it had been something more modern such as the 'Leeds' Symphonic Suite – But there – ! As Wilkins says in *Merrie England* – the time may come' –

The 'orrid ones were compensated for by a letter from a young listener in Croydon who said in a solemn and most carefully composed letter that 'after the tediousness of Mr John Ireland and the bombastics of Mr William Walton, your music came as a surprising delight to one who, young though he is, is old fashioned enough to prefer thoughtful harmony and typical English gracefulness – qualities which infuse your masterpiece.' He added that many of his contemporaries felt the same admiration for the work.

It is certainly interesting to reflect that German's editing of the 'Norwich' coincided almost exactly with Vaughan Williams' conception of the strident terrors poured into his Fourth Symphony: some say, a premonition of the horrors of totalitarian war, others the composer's thoughts on the Dorking by-pass. When the 'Norwich' was given in Birmingham, the *Birmingham Mail* made the undeniable charge that the promise of the Symphony should have blossomed into a mature talent of greater profundity and power. It unfairly suggested that the composer had concentrated on 'less important but more saleable' work; yet in lamenting the absence of later symphonies it did raise the most important aspect of German's career. If he had been solely interested in financial reward, he could have written with far less care and thought over his work yet, although his music occupies a unique place in British musical history, the grandeur and the passion of great art eluded him. To make a comparison: German, it could be argued, might have written the Strauss First Horn Concerto yet never moved forward through *Electra* to the richness of *Rosenkavalier* or the subtleties of *Ariadne*. He might, if we reflect carefully on its score (the light-hearted accompaniments to the student jollities and the two great arias of Act I not to mention Musetta's Waltz Song) have written many pages of the first two Acts of *Bohème* but he never progressed to the thrilling tonal effects of *Il Tabarro* and *Turandot*. The causes were many: a fascination with the Victorian theatre, the absence of the strong and prescient publishing support organised by a man like Ricordi, periods of excessive overwork, financial responsibilities for his family, limited views held strongly at the Royal Academy during his training, the dearth of inspired librettists, all no doubt had their effect.

Difficulties in having British works accepted were created as much by the audiences as by the management and conductors. In 1895 Francesco Berger, secretary of the Royal Philharmonic Society had written: 'The British public is *not* keen on English music, whether executive or creative; the paying public stays away when an English artist plays, or when English music is performed.'

German's life too had not been one to cultivate extremes of emotion: his childhood was as happy as Mahler's for example, had been savagely distressing. In later life he was able to recreate that comfortable world through the correspondence with his sisters and holidays with childhood friends. Yet it lacked any deeper impulse than happiness among friends, and kindness to all. Both Elgar and Strauss, despite the latter's tempestuous episodes with the formidable Pauline, had immensely strong marriages which propelled them towards ambitious creativity and positive achievement. Puccini satisfied his emotional needs with a series of low life encounters which brought forth rebukes from Ricordi despite the fact that the publisher's revenues were greatly enhanced by the results. German relied upon the advice and encouragement of Rachel, but this was sisterly and distant. His social position and delight in the society of the respectable artistic clubs and official musical organisations precluded scandals even had he wished to risk them and he had a high regard for the opinions of his friends. Within his own social circles, outside the musical world, and even within it, there was no one of particularly powerful intellect or wide experience. To this must also be added the general discouragement which, in his younger days, was given to all but sacred or semi-sacred choral works in English musical life.

Perhaps because musicology lays so heavy a stress on 'development', we overlook the fact that there may occur examples of composers in whom this does not flourish for reasons intrinsic in their own talents though what they have written may be individual and interesting in itself. Each must decide for himself whether to delight in the unique Edward German music which we have or to regret the impossiblity of carrying off a de luxe box edition of Edward German's nine symphonies from the record shop. There is no doubt that the emotional hold which much of his music exercises on his devotees, mannered and repetive as it is, points to some outreaching quality within it, which might in different circumstances have burst into flame. That is what Elgar sensed, through his own rapid ascent to predominance overshadowed and subconsciously inhibited his friend.

1932 was the year of his seventieth birthday. 'Had a quiet seventieth. Mab came over in the morning and mixed with a few 'D' and 'E's. To my surprise letters, cards and telegrams simply poured in from all sorts and conditions – had *no* idea I was so well-known. Of course, the 70th – but even then.' His health again, however, suffered a relapse. 'I am now a week old in the sacred precincts of three-scores and ten . . . Legs weak, can't walk yet.' By April he was able to move about more easily. 'What does not get better is my sense of smell – this went slap bang in the middle of the attack and has never been heard of since. Enclosing some press cuttings – read 'Mr Clever' in the *Sidcup Times*. As notice proceeds it seems to me he eats some of his own words.' There were plans for a March concert arranged by Joseph Lewis, *Coronation March* and *The Seasons*. 'It is not of a popular kind but I want to have one big work complete if only for once. The "Faithful Joe" will be calling here one day soon to go through the work with me." *Merrie England* was planned for production at the Open Air Theatre in Scarborough. ('It should be a marvellous do.') At the same time there was sadness in the death of Colonel Rogan. 'Yes, poor old Rogan has gone! Couldn't go to the funeral but sent a nice wreath. This will be the first breach in the ACM Club.' By the summer he was working again. 'I am revising and generally altering an orchestral score of my old Tarantella in A Minor which Henry Geehl has made. I have to to *slow* although publishers are waiting for it. My orb not too good.'

The second project which occupied him in the years after his knighthood was his biography. It is first mentioned in a letter of 30th August 1927.

Go up to Buckden, Yorks, to talk over proposed biography. I dare say we shall find some common ground for a little book tho' I don't quite know if it's wanted now – better have been some years ago when I was 'booming'. Still there must be some people left who would care to read it. On the whole I think it is worth doing and for that particular work there is no one better than the 'Poet' – he is so discreet!

A few days later, he asked Rachel who had always been his recorder and archivist to send all photos and letters from him to Scott. He also assured her that she would see it before publication. 'You have a good instinct in these things. Between the lot of us it should be *almost* all right.' The idea led to an attack on his accumulated papers. 'Lot of sorting out letters etc. House in muddle. Difficult to decide what to keep and what is 'dustbin' but time has come when it really must be done.'

He found that his semi-blindness did not help in the task of funishing documentary material. In June 1929 he wrote to Rachel:

You would get my card re sending the Poet what we talked about. He seems anxious about my help – letters, photos, personal touches etc. between 1890-1900and 1900-1910. I am sadly handicapped in all this. My programmes, letters, etc. seem all in a maze to me – cannot see properly – but Alice shall have another look and see what *can* be found. Sackville might oblige but he is so frightfully busy with one thing and another. As a matter of fact I doubt if I have anything of value – however Never say die. I am glad the Poet is getting on with it.

Scott who had been involved in a railway accident during the First World War suffered from poor health and was not able to start on the task as soon as he wished. German soon, however, received a letter in his own hand saying that he was better and had been out for a motor ride. 'He is a living marvel!' wrote German admiringly. On 9th March 1930 he wrote, 'I seem to be keeping well, occasionally feeding WHS (brave man!) with "Bio".' The question of photographs arose. 'Have written to WHS about the "smiling Cavalier photo". I don't like it really either, or either really. Don't think I shall have any court dress. It looks a bit fulsome. Besides I shall appear with Mac in the ACM club one.' He did in fact finally admit the court dress to the volume, but his original instinct was correct.

A lot of material was supplied by German himself and gives his mellowed version of events. It so happened that late in 1929 a selection from *The Rival Poets* was given on the wireless. 'Unfortunately I did not get the *Poets* selection last night,' wrote Scott. 'My own is only a crystal set and the wretched BBC switched us on to Manchester at 7.45 – to some northern piffle – probably not knowing that lots of people in this area know the RP.' Elgar, Landon Ronald and others were approached and asked permission for their letters to be used. Elgar supplied the verse used the in Tale of Canute and added a line to polish up his 1928 speech ('A matter of orchestration,' wrote German). Scott discovered that breaching the composer's reticence was harder than he had imagined. 'Thompson [Herbert Thompson, the music critic of the Yorkshire Post] also thinks you are a little too diffident about some of the statements, quotations, etc. that crop out of the story – and that there is no cause to be apprehensive of public interest or understanding.' To his question on 26th January 1930, 'Anything interesting to say about gramophoning or broadcasting 1919-29?' German simply wrote, 'No'. On 24th October 1929, he wrote to Rachel, 'WHS wants to know more about my life in 1906 and 1908. Surely I was writing *TJ* in 1906 but I'm dashed if I can remember much about 1908!' He supplied a certain amount of general information of limited interest.

EG was not much of a reader – he used to say he did not have time for reading but what he did read he greatly enjoyed and read slowly and very thoroughly . . . "EG's favourite recreations were watching cricket and fishing in the meres and rivers that abound in Shropshire . . . As to cricket, many is the day he has spent with his pipe and tobacco at Lords (which was hard by Hall Road) and he was enthusiatic even to being an authority on the game. Middlesex continued to be his favourite team from the 1880s onwards. . ." Before motor traffic took possession of the countryside lying around London, he would often spend a pleasant day riding in the Border Counties (sic) with Sir Frederick Cowen and that admirable singer, the late Andrew Black.

There can rarely have been a subject of biography with so little intention of using the occasion to pay off old scores, fight old battles, or advance his own theories or work, even where hints of the presence of trouble below the suface existed (e.g. Tree's 'obstinate' revival of *Henry VIII*. 'What is the point?' asks Scott. 'Is it a story? If so it should be told.')

Nothing that would endanger the impression of calm could be drawn out. He was concerned more than anything else to see that Mackenzie was properly mentioned. Yet his real personality was much more intense and his letters show a talent for words more pungent than this. It is true he never showed very great interest in European politics. The Peace of Versailles and its troubled aftermath passed on without any but the most general comments. Atonality seemed a more serious threat from Europe than Fascism. If his letters of this period were to be indexed, the only reference to Germany that I can think of would be the rather surprising announcement of a performance of *Merrie England* in Cologne, some discussion with Kalisch of a German translation of *Tom Jones* and some brief notes on German reparations. Of all the family Mab was the most interested in the outside world and tides in the affairs of mankind generally. In a letter in her old age she recalled how she had loved listening to her mother and Uncle Ted arguing over the merits of Lord Salisbury and Mr Gladstone. German did not enter into political discussion but he had outspoken conservative prejudices of the man who had risen in the world. Although his comments were not profound neither were they the sayings of a benign old hermit. 'What a mess we are in! The TUC leaders ought to swing' was his comment on the General Strike

What are we to do with fire brands like Cook and Smith flying about? But the last thing the Government ought to do is to play into their hands by imprisoning Cook – that is what they want – to make him a

martyr! Leave it alone! Every industry or big concern must pay its way or go under: if they go under the employees go under with them, and so – revolution!
P.S. The world cannot go on without capital! and all these revolutionairies want is the transference of capital and then we should find despots indeed.

In June 1929 he was amused to discover that the BBC had been relaying *Merrie England* while the Socialist gains rolled in during the Election results. 'Anyway they will do nothing very revolutionary for a year or two.' Of the National Government formed during the crisis he commented, 'I give up the Grand National! It seems a silly business – But the ballot is perhaps the best way out of it' On the October Election 1931, his style was highly personal,

What ho the election! The most momentous decision in history! Now I suppose there will be somebody or other who will be putting every possible difficulty in the way of "getting on with it". Never mind, England at heart is conservative and can always rise to a crisis. I have no words to express my feelings about LL–d G–ge but I will say this – he is a dirty damnable despicable thing – in fact a *Traitor*. That's as far as I can get at present. *Anyway, I've done with him forever.* I now see his *real* nature.

German had always had a certain suspicion of Lloyd George since the Press had once quite erroneously reported that the Welsh statesman like to support Welsh music and frequently asked Mr German to entertain his guests at his weekend house parties. He wrote to his cousins at Whitchurch approving of their decision to vote for this National Government.

In matters where he was more closely involved his outlook was not serene either, though he could remain sufficiently amused by events to accept human folly with only moderate exasperation. On the BBC publicity for his work (January 22nd 1929):

I have just received enclosed – isn't it *sickening*! First of all they had Symphony No. 1 in E Minor. I wrote on the 18th saying it was the Symphony No. 2 in A Minor and titles of each of the four movements. So much for that. Now they mess up the *March Rhapsody* with the *Welsh Rhapsody* . . . and the 'four fine *waltz* tunes' is really the limit! However, it is too late to do anything as they have already gone to press. *But* they will have their attention called to the fact that the March Rhapsody and the Welsh Rhapsody are distinct works (I will write right away.) I wish to goodness I had kept to my original title, Rhapsody on March Themes – but there again I am not going to bash my head on rocks. It is *too late* and so we have to take things in this life with the best grace we can. My new toast – (not 'all friends round the Wrekin') 'Here's to making the best of things.'

A week later, 27th January 1929:

I have written to Josephus (Lewis) as to the announcer making the programme clear. It would cost untold trouble and expense to alter the March Rhapsody title. The full score is published, the whole of the orchestral parts are published and the pianoforte duet under this title. So we must leave it and hope for the best. I am inclined to think that generally speaking Josephus is a bit careless though as he is so loyal to me I would not have him know my thoughts in this regard. Further the time chosen, 10.15 to 11.15, is just idiotic for symphonic music.

This is the style of his correspondence. The biography in much gentler mood progressed. 'The Bio is now well under way. From what I have seen of it it seems to be well put together – the only fault I have at present is that is says nothing *bad* about me. No matter.' But these were the months of the Depression and it proved difficult to find a publisher. Sixteen were approached without success. 'The Bio still seems to be wanted not – not even a nibble by a publisher but the poet still seems to think it may 'get off' one of these days. I tell him I ought to do something sensational such as getting a pretty girl to fall in love with me and joining me in placing our heads in a gas oven!' A few weeks later he lamented, 'I once wrote a song called Ever Waiting – this applies to the Bio!'

At the end of December, 1931, Cecil Palmer, a publisher, agreed to an edition of 1500 copies, with the venture partly financed by Scott and German. He was 'most favourably impressed' but the times were not normal and some sort of subsidy was thought necessary to see the work in print. He did, however, offer to share the profits equally. In fact times were so bad that Palmer's firm went into liquidation. The publication was helped eventually by Chappell's who also appear as publishers on the title page. There was a foreword by his old admirer, Herbert Thompson, who had heard German's works at the Leeds Festival and witnessed the first performance of *The Emerald Isle* in 1901 and thought that 'German went beyond his model in putting more beauty of workmanship into his music than Sullivan – who was a very practical man and knew his Savoy audience – chose to do.' In fact while Scott was approaching various pubishers, German, ever industrious, though by now badly handicapped with his 'orb' was preparing a concert version of his first operatic triumph. '*The Emerald Isle* (CV) will have its first performance by the Ealing Philharmonic Society under Victor Williams. It may or may not be successful – time will prove. Anyway, what I have done I have done. Wish there were more work for the chorus and tenor solo. It was a most difficult task.' A fortnight later, referring to his eye troubles, he wrote, 'I am all behind with my correspondence principally owing to my not wanting to overtax my orb. Here I would say I appreciate your writing to me in large hand. I wish dear Mab would do the same but I won't bother her about it.' In April, 1931, he went to hear the first performance at Ealing.

> It certainly had a splendid reception – I critically was quite satisfied with my work on it. The weak spot is the Finale to Act I but then Victor Williams took it much too slow. I'll liven up the tempi marks in the final issue. I had to go on the platform and make a little speech. I came home feeling tired. I don't suppose I shall do this kind of thing ever again – indeed there will be no occasion for it – my health keeps good but I have to go 'very slow' when walking, on account of overwhelming traffic and only half a sight.

Rachel despatched an old essay she had written many years before about his romantic ambitions. His reply ran: 'I like your 'That girl I am looking for'. By Jove and By Jove, and My Word and My Word, also What Ho and What Ho! Mind you, you have painted the ideal girl beautifully and no doubt she exists somewhere but I fancy she takes a bit of finding these days.'

When the 'Bio' was finally published in the Summer of 1932, it reminded the critics how much music he had written for the stage in the early days, especially that for Shakespearean productions. There were also some demands for good performances of his work. One comment was that his music had never needed popularising: it did that for itself. It only needed performance. 'How is it that an artist can be so widely acclaimed and yet so little regarded as Edward German has been?' said *The Literary Supplement*. He himself said, 'I have been hauled over the coals by several good folk for not having mentioned the names of many people and for not having told many stories. Well so be it! These things did not occur to me and that's all about it.' Of course, it called forth a number of recollections from old acquaintances. '15 Feb. 1933. I had a letter from Leonard Jones, the eldest son of Laura Whittingham. He enclosed a programme of an organ recital I gave at Weston Wesleyan Church on *January 28th 1880*. It gave me a real thrill. I remember it so well and the mile walk back to catch the last train from Wrenbury Station I think it must go in the archives.'

Sadly, 'The Poet' did not live more than a few weeks after his tribute to a lifetime's friendship. On 10th July German wrote, 'The last news of WHS is bad. In fact – Connie wrote me – Poor old boy.' And 18th July, 'The dear old poet passed peacefully away yesterday morning. He suffered no pain.

CHAPTER ELEVEN

To Every Cow Her Calf

When the achievements of German are counted, his work on behalf of proper rewards to composers must occupy an important place. As a young man without private means he developed a keen sense of justice and he ended his days as the most esteemed patron of the Performing Right Society. Indeed, in their study of music and its economic rewards, *The Composer in the Market Place*, Professor Alan Peacock and Ronald Weir include his photograph in the volume, the only British musician to be represented, because of his strong interest in the question. It was German who opened the new premises of the Society and it was he who wrote the preface outlining its policy to the general public in 1935 The affluent pop-star of the modern era owes him a financial debt, if not an artistic one.

Yet he was not a ruthless man of business and in his desire to have his works performed he was sometimes more lenient over royalties than many contemporaries. His principal publisher, apart from Chappells, who held rights over the operas, was Novello and that firm did not join the Performing Right Society until 1936, because it concentrated to a considerable degree upon the fields of church music and concert promotion. His own attitude, however, was greatly affected by the growth of radio and gramophone, which altered the whole basis upon which a composer's remuneration had to be judged. From 1929 onwards, as will be shown, he gave all the support he could to the Society's cause.

As a young man he was a victim of the haphazard situations and unprotected position in which a composer found himself before the Copyright Act of 1911. He disposed of his rights or endeavoured to bargain with a number of different publishing firms, and as we have seen, he was prepared to stress his worth and learnt something of the arts of bargaining. We have also noted that he frequently urged the production of cheaper copies of orchestral parts to facilitate performances. In the meanwhile his duet, solo piano and violin arrangements were a means of income, though it could be argued that these time-consuming tasks left his energies overtaxed and his pace of work was stressful.

Publishers too had their problems with the 'pirate' editions of work, as well as the unauthorised circulation of conductor's and band parts. In a letter of October 1892 when *Henry VIII* had been running successfully for three months, Novello offered ten guineas for all rights which German possessed in the music 'other than the interests covered by existing assignments between you and us'. This probably refers to an arrangement made in March whereby Novello purchased *Orpheus with his Lute* for five guineas and 'regretted' they could not enter into any arrangement for the Dance royalty until 250 copies had been sold, or the Complete Music until 500 copies had been sold. They argued that 'owing to the expense of keeping royalty accounts' they would prefer the outright purchase. They intended to put on the front page the reservation of performing rights but they did not intend to charge for performances outside theatres. They requested all manuscript copies in existence. At first they wished to make a few copies only, but when they decided to publish the Three Dances they particularly asked for a definite assurance that there were no more parts in the hands of anyone else 'as it would not be worth while publishing them if they are likely to be lent out by any so-called music lending agencies . . . We shall be glad if you will kindly assure us on this point before we proceed with the work.' They also mention the *possibility* of the violin and piano arrangement which, in view of the music's success, seems unnecessarily cautious. Within three weeks they were beginning to be enthusiastic but the composer, even when Irving's protégé, was still very much the underdog. German had sought to improve the scoring – 'Owing to the very heavy alterations you have made in the proofs of the orchestral parts of the Three Dances we shall have to charge you with the cost of making the same. In several cases we have had to re-engrave the entire plate.' They became even more admonitory about the Dances which were to bring in untold gold for decades. 'We beg to say that such heavy alterations as you have made in several parts of your Three Dances took up a very considerable amount of valuable time and we venture to hope that *if we should have to engrave any future works from your pen* you will kindly see that the MSS are carefully corrected *before* the engraving is proceeded with.' In view of these strictures it is worth noting that A.J. Jaeger of Novello (the 'Nimrod' of Elgar's Variations) once said to the composer Havergal Brian, who was urging him to publish more music by young writers, 'Do you know that the full score of Edward German's *Henry VIII* Dances is the only one that has repaid us for the cost of engraving?'

Major publishers were, of course, connected with the London concerts which they often helped to promote, but the 1880s saw a dwindling of concert audiences as new forms of entertainment developed and the halls themselves often remained archaic and uncomfortable. Novellos were pleased when they heard that the Philharmonic Society were contemplating putting the Three Dances into a programme but still had reservations about publishing the full score of the incidental music. As well as at concerts, publishers promoted music in other places. Novello told German in December that they had sent The Dances to Frascati's Restaurant, Holborn Restaurant and the manager of other important bands. At the same time they were anxious to make sure that all MS band parts had been handed over, for the opportunities of cheap exploitation of copies among London players were immense.

By May 1893 the balance of power between composer and publisher had shifted slightly. Novello's were seeking a cantata, The Spanish Gypsies, and accepted that he was at that time too busy. They mentioned, however, that they had a librettist in reserve who could supply a text 'to suit your requirements' should German ever need one. They agreed to resume the royalty system and pay three pence per copy for the piano duet arrangement of the Dances. They apologised for being too hasty in making a military band setting as they had understood the score was agreed between German and Dan Godfrey Junior who did many such tasks. They agreed that if further corrections were needed, as German had not approved the final version, these could be made when the Dances were reprinted.

By 9th November 1894 they were 'favoured' by a letter from German discussing terms for *The Gipsy Suite* (the complete work cost 3/6d of which German received threepence *after* the sale of 250 copies). The first three movements were to be published at 1/6d each (royalty twopence) the Tarantella (being considerably longer) at 2/- (royalty threepence). They agreed happily to piano and violin versions but reserved their rights on military band and string orchestra versions, as these were made – and this was true of the industry as a whole – to advertise the more saleable piano versions of the works.

For the *Romeo and Juliet* music German was offered twenty guineas for the rights in addition to royalties and the firm noted that they had received enquiries about pianoforte arrangements for *The Leeds Suite*. It is indicative of the importance of economics in art that the *Valse Gracieuse* was separated off from other movements in the financial considerations.

In 1896 they announced that their foreign representative was starting for a tour of Europe and would make The *Henry VIII Dances* a special feature in every country.

For *As You Like It* they offered the same terms as *Romeo* but received a sharp rebuke.

As I understand your letter, you ask me to part with the sole orchestral rights of these new dances which within a few months will be played by most of the orchestras in the kingdom for the sum of *20 guineas!!!* Surely the orchestral rights of these particular pieces are worth very much more. In the case of *Romeo and Juliet* it was quite different. This was of course more serious music and much less likely to sell. In the present case, the three movements of the Masque are, I am pretty sure, what every amateur society is waiting for . . . I suggest that you kindly let me know as soon as possible how near 150 guineas you care to go for the purchase of the orchestral rights.

The eventual settlement was fifty guineas for the rights plus increased royalties from threepence to fourpence. They also accepted *It Was a Lover and His Lass* for publication although their original estimate had been gloomy ('in our experience, people will not sing duets'). In 1902 when the richness of the *Henry VIII* harvest was apparent Novello published the full score.

It is interesting that German's fantasia, *In Commemoration*, was not accepted unless he agreed to forego all fees. It was a concert work and less susceptible to easy arrangements though when it re-emerged as the *March Rhapsody* in 1902 a duet version was made by A.E. Grimshaw.

He fared better with *Hamlet* for Novello agreed to publish the score but wished to postpone engraving the wind parts, keeping only some MS copies for performance until a demand was established. The withholding of wind parts was another device which publishers had to use to prevent the circulation of music between unauthorised performers. In 1897 plans went forward for the publication of a *Henry VIII* Suite in which the *Intermezzo funebre* was given the title of 'Death of Buckingham'. German was sceptical about the possibility of reducing the complete score to pianoforte solo but Novello pointed out that 'seeing that such *very* polyphonic and very difficult works as Wagner's later operas . . . and Brahms' and Dvorak's symphonies are published as pianoforte solo arrangements and yet give one a very good idea of the music, we hope some very satisfactory and effective arrangement of your music can be made'. Even so, while he could expect the royalties, German was offered five guineas only for all the work required in the reductions of each major piece. "Having regard to the rather qualified success of some of the more recent works which we have published for you" they hesitantly agreed to publish a Suite No. 2 for violin and piano (originally published for oboe by another Company). 'Although we like it very much from the artistic point of view we are not quite so sure of its success from the commercial point of view, having regard to the limited number of violinists to which it will appeal.' They agreed to a royalty but refused any additional payment. The ten guineas handed over represented a threepenny royalty on the first 840 copies sold.

The relationship was uneasy but was being consolidated and the prospect of publishing the light-hearted *Much Ado* score was not one with Novello could overlook. After accepting the *Bourée* and *Dance* (again with stipulations over piano and violin arrangements) they continued, showing the usual anxieties over security.

> We understand that there is an overture and perhaps other numbers to which your letter does not refer. May we enquire for information about these! We are assuming that whatever other portions you may desire to publish of your *Much Ado About Nothing* music, you will in the first instance offer them to us.
>
> In your letter you intimate that you will let us have the band parts 'as soon as you can get them from the theatre'. Cannot it be arranged that we send our copyist to the theatre to copy them *at once*? Any delay in bringing out the band parts must be prejudicial to the work.

Another problem which German had to face of course, was the competition from other composers, many of them eminent, whose work had to be published by an overworked staff for festival performances. He was anxious that *Much Ado* should be hurried through in order to attract attention for the new Promenade Concerts, but Novello were occupied with six new works including Mackenzie's *Little Minister* and could not be rushed. The composer was gratified, however, to learn that Sir Walter Parratt had called into the office at Novello, seen the *Bourée* and *Jig* and asked for the score to perform them before the Queen at Osborne. Novello also agreed to send out an MS copy of the 'Norwich' Symphony to seek a response but the venture does not seem to have succeeded.

Mr Littleton of Novello, in his reply to German's letter on cheaper orchestral parts again had to re-iterate the risks involved in any publication of full scores, as one orchestra could hire to another and three copies would service most orchestras in the kingdon if conductors and choral societies were sufficiently unscrupulous. German was not entirely convinced and maintained that cheaper band parts would undercut hiring agencies or illicit exchanges. He added the rather gloomy but justified note on Novello's assertion that their prices compared favourably with French and German rivals: 'It is well to bear in mind when calculating composers the public will not pay as much for British orchestral music as they will for foreign.'

The correspondence continued and Novello, in the current state of the copyright law, had good reason to lament that 'The enemies of the British composers are the music libraries and as long as they exist we have to be on our guard. They prevent us seriously thinking of lowering our prices because they are always hovering around to rob us of the fruit of our enterprise!'

After 1900 the position improved for German. From the Savoy he had his rewards for composing and conducting and the royalties were more lucrative. It is difficult to conceal a performance of *Merrie England* and Chappell needed only moderate vigilance to ensure that performances were noted. Sheet music still remained the mainstay of income and the plethora of popular songs in the Opera must have been a gratifying source of revenue. The spread of fame helped the sale of other songs produced over the years by a variety of publishers.

For the publishers themselves, however, the period 1900-1910 was one of increasing difficulty. The beginnings of mass education and new techniques is printing meant that there was a public eager for popular music and an ever increasing number of 'pirates' willing to diseminate cheap editions by the thousand. The 'pirates' even had their defenders who claimed that music should be within the reach of the poorest. This argument was countered by a humorist who brought out a penny copy of a pamphlet by the Prime Minister, Arthur Balfour, which had hitherto cost a shilling, announcing on the front page that its contents were of such value to the masses they should be priced at the lowest possible rate. Parliament responded, especially when poems by Kipling and others began to circulate in penny copies and Acts of 1902 and 1906 greatly strengthened the action which could be taken against the unlawful reproduction and sale of songs.

There were new factors, however, which influenced the economics of music and the composers' rewards. Up to 1911 performances had not been thought of as a means of providing royalties. The concerts either paid for themselves or stimulated the sale of sheet music. But with the growth of luxury hotels, restaurants, tea-gardens and promenade entertainments more means of performing music were visible on every side. And, lurking in the wings was the phonograph, which in ever more sophisticated forms would bring the mechanical reproduction of music into every home. In 1911 the Copyright Act gave to the creators of original work the right, not only to publish, but to perform or have others perform compositions. It also facilitated recriprocal agreements with other signatories of the Berlin Convention on Copyright 1908.

This Act, and the formation of the Performing Rights Association in 1914 to safeguard the interests of composers owed a great deal to William Boosey, the head of Chappell and a great friend of German's, but German himself had mixed views. The Act certainly helped writers of musical comedy and very popular music, but might well conflict with the interests of the serious musicians. 'As you know,' he wrote to Boosey,

> I have always held out at all costs for free performance. No one has been stronger on this point than I have. During the past few years however, things have changed – the advent of mechanical instruments has created a new situation and I realise something must be done to cope with it – I shall therefore be happy to join in your movement. It is quite impossible to go on old lines under new conditions.

Mackenzie, writing to Clayton at Novello, shared this view. He compared the situation with that in France.

> French composers live on performing fees chiefly, but they rarely if ever, play other than their own native music. I doubt very much if British music (of the highest class) is played as much abroad as you are given to understand. Ragtime, etc. in circuses etc . . . Yes! The fact is we are being rushed by the publishers and composers of musical comedy who think they cannot be done without. Men like myself are not on all fours with them and might be losers. Obviously if high class music is not played much gratis, it will be played less if a fee is imposed.

German noted this comment approvingly, drawing heavily on his experience and volunteered his own thoughts to Boosey.

> A composer takes say – a year, 18 months or two years to write a symphony or symphonic suite – each one performance of his work is everything to him and it is not a matter of money at all. If he has the opportunity of getting this performed by an orchestra where conductor or manager is not a member – well!!
> I have put forward the following points for consideration:
> 1) That the composer shall have the right to ask whatever fee he may wish to a conductor who is not a member of the society;
> 2) That outside this country there is freedom to perform – in America or Australia for instance;
> 3) Possibly limit protection to cinema, music halls etc;
> 4) In any case the amount charged to proprietors should not be in the least prohibitive, or at least it should be so small as to be tempting.

Broadly speaking the object of composing music is that it should be heard, but where there is money value in it, this must of course be adequately protected.

Boosey assured him that these points would be considered.

German joined the Performing Right Society in 1915 and was a committee member in 1925-6. His reservations vanished and at the end of his life he had become something of a revered figure in the musicians' crusade.

Two organisations were formed to collect and distribute revenue from mechanical rights. He belonged to the Copyright Protection Society which in 1924 amalgamated with the Mechanical Copyright Licenses Company to form the Mechanical Copyright Protection Society. He joined the new joint body but again was very careful to stipulate that membership should not affect works published by houses which were not members. These were of course his major orchestral pieces published by Novello, who remained outside the Performing Rights bodies during almost the whole of his lifetime.

He was certainly not averse to the gramophone medium and had done some recording work as early as 1916. Not all went smoothly: in 1928 he accepted to conduct a series of works for the Metropole Gramophone Company, beginning with the popular dances and *The Tempter* suite. The project was planned by Henry Geehl, who in earlier days had incurred his indignation by orchestrating the piano pieces after he had parted with the copyright to Ashdowns, but relations at this later stage seemed cordial.

On 22nd, April 1928, he wrote, 'I am going to record many of my things for a new company called the Metropole Gramophone Company. I start on Tuesday with my most popular things: *Henry VIII* Dances and Berceuse and Bacchanalian Dance from *The Tempter*. I hope it will turn out all right and that I shall be equal to it. I am not, or course the man I was – but after the Banquet and what I went through then – well anything to the good may happen.'

On 15th May there were hints of disaster. 'I was to have gramophoned to-day for the Metropole Coy. but I received a message that owing to breakdown of machinery the session had to be postponed. I should not be surprised to find they had "bust up".'

His diagnosis was correct. On 26th May he told Rachel, 'I have just agreed to do some more gramophone work with another new company but possibly it may go bust like the Metropole. I had three sessions arranged, then – bust! I have heard the records I made – they are splendid – the old evergreens and Berceuse.'

His interest was still mainly in having his music performed and heard.

When Chappells gave permission for *Merrie England* to be broadcast, Boosey strongly advised German to charge £100 for conducting as he felt the Broadcasting Corporation had more respect for works they paid for.

For the radio performances of *The Rival Poets* he seems to have ignored Boosey's advice and taken nothing. 'By the way,' he wrote in May, 'the BBC talk about doing *The Rival Poets* with two pianoforte and organ accompaniment at the end of June. It may be another "buster" as I am informing them there is no chorus. In any case it would be cut a good deal – time allowed: an hour and a quarter.'

On 16th June he confided, 'As to my remuneration for *The Rival Poets* on 25th (BBC) may I tell you that I shall go get the magnificent sum of nothing! Still it is well to have it done.'

Even with all the combined resources of the protection societies, however, copyright problems could still arise. German gave his assent to the recording of *Rolling Down to Rio* and as well as Parlophone two other forgotten companies, Zonophone and Beltona, had produced versions without payment to Kipling, who owned the copyright. German received stern letters from Kipling's solicitors:

> We shall be glad to know by what authority the recordings have been issued by you; what moneys you have in hand; and why these things have been done without any communication whatever with Mr Kipling on the subject. Mr Kipling would be entitled to take proceedings to prevent the further infringement of his copyright and further to recover damages on the basis of conversion that is to say the full value of every record which has been made.

German confirmed he had not the least idea that Kipling and Macmillan had not received their share – he had simply consented for the music to be used. Kipling agreed to German dividing future royalties equally but German and Novello had to repay fifty percent of the royalties received and costs of the legal action.

With Vocalion Gramophone Company the problem arose of whether the *Henry VIII* Dances should be treated singly or as one item. To squeeze three on to one cheap record would have meant faster tempi or cuts. In order to meet the royalty of three farthings per dance the Company would have to squeeze them on to one record. German wished them to be treated as three separate works, but history does not record how the matter was settled.

In 1930 he was dismayed to find that 'The Poet' had received nothing for the gramophone royalties of *O Peaceful Night* the highly popular part-song. The error had arisen during the amalgamation period of the Mechanical Rights Societies in 1924. Hastily German had to arrange for Scott to be paid and the amount deducted from his own royalties, as he felt this would be less embarrassing than a cheque sent by himself to his old friend. 'I confess it is very disturbing to me to think I have been innocently receiving another man's money, as in the case of Mr Kipling recently (Rolling down to Rio).' Scott's share was thirty three per cent: the amount concerned, £10/14/4d, would represent a worthwhile payment in terms of modern currency.

When the concert version of *The Emerald Isle* was under preparation, the Sullivan Estate had to be considered too. Chappell wished to place two thirds of the cost of engraving against future royalties so that both German and Sullivan's legatees would share in the original costs. They offered £50 for the task of preparing the concert version, a complicated matter as orchestral parts were involved: German requested £100. 'I certainly think the Sullivan Estate should go halves with you in this. It is not contributing a stroke of work!' Even so he was prepared to accept the £50 if Chappells thought the publication would be hampered in any way, but they agreed to the higher sum. He was determined most of all to have his music heard and financial consideration always remained secondary. There is a pair of letters very revealing of the man, concerning the Crystal Palace Choral Society; he was very keen that the Society should give the first performance, as it had of his other operas, but there were problems over the cost.

I have been surveying the matter from all points of view, and it is gradually taking shape in my mind that the Crystal Palace Society should, after all, give the first performance.

Apart from their having given first performances of other operas, I find Mr Hedgcock had already told the members about my present proposal and they are very keen about it. One member of the chorus writes to me that they are 'thrilled' at the idea. Further it now occurs to me that it was Mr Hedgcock's own project, some twenty-five years ago, that I shall make a concert version of the work. I remember he brought a copy of the opera to Hall Road one morning. Other work came along and the concert version was not made. However, at last I have done it and I admit I have a certain sentiment towards the Crystal Palace in regard to this production.

At the same time Mr Hedgcock has asked concessions that are quite unreasonable and impossible, such that no Publisher could entertain for a moment. Under these exceptional circumstances I propose:

Messrs. Chappell & Co. waive the performing fee and grant the hire of orchestral parts free of charge. This has already been done and no further concession will be expected of them. This is understood. For the rest – I am personally prepared to try and arrange matters with Hedgcock.

The letter to Hedgcock, which tells us quite a lot about his desire to hear his work performed, ran as follows:

My dear Walter,
    Although I *do* not believe what many Choral Societies say about their finances I *do* believe what *you* say about the Crystal Palace Society.
    Against what you asked of Chappells (and I am bound to say it was pretty stiff for any publisher to meet) they have taken their stand: They agree to waive the performing fee and to grant the use of orchestral parts free of charge. That is understood.
    For the rest I wonder if I personally and *privately* sent you £20 towards extra professionals in the orchestra it would be a help, and you would be able to produce the work of 28th March. If so, I should be very pleased to send it and you might call and see me one morning. If not, then I suppose we must bow to Fate and hope for better luck in the future.
        Kind regards
        As always
        Edward German

Mechanical instruments were soon to enter the debate even more deeply. When Boosey stated, 'I was gradually becoming aware that probably, eventually a composers' performing rights might be even more valuable than his publishing rights,' he was presciently foretelling the situation as it existed after the advent of radio. When the first copyright piece, *Drake Goes West*, was broadcast on 15th November, 1922, there was joy among composers who saw radio as a new means of revenue. Unfortunately the result was a dramatic drop in the sales of sheet music and gramophone records and the dispensing or what were considered scanty rewards by their new source of royalties – The British Broadcasting Corporation. Composers soon saw their earning following Drake's path all too quickly.

Yet despite the rapid drop in sales of sheet music in the 1920s there was one area in which sales were buoyant. The 'silent' cinemas required sound to accompany the films and music for the intervals between the features. As picture palaces sprang up all over the country many with orchestras and all with a pianist or cinema organist it would have been impossible to circulate scores, Much of German's music was suited to this market and his income benefited. Certainly the irksome presence of taxation became a theme rather than a diversion in his correspondence. After his first visit to the Sound Cinema (20 March 1929) he wrote in his diary 'TALKIES – No Good! but he would have been more hostile still if he had foreseen the effect they would have on orchestral music in cinemas.

Threats also came from another quarter. In 1929 a Labour M.P. W.M. Adamson brought in a Bill aimed against the 'exactions' being levied on the musical performances, the main point of which was to enable any person on payment of twopence to the proprietor of copyright to perform a piece of music as often as he wished. The fee was to cover the performance right in perpetuity of any musical work, irrespective of its extent or nature, or the nature or character of the place of performance.

The quarrel was principally between the writers of very light music and the users representing the large hotels, licensed victuallers and caterers, J. Lyons and Co. being particularly strong in the latter camp. But it struck at serious composition and older musicians joined in the fray, for as A.P Herbert pointed out in *Punch*, 'It seems odd to put the same price on the performing rights of a fox-trot, a symphony, 'Yes, We Have No Bananas' and a grand opera.' In 1924 a Private Member had tried to secure the virtual abolition of performing rights but his Bill had been rejected. The Adamson measure had the support of five other Labour MPs and at first the Bill was represented as a means of curbing gross profiteering. It passed its Second Reading without a division.

German wrote wrathfully of 'The Tuppenny Bill' in private and scorned what he considered the supine Conservative opposition. 'It is so inane and monstrous that it surely cannot pass. Yet it may if the Conservatives don't wake up from their apathy, I am sick of them.' In public he took a prominent part along with other leading composers to oppose its passage. Along with Delius, Bax, Granville Bantock, Vaughan Williams, Holst and McEwen, he signed a letter to *The Times* attacking the Bill, which, as they said, 'if it passes into Law will at one stroke immediately destroy and annul what the unremitting and practically unrewarded toil and genius of British composers has now achieved. The younger men who are entering into this achievement will find themselves thrust back to the early conditions under which artistic effort in this country was both damped and derided.

'If a composer produces a work which is included in the repertoire of a fashionable hotel and is played once a week his remuneration will be for the first year one fifty-second part of twopence and he will receive nothing at all for subsequent performances.'

Elgar was not a signatory to this letter but had written himself, independently, in equally strong terms, asserting that 'the passing of such a measure would mean the extermination of creative art in this country and the ruin of the majority of native composers.'

Shaw too, added corruscatingly to the campaign: 'That it should have passed its Second Reading is explicable only on the quite probable hypothesis that the great majority of the House of Commons are amateur vocalists who have at one time or another been caught out in the act of stealing a performing right.' Of the poor composer, Shaw wrote,

> If he is so driven by famine to relent and grasp at the two pence, which after all is an important sum to a starving man, 'he shall not,' says the Bill, 'be entitled to demand any payment other than a fee not exceeding two pence per published copy payable by any person who demands a copy upon the purchase or supply of such published copy.' What the last nine words mean I do not profess to understand, but there can be no doubt as to the well thought out lucidity of 'not exceeding'. Sir Edward Elgar may not charge more than two pence for a perpetual licence to perform 'Gerontius' but he may accept a penny. And yet, Mr Adamson is pledged, like all his Labour colleagues to put down sweated labour.

The joviality of Mackenzie which so endeared him to German comes out in his contribution to the debate, published in *The Telegraph*. After admitting to not being what is termed a 'popular' composer 'and at this period of life without great expectations of becoming one', he continued:

> We have to share our pence with the publisher, the author (if words are attached) and the collector whose services are equally indispensable. Nor let it be forgotten that in due course the Inland Revenue also claims its four shillings in the pound. Any further curtailment of this divided pittance appears to me uncommonly like robbing a corpse . . . In my youth I have seen a showman exhibiting a trained animal's struggles to climb a ladder's topmost rung and heard his invitation, 'Tuppence more and up goes the donkey'. For this identical sum the same unbusinesslike quadruped is now commanded to come down from its hard won perch.

German was a prominent member of a deputation from the

Incorporated Society of Musicians, a group as little representative as possible of what one Labour MP had described as 'the long haired fraternity which composes music', which was received by a group of MPs presided over by Sir Martin Conway. His statement with its references to *Merrie England* attracted a great deal of attention in the press, and was set out with a degree of rhetorical force that did not normally characterise his public speeches, even though private jottings on politics were in similar style:

Freedom of Contract

Why should not the composer have freedom of contract?

The author is free to negotiate with his publisher.

The playwright with his theatrical manager or syndicate.

The painter is free to make the best terms he can for the purchase of his pictures.

The sculptor the same in his own art.

Why should the composer be singled out for punishment?

Why should the composer not have freedom of contract?

The people – the community – will always want its music just as it will want its plays and pictures.

I do not like bringing up my own work into this matter, but there I am at least on safe ground: We will take the composition of a Light Opera.

I composed one some years ago. It took me some eighteen months to compose, harmonise and orchestrate it. When it was finished it was produced at a West End Threatre.

I received nothing down but I did receive a percentage of the gross receipts. This seems to me a fair way of dealing.

The Opera had a run of many months, and during that time, and during the time it was taken on tour, thousands of pounds were distributed, rightly and happily distributed – amongst the artists – singers – orchestral players, choristers, scene painters, costumiers, stage hands and so forth. Everybody was contented, everybody was satisfied, including the librettist and the composer.

Now, if this Bill had been in vogue at the time, it would have meant that I as composer would have received – let me think! 2d per copy on all copies sold. We will take it there would have been thirty to thirty-five in the chorus, twelve principals, twelve understudies and several small parts – say 100 copies in all of the opera would have been required for the production. These 100 copies would have been sold by the publishers to the producers and they (the producers) could have performed the opera in perpetuity – that is forever – without any further payment to the composer. That means that I as composer would have received 16/8d. The librettist would here have had freedom of contract with the management but the composer would *not*.

There is another aspect of the matter: with the advent of mechanical devices, wireless and BBC etc. the sales of *sheet music* have become practically *nil*.

Where in the old days 100 copies of a song were sold, now there is only a sale of two or three. *Therefore* unless the composer has some form of protection in the way of fees for the *performances* of his works, I can see nothing but starvation and death to the composer.

If you kill the Performing Right Society you at the same time kill the composer. The composer has nothing else to look to under modern conditions. I am sorry to end on a tragic note but that is really how things appear to me!

[A.P. Herbert made the same point: 'Let us give 2d to Mr Shaw for *St Joan*, 2d to Mr John for a picture, 2d for *The Forsyte Saga*, 2d for a Chaplin Film . . . and later – Why give them 2d? Why not 1d? Why not ½d? Heavens! Why not make the composers pay?']

German's performance was sufficiently dramatic to persuade one Labour MP 'that he did not want to think there may be a Mozart moving through England who might find a pauper's grave'.

A special Select Committee of the House of Commons quickly saw the absurdity of the twopence payment, although it was cautious over the monopolistic nature of the Society's position and suggested appeals to arbitration where it was considered that licences to perform music had been unreasonably withheld or granted on inflated terms. The proposed tribunal was difficult to establish as a re-wording of the Berlin Convention would have been needed and international problems in the 1930s held up changes. The 'Tuppenny Bill', however, was 'reported without amendment.' It met its end and could not be proceeded with. Once it was rejected a storm of criticsm burst over the heads of its unfortunate authors. It was discovered that the proceeding of the Select Committee had cost £456 – 'enough to support an ordinary family in comfort for twelve months,' declared *The People*. *The Evening Standard* said of the measure. 'The committee examined it, heard witnesses and finally reported roughly speaking that it could not be

Presentation at the opening of the Performing Right Society Building (Performing Right Society)

Edward German in later life (Performing Right Society)

passed as it was and that it could not usefully be amended – a conclusion which might have occurred to anyone who spent five minutes in the perusal of its three short clauses.'

For the rest of his life German was an ardent champion of the Performing Right Society. When it moved to its new premises he was invited to perform the opening ceremony, before a gathering of publishers, authors and composers of such widely differing talents as Frank Bridge, Nŏel Gay, Billy Mayerl and Roger Quilter. In his speech he said again that he personally was in favour of the highest possible quality in music and hated poor quality. 'But,' he continued, 'this has nothing to do with the justice of the principle that a composer should be paid for the public performance of his work.' The work of the Society had grown to monitor twenty-six million performances. 'No wonder,' he observed

it has become necessary to have new and enlarged premises. I understand the P.R.S. does not work on the number or performances alone. It converts the number of performances into 'points'. Of these points so many are allocated for songs, so many for dance or light music and so many say, for a full symphony.

Last year the total number of points recorded was more than 111,000,000 and the number of programmes and returns received from licences was more than 35,000. (At this point I may say in parenthesis that I feel very much like the Chancellor of the Exchequer in the House of Commons on Budget Day. I am informed that the values of these points are worked out to the fraction of a penny.)

Now, how is the intricate matter of accountancy done? That is, what method is adopted to allocate the appropriate fee to the appropriate member? I confess this has always been a mystery to me. But I am looking forward to going through the new offices with you in a few minutes time: then we shall all see just what happens.

He rarely resorted to anecdote in his very straightforward speeches but on this occasion he relaxed. 'Before I close,' he added.

I would just say a word about copyright law (not that I personally am an authority on it) but according to my information it dates back to a period even much earlier than the reign of Queen Anne.

A pamphlet recently published by the equivalent society in America states that it was in the ancient Kingdom of Tara – in Ireland – that the principle of copyright was first estabished. Here is the little story:

In that ancient Kingdom of Tara there were two monasteries and they 'competed for the tourist trade of the day. In one monastery lived an artistic monk who designed a very beautiful psalter which so pleased the abbot that he had it hung over the altar. People went in large numbers to see it. The monks in the other monastery wondered at the decline in the number of their visitors and sent to find out the reason for the popularity of their rivals. When the abbot of this second monastery was told of this psalter he ordered an exact copy. The abbot of the first monastery then appealed to the King whose judgement was, 'To every cow her calf' and ordered that this infringing copy should be destroyed. Thus was established the principle of copyright which is now organised throughout the world.

The 1930 furore averted disater but it had still not made a material difference to a composer's rewards which had been dwindling since the advent of radio. While singers like John McCormack, Gigli and Chaliapin could command fees of £1,000 for a single concert, and the Mayfair Hotel paid Ambrose and his Orchestra £412.10 per week, his share of the profits remained small. It was estimated that six hotels in the year 1934-5 paid their bands £96,000 of which only £600 went to the writers of songs and dances performed. The Society also failed to share in the growing popularity of radio music for its share of the licence revenue was comparatively small and could only rise as the number of licences rose. As the BBC also held a monopoly the society were not in the most advantageous bargaining position. All these points were included in a publication: *Radio and the Composer* issued in 1936 and Edward German wrote the foreword. It coincided with a report by the Ullswater Commission which its cause had done much to influence and which recommended a 'liberal treatment of creative artists' and a tribunal for disputed matters.

German's foreword was his last public statement.

It paid tribute to the work of the composer and the work of the Society on his behalf. It re-iterated his belief in the justice of rewarding all composers whether their work should be a fine symphony or a simple dance tune, and concluded, 'If it can be shown how much their public owes to the composer in these days of mechanical music when for less than a halfpenny a day the best of the world's music can be brought to its very door, it will not have been written in vain.'

CHAPTER TWELVE

Here's to Making the Best of Things

When German opened the new home of the Performing Right Society he was presented with two ebony paperweights inscribed with treble and bass clefs in silver. The chairman, Leslie Boosey, expressed the hope that they would be a reminder to Sir Edward that the world was always eagerly awaiting more music from his melodious pen. The days of composition were over, however, though interest in his pre-war works continued.

Early in 1933, 18th February, *A Princess of Kensington* was peformed under Joseph Lewis in an old converted wine warehouse down by the side of Waterloo Bridge. When the BBC moved to Broadcasting House, this gloomy setting had survived as a concert hall and a possible venue for experiments to turn opera into ordinary radio fare. It was reached by a long flight of steps from the Surrey side of the bridge and a grimy land arch. 'Great lorries rumbled over the pavements, street children are playing outside mean houses,' said the *Radio Times*. 'A light sign BBC No. 10 Studio stands out in striking modernity against its dirty background.' Inside, many experiments were made for the broadcast with the placing of the forty instrumentalists occupying two sides of a right-angled triangle with the microphone at its apex. The first violins were placed in front for better definition and then, after the rest of the strings, the woodwind with the brass and percussion spilling over the originally marked area. To us, the idea of broadcasting opera has no novelty but it was the BBC's intention to copy the pioneering work of the German producer, Cornelius Bronsgeest, who had condensed libretti and even had works rescored to gain the maximum effect over the air. Most operas run for three hours or so and without the present choice of radio channels the Corporation could not allocate more than one hour and a half at the most. It wished to try to allay popular suspicions about opera in a country that had no operatic tradition apart from 'social seasons' at Covent Garden and the occasional touring company. Moreover there were few singers who could act with their voices and even fewer teachers of the art. Singers would sometimes move from their places during the performance and had to be coaxed back by the control man employing frantic mimes. *Merrie England* and *Tom Jones* had already been given radio performances singly, but *A Princess of Kensington* was intended to be the first of a series which would present condensed versions of light operas by Dibdin, Cellier, Offenbach and others. The plot which had required twenty-two characters in 1903 now only needed seven. Two narrators, both of them microphone artists rather than singers, played the parts of Puck and Mustard Seed linking the musical numbers together. On the whole, the effect went some way towards meeting the suggestion made many years earlier by Rachel that the whole work would benefit from a prologue preparing the plot. The new version was given subsequently on a number of occasions.

In March there was a dire blizzard which reminded German of a journey he had made up to London with his mother fifty years before when a train had come to a halt in the snow near Tring and they had to be dug out. Family illness occupied much of his correspondence and he himself found his eye troubles worsening. 'My eye tires, so no more, Dear Dick' is the refrain which closes several of his letters.

In April he was grieved at the death of William Boosey. 'The whole *musical world* owes him a tremendous debt.' he wrote, 'But for him there would have been none of the protective measures that have now become law and *without* them the profession (broadly speaking) would now have been starving.' The *Just So Songs* were broadcast in April, 'I don't agree with *The Star* man that every word . . . came over. But I enjoyed the musical part and the pianoforte playing.' His attention was still closely fixed upon the *Radio Times* and his standards about the performances of his own works unsparing. 'As Godfrey raced the 'Norwich' it ought to have been called the 'Derby' Symphony. Well, Well, so be it.' And on another occasion even the faithful Lewis was censured. 'Yes, Joe took the fiery section of *Romeo* as though he were in a Sunday School. Otherwise the serious parts were most impressive and on the whole it was good rather than bad – but Lord! we have to be thankful for anything in these days of composers by the millions.' Modernism went on depressing him. 'Things musical – that is *ultra*-modern musical don't bear thinking of. I have heard some sinful stuff lately . . . 'YE GODS. SCHÖNBERG 8.15,' he wrote in capitals in his diary when the dodecaphonic cloven hoof was first spotted in the advertised programmes. He made some effort to come to terms and put down a note to listen to Schönberg's *Pierrot Lunaire* in November but his reactions are not recorded.

The production of *Merrie England* at the Open Air Theatre at Scarborough was to be followed by *Tom Jones* in 1933. He wrote to Rachel:

'Scarboro' seems to have been a great success. Of course, you would have liked me to be there, but as was the case in *Merrie England* last year I didn't feel equal to it. I sent a message to Haydn Coffin for him to read to the company. M.E. was a record success without me so will *T.J.* be so do not feel worried about it. Besides too much excitement as I get older is not good for me. So again I say – please do not feel worried about it. . . . Lord, how time flies! It is just about four months Saturday, since you and I heard the Boat Race described on my wireless.

Then I went to bed for a few weeks with gout and rested my foot. I have been alright again for some time now and have been to Lord's with Ham and Sackville and Roberts two or three times. I recently went with Sack and Hagelman for a motor ride (in Sack's motor) to Buckingham and back. It tired me but I enjoyed it.

One new task which occupied him, despite the difficulties he had with reading notation, was the Cloverley Suite. 'I have just finished scoring or rather re-scoring an orchestral arrangement of my violin and piano. Three Sketches,' he wrote in March, 1934.

It will appear as "Orchestrated: Arthur Wood" tho' actually all the colouring and detail are *mine* – it has taken me months to do it – it really amounted to me making a new score so carelessly had the work been done. Now I have finished – so says my orb. No more of that kind of thing. Instead of calling it Three Sketches it will come out as Cloverley Suite. *Valsette, Elegy, Bolero.* . . . Do you remember Mr Jones of Cloverley Hall? We used to think him a very important person: he was head gardener there.

'I am so fond of shaking hands with the past,' he wrote to his cousin Mrs Johnson, who had unearthed some old papers of the Dodington Discussion Society. 'I remember I was a member of it *but never spoke.* I can recall many exciting evenings – principally the occasion when Mr Tongue opened a debate on 'Is Woman equal to Man?' 'I remember Mr Clayton (a jeweller) championed the Woman.'

Each spring his cousin Winifred sent him flowers from the Shropshire countryside. 'Beautiful, beautiful snowdrops!' he replied in 1935' and from Combermere Woods too. I seem to know exactly where they grew there.'

He was not pleased with the *Radio Times* when a March, 'President', by another composer called German was slipped into the programme with his

Christian name inadvertently added. Nor when two 'Tango Movements' were advertised 'Arranged German'. 'To many the matter may seem of little importance,' he wrote to the BBC, 'but from my point of view I fear I think differently.'

Rachel continued her campaign to keep his works before the public:

Own up Dicky Bird –
Did *you write*
Stanford 'Robin' on
Monday night?

Because he writes me, in answer to a card of thanks I sent for *Much Ado*, that a 'Midland listener' had said some charming things about it and had suggested he should perform *The Tempter*. I don't mind if you *did* or *didn't* but if you *didn't*, it makes it all the better doesn't it!
Fondest love, Jim.

Both continued to scan the papers for broadcast performances. When the *News Chronicle* referred to 'the veteran composer' the reaction was predictable:

Well, dash my rags
And blow my buttons
I *am* a veteran!

Fancy you hearing the N.G. Dances from Luxembourg! They seem to go 'marching along' like John Brown's body. With each *Weekly Exam*. I get my weekly surprise, for there's always something of mine down.

For some time the reader is mystified by references to 'the horse' in the Jim – Dick correspondence, for its performance seem distinct from those of genuine runners, such as Carioca, when German placed as occasional bet. Eventually, enlightenment comes and it transpires that 'the horse' is the frequency of E.G. on radio. Some weeks its form was better than others.

The horse wants a feed of corn! Still I am thankful for all mercies . . .

Old M.E. seems the best horse despite that nasty man Eric Blom. At the same time I quite see he is after the *very* best in art and he writes well. So be it! . . .

I have heard no more about the song selection. With the positive plethora of music available today it is a marvel that the poor old horse has a tail to wag with at all!

Although he was greatly affected by Elgar's death – 'Elgar's burial was beautiful in its simplicity,' he was also deeply moved by the award of a further honour which seems to have been unexpected and was certainly unsought.
In March 1934, he wrote to Dick:

> Now I have a bit of news for you! I am to receive the Royal Philharmonic Society's gold medal 'in recognition of your great services to English music'. The presentation will take place at one of the remaining concerts of the present season, and the committee hope that that one of my works may be included in the programme that night. This seems to depend on whether Beecham can alter one of his programmes to allow of it.
>
> If so, I should ask him to conduct *March Rhapsody on Original Themes*. All things considered I think this is·the best choice – but of course it may not come off at all. Anyway I shall get the 'Blue Ribbon' – the Gold Medal.

It was in 1870 when the Centenary of the birth of Beethoven was being celebrated that the Directors of the Philharmonic decided to have a gold medal struck to be presented to composers and executive musicians who had rendered eminent services to musical art and society. Wyon, a sculptor and numismatist, in designing the medal made use of the Beethoven bust in the Philharmonic's possession for modelling the head in profile which is on the obverse side. The first musician to receive it was Sir William Sterndale Bennett at a concert in 1871. In the same year, it was given to Joachim, Gounod and Charles Santley. Sir Thomas Beecham who was to make the presentation to German liked to recall a former occasion when he had bestowed the medal on the eccentric Pachmann. 'Pachmann,' said Sir Thomas, 'was a great judge of precious stones and the first thing he did on receiving the medal was to bite it.' The next thing he did was to chase Beecham around the platform in a keen desire to embrace him. The conductor, then young and active, eluded his pursuer and took refuge below the stage platform. When Rachmaninoff was presented with the medal he was apparently stricken with terror by the grave and funereal appearance of the Philharmonic Directors.

Although there is no hint of anything amiss in the press reports, the occasion produced an almost overpowering ordeal for German. All appeared to be planned. On the 16th April he wrote to Rachel: 'Sackville will call at about 7.30 and we will all four go together to the Queen's Hall. You and Mab in your two seats in the front row (Dress Circle) and Sack and self at the back near the stage door.' It was arranged that they would go round to Sackville's after the concert and have a glass of wine and Rachel was then to stay overnight with some friends in Maida Vale, 'then you come on here for our day's outing. Everything will be perfectly all right and here's to our merry meeting.' The Concert began with the Berlioz *Te Deum* and closed with Borodin's Polovstian Dances. 'The Frenchman's pious and the Russian's pagan orgy,' as one critic commented. German's hopes of having some of his music played were callously dashed.

Sir Thomas was nevertheless in fluent form when he made the presentation during the Interval. 'Not many people possess it,' he said of the treasured medal, 'and even if in the past the Society has been guilty of some errors of judgement it has always acted with the best intentions. In the case of Sir Edward, I think there can be no scope for error of judgement.' Sir Edward had appeared like a comet in the English musical world and he had won a public that had remained faithful to him ever since. 'It is possible,' Sir Thomas added, 'that no other composer who makes music of the quality of yours has the same public.' German responded by saying that when he remembered the names of the distinguished artists whom the Society had already honoured, he was more grateful than he could express. 'I shall honour this in my old age more than any other treasure,' he added. A great ovation followed and according to the fullest report: 'Sir Edward German, obviously moved by the reception the audience gave him, seemed almost overwhelmed by the conductor's personality. Sir Edward is an old man now but although a companion hovered at his elbow ready to give the aged composer his arm, he walked slowly, if firmly, on to the platform with a fine gesture of independence.' There was not surprisingly some indignation expressed by the critics that the Concert had contained no item by the man of the hour. Richard Capell in *The Telegraph* felt that a piece by Sir Edward should have rounded off the occasion although it must be said that the Polovstian Dances would be a difficult penultimate item to follow. *The Star* commented, 'German has also written some very charming dances and under the peculiar circumstances – still! enough said.' In fact the Philharmonic promised German that this omission would be replaced in the following year, but it did not do so and no work had been selected for performance by the time he died. He felt the same as the critic in *The Star*.

The familiar combination of honours bestowed and his serious music unappreciated was nothing new. It was at this moment that he penned the sad note which lies among his papers:

> I die a disappointed man because my serious orchestral works have not been recognised.
>   This has nothing to with my Lighter Works which have been recognised. The latter however are as serious artistically as my heavier works.
>   E.G. 1934

However independent of help he may have seemed in negotiating the Queen's Hall platform, he was in acute pain and found the occasion almost unbearable. The next message to come from him after 'Black Thursday' as he called it was written from his bed on the 22nd April where he was laid up 'with a little gout'. On the 28th he made a laconic entry in his diary: 'Thunderbolt'. On the 30th he added that trouble had been diagnosed with the prostate gland. On 6th May 1934, he wrote to Rachel,

> I told Dr Ham who called this morning that it was the most cruel, painful, hopeless and God-forsaken day in the whole of my long life – and so it was! Now I'll try and bury it although I can never forget it was Ham who saved the situation. An account of the presentation dictated by me and written and posted by Sackville was sent to the *Herald* (Whitchurch) but I have heard no more about it.

Immediate medication had rescued him on Black Thursday but he continued to find walking difficult. 'Thank you for yours but please write *large and not in pencil* – I just can't read it. In this regard, dear Mab is usually the culprit. Looking back in the last fortnight or so I seem to be waking from a horrible nightmare!' The crisis was kept from the press and public and after a few weeks his spirits revived. 'Black Thursday' became 'BT' in the usual German style and he warmed to Rachel's accounts of the flowers and spring colours in her garden.

He was further cheered as plans unfolded for a major revival of *Merrie England* at the Prince's Theatre by Claude Jenkins. As people pondered the Wall Street Crash and the Depression, the jazz frivolities of the 1920s lay temporarily under a cloud and there was a call for a return, if not to 'Victorian values' at least to Edwardian graciousness. A series of opera revivals was planned and German was well enough by July to attend a reception at the Theatre. Although some operettas were given at that period with cheap and shoddy costumes and scenery and with a depleted orchestral force, it was the intention of Jenkins ('Ap Jenkins' as he came to be in the correspondence) to mount a worthy and spectacular version. Herman Finck was to direct full chorus and orchestra and the distinguished tenor, Joseph Hislop, was engaged for the part of Raleigh. It is doubtful whether German worked regularly nine hours a day at the theatre, as one newspaper reported, but he took a close interest and was often there from an early hour.

July 29th 1934, M.E is all anyhow for the moment but according to Ap Jenkins' last letter, the principals (except Jill) are chosen: he hopes to get Joseph Hislop for Raleigh. On Tuesday from 10 to 1 there will be an audition for smaller parts and chorus. I hope to be present.

2nd August. Have just returned from meeting all the *M.E.* principals: they are certainly a nice lot to look at; but I don't know whether they can sing. Anyway you will be pleased to learn that Joseph Hislop is engaged for Raleigh: *he* will be all right vocally. It is announced for production on the 6th of next month; the time is too short – however we can only hope for the best.

Rachel sent some suggestions for improving the work as there was always a certain unhappiness about the dramatic implausibility of it all. German responded:

Your idea is nice and I like it; but the management are so pressed and pestered with getting the thing done in time, that if I mentioned it to them they would one and all have a fit! You have no idea what a rush it all is!

You see in these 'fighting against time' days there seems to be no time for working out pretty ideas like yours.

Alas and alack!
Alack and alas!

But do not let this prevent you from telling me of any ideas you may have. They are always worth taking seriously!

Shall be thankful when the prod. is over. On Tuesday Sackville comes down with me to Bournemouth. I feel the programme on the following day is too long: anyway Godfrey expects me to appear on the platform at the end of the concert.

Again I say: Shall be thankful when it is over

Yes, I remember the Snap cards (and see the pictures):

'My heart is in the Highlands'
'Look out! the Police are coming'
'Another gash of my poor chin'
'Who would be a Doctor?' etc.

Well, no more now dear Dick.

Sometimes Rachel's ideas were taken up. In 1935, Walter O'Donnell put together three of the composer's pieces: Valse Gracieuse, Souvenir, and Gipsy Dance into a Grand Suite and at Rachel's suggestion it was entitled *Three Memories*.

Merrie England duly opened on 6th September and proved highly successful. Over a hundred costumes were designed and that worn by Enid Cruikshank as Elizabeth was copied from the portrait by Zuccaro. The morris dancers costumes were copied from manuscripts in the British Museum. However, it should be added that on the backcloth Windsor Castle appeared in all the amplitude of its completion by George IV more than two centuries later.

As Bessie Throckmorton, Nancy Fraser played the part her mother Agnes Fraser had done in the 1902 production. Her father was Walter Passmore, the first Wilkins and Puck in *A Princess of Kensington*. German himself signed a statement to the press that he considered it superior even to the 1902 Savoy production and he took a close interest in its welfare. He fretted, 'Cochran's Revue will certainly do us no good: but we hope to be prepared for all sorts of competition. I believe there is another so-called comic opera coming up next week . . . on account of the success of *M.E.* Well let 'em all come.' Towards the end of the first month of the run those expectations seemed justified. 'Everything is difficult now owing to enormous competition but *M.E.* still holds on. All the same we must not expect too much.'

In fact it held on well, though Hislop as Raleigh did not ease the paths of the others with the same grace as his original.

You ask me about the theatre! Well, JH is still a difficulty but he, Herman (who by the way is in bed for lumbago) and I are getting things straightened out. The tour starts about the middle of February. For the rest – *The Rose of Persia* (an opera by Hood and Sullivan) is proposed for production next. After that *Tom Jones* is, I hear, to come along at the Princes but . . . In any case thank the Lord there is no *tenor* part!

At one Matinee performance German was accompanied by 'Faithful Joe', who reported:

> Most of the time he sat back in his chair, eyes closed, but face lit up, beating time on the edge of the stage box and occasionally saying quietly. 'Beautifully sung – lovely playing'. I was poignantly reminded of his failing eyesight when after Enid Cruikshank had sung 'O Peaceful England' he leaned over to me and said, 'They tell me she looks very beautiful.'

His critical faculties did not diminish. At the last performance he attended he wrote across his programme on the synopsis page, 'Yeomen too fast. Dialogue not Distinct!' After the play passed its fiftieth performance, he gave an interview, a rare occurrence, to the columnist, Jesse Collings, of the *Daily Sketch* in which the salient qualities of his public persona struck the journalist: 'Shy, retiring, dreading publicity. He made an interesting remark about his refusal to consider writing another opera. He blamed his eyesight but declared that he would not trust anyone to set down a score for him.'

His reference to the difficulty of approving an anamuensis arose from problems with the Cloverley suite. While the casting continued for *M.E.* he wrote:

> My real worry for the moment is correcting and altering the 2nd proofs of 'Cloverley Suite' – they have been most carelessly done by Arthur Wood, hence I am putting in every hour I have to make them right: it is a really terrible job. MORAL – Never trust *anybody* to your own work. Anyway it will sound very different when next you hear it.

He gave the same exact notice to radio performances.

> I wrote (Oct. 29) Leslie Heward thanking him for his excellent renderings of Sunday last. Of course, the Scherzo from the Symphony was much too slow and uninspired, but the *Welsh Rhapsody* was splendid. The Faithful Joe called on me on Friday to get my ideas re The *Tempter* Suite. I believe he is a real genuine chap and I feel grateful to him.

There had been a short period when it was felt that Joe's 'faithfulness' was being diluted, and that Warwick Braithwaite would prove the stronger champion of the orchestral works but that episode had been forgotten. HMV gave him as a gift for his seventy-third birthday one of their new radio-gramophones. 'Very kind of them. I have given up my old one to Mab as she has had a pretty poor one up to now.'

During the early part of the run of *Merrie England* he was confined to bed with lumbago and sciatica but he kept up an intermittent round of engagements. He had a photograph taken with Landon Ronald and McEwen which invoked the usual assualt on the veracity of the camera: 'It is so terrible that I expect you will have a fit when you see it. Landon and McEwen are good but I look not 72 – but 172 – I had no idea I had so many double chins – but there it is! A.D! I don't look much of 'as dapper as a Spy Cartoon!' In March 1935 he went to a dinner in honour of Marie Tempest. He always collected the large panoramic photographs of these musical and artistic gatherings, and this particular one shows him sitting next to George Robey, which he considered a great distinction. 'What do you think of that?' he wrote to Rachel. 'I found him a nice man to talk to – he makes violins as a hobby.' He was ill again shortly afterwards with a rheumatic and gouty chill. He also heard in March that plans to present *The Rose of Persia* had collapsed. 'It is a bad thing for high-class comic opera that *The Rose* has failed to bloom. One can't help feeling that the theatre may now go to the devil in the usual way – CINEMA! I hope it may not be so. I think *M.E.* is doing pretty well on tour – that is from notices I have seen – have no statistics.'

In May, the A.C.M. Club lost another quarter of its membership with the death of the octogenarian Mackenzie. 'Yes, the G.O.M. of Music has gone and I have just returned from his funeral. He was a great man and a great friend!' A win on the Derby enabled him to send Rachel an enhanced cheque the following month but he was not at all interested in racing, nor in increasing demands on his generosity. 'What you say about money troubles in the family touches me, but really, dear Dick, everyone seems to be in the same plight – especially as we all get older!'

As the 1930s proceeded he did not take the frequent place in music programmes that had been occupied at the start of the broadcasting era. 'I often wonder when I shall cease to be heard on the wireless. I am always waiting for Alice to come in and say, 'Nothing this week, Sir'. It is really extraordinary but there is always *something* in! Well, I am indeed thankful.' In Rachel's company he made an enjoyable excursion to the Kew Botanical Gardens and he fell into the habit of taking his friends and visitors there.

When performances were given his critical faculties remained alert. When visiting Mabel in Pinner in August 1935, they had listened to a performance of the *Welsh Rhapsody*. 'A fine performance except the Harlech March: this was too slow and un-rhapsodical!'

He enjoyed his record collection but appeared to be willing to dispense with at least one item in the collection. Writing to congratulate his brother-in-law Edwin on having returned to Whitchurch to preach a 'Jubilee' Sermon fifty years after his appointment at the Chapel he invited Mab up to see him and concluded: 'Take Arthur Bliss away!'

Rachel was worried about his attending the Landon Ronald Jubilee Dinner on 3rd November 1935 for which he had undertaken a great deal of the organization and where he was expected to make a short speech. Ronald was to receive a loving cup as a token of gratitude for his long reign at the Guildhall School:

> Am much worried about this Landon dinner (could wish now that I had never taken it on) – it is almost too much for me. You were right, however, when you said, 'I expect you will end by going', Developments have made refusal impossible. But all will be quiet *here*. As a matter of fact not a single friend of mine will be coming. Shall be jolly thankful when it is all over. Never again!

He had planned to to into a nursing home the day after the dinner for a check and overhaul. 'I don't think there is anything serious the matter. Anyway, I thought I had better just tell you. Lella will let you know how I get on during the week. So 'be not afraid if I don't write myself.'

The speeches were to be made by Hugh Allen, Lord Justice Greer, and Seymour Hicks. After these Ronald was to reply and call upon German for a few closing words. German was upset by the fact that an invitation had been sent to Sir Harold Boulton, of whose death he was unaware. 'I hasten to say that I did not know of the death of your distinguished father,' he wrote to the son. 'This may seem strange but it is true. He was one of the few great men in the world, both as poet and friend – and I feel very bitterly this terrible misunderstanding – He and I worked together in artistic friendship for so many years. I am very sad about it all.' Numerous letters to people in the musical world were necessary and he felt increasing fatigue. There were also donations and testimonies of friendship of Ronald to be acknowledged.

In fact he had to be rushed on the evening of the dinner itself to the Wimpole St Nursing Home and underwent an operation. This was more serious than he himself was aware. It was during his stay in the Home that Arthur German wrote to Joseph Lewis in the hope that a concert of his music would be a 'source of spiritual joy and comfort to the composer whose illness is of a very grave nature'. He suggested *Hamlet*, the *Leeds* Suite or the *March Rhapsody* for inclusion. Lewis replied that he had been very distressed to hear of the illness and while he would make enquiries of the programme committee the family could rest assured that German's music would be included in his programmes as usual.

Yet by the early spring of 1936 he was apparently recovering once again and his letter book was resumed. He was delighted to hear from 'the redoubtable Mrs Crosthwaite,' a lady in India, that *Merrie England* had been given in New Delhi, and a production was destined for Calcutta.

In February 1936 at the time of his birthday, he wrote to thank Rachel for her card

> 74!! Well I suppose I am 74! I am feeling better but Lord! How slow it all is and I mean the improvement . . . I am looking forward to another gathering of the 'remaining three' – it should be before long – each of the 'R.T.' has I suppose to make the best of things.

The Allied News Agency sought an article from him in February – in a series called 'Reminiscences': He replied

> Please be sure I fully appreciate the compliment you have paid me! I have thought over the matter of my Reminiscences as you suggest and feel at least for the present, I would prefer not to publish anything of a personal nature (not that my past has been too dreadful!)

He found a new champion in one of the BBC's most energetic and sympathetic young conductors, Stanford Robinson. It was he who arranged a 'Sullivan and German' programme. German enjoyed it greatly, 'Partly because I didn't know what would happen next. Anyway S.R. had selected a good programme and the performance was just perfect.'

On 25th April, 1936, in recognition of his eminent services to the art of music, he obtained the rare honour of admission as an Honourary Freeman of the Worshipful Company of Musicians. He had at first, when this distinction was offered, stipulated that he would not be able to attend in person. But by April he felt well enough to do so. He described the event prospectively to Rachel:

> Scene: Stationers' Hall. Met by Beadle – escorted by him to two Wardens at door or court room – *They* will escort me to the Worshipful Master – *he* will present me with the Scroll of Freedom and after his speech *I* have to say: 'This do I solemnly and sincerely declare.'
>
> Then I have to make *my* little speech of appreciation and thanks. That ends the ceremony. I am not staying for the dinner that follows. So

now you know what is happening. *Afterwards* I just go with friend Sackville and have a little meal and then all will be over and jolly thankful I shall be!

I don't suppose there will be any account of it in the papers – these City affairs seem to be so 'self-contained'.

After the ceremony he wrote to Mr Crewdson, the clerk:

I feel that in my few words on Tuesday evening, I have not adequately expressed my appreciation of the honour done me by the Worshipful Company of Musicians. I now wish to assure you that the Scroll (the beautiful Scroll) will ever remain with me and I would like you to convey my thoughts to the Worshipful Master and to all members of the Company.

This was his last appearance in public. He presented the MS of the Masque from *As You Like It* to the Company.

To Chappell's he wrote in April urging them to keep a watchful eye upon the proposed *Merrie England* at Scarborough. 'By the way I hope that you have made it plain to the Scarborough people that if they are enlarging the ballet, not a note by any composer but myself can be allowed.' Humour crept back in an arcane discussion with a friend over rival appeals of the names of the two singers, Clara Butt and Carrie Tubb. 'Well my dear Barnes, what a name to have! What can be done with such a name! or said of!'

Joseph Lewis was keen to arrange a meeting with a wealthy amateur composer, the Baron d'Erlanger but it had to be postponed. When Lewis asked for a rare item for a concert he suggested The Death of Buckingham (*Henry VIII*) and the Saltarelle (*Leeds Suite*) adding of the latter, 'as you know, wants a bit of playing'.

In May he had the delight of delving into a biography of his favourite composer Bizet, and he wrote to congratulate the author, D C Parket, eliciting lavish compliments in return.

German also wrote to thank Joseph Lewis for a concert of his work given on 16th May: 'I feel I owe you a debt of gratitude for the loyal way you have from time to time revived my more serious works. This now dates back many years. *I do not forget.*

At the end of May he was able to thank Lewis for a performance of *The*

Tempter Suite. 'I am glad my sister thanked you for it. She is a real critic.' To the conductor Foster Clark, he praised a performance of the 'Norwich': 'Yes it is difficult to get just the right tempo in movement 1. In my young days I often marked it a little faster than I ought to have done. Anyway the 'Norwich' you played on Friday afternoon was just right from beginning to end.'

In June 1936 hearing that Stanford Robinson was to move from the BBC Theatre Orchestra to be Director of music productions, he wrote to thank him 'for the many splendid renderings of my music . . . It is pleasant to think that in your wanderings and new experiences you will not leave me (speaking for myself) forgotten.' His hand was by now very shaky upon the page but he wished his friend every success.

All this was carried on against a great deal of pain. A 'bad attack' or rheumatism worsened his condition and the troubles resulting from his November operations returned with greater complications. He had hoped to see his sisters in London and take a cab-ride. 'You, Mab and I will have our lunch here after having taxied Regents Park or anywhere else you may fancy. Somewhere, anywhere,' but their visit had to be postponed.

To Richard Austin, who was conducting 'The Norwich' in July, he sent one of his familiar snippets of advice. 'Now that I am writing I would say that the very first opening bars generally seem to drag: you might "whip it up" a bit for those few bars and tell the trombones to "bite" their notes. I send my best wishes to you and to each other member of the orchestra.'

In July a friend suggested a holiday in North Wales.

Good! good! good! Wish I could come with you but, my dear boy, I don't think you realise how weak and uncertain my health is. I am sure your Cliff is an excellent and careful driver – all my friends have cars now – for some stupid fad of mine I do not go out with any of them. I repeat *stupid fad* – for so it *is* but there it is! I do appreciate your kind thought! Give my love to old Whitchurch as you pass through – What memories! fishing! cycling, Brown Bank, etc . . . Now I am going to get back to my old self – and be ready for our next meeting.

Amazingly he began work again, even contemplating fresh fields. 'I really do not know anything about the instrument – the accordion,' he told a publisher, 'but since you are desirous of publishing an arrangement of the *Henry VIII* Dances for it. I am wishful to fall in with your proposal. Perhaps I could see a specimen arrangement for the instrument, showing its chromatic capabilities.' At the same time he sent six bars of his orchestal arrangement of the *Merrie England* Dances to Arthur Wood to give some guide for a setting for military band. He was not altogether happy with the result. 'They seem to be so complicated that I fear I cannot hold myself responsible for having 'passed' them. The engraver may be better able to judge tham I am!!' His good nature would not allow him to be censorious. Having scribbled in a postscript that he thought No.1 'The Hornpipe' was 'the worst' he altered that to 'most difficult' and finally left it as 'the serious one'. He felt that the work was impeding his efforts to arrange a reunion of the Remaining Three. 'I am being driven crazy with the new arrangement of the *M.E.* Dances – I am having virtually to re-write them. I ought to be free by the 28 Aug. – Anyway let's make for it. All would have been simple but for these D-D D-S'

Throughout August he was fortified by pain killers and other medicaments, under the ministrations of 'Dr Benjie Balsam'. There were lapses. Mabel unfortunately never acquired he habit of dating her letters but usually headed them with a vague time signal such as 'Early Sunday Morning' or 'After Supper'. From what would appear to be August she wrote to Rachel:

The latest news of Jim is very good – and quite satisfactory so far as it can be. It seems he was feeling so much better on Wednesday that he went to the bank by himself (Sack being away). While there he felt rather ill and was helped back to a taxi by the driver, went straight to bed and has remained there ever since. He has been in awful pain, this time it seemed all over his body like acute rheumatism. – He seems to think he won't be able to walk again and I shouldn't be surprised if he becomes bed-ridden. I was very upset aout him on Friday night and couldn't sleep – phoned before 9 a.m. in morning yesterday. Alice replied he had had good night (after tablets) and pain was better. I asked her to put Dr Ham on to phone when he came so at quarter past 12 he rang me up and was altogether reassuring so far as I could hear, but he talked *so* fast and had so much to say. But I got this – Jim had had good night and was *tons* better, that pain had gone and that it was caused by rheumatic deposits . . .

I am going over this afternoon and will send latest news. After this I really feel it is foolish to get so upset about him, and he may live for a few years. Yet *I don't know.* Sometimes I think it must wear him out for he has definitely changed for the worse since you found him so bad a few weeks ago. He certainly has had two attacks since but each time made a good rally – and that is how he will go on it seems to me . . .

Sack is back now I'm glad to say. Alice is looking fine after her holiday and Jim says she is a 'tower of strength' and both women are devoted to him.

Further memories returned among the final group of letters when Nancy McIntosh wrote to recall *Fallen Fairies*. She had returned to look after Lady Gilbert in her old age, and wrote to say how much they had both enjoyed listening to German's music on radio. 'It is indeed a truly wonderful invention,' he replied. 'I was grieved to hear of Lady Gilbert's indisposition. I suppose we all have to bow to the inevitable – I know *I* have! I'm sure she owes her splendid record to your own careful keeping.'

In September he entered a nursing home again and underwent another operation. After a few weeks during which anxiety was felt for his condition, he was able to return home on 7th October. The last press cuttings which he collected recorded a performance of the *Theme and Six Diversions* under Joseph Lewis at the Swansea Festival and, a few days before he died, a photograph of *Merrie England* performed appropriately in the folk hall of Rowntree's model village near York.

Sackville now wrote his letters for him. One of the last messages dated 4th November 1936 was sent to his Johnson cousins at Whitchurch when he learnt of the death of Maggie, of Ted Jone's family, who had joined in the annual entertainments above the Grocery.

> And so dear Maggie has gone!
> I understand it is a happy release – therefore let us be thankful.
> Very fondest love to you Winifred and Ernest – God bless you!
>   Cousin German.

He could no longer add his own signature and the note sounds its own farewell.

He died on Armistice Day, November 11th. Rachel was with him. The cause was given as Carcinoma of the prostate. The date was the same as that on which he had lost his eyesight nine years earlier.

★　★　★

In the evening Rachel wrote to her husband, Will,

> My dearest Boy,
> Jim's end was beautifully peaceful and I thank God it is all over. I am trying to think it is his *birthday*. I was with him, also Sackville, Dr

Ham, Lella Davies and the two devoted women. Tho' I phoned Mab she was just too late.

This has been a dreadful day, with all sorts of business to be done . . . I have written Arthur (he is sure to get the day off tomorrow) asking him to go to Whitchurch early, see the Rector, and tell him that Ted is to conduct the little service at the graveside and see about the casket resting in the church on Friday night. Funeral is fixed for two pm. on Saturday.

Arthur will have plenty of time to get here tomorrow night after the business is settled.

Mab and I deeply regret that Jim wished 'No flowers'. He loved them so and his many friends here and in Whitchurch will be so disappointed. But it is characteriscally modest of him – he didn't want to put people to any expense or trouble . . .

I hope you will hear Landon Ronald's tribute after the 10.00 news to-night. He is greatly cut up (have just had a talk with him over phone).

Can't write more,

As always

R

Landon Ronald did indeed broadcast a memorable tribute that evening As it followed the Armistice Day Service of Remembrance, his words came into homes already full of poignant memories. As one listener wrote,

Please forgive these few lines – but – when you spoke last night of our great loss – and it's really a great loss to us all who are music lovers to hear that our beloved Edward German had left us on the Great Day of Armistice, it will be a double remembrance for some of us – War – Hell, our hearts torn with grief – the other – Music – Heaven. Our beloved Elgar and German, two we have all loved and admired, taken from us. It was fitting that you should speak of them: I admired the way you brought them together and spoke of dear Elgar's tears when he heard E.G's Pastorale in the Three Dances, a really marvellous movement. It will live for ever.

'It is hard indeed to realise.' Ronald had said, 'that that great little man, Edward German, whom I loved so well and the composer whose works gave me such pure joy, has passed away. It is good to know that he has been spared much suffering and that he is at rest. But the void he has left behind in the hearts of those who loved him will not easily be filled.' Having declared that *Merrie England* would live as long as this country existed, he concluded an emotional peroration. 'We are left behind to taste the sting of death and to mourn the loss of a dear friend and a great musician.'

Of German the man, he repeated the strange assertion that he was 'almost a recluse'. This is hard to believe. Beside flamboyant conductors and temperamental singers he may well have seemed quiet and he disliked probing personal interviews. Yet he was the centre and mainstay of a very dependent family with whom he maintained a lifelong correspondence full of jokes, happy recollections and warm sympathies. He struggled throughout his life to focus more attention upon his compositions and had a busy career as a conductor of his works enjoying a happier relationship with the playing musicians than most. He belonged to several impeccable musical bodies which he attended regularly. He loved the theatre, Lord's, billiards and convivial meals with the A.C.M. Club. His cupboard was stacked with photographs of star-studded dinners attended at the Café Royal and elsewhere. He had a private circle of friends such as Bert, the sporting cartoonist, with whom he relaxed and escaped from the cares of his work. In his dealings with publishers, the BBC and the makers of copyright law, he was a bombadier rather than a hermit. His friendships were intense and in early days he passed through several periods of turbulence not unknown to the gifted and the popular when pre-eminence among his friends was disputed. Yet the public who knew his music knew little of the man. He undoubtedly enjoyed cultivating the picture of the recluse and it is true, as Landon Ronald continued, that he never expressed unkind views about anyone and within the artistic professions this denotes several steps towards sanctity. His letters sometimes display indignation, but it is always in a slightly amused and dramatised form. There is no trace throughout his whole correspondence of any anecdote or gossip told against another with malice or the deployment of unfair comment against opponents and rivals.

The Times wrote appreciatively of his contribution to British music saying that in the early days of *Merrie England* and *Tom Jones* he had been

so frequently spoken of as Sullivan's successor that his generation tended to forget that he was something more than that – an artist of genius. The kind of music in which German excelled is commonly called 'light music' and its composer is apt to be lightly regarded. If that with which it contrasts were called with equal frankness 'heavy music' the virtues of the light hand might be more widely recognised. German unlike Sullivan was incapable of heavy handedness in his art.

It was *The Times* too which pointed to his incidental music now forgotten. 'The English Stage of the '90s, dominated by Irving, Tree and Alexander, adopted music as an element of its decoration and no composer of the period showed so sure an instinct for what was wanted of music in that capacity as German,' The *Manchester Guardian* made the same points, 'In Vienna, the grave of Johann Strauss lies not far from those of the great masters . . . Edward German wrote two operas which are in their way as fine as the best of Messager and Johann Strauss' The *Guardian* saw the Savoy tradition as an encumbrance to German's career rather than an advantage.

When German came to mastery over his technique no idea of light opera was possible to England if it ran counter to the Gilbert and Sullivan idea. The Savoy opera established not so much a tradition as monopoly. It was almost bad luck that German was called in to finish *The Emerald Isle* at the death of Sullivan; his orchestration surpassed in richness of harmony anything ever done by Sullivan but German lacked Sullivan's nimbleness of wit and familiarity of sentiment; these traits of style were not relevant to his bent. *Merrie England* was an attempt to sustain the Savoy school: German even vies with Sullivan in this work at the patter song and as music, pure and simple, the Neptune ensemble is felicitous enough. But it is in the warm melodic and harmonic flush of 'It is the Merry Month of May' that we can feel the German who in a more favourable environment might have given us a masterpiece of the lyric stage.

The cremation took place on the 13th November at Golders Green and a service at Whitchurch Parish Church in the same week. After the funeral service the ashes were taken to Whitchurch by German's sisters where their arrival at St Alkmund's was seen only by a few late evening passers-by. They rested overnight in the Parish Church and a service was held the following day. Among the wreaths was one in the form of a musical stave from the taxi drivers of Elgin Avenue near his home.

The Service was the simplest possible, and comprised Psalm 23, the hymn Abide With Me and the *Nunc Dimittis*. Of his own music the *Diversions* Four and Six, a *Song without Words*, the *Bourree* and *Elegy* from the Pianoforte Suite, and the melody of *David of the White Rock* were included. It will be remembered that the *Elegy* contained the contribution from his young pupil at Wimbledon School, fifty years before, Theodore Holland. At the close the Coronation March was played upon the organ where he had received his first official lessons as a child.

The Whitchurch Cemetery, unlike the Congregational Burial Ground in the centre of the town where his mother and father lie, is high on a windswept hill in the countryside. At the summit, from which stretches away the scenes of his boyhood, is the simple grave bearing the inscription 'Edward German Knight, 1862-1936'. Seeing it one thinks immediately of the words of Masefield which German himself had set, capturing the joys of escape from London Town:

So hey for the road, the west road, by mill and forge and fold,
And scent of the fern and song of the lark by brook and field and wold.
To the comely folk at the hearthstone and the talk beside the fire
In the hearty land where I was bred, my land of heart's desire.

Epilogue

The constant theme of the tributes paid to German during his lifetime was his popularity throughout all sections of society. When the cast of *Merrie England* left London for the provincial tour in March 1935, the old gentleman himself went to Euston Station early on a Sunday morning to wave off the train. They in turn thanked him for all he had done since the beginning of rehearsals to this 'last graceful act . . . We have enjoyed very much being associated with you in bringing more to the notice of the public your beautiful music,' wrote one. 'I do not think you know that there were two people on the platform yesterday, one a taxi-driver and the other a nurse, and they prided themselves on having attended *Merrie England* performances at the Prince's 37 and 68 times respectively.'

The same devotion shows in many of the letters which came to Biddulph Road and to Landon Ronald after his death. Some correspondents reported that they too had stood in silence by their radios while The Shepherd Dance was played that evening. A young man in Dewsbury who worked ten hours a day in a woollen factory to keep himself and his mother told Ronald how he came home in the evening exhausted and listened to German's music:

> In order to buy records you would be surprised at the things I have done. I have entered boxing tournaments, sung at concerts, sold my few birthday presents, etc. Most of my friends are mad about jazz music . . . it is very seldom I have the opportunity to talk to anyone about my favourite subject.

This echoes a letter received by German himself on his knighthood some years before:

> Among living composers there may be some more admired, more to be wondered at, but your music speaks with so friendly a tone that we love it best. Your melodies have captured in some way the dainty sweetness of the English countryside, meadows, streams, and woods. To people immured most of their time in noisy factories and such

places they are magically refreshing – a sort of mutual elixir. You must have cheered thousands like myself and that is a fine thing. I am afraid I have expressed myself rather stiffly. I am no musician – merely a young fellow that happens to be a music lover.

The gardener who tended the graves in the Dodington Burial Ground had once written, 'Words fail me, Sir, to express my appreciation of your music and my earnest wish is that you will long be spared to continue to work I know you love. It is our privilege to attend to the spot which I know is sacred to you in Whitchurch.'

Simple unaffected tributes such as these, both in life and in death, have to be recorded beside the stately and more formal tributes that came from august musical bodies. The Royal Philharmonic Society declared: 'The loss of an old and valued member of the society, a gold medallist and a composer of genius is a real sorrow to us all and a personal one to many.' Sir John Reith wrote from Broadcasting House to Ronald 'A line of appreciation and congratulation to you on your very good and moving tribute to Sir Edward German last night. While you were speaking, I hoped very much that some of his music might follow. It was all most impressive.' The directors of the Performing Right society wished to place on record 'their deep sense of the value of his work to British music and to their high appreciation of the many services he rendered to the society throughout the many years of his membership.' There were many echoes of the past in the letters received. One of the trio who had sung *Orpheus* in Beerbohm Tree's *Henry VIII* and who had danced in the banqueting scene told how German, after he had finished conducting the orchestra on the first night 'actually took the trouble to come up to our dressing room and thanked us personally'. Angela Vanbrugh, one of his pupils when he was sub-professor of violin, recalled his last public performance on the instrument when he played with her the Bach Double Concerto. He had also dedicated two violin solos to her 'which are much treasured'.

In the Bank Buildings at Whitchurch, his cousin, Mrs Johnson placed a large board in the window of the Grocery below the rooms where he had played in the early entertainments, announcing the death. Other tradesmen in the High Street followed suit and soon the town centre was in mourning.

His estate was valued at £57,117. He left gifts to his godchildren and smaller gifts to various friends. The MSS of his full orchestral scores he gave to his sisters, desiring that only the *Marche Solennelle* and the *Richard III entr'actes* should be published. After generous gifts to his housekeepers he bequeathed the residue of his property to his sisters during their lives with remainder to their children. Speaking of the *Richard III* music early in 1937 when the Will was published, Sackville Evans said that for some reason this music had been held back.

A strange little collection of cuttings was found in his wallet when he died. Along with a few extracts which describe his reception at the Whitchurch *Tom Jones* in 1931; a photograph of his appearance at rehearsal and a report on the 1932 Promenade Concert performance of 'The Norwich'; a newspaper photograph of his laying of the wreath at the Sullivan Memorial and a record of a brief speech he had made at the Shrewsbury performance of *Tom Jones* 'I believe there is a tradition that we are called proud Salopians. I do not know that I have ever been considered a proud one myself, but after tonight's performance I should not be surprised if I am converted.' there was an old newspaper photograph of Roome, the signaller who had hoisted Nelson's last message at Trafalgar and was an octogenarian pensioner at Greenwich. Another cutting told quite erroneously that Lloyd George liked to entertain German at Criccieth where he had in turn entertained Churchill, Rufus Isaacs and others with music in Welsh (underneath which the composer had written 'Good heavens!!') There was one of those horoscopes beloved of the press astrologers where a celebrity is chosen to represent the birthday (Somerset Maughan was next in the series), which described him as a keen character-reader, not demonstrative but feeling deeply with a highly strung nature, and promising in business and finance. The collection included a statement of Neville Chamberlain on the diminishing returns of high taxation, a comment on Destiny, and a joke copied from an L.N.E.R. advertisement:

If you want to see this world go by train
If you want to see the next, go by road.

Before the departure of his effects from Biddulph Road, the neighbours were alarmed by the great quantity of incineration which was performed in the garden and felt so strongly that valuable music might be being destroyed that a petition was considered. Of course, many of the numerous arrangements made of his music must have involved sketches and discarded versions which would have had no value. There are still a number of unpublished works which remain, including the early *Nocturne* for Violin and his *Piano Sonata*, first movement, from Academy days, together with songs across which he firmly wrote 'Not to be published', though whether for musical or sentimental reasons is not known. There were certainly no large-scale compositions left at his death which may have been lost.

Nevertheless, the whereabouts of much of the incidental music except for the extracts which we have in Suites remain a mystery; the Victorian Theatre, however haltingly, had caught some glimpse of the effectiveness of music which the worlds of film and television were later to exploit.

German's baton presented to him by the Leicester Oriana Society was given by the family to 'Faithful Joe'. 'I am really so glad to be able to do this,' wrote Arthur German. 'I only hope you may find this little souvenir of practical use . . . your own unfailing loyalty we shall always remember with gratitude. In conclusion I will use Sir Edward's favourite words together with my own sincere thoughts for your love of his music – Every kind thought.'

Lewis replied: 'The parcel has arrived and I cannot tell you how proud I am to receive it . . . I can have a glass case made for it and you may be sure it will be Exhibit No. 1 in my own personal effects.'

Although there was no major memorial concert, Lewis continued to correspond with the ever vigilant Rachel.

I always enjoy the *March Rhapsody* and although I know all about that gramophone cut, I cannot bring myself to take away a single bar. I had more than an affection for Edward German. He so embodied my ideals of what music ought to be, and the music maker, that I should hate to take away a single note. I did however do something which he and I had often discussed and, in fact, he had intimated the parts in the score where it should take place, and that is we used the *organ* in the big *tuttis* and at the end, and I am told it has a very fine effect.

As further plans for broadcasting German's works proceeded he wrote to Rachel, 'You may be sure that my programmes will always find a place for the dear man's great works because, to tell you the truth, there isn't anyone quite like him.'

It was not easy to persuade the programme planners to agree to a concert including the 'Norwich' Symphony. 'I have asked on many occasions,' wrote Lewis. '(I *do* have to ask you know, and what is worse, ask young gentlemen of twenty-five years of age!) to be allowed to do the 'Norwich' and on this occasion I have been promised "when a suitable period can be found".'

'Now that Sir Landon has passed away,' he wrote in September 1938, 'I feel that *all* my old friends have passed and I have no interest in all of the present generation. However, that only serves to add to the joy I get in playing the music of my dear friends of which category as you know your dear brother stands first.'

In October of that year, the 'Norwich' was included in a concert which included 'Autumn' from *The Seasons* and the *Valse Gracieuse*. It was given in Broadcasting House and Rachel and Arthur attended.

During the War Arthur attempted to gain an opportunity of conducting on the radio for a young Czech refugee, Vilem Tausky, whose credentials had all been left behind in his native land, and who appeared to be without friends or influence. It was the kind of gesture of which his uncle would have approved. By then, unfortunately, Lewis's connection with the BBC was almost ended. 'I know that if I intervened I should do more harm than good – you see I am not now on the staff just an old cast-off who must not interfere.' Tausky – pupil of Janacek and Suk – did in fact become a popular conductor. Joseph Lewis, who is not mentioned in the new Grove, wrote two books on 'Conducting Without Fears' in 1942 and 1945, which are well regarded by choral and orchestral society conductors.

The publication of the *Richard III* extracts and the *Marche Solonnelle* proved more difficult that was at first supposed. Ashdown had already published a piano selection from the incidental music arranged by German himself in 1920. Chappell were interested in the full score and Ashdown do not appear to have claimed rights over the originals. Mabel, much bothered by her new responsibilities, did what she could to further the project but the task of collating the 1920 Selection with the MS was a difficult one. The Marche appeared as a separate work in a military band arrangement appended to 'Sketches' from Sullivan's *Kenilworth* and without German's name on the title-page. The War delayed further work and the precious MS disappears from the records, probably lost in the fire at Chappell many years later. If they were returned to Mabel they must have been lost in the fire which destroyed the house of her daughter, Ruth, for they were not among the music salvaged which she was later persuaded to deposit with Southampton University Library.

In 1937 a memorial tablet to John David Jones, Betsy his wife, and Sir Edward German was dedicated and unveiled in Dodington Congregational Church. Rachel unveiled the tablet as her sister was indisposed, and *O Peaceful England* and the *Coronation March* were played on the organ where, along with Rachel and two friends, the young German had scratched his initials. The pastor spoke of John David and his thirty years as organist of the church and his wife who had taught for so many years in the Sunday School and brought an invaluable influence for good upon all those to whom she ministered. Within St Alkmunds a week later another tablet was dedicated and the *Herald* referred to a gift to the Cottage Hospital which would perpetuate in the town his affection for his birthplace.

In 1952 his sword of honour and court dress were given to the Whitchurch museum by Arthur German and his brother, where they remain beside the Edward German Room and the happily named *Merrie England* Bar, though re-arrangement of museum exhibits has carried off his portrait elsewhere. For his sisters the death of 'Dear Jim' left a gap which was quite irreparable. Both kept a vigilant ear to the radio and exchanged their feelings.

'I with you,' wrote Mabel, 'felt a big ache that dear Jim was not represented at the Command Performance. I listened to it, every bit . . . I longed to hear Jim's Coronation March and Hymn, and it had to end in longing.'

She recalled the days when Jim had set poems by friends in Whitchurch, including *Mabel*, words by John Elliott Bsc., and music by J. E. German, and *Secret Voices*, words by her husband, then the young minister. She remembered when girls from the Academy had sung to his family in his 'old rooms with Miss Friswell'. Her lot was in many respects a sad one. The young poet of Dodington had become a scholar and recluse, who did not enjoy listening to music. Like Rachel's husband, he was wracked with arthritis. Both sisters had wretched health and bulletins passed between them weekly as the list of ailments grew. Mabel guarded too the memories of her child, Edward Barrett, who died young ('That was a tragedy that should never have happened'.) Her surviving son, Eric, was in the colonial service in Uganda and his duties and the advent of war meant years of separation. Her daughter Ruth was strong-willed and independent with little care for domestic pleasures. [She was capable of generous gestures. On her parents' Golden Wedding she filled the house with gold and yellow flowers with the card 'a golden bouquet for a golden wedding from a brazen daughter.'] War brought the air attacks on London and these were especially frightening to elderly people with invalid relatives.

Mabel used some of the wealth which her brother's death had given to help those known to her who were in need.

> I feel sometimes instead of our big fortune if we could have had say £200 a year more, life would have been happier if he had been with us still in health. And now the money is a constant care to me because I see to everything. But I feel it is simply hateful to let it be a burden. It is very wonderful blessing and I find my greatest pleasure in life in helping others – that I do appreciate.

She died in 1942, not having witnessed the downfall of Hitler which was another absorbing pre-occupation of her family letters. Her husband wrote touchingly to Rachel:

Believe me I feel for you much in the bereavement you yourself have experienced in dear Mabel's death. Not only does it leave you the last tree standing in the little plantation that adorned and distinguished Alkington Road for many of us in those dear old distant days, but a very big thing has been taken out of your life in these recent days and indeed years. You were devoted sisters and occasional visits and constant correspondence filled a large place and was a chief interest with both of you.

. . . And, it will be as life advances the earlier days grow more vivid, not so much St Mary St. curiously as Alkington Road – the old drawing room, music and crambo and Jim and you – all of us wasting too many hours but enjoying talks and laughter. . . . Oh! Life is but a short Play: and varied are its scenes and characters. There's much comedy in it, not a little melodrama; and always, always something of tragedy – perhaps a great deal. Even though it means that some few of us are left to do the monologue, standing solitary, lonesome, it is on the whole a wonderful drama, and great. And have we not known charming stars in our company and watched their exits with loving reverence?

Rachel lived on for another decade and died peacefully in 1951.

★   ★   ★

For many years after his uncle's death, Arthur exercised the supervision over matters to do with performance and copyright. As early as 1934 the Columbia Gramophone Company had recorded a sharp drop in sales of German records, especially the selections from *Tom Jones* and *Princess* and they did not feel justified in risking the recording of other works. During the war years the jaunty patriotism of his operas ensured numerous revivals by local societies and on the radio Stanford Robinson did noble work to keep German's name before the public. In September 1940 during the Battle of Britain, a two-part radio biography was given with musical extracts. Arthur German took down the details hastily on the back of a pamphlet entitled *Your Home as Air Raid Shelter* issued by the Ministry of Home Security. The programme included Selene's aria from *Fallen Fairies*, Partridge's song from *Tom Jones* and music from *The Conqueror*, the First Act Finale from *Princess* and the *Valse Gracieuse*.

On the day that France fell, the Governing Body of Charterhouse were due to hold a meeting in London, and the Archbishop of Canterbury, the chairman, confided the news at the start of proceedings. They then settled down for more than two hours to discuss the boarding house drains at this particular school. Years later, when the headmaster recounted the story in a lecture on public schools in Germany, an ex-Luftwaffe officer who had been concerned in the plans for the invasion of Britain came up and wryly said that he now understood why Hitler had lost the war. One cannot help feeling that listeners to the *Valse Gracieuse* during the Battle of Britain gave further proof of unconquerable optimism.

Professional representations of *Merrie England* were much rarer. A production mounted at Croydon in the war years was defeated by the bombs and the blackout. The press noticed with approval that the heart-stirring verses of The *Yeomen of England* were delivered by an Earl of Essex who served as a member of the Police Force by day. At the end of the War when national feeling was still running high a film version was mooted. In 1936 German himself had agreed to the use of his *Nell Gwyn* score for a Herbert Wilcox film, *Peg of Old Drury*, though he was somewhat baffled by the change of story. The actor Raymond Massey was enthusiastic over a *Merrie England* film, and it seemed a hapy augury when a party of J. Arthur Rank officials arrived at Waterloo Station to discuss the project to the strains of German's music coming over the loudspeakers. Edward Dryhurst, the producer, was a relative of Dr Burnett Ham who had attended German during his final illness, and for some unaccountable reason had failed to collect his fees, finally submitting a bill for £1,000, for several hundred visits, to the astonished executors. Chappell, however, did not warm to the idea of a film, for there were still many amateur performances given every year. A film of *The Mikado* had been only moderately successful, and the costs appeared likely to be great. Dryhurst revived the idea from time to time but was unable to raise the necessary capital.

A more fruitful attempt to celebrate the victory year was made by the impresario Jack Waller, who commissioned Edward Knoblock, a dramatist known for his collaboration with Arnold Bennett in *Milestones* to write an entirely new play, *Elizabeth of England*, using the original music. Knoblocks' version did not win favour with Chappell and he was over-critical of the original. 'Believe me,' he told Arthur,

I have worked very hard to make something effective with the incomprehensible book which I am convinced must have bewildered the original company as much as it does nowadays. I do not know Mr Goodman at all. He looked at my book which has worked in all the songs in a much more effective way, though of course, not in the same sequence, and finding that I had invented a new story was (as he told Mr Walker) 'shocked'. I wonder how he could expect me to re-write the story without changing it.

The new production had the advantage of some fine singing from tenor, Heddle Nash and baritone Dennis Noble, but it did not meet with universal approval. The critic Stephen Williams wrote,

> Was it Oscar Wilde who said after seeing what he thought was a bad performance of *Hamlet* that it would solve once and for all the ancient problems as to who wrote the great tragedies. All they had to do was open up the graves of Shakespeare and Bacon and see which one had turned over. I propose that a similar test be applied here by exploring the honoured remains of Edward German and Basil Hood. I think that both will have been caused a certain amount of unrest by this production.
>
> The plain truth is that this is not a new version of *Merrie England* at all, it is an entirely new play into which the principal numbers of German's score are introduced by timely and accommodating tricks in the libretto. Windsor Castle, the sturdy foresters, the May Queen, and that green-mantled Arcady which is for ever England, are all swept away. We are given instead a complicated story of Spanish spies and court intrigues in Whitehall and the Mermaid Tavern. Shakespeare, Jonson, Dekker and Lord Burghley are there and not one is given a single line that could earn his place in history. Burghley, a losing battle fought valiantly by Douglas Stewart is especially unlucky. He has a great many words to speak and nothing to say . . .
>
> Not for a long time have I heard so much costume play jargon, so many witticisms at which the players laugh so much more heartily than the audience.

Yet the vivid score survived the transplant.

> The music is still there, and very enchanting music it is as we all know. The *Yeomen of England*, sung with immense ardour by Dennis Noble, is one of the finest patriotic songs ever written and the finale of Act I (I refer in terms of the original score) rises like certain things in *The Yeoman of the Guard* to the level of grand opera. *The English Rose*, sung by Heddle Nash with the customary but unauthenticated high B flats can still move me after a whole life-time.

Knoblock, like the critics of 1902, had not realised that the chief protagonist in *Merrie England* is the English Spring, with its rushing pulse and sudden delights and regrets. The action could not be moved into the city, and the music was ill fitted for a plot that required the score of *Don Carlos*.

Knoblock died before the opening of *Elizabeth of England* and his libretto was never published. It had a successful tour but operatic societies were lukewarm in accepting it and the costs of publishing an entirely new set of parts for the orchestra would not have been justified. It had, however, reached the stage, which a new version of *A Princess of Kensington* had failed to do. A radio programme in 1938 had revived interest in the score and a Mr Avalon Collard was commissioned to revise the book and amend the lyrics which he did in 1939. The result was sent to Ruth Tongue who made further alterations of her own. 'My opinion,' wrote Arthur German, 'is that when Ruth barged in Collard barged out, satisfied to forego his fee, if he could escape with his life.' The war delayed further action, Ruth mislaid the script and the project foundered.

In Coronation Year hundreds of performances of *Merrie England* were given, and brass and military bands settings were made of *Long Live Elizabeth*. A very impressive version was given at Luton Hoo by over 1,000 performers, and a lavish display of spectacular effects in an open-air production. For Sadler's Wells in 1961 Dennis Arundell re-worked the plot, employing rather less drastic surgery than Knoblock. To remove the Queen's plot to poison her rival, the details of one of the many conspiracies against the life of the historical Queen were included from the story of Dr Lopes and foreign factions at court. It was to assist in checking the score that Mrs Winifred German took the original MS up to Chappell. She was asked to leave it for some copying work but decided to take it home. She learnt the following day of the fire at Chappells in which it would undoubtedly have perished. In the new version Anna Pollak enjoyed a great success as the Queen, but once again local operatic societies were conservative and the expense of a published score was not thought to be justified.

The early 1960s were not years of patriotic fervour and critics were quick to deride 'old chest-beating tush-mush about English yeomen, English roses, English ale and English folk dancing'. Even the critic Edmund Tracey however, though he called the work a 'Podsnappian-gloss' on Elizabethan times and was quite unmoved by the score, admitted that 'the theatre seemed to be filled with Empire Loyalists' cheering as they hadn't cheered since *Cavalcade*.' In recent years performances of *Merrie England* have been reported from both Japan and Russia where one wonders what the translators have made of *O Peaceful England*.

Arthur German continued to be a zealous guardian of his uncle's reputation. In 1958 an impression that *Merrie England* had been slightingly referred to in Kingsley Amis's novel *Lucky Jim* led to pressure on Chappell who ascertained that the reference had been generally historical and did not apply to the opera. He had something of his uncle's epistolary style. During this exchange he made reference to a brand of tinned peas that went under a 'Merry England' label. 'But we don't mind that, do we?'

He also made every effort to keep Edward German's name before the public, and when the film *Tom Jones* was mooted, suggested that the opera music might be used, though in the event it would have been a chaste accompaniment to a version of Fielding's novel that gave a much racier flavour of the original than Courtneidge had attempted.

In German's Centenary year 1962, the concert version of *Merrie England* was given by the Hallé Orchestra and Sheffield Philharmonic Society. Barbirolli was a great admirer of the composer. He had performed the 'Norwich' Symphony in 1936 shortly before German's last illness and he wrote to Arthur, 'I treasure the letter I received from him just afterwards in the following words: "Your interpretation of my Norwich Symphony tonight was indeed a splendid one. I thank you for your lead and every member of the orchestra for their follow. No detail was missed and the work was performed most sympathetically."'

In 1956 when Barbirolli himself was in hospital and there had been some correspondence, Evelyn Barbirolli wrote, 'He is the greatest admirer of your uncle's genius and asks me to tell you that his music gives him more pleasure than most. He really does love it!'

The tides of fashion had by then set against it. As late as 1949 the *Radio Times* could still write truthfully that millions of listeners had been captivated by the art of Edward German and of 'the spell he has cast over so large a section of the public'. In introducing a BBC Light Music Festival in that year, Harold Rutland wrote: 'Edward German was the first composer whose music I fell in love with as a boy. I remember borrowing from the local library the vocal scores of *Merrie England* and *Tom Jones* and playing them through so often that within a short time I knew them from memory.' The present writer experienced exactly this reaction. Rutland recalled going to his first Promenade Concert at Queen's Hall when German conducted the *Welsh Rhapsody*: 'While it was being played I gazed in a glow of excitement at the trim unassuming figure on the rostrum and I said to myself, "Is it you? Are you really there?"'

Now that all the world's great operas can be brought into homes in vivid and well-nigh impeccable recordings, it is hard to imagine the devotion which German's music, accessible and rewarding, brought to communities in the most far-flung towns in the country. 'So long as the resounding notes of Wagner and Beethoven float down the misty vales of this old England of ours,' wrote one reporter, 'So long as men gaze on the paintings of Rembrandt, while there is still a love of Shakespeare, Shelley and other immortal poets; so long will the music of Edward German shine forth as a bright constellation in the firmament of art.' This sweeping survey of European culture was the prelude to a review of *Tom Jones* by the Augmented Wesleyan Choir of Penzance. Yet the words were not insincere.

When music sprang from the home, the chapel, the choral and operatic societies, Edward German's music was indeed known to millions to whom some of the most frequently heard composers of to-day, Mahler, Richard Strauss, Stravinsky, Prokofiev, were quite unknown. Even if the average music-lover heard the occasional Puccini aria or Verdi's *Miserere* sung in the local church halls, the dramatic impact of the great operas themselves could not be felt. To countless numbers, German was the gateway through which they passed to gain a knowledge of wider horizons and different musical languages. To others his work remained a joyous and lively contrast to the stereotyped religious music that formed a great deal of their diet, and a summit on which they were happy to rest.

The Llandudno local paper, using the epithet as a compliment, declared that *Tom Jones* was the most 'pretentious' work the local society had so far attempted. And did not Elgar himself summarise his works as 'the highest and most beautiful of the lighter forms of music?'

Yet as knowledge and discernment have spread it is strange that a veritable glacier of neglect has crept over his impressive orchestral work. In the record catalogues he is no longer represented even by *Merrie England*, leaving aside *The Leeds Suite*, *The Seasons*, the Symphonies, and the *Rhapsody on March Themes*. Stranger too, is the fact that in a period when musicology is strong and interest in the history of music has led to some outlandish places, his unique corpus of Shakespearean stage music should have been passed over with total disregard. A great deal of it may have been lost, but the overtures to *Richard III*, *Henry VIII*, *Romeo* and *Much Ado* as well as much else remains unplayed, unrecorded and unknown, while recondite works find their way into the catalogues. It is the music of an era and worth resuscitating on historical grounds alone, not to mention its excitement and its skilful sense of the darkened theatre and the tenseness of drama. Many a spectacular television series made on a huge budget has reached an appreciation of the importance of the musical score which Irving and Forbes-Robertson divined almost a century ago.

German has suffered, too, from the willingness of modern minds to award the gold, silver and bronze metals in the arts as well as in the world of sport where such concepts are viable. The ten greatest composers, the ten greatest novels, the ten greatest paintings, impart the concepts of the supermarket into areas where distinctiveness and originality, a blending of excellences and incongruities have to be judged with finesse. The search for hierarchy has obliterated our sense of the unique. There is much to be gained from a revival of interest in and appreciation of German's music and not just for a small group of devotees but in a wide enough sense to show the unique part he played in British music when its links with the past as well as its beauty held sway.

The last word must rest with Alec Rowley, musician and teacher, in words written shortly after German's death:

And so, Edward German, you lie quiet now, but your music is alive in our hearts and we are eternally glad that you gave so much artless joy and hope to the world. Your simple life is told in music, and your kindliness of spirit is ever with us. You were a musical peace-maker and would that the world of today had listened to your voice and translated it into action.

List of Compositions

German's compositions appeared in many different forms, vocal and instrumental. I have not included the many Tonic Sol. Fa additions in this list.

Work	Version	Date Written	Date Published	Publisher	
OPERAS The Rival Poets. Operetta.	Vocal Score. Selection Arr. V. Hely Hutchinson Arr. Military Band. Gerrard Williams Duet: Love in her Boat Happy Days	1883-6	1900 1930 1901	Boosey Boosey	
The Emerald Isle (A. Sullivan and E. German)	Vocal Score Concert Version Selection	1901	1901 1931 1901	Chappell Chappell Chappell	
Merrie England	Vocal Score Arr. Wilfrid Bendall Vocal Score Arr. Wilfrid Bendall Concert Version Concert Version (Final Edition) Concert Version (Choruses only S.S.A) Arr. Felton Rapley	1902	1902 1903 1908 1930 1951	Chappell Chappell Chappell Chappell Chappell	Arr. from Full Score

Work	Version	Date Written	Date Published	Publisher	
	Pianoforte Solos		1902	Chappell	
	Selection for Orchestra Arr. Carl Kliefort		1902	Chappell	
	Military Band Selection		1902	Booseys' Military Journal	
	Fantasia Military Band		1914	Chappells' Army Journal	Arr. D. Godfrey
	Second Selection		1927	Chappell	
	Second Selection Military Band		1927	Chappells' Army Journal	Arr. D. Godfrey
	Second Selection. Piano Forte		1926	Chappell	
	Six Easy Pieces for Piano Forte		1925	Popular Opera Series	
	Selection. Violin and Piano		1902	Chappell	Arr. T.F. Dunhill
	Four Dances Military Band		1902	Chappell	Arr. H. Tolhurst
	Orchestra		1937	Chappell	
	Military Band		1936	Chappell	Arr. Arthur Wood
	Four Dances (continued) Violin and Piano				Arr. Composer
	Piano		1902	Chappell	
	Songs etc.				
	Duet: Come to Arcadie		1902	Chappell	
	Duet: It is the Merry Month of May		1902	Chappell	
	Duet: She had a letter		1902	Chappell	
	Duet: Waltz Song		1902	Chappell	
	Fantasia on E. German's Opera Flute and Pfte.		1902	Chappell	Arr. F. Griffith
	Waltz on Melodies by E. German		1902	Chappell	Arr. C. Kiefert
	Lancers on Melodies by E. German		1902	Chappell	Arr. N. Williams
	Quintet. Love is meant to make us glad		1902	Chappell	

Work	Version	Date Written	Date Published	Publisher	
	Arr. as Song (S)		1902	Chappell	Db. Eb. F.
	Arr. as Quartet		1902	Chappell	
	Arr. as Duet. (S and B)		1915	Chappell	
	Arr. as Trio (SSA)		1927	Chappell	
	Solo: O Peaceful England		1902	Chappell	
	Arr. as Two Part Song		1935	Chappell	Arr. C. Lucas
	Arr. as Chorus (SATD)		1947	Chappell	Arr. C. Lucas
	Solo Yeomen of England		1902	Chappell	Arr. C. Lucas
	Arr. as Quartet (T.T. BB)	1947			Arr. C. Lucas
	Solo: English Rose	1902			G & Bb.
	Arr. Part Song (SSA)	1953			Arr. by Felton Rapley
	Quartet: In England Merrie England				
	Arr. S.A.B.	1902	1964		Arr. by Felton Rapley
	Chorus: Long Live Elizabeth	1964	1964		
	Arr. Female Chorus SSA and SA				
	Part Song TTBB		1953		Arr. Felton Rapley
	Military Band		1953		Arr. W.J. Dutheit
	Brass Band		1953		
A Princess of Kensington	Vocal Score	1903	1903	Chappell	Arr. Wilfrid Bendell
	Pianoforte Solo		1903	Chappell	Arr. Dan Godfrey Jnr.
	Selection		1903	Chappell	
	Selection (Pfte)		1903	Chappell	
	Lancers on Melodies		1903	Chappell	Arr. Sir D. Godfrey
	Fantasia on Airs for Fl. & Pfte		1903	Chappell	Arr. H. Leclire
	Five Easy Piano Pieces		1925	Chappell	Arr. T.F. Dunhill
	Concert Selection		1909	Chappell	
	Quartet: Four Jolly Sailormen		1903	Chappell	

Work	Version	Date Written	Date Published	Publisher	
	Arr. as Song		1905	Chappell	
	Solo: He was a simple sailor man		1903	Chappell	
	Solo: The Happy Man		1903	Chappell	
	Solo: Oh what is Women's duty		1903	Chappell	
	Duet: Seven O' Clock in the Morning		1903	Chappell	
	Solo: A Sprig of Rosemary		1903	D Eb. F	
	Twin Butterflies		1903	Chappell	
	Sextet Where Haven Lies		1903	Chappell	
	Who that knows how I do love you		1903	Chappell	
	March. The Red Marines (Piano Duet)		1903	Chappell	Vocal List of Part Songs
Tom Jones	Vocal Score (First Edition)	1907	1907	Chappell	
	Concert Version (Final Edition) (Choruses only)		1908	Chappell	
			1913	Chappell	
			1930	Chappell	
			1913	Chappell	
	Pianoforte Solos		1907	Chappell	Arr. Wilfred Bendell
	Pianoforte Selection		1907	Chappell	Arr. H.M. Higgs
	Orchestral Selection		1907	Chappell	Arr. Dan Godfrey. Full and Small Orch.
	Three Dances. Morris Dance Gavotte Jig.		1906	Chappell	Full and Small Orchestra
	Three Dancers. Pianoforte		1907	Chappell	Arr. by Composer
	Five Easy Pieces for Pfte		1907	Chappell Popular Opera Series	Arr. Thomas Dunhill
	Songs: By Night and Day		1907	Chappell	
	Dream O'Day Jill		1907	Chappell	
	Green Ribbon		1907	Chappell	Eb. F.

Work	Version	Date Written	Date Published	Publisher	
	If Love's Content		1907	Chappell	C. Db.
	On a January Morning		1907	Chappell	
	Today, my Spinet		1907	Chappell	C. Db.
	Waltz Song		1907	Chappell	C. D.
	We Redcoat Soldiers Serve the King		1907	Chappell	
	West Country Led.		1907	Chappell	
	Madrigal: Here's a Paradox For Lovers		1907	Chappell. Vocal Library of Part Songs	
	Tom Jones Lancers, Melodies by E. German				Arr. L. Williams
	Valse on Melodies by E. German				
Fallen Fairies or Moon Fairies	Vocal Score	1909	1909	Chappell	
	Selection (Orchestra)		1910	Chappell. Operatic and Popular Sel. For Orch.	Arr. D. Godfrey F. G.
	Songs: Oh Love that Rulest		1910	Chappell	
	Waltz: Poor purblind wayward youth		1910	Chappell	
	Thy Features are Fair and seemly (Duet)		1910	Chappell	
	When Knight loves Ladye (Song arr. from Duet)		1910	Chappell	
	With all the Misery		1910	Chappell	
ORCHESTRAL & INCIDENTAL MUSIC The Guitar	Pizz. Strings	1883	1885	London Publishing Co. (Ashdown)	

Work	Version	Date Written	Date Published	Publisher	
Music To 'Richard III'	Overture Full Score	1889	1902	Novello	Arr. G. Miller
	Military Band		1896	Novello	
	Piano Duet		1891	Novello	
	Selection for Pfte		1890	Ashdown	Arr. Composer
	Selection for Pfte		1920	Ashdown	Arr. Composer
	Intermezzo Funebre for Pfte		1890	Ashdown	Arr. Composer
	Processional March for Pfte		1890	Ashdown	Arr. Composer
Symphony No. 1 in E Minor	Full Orchestra	1890	1904	Novello	Based upon earlier R.A.M. Version
	Arr. Pianoforte Duet		1904	Novello	Arr. by Composer
Marche Solonnelle		1891	1940's	Chappell	Military Band Arr.
Music to 'Henry VIII'	Suite from Music (Pfte. 4 bands)	1892	1892	Novello	
	Overture. Preludes Act II, III, IV		1893	Novello	String Parts only
	Intermezzo. (Pfte)		1897	Novello	Arr. Composer
	Coronation March. Prelude. Act IV		1898	Novello	String and Wind parts published separately
	Coronation March. Arr. Military Band		1898	Novello	Arr. Dan Godfrey Jnr.
	Coronation March. Arr. Organ		1904	Novello	Arr. J.E. West
	Coronation March and Hymn (Orch)		1911	Novello	
	Coronation Arr. Pfte		1911	Novello	Arr. Composer
	Coronation March Arr. Military Band		1911	Novello	Arr. D. Godfrey. Jnr.

Work	Version	Date Written	Date Published	Publisher	
	Three Dances		1893	Novello	Orchestral Parts
	Full Score		1901	Novello	
	Military Band		1893	Novello	Arr. D. Godfrey Jrn.
	Quintet. Pfte & Strings		1892	Novello	Arr. Composer
	Violin and Piano		1893	Novello	
	Pianoforte		1900	Pirated Edition	
	Pianoforte		1892	Novello	Arr. Composer
	No. 1 Morris Dance. Arr. Organ		1928	Novello	Arr. E. Lemare
	No. 2 Shepherds Dance (Orch.)		1922	Novello	
	No. 2 (Words by W.G. Rothery)				Arr. Composer
	Two Part Song S.A.		1920	Novello	
	Two Part Song Children's Voices		1920	Novello (School Song Book)	
	Unison Song Children's Voices		1937	Novello (School Song Book)	
	Four Part Song. SATB		1954	Novello (Part Songs)	Arr. H.A. Chambers
	No. 3 Torch Dance. Organ Solo		1928	Novello	Arr. E.H. Lemare
	Intermezzo. Prelude Act III				
	Wind Parts		1897	Novello	
	String Parts		1898	Novello	
	Organ Solo		1907	Novello	Arr. E.H. Lemare
	Prelude Act V. Hymn (Strings)		1898	Novello	
	Organ		1899	Novello	
	Trio. Orpheus with his Lute. Female voices		1892	Novello (Collection of Trios)	
	Arr.: Four Part Song (Mixed)		1921	Novello (Part Song Book)	Arr. Composer

Work	Version	Date Written	Date Published	Publisher	
	Arr.: Two Part Song		1933	Novello. School Songs	Arr. H.A. Chambers
	Arr.: Women's Voices (Three Parts)			Galaxy Music Corporation. N.Y.	Arr. A. Walter Kramer
Gipsy Suite	Full Score	1892	1902	Novello	
	Arr. for Military Band (Four Characteristic Dances)		1894–5	Novello	Arr. Dan Godfrey. Jnr.
	Arr. Solo and Duet (Pfte)		1894–5	Novello	Arr. Composer
	Arr. Violin and Pfte				
	Valse Melancholique. 'Lonely Life' Unison Song		1934	Novello. (Part Songs)	Words by M. Sarson
	Allegro di Bravura. Two Part Song		1935	Novello (School Song Book)	Words by M. Sarson
Symphony No. 2 in A Minor (The Norwich)	Pianoforte Duet	1893 Full Score and Parts	1931	Novello	Arr. Composer
			1899	Novello	
Music for 'The Tempter' Play (H.A. Jones)	Suite. Overture. Bacchanalian Dance. Berceuse. Orchestra	1893	1900	Ashdown	

Work	Version	Date Written	Date Published	Publisher	
	Military Band		1917	Chappell	Arr. Dan Godfrey Jnr and Composer
	Piano Solo		1894	Ashdown	Arr. Composer
	Piano Duet		1894	Ashdown	Arr. Composer. Re-issued 1913
	Violin & Pfte		1894	Ashdown	Arr. Composer
	Selection of Themes (Pfte)		1894	Ashdown	Arr. Composer
	Berceuse. Words by Helen Taylor		1948	Ashdown	Arr. as Part Song. H. Geehl. 1948 (Ashdown)
Symphonic Suite in D Minor. (The Leeds)		1895			
	Orchestral Parts		1895	Novello	
	Four Hands Pfte		1907	Novello	Arr. Composer
	Valse Gracieuse. Full Score		1902	Novello	
	Solo Pfte		1896	Novello	Arr. Composer
	Duet Pfte		1896	Novello	Arr. Composer
Music for 'Romeo and Juliet'	Selection of Themes (Pfte.)	1895	1895	Novello	Arr. Composer
	Suite. Pfte. (Four Hands)		1896	Novello	Arr. Composer
	Suite. No. 5. Dramatic Interlude				
	Orch. Parts		1896	Novello	
	No. 4 Nocturne		1896	Novello	Arr. Composer
	Orch Parts		1895	Novello	Arr. Composer
	Pfte Solo		1909	Novello	
	Violin and Pfte.				
	No. 2 Pastorale				
	Orch.		1896	Novello	Arr. Composer
	Pfte.		1896	Novello	

Work	Version	Date Written	Date Published	Publisher	
	Violin and Pfte.		1895	Novello	Arr. Composer
	No. 3. Pavane				
	Full Score		1902	Novello	
	(Parts)		1896	Novello	
	Arr. Pfte.		1895	Novello	Arr. Composer
	Pfte. Duet		1895	Novello	Arr. Composer
	Violin and Pfte		1895	Novello	Arr. Composer
	No 1. Prelude				
	Parts		1896	Novello	
	Full Score		1902	Novello	
Music for 'As You Like It'		1896			
	Duet: It was a Lover and his Lass		1897	Novello	
	Two Part Song		1926	Novello	
	Two Part Song		1933	Novello (School Song Bk)	
	Solo. It was a Lover and his Lass		1919	Novello	G & Bb.
	Masque. Full Score		1902	Novello	
	(Orch Parts)		1897	Novello	
	Military Band		1898	Novello	Arr. Dan Godfrey Jnr.
	Pfte.		1897	Novello	Arr. Composer
	Pfte Duet		1898	Novello	Arr. Composer
	Violin and Pfte.		1897	Novello	Arr. Composer
Church Music for 'Michael and his Lost Angel'		1896	–	Unpublished	Ms. existed in 1920's

Work	Version	Date Written	Date Published	Publisher	
Symphonic Poem Hamlet	String Parts	1897	1899	Novello	
	Wind Parts		1899	Novello	
	Arr. Four Hands (Pfte.)		1904	Novello	Arr. A. E. Grimshaw
English Fantasia. In Commemoration	String Parts	1897	1897	Novello	
Music for 'Much Ado About Nothing'	Selection of Themes. Arr. Pfte.	1898	1898	Novello	
	Overture. Orch. Parts		1898	Novello	Arr. Composer
	Arr. Pfte Duet		1898	Novello	Arr. Composer
	Bourrée and Gigue Full Score (Parts)		1902	Novello	
			1898		
	Arr. Military Band		1899	Novello	Arr. Dan Godfrey Jnr.
	Pfte. Solo and Duet		1898	Novello	Arr. Composer
	Violin and Pfte.		1898	Novello	Arr. Composer
Symphonic Suite 'The Seasons'	Orchestral Parts	1899	1900	Novello	
	Full Score		1912	Novello	
	Harvest Dance (Summer) Arr. Military Band		1900	Novello	Arr. Dan Godfrey Jnr.
	Solo and Duet Pfte		1899	Novello	Arr. Composer
	Autumn Arr. Pfte		1900	Novello	Arr. Composer
Music for 'Nell Gwyn' (Play by A. Hope)	Overture	1900			

Work	Version	Date Written	Date Published	Publisher	
	Full Score		1901	Chappell	
	Parts		1901	Chappell	
	Arr. Pfte. Duet		1901	Chappell	Arr. Composer
	Piano Conductor Score		1939	Chappell	
	Three Dances				
	Full Score and Parts		1900	Chappell	
	Arr. Pfte. Duet. and Solo		1900	Chappell	Arr. Composer (Pirated Edition also 1905)
	Arr. Pfte. and Violin		1900	Chappell	Arr. Composer
	Arr. Piano Accordion		1939	Chappell	Arr. H. Anderson
March Rhapsody (Based upon 1897. Fantasia 'In Commemoration') or Rhapsody on March Themes	Full Score	1902	1912	Novello	
	(Orch. Parts)		1902	Novello	
Welsh Rhapsody	Arr. Pfte. Duet.	1904	1902	Novello	Arr. A.E. Grimshaw
	Full Score (String Parts)		1905	Novello	
			1904	(Novello)	
	Arr. Military Band		1906	Novello	Arr. Dan Godfrey Jnr.
	Arr. Pfte. Solo		1904	Novello	Arr. Composer
	Duet. Pfte.		1905	Novello	Arr. Composer
	Band Score		1941	Boosey and Hawkes. N.Y.	
	March Para phrase. 'Men of Harlech'				Arr. T.C. Brown
	Full Score		1918	Novello	
	Arr. Brass Band		1954	Novello	Arr. Denis Wright

Work	Version	Date Written	Date Published	Publisher	
Music for 'The Conqueror' (Play by Millicent Duchess of Sutherland) (R.E. Fyffe.)		1905			
	Selection from Full Score		1905	Chappell	Arr. Composer
	Romance and Two Dances		1905/6	Chappell	Arr. Composer
	Three Songs: a) Evadne's Song b) O Love that knew the morning c) Cupid Fickle		1905	Chappell	Arr. Composer
	Chant of The Watchmen		1905	Chappell	
Coronation March and Hymn (See 'Henry VIII' above)					
The Irish Guards. Military Band		1918			
Theme and Six Diversions		1919			
	Full Score		1920	Novello	
	(String parts)		(1919)	Novello	
	Arr. Pfte. Solo and Duet		1919	Novello	Arr. Composer
The Willow Song (Othello)					
Tone Picture for Orchestra		1922			
	Full Score		1922	Novello	Arr. Composer
	Arr. Pfte. Solo		1922	Novello	Arr. H. Gechl.
Early Piano Suite					
Cloverley Suite	Orchestrated	1934	1933	Ashdown	

Work	Version	Date Written	Date Published	Publisher	
(Earlier Pieces Orchestrated.)	Pfte. and Orchestral Parts				
Edward German Melodies	Selected: Stanford Robinson Arr. Military Band		1934	Kramer	Arr. A. Wood.
			1944	Chappell	Arr. W. Dutoit
			1940	Chappell	

Songs	Words by	Published	Publisher	
Fine Feathers	J.E. Carpenter	1886	Boosey and Co.	
Fancy Free	A. Chapman	1887	R. Cocks and Co.	
Lady Hilda's Song	W.S. Gilbert	1888	Chappell	
Little Sweethearts	R.S. Hichens	1888	Phillips and Page	
His Lady	R.S. Hichens	1889	S. Lucas. Weber and Co.	
The Banks of the Bann.	S. Lennox	1890	Phillips and Page	(See Part Songs)
Little Boy Blue	F.E. Weatherley	1891	Boosey and Co.	
Little Lovers	R.S. Hichens	1891	R. Cocks and Co.	3. C. Eb. F.
Ever Waiting	G.H. Newcombe	1893	R. Cocks and Co.	2. Eb. G.
In a Northern Land	F. E. Weatherley	1893	Chappell	
In the Merry May time	M. Blackett	1894	Boosey and Co.	
Who'll buy my Lavender?	C. Battersby	1896	Boosey and Co.	(See Part Songs)
Three Spring Songs:	H. Boulton	1898	J.B. Cramer and Co.	1912 Edition also
1. As the World awakes today				Eb. F.
2. The dew upon the Lily				F.G.A.
3). My Song is of the Sturdy North				C.mi. D.mi.
Woo me not	C. Battersby	1898	Boosey and Co.	
Love the Pedlar	C. Battersby	1898	Boosey and Co.	
Sweet Rose	C. Bingham	1899	Enoch and Sons	Also Pirated Editions

Songs	Words by	Published	Publisher	
Early One Morning	–	1900	Chappell	2. Eb. F.
Four Lyrics:	H. Boulton	1900	Chappell	2. Ed. High, Low Voices
1. Sea Lullaby				
2. Birds on Wing				
3. Fair Flowers				
4. In Summer Time				
Six Lyrics	H. Boulton	1900	Ricordi	
1. Wake up my Nestling				
2. White Snowdrop				
3. Over the Heather				
4. A Wild Rose				
5. Meadows Green				
6. From Wave to Wave				
Daffodils a. Blowing	C. Battersby	1901	Boosey and Co.	Also Arr. Duet. and
Restless River	C. Bingham	1901	Boosey and Co.	Two Part S.A. Alec Rowley 1932 Violin. Ad Lib. See Also Part Songs
Roses in June	C. Bingham	1903	Macmillan	
Just So Song Book	Rudyard Kipling	1903	Macmillan and Co.	
1. When the Cabin port holes			Doubleday. Page and Co. N.Y.	
2. The Camel's Hump				
3. This Uninhabited Island				
4. I keep six honest serving men				
5. I am the most wise Baavian				
6. Kangaroo and Dingo				
7. Merrow Down				7. Also Novello. 1904
8. Of all the tribe of Tegumai				
9. The Riddle				

Songs	Words by	Published	Publisher	
10. The First Friend				Arr. Gordon Jacob
11. There never was a queen like Balkis				10. Also Novello. 1904
12. Rolling Down to Rio				12. Also Novello. 1904
Rudyard Kipling's 'Just So Songs'	(Arr. For Chorus and Orchestra)			
Rolling Down to Rio	(Arr. Unison Song)	1947	Novello	
Cupid at the Ferry	C. Battersby	1955	Novello	
Land of the Past	C. Bingham	1904	Boosey and Co.	
Two Lyrics:	H. Hammond Spencer	1904	Phillips and Page	
1. A Fancy		1904	Chappell	
2. High Ho				
Three Baritone Songs				
1. Come to the Woods	S. Waddington	1905	Boosey and Co.	
2. My Lady	F.E. Weatherley			
3. Glorious Devon	H. Boulton			
Separate publication				
2. My Lady		1905	Boosey and Co.	
3. Glorious Devon		1905	Boosey and Co.	
Arr. Cornet Solo & Military Band		1908	Boosey's Military Journal	
Voice Part only!		1936	Boosey and Co.	
Arr. Orchestra		1946	Boosey and Co.	
When Maidens go a 'Maying	H. Boulton	1906	Chappell	Arr. George L. Zelva
This England of Ours	H. Boulton	1907	Chappell	F. Ab.
The Drummer Boy	H. Boulton	1908	Chappell	D. Eb.
Little Girl in Red	A. Wilkins	1908	Boosey and Co.	
Love's Barcarolle	Basil Hood	1908	Chappell	3. F. Ab. Bb.

Songs	Words by	Published	Publisher	
To Katherine Unkind	Basil Hood	1908	Chappell	3. D. E. G.
Memories	H. Boulton	1909	Chappell	3. D. Eb. F.
Bird of Blue	'Chrystabel'	1910	Boosey and Co.	
Love in all Seasons	Basil Hood	1910	Chappell	3. D. E. F.
Moorish Lullaby	M. Byron	1910	Boosey and Co.	
An Old English Valentine	Mary Farrah	1911	Chappell	
Big Steamers	R. Kipling	1911	Metzler and Co.	(See also Part Songs)
Arr. Unison		1939	Cramer Lib of Uni. and Part Songs	
What 'Danegeld' means	R. Kipling	1911	Metzler and Co.	
When we grow old	H. Hammond Spencer			
Alistair	Lady Sybil Grant	1911	Ricordi	
Court Favour	Basil Hood	1912	Metzler and Co.	
Lady Mine. Serenade	M. H. Pollock	1912	Chappell	
Three Songs of Childhood	M. Lawrence	1913	Chappell	
1. Wondering		1914	Chappell	
2. The Nodding Mandarin				
3. Byelow Land				
To Phyllis		1914	Chappell	Only reference in E.'G's list
Second Portrait Album		1914	Chappell	Only reference in E.'G's list
Countrymen's Chorus	H. Taylor	1916	Enoch and Sons	
Be Well Assured (Fringes of the Fleet)	R. Kipling	1916	Chappell	
All Friends Round the Wrekin	W. H. Scott	1917	Chappell	
Have You News of my boy Jack?	R. Kipling	1917	Gen. Publishing Society	Also Arr. with Orchestra and for Female Voices

Songs	Words by	Published	Publisher	
Charming Chloe	R. Burns	1917	Novello	
The Irish Guards	R. Kipling	1918	Chappell	
The Lordling's Daughter	Ballad (Elizabethan)	1925	Novello	
Songs of Edward German	—	1933	Boosey and Hawkes Military Journal	Selected and Arranged. V. Hely Hutchinson

N.B. A list in E. G.'s handwriting refers to other songs which have not survived:

Ode to the Woodlark
Story of a Monk
A Summer Idyll
Love me Nevermore
A Midsummer Ghost
Three Heavens
A Wayside Story
Molly Maloney

CHORAL WORKS AND PART SONGS (excluding numbers from stage works)				
Te Deum in F.	—	1899	Novello Parish Choir Book	
The Chase	E. Oxenford	1886	S. Lucas Weber and Co.	Lucas Prize Composition 1885
Antigone. Chorus and March	Sophocles	1900	Novello	
		1887/8	Noted as pub. by Novello, but no other record exists	

Songs	Words by	Published	Publisher	
O Lovely May	H. Wethered	1894	Novello	
Also Arr. Female Trio:		1921	Novello	Arr. Composer
Who is Sylvia?	W. Shakespeare	1894	Novello	
Also Arr. Two Voices & Pfte		1928	Novello	J. Pointer
		1933		
Banks of the Bann	S. Lennox			
(See Songs)				
Arr. Part Song		1899	Phillips and Page	Arr. L. Kingsmill
Just So Songs (See Songs)				
The Camel's Hump	1927	Novello		Arr. Composer
Arr. 4 part		1933	Novello	
2 part				
Rolling down to Rio				
Arr. Men's Voices		1916	Orpheus New Series	Arr. Composer
SATB		1918	Novello	Arr. Composer
2 parts		1925	Novello	Arr. Composer
SSA		1963	Novello	
Canada Patriotic Hym	H. Boulton	1904	Chappell	
Also Solo and Chorus		1904	Chappell	
O. Peaceful Night	W. H. Scott	1904	Novello	Arr. Composer
Also Arr. Female Trio		1921	Novello	H.A. Chambers
Arr. 2 Parts				
Introit. Bread of Heaven	J. Conder	1908	Novello	
Grace. 'Non Nobis Domine'		1911	Novello	
Pure as the Air. Trio Female Voices	W.S. Gilbert	1911	Chappell	Noted 1911 by E.G.
The Three Knights	A. Cleveland	1911	Novello	
Also Arr. Men's Voices		1922	Novello	Arr. Composer
Beauteous Morn.	O. W. Holmes			
3 Parts Female Voices		1912	Novello	
Also Arr. 2 Parts		1933	Novello	H. A. Chambers

Songs	Words by	Published	Publisher	
In Praise of Neptune	T. Campion	1912	Novello	Arr. Composer
Also Arr. Unison		1925	Novello	
My Bonnie Lass.	Trad.	1912	Novello	Arr. H. A. Chambers
Also Trio		1924	Novello School Songs	
2 Part		1933		
Sleeping	Old English	1912	Novello	
Men's Voices			Orpheus Series	
Sweet Day So Cool	G. Herbert	1912	Novello	Written for High School for Girls. Whitchurch
Morning Hym.	Anon	1912	Unpublished	
Intercessory Hymn	W. H. Scott	1915	Novello. Parish Choir Book	From 'Homage to Belgium'. King Albert's Book. 1914
Father Omnipotent				
London Town	J. Masefield	1920	Novello	Arr. Composer
Also Arr. Men's Voices		1921	Novello	Arr. Composer
Song		1926	Novello	

PIANO WORKS	Published	Publisher
Suite for Pianoforte	1889	Ashdown
1. Impromptu.		
2. Valse Caprice		
3. Bourrée		

PIANO WORKS	Published	Publisher	
4. Elegy			
5. Mazurka			
6. Tarentella			
No. 6 Arr. Pfte Duet	1925	Ashdown. Novello	
Four Pianoforte Duets	1890	Ashdown	Omitted by E.G. in his 1925 Listing of works
Graceful Dance in F.	1891	Ashdown	
Polish Dance	1891	Ashdown	
Valse in Ab	1891	Ashdown	
Arr. Duet	1916	Ashdown	
Album Leaf	1892	Ashdown	
Intermezzo in A Minor	1892	Ashdown	
Valsette pour Piano	1892	Ashdown	
Minuet in G.	1893	Ashdown	
Second Impromptu.	1894	Ashdown	(First in 1889 Suite)
Concert Study in A. Flat.	1894	Ashdown	Altered to Etude de Concert in E.G.'s writing
Melody in Eb.	1895	Ashdown	Arr. for Organ. J. W. Elliott 1909 Violin & Pfte 1910 J. Fontaine
Suite for Four Hands	1896	Ashdown	Omitted by E.G. in 1925 listing
"The Guitar"	1897	Ashdown	Transcription of Academy composition
Melody in Db.	1898	Ashdown	
"Columbine" Air de Ballet	1898	Enoch and Sons	Included. R.H. Bellairs. 'The Progressive Pianist', 1905
Abendlied 'Evensong'	1900	S. Lucas and Son	
Arr. Military Band	1907	Boosey and Co.	
Violin and Pfte.	1914	A. Lengnick and Co.	
Melody in E. 'The Queen's Carol'	1905		Arr. A. Moffett
Edward German's Pianoforte	1910	Ashdown	

PIANO WORKS	Published	Publisher	
Compositions	1913 (Two Volumes)		
Early Piano Suite			
Arr. Full and Small Orch.	1933	Ashdown	Arr. H. Geehl.
English Country Dances	1941	Chappell	Arr. of Opera Dance Movements etc.
VIOLIN WORKS &			
Nocturne	1882	Unpublished	
Chanson d'Amour	1880's	Unpublished	
Barcarolle			
Album Leaf			
Sprites' Dance			
Bolero	1883		
Orch. Ar.	1885	London Publishing Co. Ashdown Ashdown	
Violin and Pfte.	1912		
Scotch Sketch 2 Viol. Pfte	1890		
Arr. Full Orch.	1890/1935	Ashdown	Arr. H. Geehl
Moto Perpetuo	1890	F. W. Chanot	
Pour Violin accompagnement de Piano			
Souvenir Vl. and Pfte.	1896	Stanley Lucas & Co.	Ed. J.C. Beale. EG's list suggests Fl. versions First
Song without Words	1898	Augener	E.G.'s list suggests Violin was first version
Also Arr. Cl. & Pfte	1898	Augener	
Organ	1906	Chappell	Arr. H.M. Higgs
Pfte		Sir H.B. Tree's Charing Cross Hospital Bazaar Souvenir	
Three Sketches	1897	Metzler and Co.	With portrait
1. Valsette			

PIANO WORKS	Published	Publisher	
2. Souvenir			
3. Bolero			
WOODWIND			
Saltarelle. Fl. and Pfte.	1889	Rudall Carte and Co.	
Also Arr. Viol. and pfte	1890	Augener	
Pastorale and Bourrée Ob and Pfte.	1891	Oboe Player's Jounral (R.C. & Co.)	
		Charnot	
Also Arr. Viol. and Pfte.	1892		
Fl. and Pfte	1892		
Cl. and Pfte.	1895	Clarinet Player's Journal (R.C. and Co.)	
Suite: Three Pieces Fl. Pfte.	1892	Rudall Carte and Co.	
Andante and Tarantella Cl. and Pfte.	1892	Rudall Carte and Co.	E.G.'s 1925 List refers to Two Romances and gives 1889 as date
Romance. Cl. and Pfte	1892	Rudall Carte and Co.	
Intermezzo Fl. and Pfte.	1894	Rudall Carte and Co.	
		Stanley Lucas and Co.	
Early One Morning Fl. and Pfte.	1900	Chappell	
ALSO			
Trio in D. Vn. Vc. Pfte.	c.1883	Unpublished	
ORGAN			
Andante in Bb.	1880's	Unpublished	E.G. Listed Three Pieces for 'American Organ'.
ENSEMBLE			
Serenade. (Voice) Vln. W. Wind	1890's		Missing

Bibliography

GENERAL

W.H. Scott Edward German. An Intimate Biography. (Cecil Palmer. Chappell) 1932.

Kathleen Barnard. Eminent Men of Whitchurch 1982.
Ernest Clark. Famous son of Whitchurch. Edward German. Shropshire Magazine. 1951.
Dennis Earnshaw. Whitchurch Archaeological Society. Newsletter 17. 1982.
Dominic Guyver. Elgar Journal.
Royal Academy of Music Club Magazine. 1926. J.A. Forsyth.
                                    1937 Theodore Holland.
New Grove Dictionary of Music and Musicians. (Edward German). Andrew Lamb. 1980. Macmillan.
[Earlier Editions of Grove make much play with the interposition of a Burlesque into 'A Princess of
    Kensington' an isolated incident which German deplored.]
Dennis Anndell. The Story of Saller's Wells. 1965. Hamish Hamilton.
Hector Bolitho. Marie Tempest. 1936. Colden.
William Boosey. Fifty Years of Music. 1931. Benn.
A. Brereton. The Life of Henry Irving. 1905. A. Trehome.
Cicely Courtneidge. 'Cicely'. Reminiscence. 1953. Hutchinson.
Robert Courtneidge. 'I was An Actor Once'. 1930 Hutchinson.
Robert Elkin. Royal Philharmonic. The Annuals of the Royal Phil. Society. 1947. Rider.
Robert Elkin. Queen's Hall. 1893-1941 1944. Rider.
Herman Finck. My Medodious Memories. 1937. Hutchinson.
C.H.F. Irving. Henry Irving. The Actor and his Work. 1951. Faber.
Henry A. Jones. The Tempter. 1898. Macmillon.
Henry A. Jones. Michael and his Lost Angel. 1895. Macmillon.
Henry Lytton. The Secrets of a Savoyard. 1921 Jarrolds.
Henry Lytton. A Wandering Minstral. 1933. Jarrolds.
A.E.W. Mason. Sir George Alexander and the St. James Theatre.
A.C. Mackenzie. A Musicians Narative. 1927. Cassell.
Julia Neilson. This For Remembrance. 1941. Hurst and. Blackelt.
Peacock and Weir. The Composer in the Market Place. 1975. Faber.
Hesketh Pearson. Gilbert. His Life and Strife. 1957. Melhues.
Bernard Shaw. Music in London 1890-94. 1932 Constable.
Bernard Shaw. How to become a Music Critic. Ed. Dan H. Laurence 1960 Hart Davis.
Bernard Shaw. Shaw's Music. Ed. Dan H. Laurence. 1981 Bodley Head.
Dennis Stuart. My Dear Duchess. 1982. Gollancz.
Sir Henry Wood. My Life of Music. 1938. Gollancz.
Reginald Pound. 'Sir' Henry Wood. 1969. Cassell.

Index